ACROSS THE CONTINENT

ACROSS *the* CONTINENT

The Union Pacific Photographs of Andrew J. Russell

DANIEL DAVIS

UNIVERSITY OF UTAH PRESS
Salt Lake City

UTAH STATE HISTORICAL SOCIETY
Salt Lake City

Copublished with the Utah State Historical Society.
Affiliated with the Utah Division of State History,
Utah Department of Heritage and Arts.

The Defiance House Man colophon is a registered trademark of The University of Utah Press. It is based on a four-foot-tall Ancient Puebloan pictograph (late PIII) near Glen Canyon, Utah.

Library of Congress Cataloging-in-Publication Data
Names: Davis, Daniel (Photography curator), author.
Title: Across the continent : the Union Pacific photographs of Andrew Joseph Russell / Daniel Davis.
Description: Salt Lake City : University of Utah Press : Utah State Historical Society, [2018] | Includes bibliographical references and index. |
Identifiers: LCCN 2018017664 (print) | LCCN 2018021575 (ebook) | ISBN 9781607816386 | ISBN 9781607816379 (pbk. : alk. paper)
Subjects: LCSH: Russell, Andrew J. | Photography of railroads. | Union Pacific Railroad Company--History--Pictorial works. | Central Pacific Railroad Company--History--Pictorial works. | West (U.S.)--History--Pictorial works. | Railroads--United States--History--19th century--Pictorial works. | Photographers--United States. | LCGFT: Photobooks.
Classification: LCC TR715 (ebook) | LCC TR715 .D38 2018 (print) | DDC 779/.9385--dc23
LC record available at https://lccn.loc.gov/2018017664

Printed and bound in the United States of America

CONTENTS

ACKNOWLEDGMENTS

THIS BEING MY FIRST BOOK, I was astonished at how much human debt one racks up with this sort of endeavor. It took the Union Pacific about four and a half years to build its line once it got started. It took me considerably longer than that to write this book. Like that railroad though, once I built up some momentum I was in a hurry and I completed a hasty rough draft full of problems and rough spots that had to be reworked and redone. The man mostly in charge of this "finishing" work was John Alley, first at the Utah State University Press and then the University of Utah Press. My father John Davis, as well, in addition to passing on his love of history, read it and provided invaluable comments. I was especially fortunate to make the acquaintance of Dr. Glenn Willumson. Dr. Willumson was generous with his sources and encouragement and I bounced many ideas off him. He also secured access for me to an invaluable document, the transcription of O. C. Smith's diaries. After Dr. Willumson published *Iron Muse* in 2013, I was both in awe of his achievement and somewhat intimidated. Yet I still felt that Russell deserved his own biography with a chronology of his Union Pacific photographs and a separate catalog. I hope that my book can be a companion to his, and that it complements and extends the themes of *Iron Muse*. At Utah State University, administrators in the Merrill-Cazier Library (Richard Clement and Brad Cole) were not only encouraging intellectually but also supported me with time away from my daily duties in Special Collections. My colleagues in Special Collections (Liz Kline, Clint Pumphrey, Becky Skeen, Jennifer Duncan, Robert Parson, Sara Skindelien, Randy Williams, Rose Milovich, and Steven Sturgeon) encouraged me to keep grinding away and took up the slack from my many absences.

Being an archivist myself, I appreciate those who labor tirelessly to make primary sources available to the public. Russell's images are strung from coast to coast and an astonishing number are available online in dozens of museums, archives, and libraries. Though the people (usually students, staff, and technicians) who do this work are rarely acknowledged, their work was vital for my book. In particular I must thank Sarah Langsdon at Weber State University Special Collections, Scott Christensen and William Slaughter at the Church Historical Department of the Church of Jesus Christ of Latter-day Saints, Doug Misner at the Utah State Historical Society Library, Tom Wells at Brigham Young University Special Collections, and most of all Patricia LaBounty at the Union Pacific Railroad Museum. My old friend Mark Nelson at the Sweetwater County Historical Museum gave me access to their photographic reference collection. Lorraine Crouse and Crissy Giacoletto at the University of Utah Special Collections were especially generous, after I initially stood them up, in giving me a second chance. Dale Hansen granted me access to his land where once stood the mighty Dale Creek Trestle and provided me and my father with an amazing morning. The Redd Center at Brigham Young University generously funded my summer of travel and discovery along the old Union Pacific line and a later trip back to Omaha. My former colleague Noel Carmack traveled with me for part of the journey, providing encouragement and great conversation over the long, long miles of I-80 in Wyoming, Nebraska, and Iowa. My poor daughter Emilee will, in later years, recall being raised mostly by her grandparents Semm and Max. Most of all I have to thank Emilee's mother and my wonderful, patient, and supportive wife, Ashlee. She helped me emotionally and did much of the final manuscript preparations. Without her support and encouragement this book would simply not have happened.

INTRODUCTION

The Forgotten Photographer

"The construction of photographic archives is not a simple process."

—Glenn Willumson

On June 28, 2010, I realized that Union Pacific Railroad photographer Andrew J. Russell[1] was not infallible. I had just climbed partway up a mountain above the Weber River in Utah. I crested the hill and was now looking down at the west entrance to tunnel no. 3. At that point I was attempting to re-photograph a Russell image, "View of Tunnel No. 4, from an Elevation of 1,000 Feet."[2] I groaned as it dawned on me that I was apparently on the wrong part of the mountain. My car was parked, probably illegally, just off I-80. While I had not seen a No Trespassing! sign, it is best not to linger too much after jumping a fence. "Well, damn," I thought. My first reaction was to blame myself: sloppy preparation. I sat down on a rock to look again at my copy of the stereo-view and realized that what Russell called tunnel no. 4 was most definitely not tunnel no. 4 and was instead tunnel no. 3. The other thing I noticed was that Russell photographed from far higher up on the mountain. Of course there were no trails leading up there and he would have had to make his way through the dense scrub oak and up steep, slippery rock slopes. He did that while carrying a thirty-pound stereo camera and tripod no less. "Wow!" I said out loud as I looked up the mountain.

I first became interested in A. J. Russell after starting my new job as the photo archivist in the Special Collections Division at Utah State University in 2000. I knew little about Russell except he had taken several well-known photographs of the Union Pacific Railroad in 1868 and 1869. I found a copy of *Sun Pictures of Rocky Mountain Scenery*.[3] I looked through Russell's thirty photographs included in this volume, only dimly aware of the skill and patience needed to create high-quality collodion wet-plate negatives in such primitive conditions. As I did more research, I discovered that Russell had taken hundreds of images, mostly stereo-views, yet there were few scholarly publications about him.

I completed more research on Russell and viewed more images, but he always seemed shrouded in mystery. I knew the name, and the basic story, but who was he as a person? More was known about other western photographers such as William Henry Jackson, C. R. Savage, and Timothy O'Sullivan, but these photographers were, with the glaring exception of William

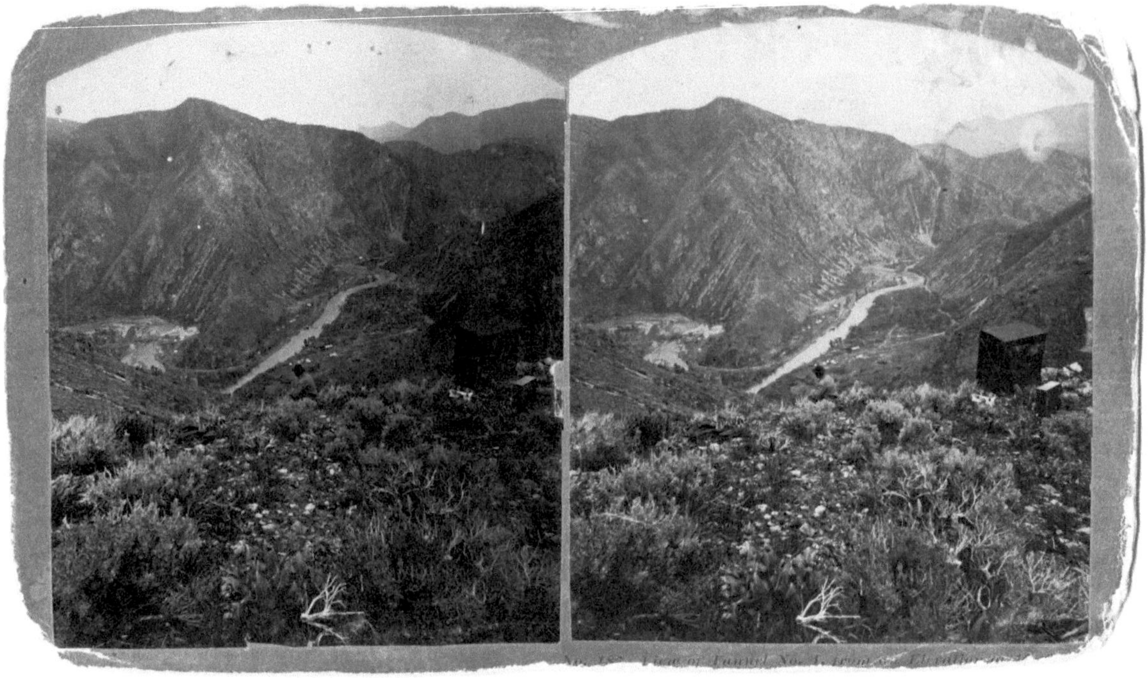

0.1. Looking down on Union Pacific tunnel no. 3 in Weber Canyon, by A. J. Russell, stereo-view no. 385. *Courtesy of the Union Pacific Railroad Museum, Union Pacific Collection, Photography Archives, A. J. Russell Views.*

Henry Jackson, mostly silent. Physically they operated in the background. They provided the public with a rendering of an expedition or a railroad company, but were, officially, an ancillary endeavor.

Another mystery for me was what the public of 1868 and 1869 saw in these images. As a photograph archivist I am fascinated with how people view images. At first that may seem like an odd comment. Of course people view images the same way! What does it matter that one person sees an image of a gold (or is it blue?) dress on the internet from her work computer and one person views it on his phone on a bus?[4] What difference does it make if someone sees a small, physical image held in his hand or the same image on the wall of a museum? But I have noticed that people view images in profoundly different ways contextually, emotionally, and conceptually. Context matters with images. Is the viewer looking at an image in a group, and does the group commentary change his or her understanding? What are the written words that accompany the image? Is the image in an archive or museum or is it in a family photo album? What meaning do we then ascribe to the image based on how we physically view the image and hear or read words meant to explain that image?

Photographs also have the power to provoke an emotion, much more so than words alone. An injustice becomes more "real" and more immediate with an image. When viewing photographs of badly injured Syrian children, the plight of refugees becomes something more than just

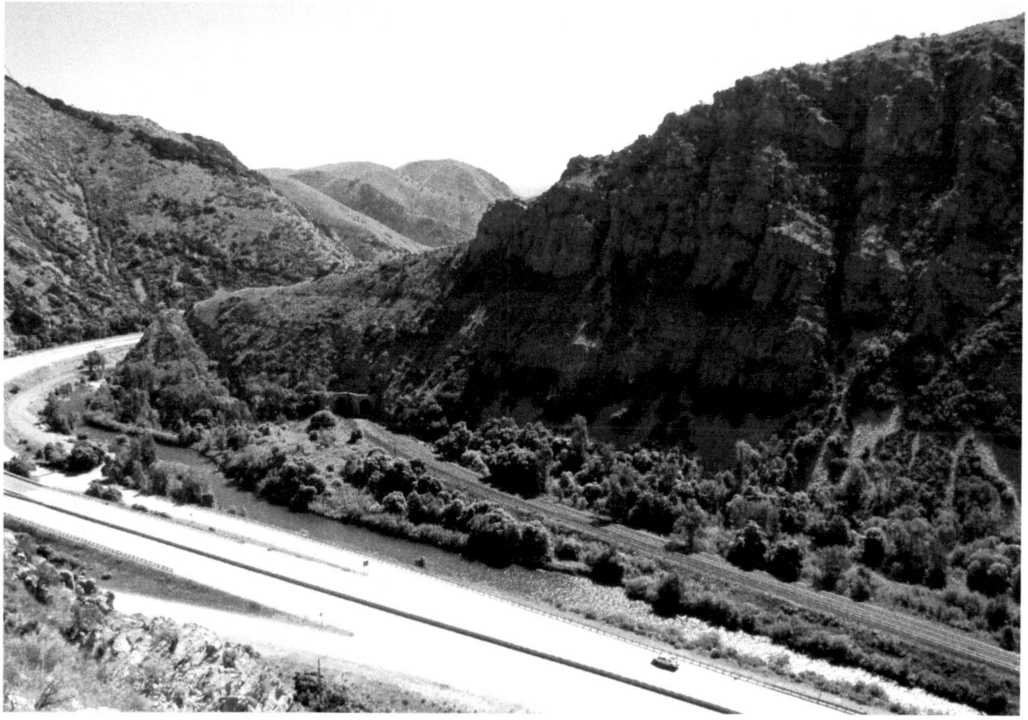

0.2. View of old Union Pacific tunnel no. 3, June 28, 2010. *Photo by author.*

a story in a newspaper. We bring our personal assumptions and ideas to these kinds of photos as well. A foreign aid worker for the Red Cross might see the plight of a refugee through world-weary eyes. Someone else, however, might see a potential terrorist and, for yet another person, the photo might evoke pity and prompt a donation.

Conceptually we all have different backgrounds, experiences, and knowledge that we bring when viewing a photo. One image of a celebrity might provoke disgust in the first viewer and adoration in another. An image of your favorite hometown haunt puts a smile on your face but is meaningless to anyone not from your hometown. A car enthusiast might see a photograph of a Ferrari and know the car's year, the specific options it has, how much horsepower the engine produces, and how fast it is from 0 to 60 mph. Some people, however, would just note that it is a sporty car, rarely seen in Utah. An image also has a certain meaning based upon the time you view it. If you view an old image of your parents or grandparents you might find the clothing and hairstyles amusing, but maybe they took the photo expressly to show off how trendy they were at that time. Most importantly, here, if you were alive in 1869 and viewed an image of the transcontinental railroad, you had a completely different set of assumptions than a contemporary viewer.

When you take the time to analyze the Russell photograph of a windmill in Laramie, Wyoming (see figure 0.3), what do you think of first? If you are a railroad enthusiast, you probably

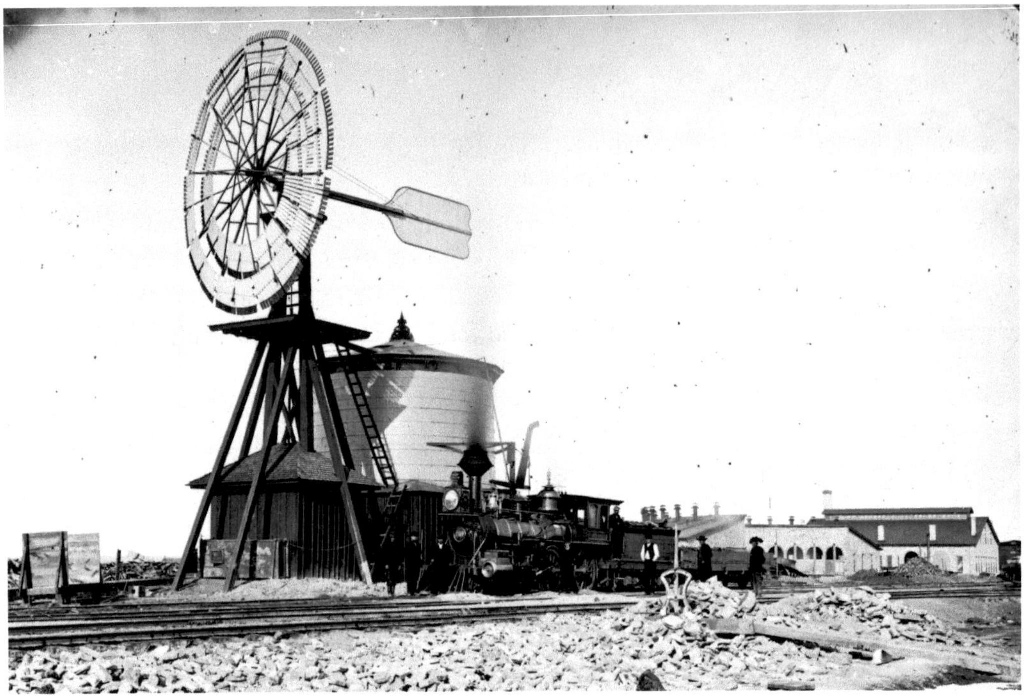

0.3. "Wind Mill, Laramie City," by A. J. Russell, large-format view no. 51 1/2. *Courtesy of the Oakland Museum of California, A. J. Russell Collection.*

note what kind of engine it is and think of the complex process of creating movement from coal and steam. My wife would note how uncomfortable the clothes look. An art historian might analyze the contrast between light and dark and the interplay of lines and shapes. For me, after viewing Russell's photographs many years ago, I wondered, who are the people in the images and where did they go after completing the great national project? What did they tell their spouses, children, or grandchildren about their time working on the transcontinental railroad? Were they proud to be part of a great national project that restored faith in American exceptionalism or, after the Credit Mobilier scandal, did they view their work as enabling already wealthy men to grow even wealthier? My final question regarding Russell's images was simple. I have spent over twenty years as a photograph archivist and a big part of my job is putting names to faces. Who, then, are the people in his images?

Armed with these questions, I began my research. Luckily, historians love a good mystery. The thrill of discovery through dogged research in obscure records and photographs and then the subsequent construction of a forgotten story stayed with me for many years. I read the available primary sources written by Russell but the problem was that he, like most western photographers, did not leave a diary or even a cache of revealing correspondence. This made it hard to decipher a sequence for his images, or even what he wanted to photograph and why. The writings Russell did publish were more about the adventures he had taking the pictures or about "strange" peoples such as Mormons, the Chinese in California, and "Snake" Indians. Eventually, however, I realized that my research about Russell would only get me so far. I needed to see the places that Russell saw and stand in the places where he stood. More, I needed to view the locations of the railroad in person with copies of his photographs. In 2010 I was awarded a summer sabbatical from my usual duties in the Merrill-Cazier Library at Utah State University, as well as a travel grant from the Redd Center at Brigham Young University. My initial idea was that the sabbatical would help me to create a website that brought together all of Russell's images from various repositories to create a master online catalog available for free to the public. This website, in modified form, is now a companion to the book (see dansrailroadphotos.com), but at that point in 2010 it was not feasible for a variety of reasons. Instead, I created binders with photocopies of all the Russell images that I could find.

I made four binders that re-created Russell's original numbered series of stereographic images (a series of over six hundred images he entitled Across the Continent, West from Omaha) as well as his large-format views. I found images (both in person and on the internet) at the Oakland Museum of California, the Union Pacific Railroad Museum, Weber State University, the University of Iowa, the Beinecke Library at Yale, the Denver Public Library, Brigham Young University, the University of Utah, the Library of Congress, the History Division of the Church of Jesus Christ of Latter-day Saints, the University of Wyoming, the Utah State Historical Society, the George Eastman House, Utah State University, and even on eBay. These binders form the most complete set of Russell reproductions in existence and they are now a collection at the Utah State University Special Collections in the Merrill-Cazier Library.[5]

The rest of my sabbatical was consumed with traveling back and forth along the original route of the transcontinental railroad, from the Golden Spike National Historic Monument to the Union Pacific headquarters in Omaha, Nebraska. I put over 6,500 miles on my car, and visited thirteen museums and archives. Although I am not a trained photographer, I thought that I should try to think like a photographer, so I took nearly two hundred re-photographs of Russell's images. After the fun and adventure of my sabbatical had ended, I started to put together a biography of Russell and reflect on what I had learned.

During my time on the road, I viewed the immense open spaces of Nebraska, Wyoming, and Utah. I marveled at how raw and untamed the West must have felt for someone who grew up in upstate New York. But I also saw how Russell mostly turned away from these spaces and focused on the intimate and the personal. He photographed the people he knew who had worked so hard to build the railroad. It is not too much of a stretch to say that he primarily photographed people with the Union Pacific as a backdrop. I then wondered what Russell could tell us about the smaller, more intimate stories of these people in his photographs. The key to answering my initial questions about Russell, I discovered, was through his images—not just a handful of his images, but his entire body of work. And in order to understand his images, I needed to understand his literal and intellectual thinking. Every thoughtful photographer is trying to "speak" with their images, and they have a certain interpretation in mind. It turns out, in fact, Russell's images have much subtlety and nuance. I realized that if I could not find answers to my questions through traditional sources, maybe if I paid attention, and knew the history, I could start to learn his photographic language. And if I could discover what one western photographer was saying, I could reveal something more about the history of the transcontinental railroad beyond the standard corporate and chronological histories.

I still struggled, however, to answer two big questions. Given numerous options, why did Russell take the photographs that he did, and in what chronology were these photographs taken? I was immensely helped when I connected with Professor Glenn Willumson. Dr. Willumson was generous with his ideas and sources. But most importantly, he aided me in obtaining access to the transcript of O. C. Smith's diaries, held by a private individual. After reading the transcript, I was able to create a rough timeline for what Russell photographed and when. After creating this chronology it became clear that the second question, more than I could have imagined, was influenced not by personal whims, but by what the Union Pacific wanted him to photograph.

In my mind I have answered most of my initial questions satisfactorily. Unfortunately, my questions about the men who did the work of building the transcontinental railroad remain mostly unanswered. The history of the transcontinental railroad focusing on the wealthy men who financed and managed it has been written and written well.[6] Also the technical details of how the line was built and where it was at any particular point are well known. It is a shame, however, that we do not know more about the stories of everyone else: the laborers, graders, tie hacks, clerks, surveyors, and so forth, who labored under such extreme circumstances. Creating this kind of history is the next step in understanding the first transcontinental railroad. I believe this book will help begin that process and I urge my readers to view the companion website and even to conduct their own research. My hope is to create an ongoing dialogue about Russell's many lesser-known photographs and the people in those images.

Finally, I have to say that I grew to like and appreciate Russell even while I strained to remain neutral and objective. He came out West as a commentator, not a conqueror, with no big dreams of creating a personal fiefdom in the West. He was a warm and personable fellow and, like me, he was an employee with a job to do and bills to pay. Also like me he had an ironic, self-deprecating sense of humor. Russell was not terribly ambitious by the standards of mid-nineteenth-century America; yet he rose to the occasion when needed. He went to extraordinary lengths to take his photographs when the moment called and then, like so many other employees of the Union Pacific, just faded into the background.

CHAPTER 1

A. J. Russell and the Golden Age of Western Photography

"Photographs are primary source documents that can be encountered both *in* history and *through* history."

—Martha A. Sandweiss

You know the photograph even if you do not know the photographer. It has been used in countless coffee table books, documentaries, textbooks, exhibits, and promotional brochures. Union Pacific Railroad chief engineer Grenville Dodge shakes hands with his counterpart on the Central Pacific, Samuel Skerry Montague. Behind them two men lean towards one another, each with one hand grasping their respective locomotive and the other around a bottle of champagne. On the right, with Dodge, stand the Union Pacific employees. On the left is Montague's Central Pacific crowd. Behind them are the two engines available that day, Engine 119 on the Union Pacific side and the Jupiter for the Central Pacific. On May 10, 1869, the great transcontinental railroad, the "work of the age," linking East and West, came together in northwest Utah in a remote spot known as Promontory Summit. What you may not know is that this famous photograph was just one image in a remarkable body of photographic work. The photographer, Andrew J. Russell (or A. J. Russell), took nearly one thousand views in 1868 and 1869 of the Union Pacific and the sights along the line.

In the early spring of 1868, while there was still snow on the ground, Russell began the great project of photographing the Union Pacific Railroad. He would make at least two trips out West and away from his home in New York City. He would travel from Nebraska to Wyoming to Utah and eventually to California in 1868 and 1869, taking over 250 large-format images and at least 650 stereographic views (a stereographic camera uses two lenses to capture the double images on a card that, when placed in a stereographic viewer, provides the illusion of three-dimensionality) on collodion wet-plate glass negatives.[1] These images were either used as the basis for graphic illustrations in the popular magazine *Leslie's Illustrated* or mass-produced in at least nine series of stereographic cards or as albumen photographs tipped-in to two publications, *Great West Illustrated* and *Sun Pictures of Rocky Mountain Scenery.*

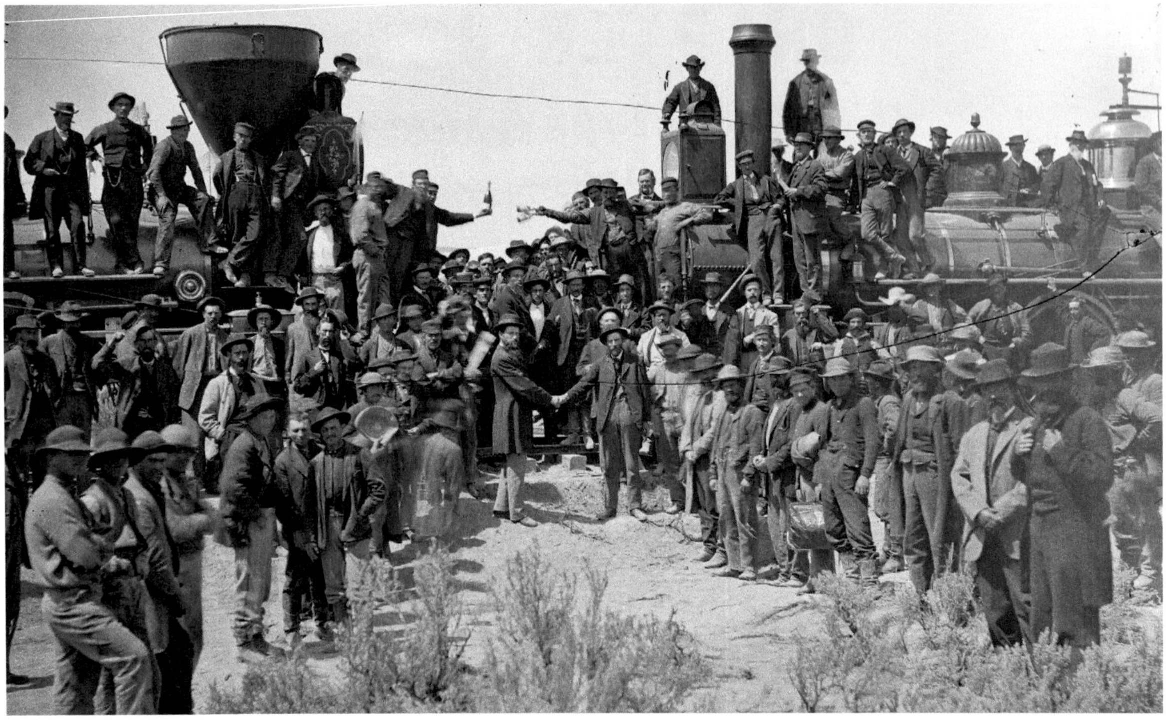

1.1. "East and West Shaking Hands at Laying Last Rail," by A. J. Russell, large-format view no. 227. *Courtesy of the Oakland Museum of California, A. J. Russell Collection.*

Although Russell photographed the construction of the Union Pacific, this statement might seem misleading by today's standards. The technology for and public expectation regarding capturing people in motion had not yet arrived. The images Russell did take of the actual laying of rails are blurry and overly busy. Too much was happening, too quickly, for Russell to capture, with his equipment, compelling photographs of men in action. Today we have expectations of what a photojournalist can do that Russell's images do not match. Moreover, of the images used most frequently to show track laying, none were taken by Russell.[2] Russell should still be considered a pioneering American photographer; his images introduced a nation to the transcontinental railroad. Although his equipment did not allow him to stop motion, he did set up scenes to show the daily work of the laborers. Russell pushed the available technology to its limits. His capture on glass of even a small portion of the chaos, confusion, and energy that accompanied the building of the transcontinental railroad is a significant historical accomplishment. Russell's work is even more impressive when one considers that all of his negatives had to be sensitized, exposed, and developed in about one hour. In effect, Russell had to employ a portable, rapid-action darkroom. He moved his wagon-based darkroom by train or mules.

Russell did not confine his picture making only to the Union Pacific line. He also ventured into the Medicine Bow and Uinta Mountains, as well as Salt Lake City and nearby

Cottonwood Canyon, Bingham Canyon, and Parley's Park (now Park City). Even though Russell used the railroad to travel greater distances, he still had to travel frequently by means of a photographic wagon and even employ pack mules at times.

Russell had already garnered some impressive credentials before 1868. He was an illustrator for popular moving panorama shows, which toured New York state in the 1850s and early 1860s.[3] During the Civil War he was a military photographer for the Military Railroad Construction Corps of the Union army. Initially his images were used by General Herman Haupt to illustrate Haupt's reports on new and innovative bridge and railroad construction techniques, but after Haupt retired in September 1863, Russell assumed a broad range of documentary duties, showing fortifications, railroads, bridge building, supply operations, and the destructive aftermath of battle. President Lincoln was supposedly given an album of his images.[4] Russell brought his skills from these previous experiences to his new position in 1868. Certainly he recognized the need for flexibility. He seemed quite comfortable taking images that were meant to be artistic, others that were meant as a documentary record, some that were meant for the tourist trade, and others that were meant to be working documents. These photographs are priceless not only because of the power of photography to provide an emotional link to another time and place but also because they are historical fragments that give us remarkable insights into the story of the railroad. Many of the images depict towns, stations, structures, and even geological features that no longer exist. Today, on the entire line from Omaha to Promontory, no original Union Pacific buildings remain from the 1865 to 1869 construction of the line.[5]

Russell meant for his stereographic images, much more than his large-format views, to provide useful contemporary information. These stereo-views give a sense to the prospective traveler of where they would and could stay overnight, what the dining halls looked like, and what towns and stations were along the route. They provided the people back East (such as company directors, trustees, investors, and government officials) a sense of what was happening on the Union Pacific during its construction. About one-third of Russell's stereo-views were taken in a stretch from the head of Echo Canyon to the mouth of Weber Canyon in Utah territory. During the fall of 1868 and early spring of 1869, a dispute erupted between the Union Pacific and Central Pacific over who would lay rail through these canyons. Both railroads wanted to build into the canyons because of potential coal deposits in the Wasatch Mountains and the opportunity to gain control over Utah traffic. The secretary of the interior, Orville Hickman Browning, was consistently more accommodating to the Central Pacific, but the Union Pacific was already in Utah and had begun the work of grading and building tunnels and bridges.[6] Russell's time in this area makes sense because the Union Pacific was desperate to show just how much work they had done.

Even with these stereographs, it is apparent that Russell was mostly photographing people. This is the only conclusion that can be reached after examining the hundreds of images he took from 1868 to 1869. He shot the whole human panoply that was building the transcontinental railroad, from the future president of the United States, to the lowest-paid Union

Pacific laborers. He shot Mormons, station attendants, soldiers, surveyors, engineers, travelers, and Union Pacific directors. But most importantly, he photographed the men who labored under sometimes extreme conditions to get the job done. He focused on their living accommodations, their trade, and on the end product of their work; he even staged fake action shots, as if he were a simple observer of work that never stopped. Clearly Russell felt an affinity towards the people who worked for the Union Pacific. He thought of himself as one of the men working not only for a payday, but to play a part in the completion of this great national project.[7] Russell was not hired by the Union Pacific to photograph people, but he never lets us forget who built the machine. His West is fundamentally a landscape that he understood through human needs. In the end, people built the railroad, and those people are all over his photographs, even if many of them remain anonymous.

The building of the transcontinental railroad by the Union Pacific and Central Pacific generated enormous interest among the American public and, by creating a market for photographic images of western America, also created not only a means but an incentive for photographers to transport bulky equipment to remote regions. Russell's images would also be used by the Union Pacific to promote tourism along the line. So A. J. Russell became one of many to follow who would take advantage of interest in the railroad and the sights along the line. He was part of a group of photographers who visually introduced the West to the East in the 1860s and 1870s. This was the "golden age" of western photography (which lasted less than twenty years). The interior West was still an exotic concept to the rest of the nation and the public clamored for a realism that it reasoned could only be provided by photographers. Russell capitalized on the visual interest of the West through his stereo-views, which, in the 1860s and 1870s, were actually seen by more people than the visually impressive, large-format views. Western photographers like Russell played a large part in creating a more positive public vision of the West, not as the great American desert, but as a land of limitless opportunities.

Russell did not leave behind a diary or voluminous correspondence, which leaves the questions, what instructions did he receive from the Union Pacific and how did he deviate from those instructions? His motivation, movements, and rationale during this year and a half are a matter of calculated guesswork. Unfortunately for the historian, the railroad's reasons for hiring one photographer among its ten thousand employees have become obscured, and this minor detail, which became so crucial to the way we envision the transcontinental railroad, is a matter of speculation. There are very few corporate records from this time and the company had more pressing problems (financing, construction, legislation, litigation, hostile American Indians, and so forth). As 1868 began, however, the Union Pacific's photographic efforts were definitely behind the curve. Several photographers had already been on the line and at least two of the railroad's competitors had begun to photo-document its construction efforts. The large archive of Russell images helps us understand his motivations, movements, and rationale.

In crafting a new understanding of his photographic legacy, though, we need to consider the whole body of work rather than just a part. A catalog of all his Union Pacific images should encourage greater use and appreciation for his images. As well, their scattered locations call for a comprehensive catalog. The original Union Pacific line stretched across three states and ventured, ever so briefly, into Colorado, but it was headquartered in New York City and Boston. Also, the majority of images were sold in the East. Major repositories with original Russell prints are located from coast to coast. The largest collection of original images is held by the Union Pacific Railroad Museum in Council Bluffs, Iowa, but the Oakland Museum of California has the majority of original negatives (a handful also reside in the National Archives in Washington, D.C.). Many of the images that are in Oakland are not in the Union Pacific Railroad Museum and vice versa.

Resurrecting Russell's legacy has been a slow and laborious process. There were three photographers at Promontory (Russell, Charles Roscoe Savage, and Alfred A. Hart) and for years confusion persisted about who took which photograph. In this confusion Russell's famous image "East and West Shaking Hands at Laying Last Rail" was usually credited to Savage (a Mormon photographer and friend of Russell). Misattribution was a common problem for Russell during his photographic career. His Civil War images have often been attributed to Matthew Brady. Many of his images from a trip to the Uinta Mountains in August of 1869 were credited erroneously, but understandably, to Timothy O'Sullivan.[8] Even with the stereographic views, O. C. Smith and Stephen Sedgwick, two of Russell's financial partners, are sometimes credited instead of Russell. Today, Russell is primarily known either through the famous Golden Spike image or through a small handful of images that have been used repeatedly to portray the builders of the line in almost mythic, heroic terms. It is time to delve deeper into the intricacies of the transcontinental railroad, to flesh out the details of its construction, its operation, and the men who lived (and died) building it. It is also time to acknowledge that its chief photographer created more than one image, or just five or six images. It is my hope that through this publication scholars, publishers, museums, and the media seeking transcontinental railroad images will spend the time to explore fully and use Russell's remarkable body of work.

CHAPTER 2

Russell in New York and during the Civil War (1829–1865)

"Pictured with a truthfulness scarce ever equaled."

—*Nunda News*

Russell was, it turns out, an ordinary man caught up in extraordinary events. He was a capitalist, but not an adventurer, by nature. He was modest, flexible, and unassuming, with a wonderful, dry sense of humor. Time and again he let others take credit away from him, but clearly he liked people and they liked him. He preferred to work in a collaborative environment, with other photographers, in a corporation, or with a partner. He showed artistic promise early in his life, but today his work on canvas is nearly forgotten by art historians. While many of his large-format images are visually stunning, there are many others that are dull and mundane. He took most of his Union Pacific images for promotion, for tourism, and even as a result of petty "trash talk" between the Union Pacific and the Central Pacific. Yet no one can claim that Russell did not rise to the occasion. He was an ordinary man who went to extraordinary lengths to capture the right image from the two great events of his life: the Civil War and the settling of the American West. What he accomplished through sheer will and determination is impressive. Russell might have preferred the quiet, thoughtful life of an artist but the Civil War began a chain of events that he, no doubt, never saw coming.

Russell was born on March 20, 1829, in Walpole, New Hampshire, but grew up in the small upstate town of Nunda, New York. He was a younger, perhaps even the youngest, sibling in his family. His older sister Priscilla married Syrannus Britton before Russell's birth in Walpole. The family moved to Nunda around 1840, probably to work on the Genesee Valley Canal where "Brit" supervised the construction of a deep cut in the canal and later formed a stagecoach business with three of the older Russell brothers.[1] In addition to portraiture and landscape painting, Russell found employment in other artistic odd jobs, such as house decorating and sign painting. He was also both a student and teacher at the Nunda Literary Institute where he taught penmanship starting around 1855.[2]

Little is known about Russell's wife and daughters. He married Catherine Adelia (or Delia) Duryea, and the couple had two daughters born in Nunda: Cora Phillips on July 20,

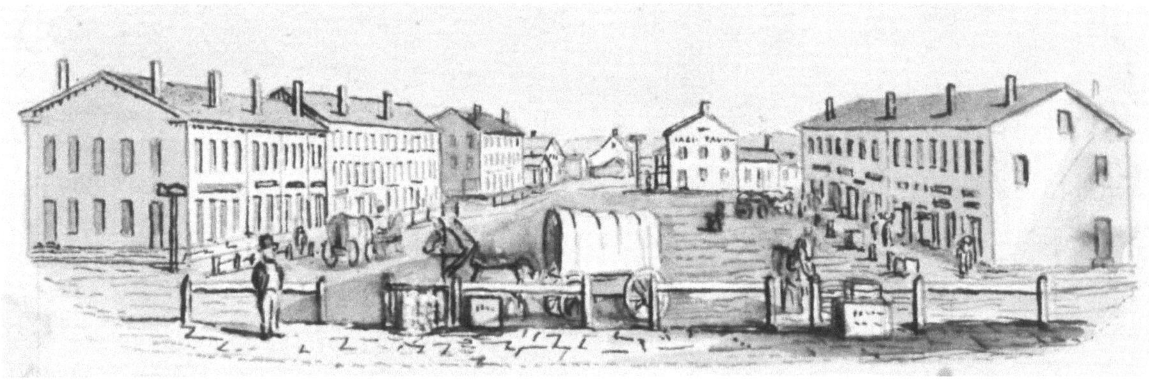

2.1. Central park of Nunda Valley Village, around 1839. *Courtesy of the Nunda Historical Society.*

1853, and Hattie in 1859. Interestingly, his wife and daughters maintained a home in Nunda throughout his career while he lived (mostly) in New York City. Theirs was probably not a happy union. Russell's visits to Nunda were infrequent enough that his presence was commented upon in the local paper. Even after his career was over and he lost his eyesight, he maintained a residence in Brooklyn, New York.[3]

From early on, Russell began an artistic relationship with railroads. While in Nunda he received commissions for portrait and landscape work from railroad employees, probably from the Attica and Hornellsville Railroad built in 1852. He made two landscapes of the waterfalls at Portage and the trestle railroad bridge over the Genesee River around 1854.[4] By 1859 Russell was a noted artist in the Genesee valley who judged art at the Livingstone County Fair and who painted moving panoramas that were exhibited to the public.[5] In upstate New York, Russell was best known for these moving panoramas, which were immensely popular from the late 1840s to the late 1860s. These panoramas consisted of huge lengths of painted canvases that were unrolled slowly on giant spools (hidden by stage curtains), thus revealing a moving montage of images that were considered middle-class art and entertainment. Topics varied widely, but travel narratives were especially popular in the United States. These panoramas were accompanied by a speaker, who explained the significance of the images, frequently with music, special lighting, and atmospheric effects.[6] In 1858 he painted a panorama of David Livingstone's travels in Africa based on sketches brought from Africa to London. The Africa panorama took two hours to view with narration and cost fifteen cents.[7] Russell, as well, would paint panoramas of Niagara Falls and of Dr. Elisha Kane's arctic explorations in the 1850s.[8]

Like many artists before and after him, Russell moved to New York City to further his career in June 1860. Despite leaving his hometown permanently, he obviously felt an affinity for its residents and they for him. Russell remained a noted personality in the town for nearly twenty-five years, first as a talented painter of panoramas, then as a captain in the Union army, then as the photographer of the transcontinental railroad who wrote interesting travelogues to the *Nunda News*, and, finally, as an employee of the popular magazine *Frank Leslie's Illustrated*

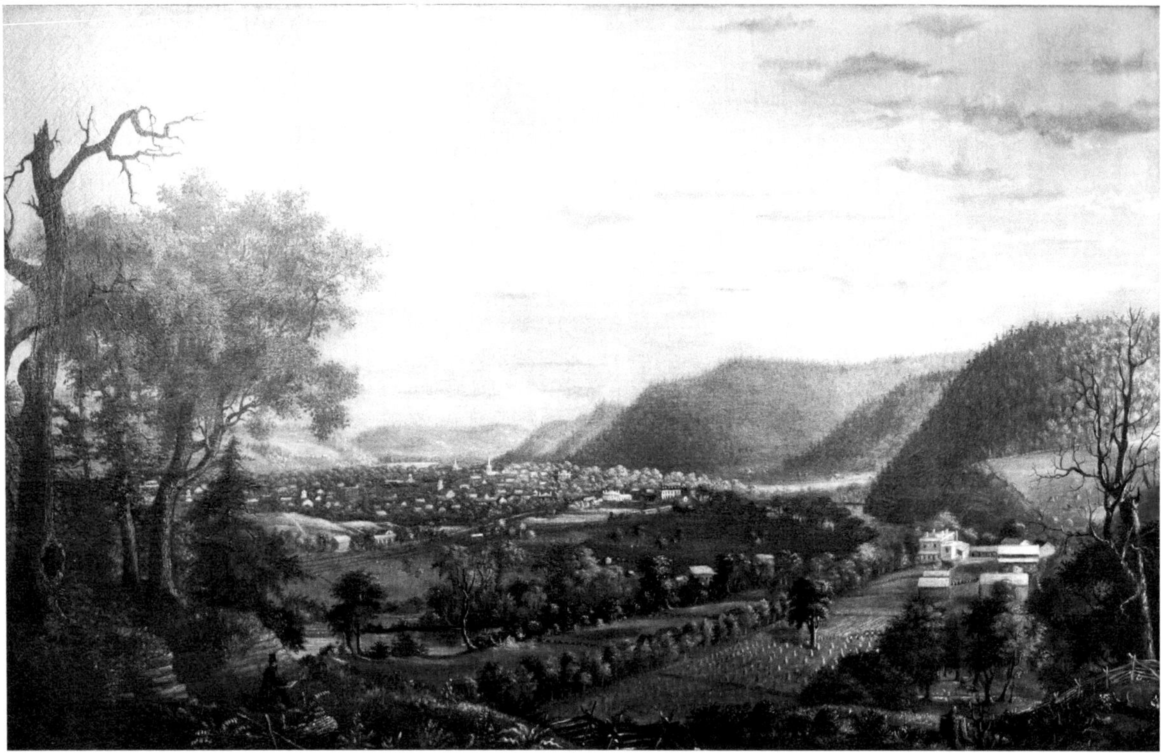

2.2. View of Bath from the west, by A. J. Russell, 1859. *Courtesy of the Steuben County Historical Society in Bath, New York; photo by Joshua House.*

Newspaper. Even seemingly mundane events like donating photographs to the local library in Nunda were dutifully recorded.[9] Before he left for New York City he received an endorsement in his local paper, which fairly burst with pride in their local boy: "[Russell's art] exhibit[s] in a high degree the indications of true genius for the art, and we trust will give him a sure passport to that success to which his character, his genius and attainments [pre]eminently entitle him."[10]

In New York City he continued his budding career as an artist and, while he had moved beyond earning money from teaching penmanship and house and sign painting, he still maintained a remarkable versatility. Russell had mastered sketching, watercolor, and oil portraits. He also created oil paintings of picturesque landscapes around Nunda. The *Buffalo Express* wrote: "During a recent sojourn of a few days in New-York, we strolled into the studio of A. J. Russell, where we spent an hour most satisfactorily in examining the productions of his pencil. They are mostly landscapes of American scenery with drawings from nature. One struck our attention as particularly meritorious. It is a view of the Cohocton Valley, near Bath, in Steuben County, and is exceedingly truthful in its representation. It is a summer scene, and never did the golden harvest appear in richer luxuriance and perfection, or the forest foliage more beautiful, or the summer sky more enchanting than they rest in this instance upon the canvas, as

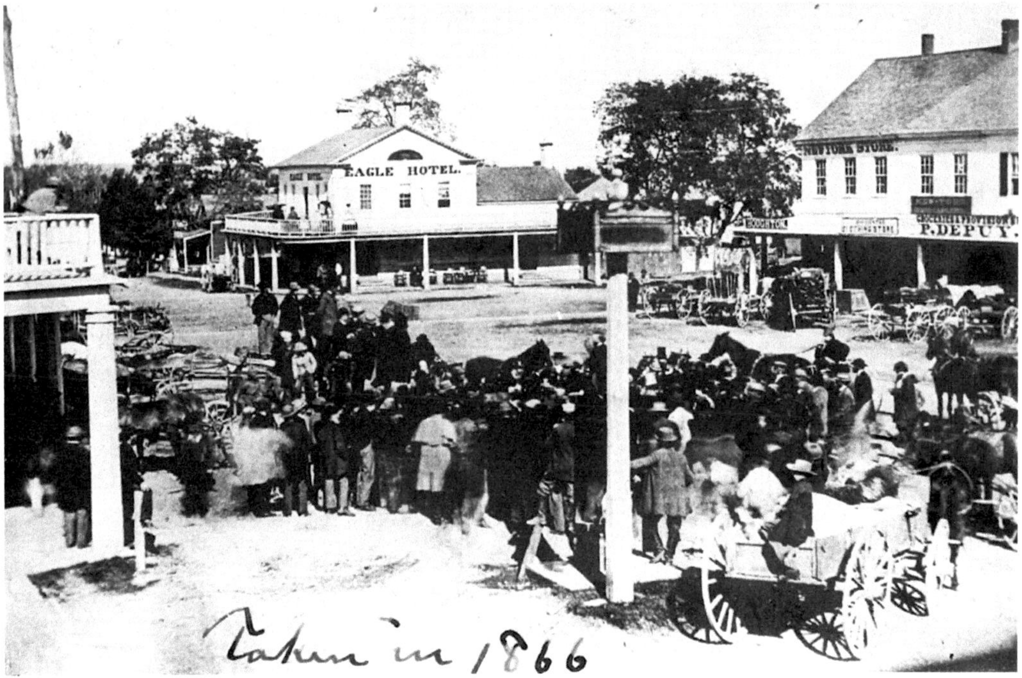

2.3. Nunda village square in 1866. *Courtesy of the Nunda Historical Society.*

the achievement of a wonderful art. This picture speaks volumes in praise of the artist, whose prospects are just budding, and whose future, if life and health shall be spared him, is full of honorable success."[11] According to the *Nunda News*, he planned to visit Europe to further his art study, but it seems he never made this trip. In fact, Russell only stayed in New York City for about a year before opening a studio in Hornellsville (now Hornell) located only a few miles from Nunda. The move is especially unexpected given that he had been commissioned to produce a series of landscapes of the Cohocton Valley for the wealthy lawyer Robert B. Van Valkenburg. Van Valkenburg and Russell grew up only a few miles from one another so it is not surprising that they made a connection.[12]

RUSSELL'S "PANORAMA OF THE WAR FOR THE UNION"

Russell's life changed, however, in ways that he never could have predicted through the four-year carnage that was the Civil War. Panoramas of the Civil War were immensely popular and in late 1861 he began painting "Panorama of the War for the Union," which was first shown in Hornellsville on December 9.[13] The *Nunda News*, quoting from the *Hornellsville Journal*, sang its praises: "His pictures speak volumes of truth relative to camp life, battle scenes, showing the extreme of excitement, as well as the resignation of the wounded and dying, and the marble-cold expression of the up-turned faces of the dead. All these show—alas! But too faithfully—the stern realities of war. The battle-fields are pictured with a truthfulness scarce

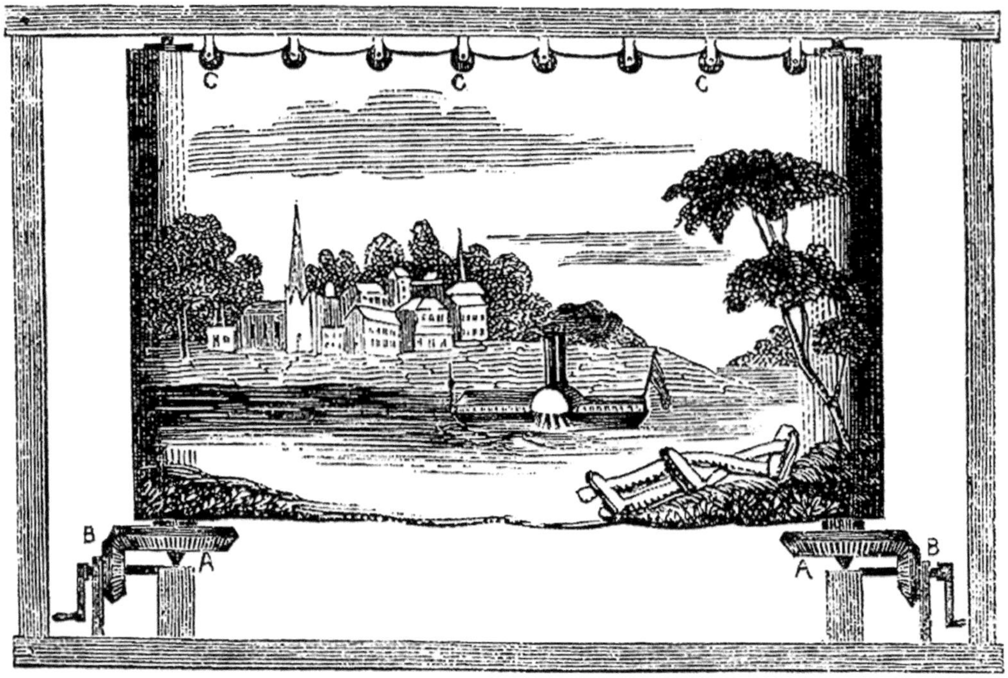

2.4. Illustration of a moving panorama designed by John Banvard, appeared in *Scientific American*, December 16, 1848.

ever equaled, and in gazing upon them one forgets that he is looking at an inanimate piece of canvas, and is transported to the field of strife."[14] Unfortunately this panorama burned not long after on December 26 in a fire in Hornellsville.[15]

Russell shrugged off this setback and had a new panorama painted by February that was enlarged in May.[16] In 1862 the panorama was shown throughout upstate New York, including Hornell, Nunda, Warsaw, Binghamton, Rochester, Schenectady, Elmira, Mount Morris, Medina, and Oneida. The narrator and manager (and perhaps owner) of the panorama was not Russell, but a man named J. H. Lillie.[17] The panorama depicted "24 distinct views besides a large portion of moving Panoramic Scenery of Skirmishes, Battles, Encampments, Cities, Shipping, Harbors, Bombardments, and nearly every principal place and battle of interest connected with the war of the present time."[18] This panorama encouraged enlistment and pride in the unified United States before the Civil War. The *Medina Tribune* wrote: "The opening scene . . . is a splendid picture, and represents Fort Sum[ter] on fire . . . and volunteers coming from every section of the loyal portion of our country: the farmer leaving his plow in the furrow, and the smith leaving his anvil and forge. One is instantly carried back to the commencement of the rebellion, and to the days when our beloved country was at peace, and we a united and prosperous people. We cannot enumerate each piece, but the affect of this Panorama is to arouse one's patriotism, to teach us more about the country, and impress strongly upon our minds the value of the Union."[19] In fact the panorama took on a life of its own after Russell joined the army as it continued to tour throughout New York and even into Ohio and Pennsylvania.[20] The panorama was sold at auction in Rochester in 1865 to raise money for charity but amazingly it resurfaced in 1879 to be shown in Naples for twenty-five-cent admission.[21] There were, in fact, many Civil War panoramas. Russell's "Panorama of the War for the Union" was not as popular as others produced by artists such as William Travis, Thomas Clarkson Gordon, and George W. Williams, which were shown in large cities rather than towns.[22]

Russell's panoramas were important to his career as a photographer in two ways. A moving panorama could use a series of images that mimic a trip from point A to point B. Later Russell would use the same concept of overland travel through sets of stereoscopic views. The second benefit was suggesting that a single image was not able to convey the ideas that a group of paintings accompanied by narration (either spoken or written) could. Photographs, as well, were important for panoramas because of the greater accuracy they bestowed (in the mind of the public) when they were copied to paint. In advertisements it was stressed that Russell's panorama was based on photographs taken by several photographers, including Mathew Brady. In truth, Russell also probably used battlefield illustrations that could be found in contemporary journals.[23]

Russell took heed of his own message and entered the army with the rank of captain. He recruited a company of soldiers (Company F, the 141st Regiment of the New York Infantry Volunteers) in Hornellsville on August 19, 1862.[24] Russell's art patron Van Valkenburg was in charge of volunteer recruitment for New York, which was headquartered in Elmira, where Russell officially joined the army. One local paper praised Russell's recruiting services as "almost beyond precedent having enlisted 90 men in four days."[25] Russell did not immediately become a photographer in the war. He spent December near Washington, D.C., where he served in his unit north of the Potomac River as part of the defenses of the Capitol. The 141st was then deployed south to Belle Plains, Virginia. He was detached from this unit on March 1, 1863.[26] General Haupt requested that Captain Russell be assigned as a special assistant to the Military Railroad Construction Corps for the Union army.[27] Later, the *Nunda News* speculated that Russell did dangerous work sketching important Rebel defenses while operating behind enemy lines.[28] While some artists did this kind of work, there is no evidence that Russell was used in this way.

The Civil War offered new opportunities for enterprising photographers, many of whom left their studios to follow the various Union army camps, selling portraits or group shots of the soldiers that could be sent home to nervous relatives. Others contracted with illustrated newspapers such as *Harper's Weekly, New York Illustrated News*, and *Leslie's Illustrated* to provide images that were used as the basis of printed engravings. In 1861 and 1862 there was tremendous public interest in the military sites, generals, and politicians associated with the conflict, leading to a boom in mass-produced cartes de visite and stereographic images. Some photographers, in fact, contracted with large-scale distributors such as Anthony's of New York City.[29] The Union army also hired several photographers

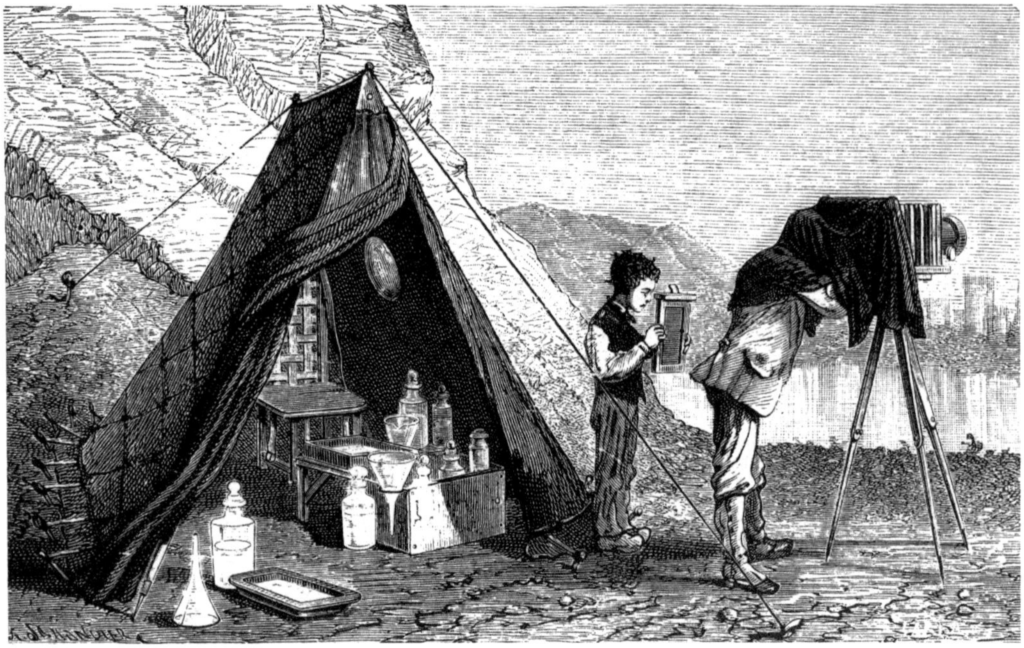

2.5. "Photography and Exploration," from *A History and Handbook of Photography.*

on a temporary basis to document campaigns, military structures, and construction techniques.[30] Russell, however, occupied a unique niche, as the only officer whose major duty was photography. Russell was more constricted because his image taking was, no doubt, directed by his superiors. But he also enjoyed more financial security, knowing that he would have a steady paycheck.

Russell's detachment classified him as government artist. He established the photographic department in the railroad roundhouse complex in Alexandria and served as acting assistant quartermaster.[31] Whether Russell was detached from his unit for this specific assignment is unknown. Russell had to learn the art of wet-plate photography from a Baltimore man named Egbert Guy Fawx (or Faux). Fawx agreed to teach Russell the collodion wet-plate process for the sum of $300.[32] As subsequent events would show, Russell would practice the form at a high level, and it is not hard to imagine that the pupil quickly became the master.

Creating a collodion wet-plate glass negative was a tricky business that discouraged the amateur. The process required a number of steps, any one of which could go afoul, which had to be completed in a prescribed order. Frederick Scott Archer invented this new photographic method in 1851. He experimented with the recently invented collodion compound in liquid form and discovered that it tightly adhered to a glass sheet. After the collodion dried, however, it could not be developed and fixed. Archer realized that the negative needed to be sensitized, exposed, and developed while it was still wet. Iodized or sensitized collodion was prepared shortly before the image was taken by mixing plain collodion and an iodizing solu-

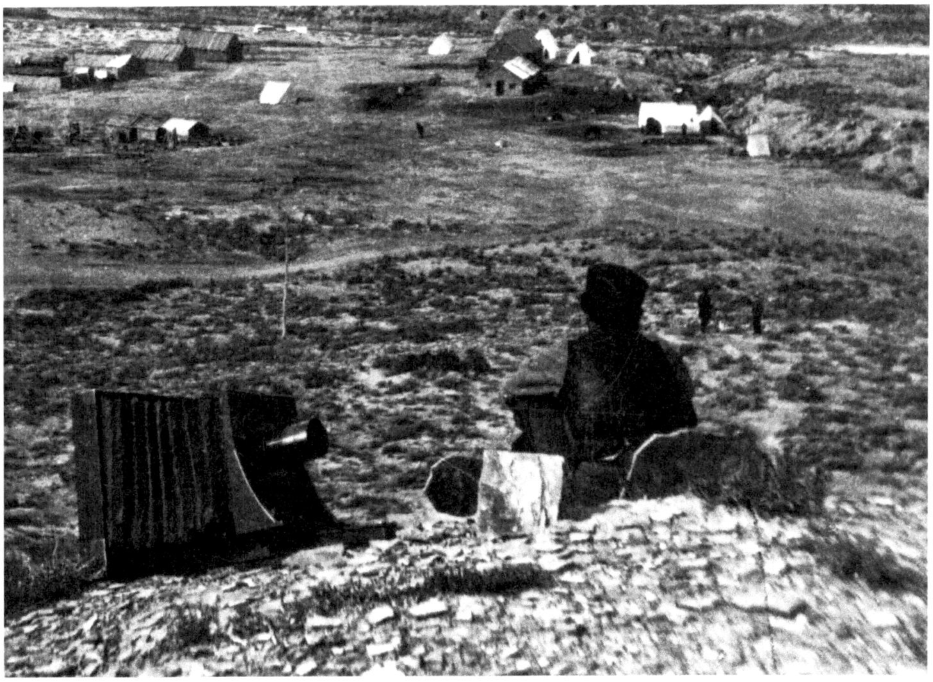

2.6. Cropped version of A. J. Russell stereo-view no. 168 (Russell's large-format camera). *Courtesy of the University of Iowa Libraries, Special Collections, Levi O. Leonard Railroadiana.*

tion. The plain collodion was a mixture of gun cotton (cotton, potassium nitrate, and sulfuric acid), alcohol, and ether. The iodizer was created by dissolving cadmium iodide and cadmium bromide in alcohol. After mixing the two compounds the photographer now had sensitized collodion and it was ready for use.[33]

Russell used plate glass for his views. Plate glass surfaces were ground flat with the edges smoothed with a diamond-point glass cutter. These plates were immersed in dilute nitric acid and then washed and dried in a, preferably, dust-free space. They were then polished on the emulsion side and coated with a mixture of tripoli powder and alcohol spread with cotton. The iodized or sensitized collodion was slowly poured onto the plate while it was tipped back and forth so that the collodion was evenly distributed. In a darkroom the plate was then dipped into a silver nitrate solution, loaded into a plate holder, exposed in the camera (within five minutes), and removed from the camera. The plate was then washed and developed using iron sulfate, water, glacial acetic acid, and alcohol. Silver nitrate and more developer were applied as needed to attain the right contrast or intensity. The plate was washed again, fixed with hyposulfite of soda, and washed again with a fine spray of water. Having distilled, or very clean, water was critical for the process.[34]

Although all the steps had to be performed while the negative was wet (in one or two hours), this process had definite advantages over the daguerreotype. Collodion wet-plate glass negatives had an exposure time that was ten times faster than the daguerreotype and

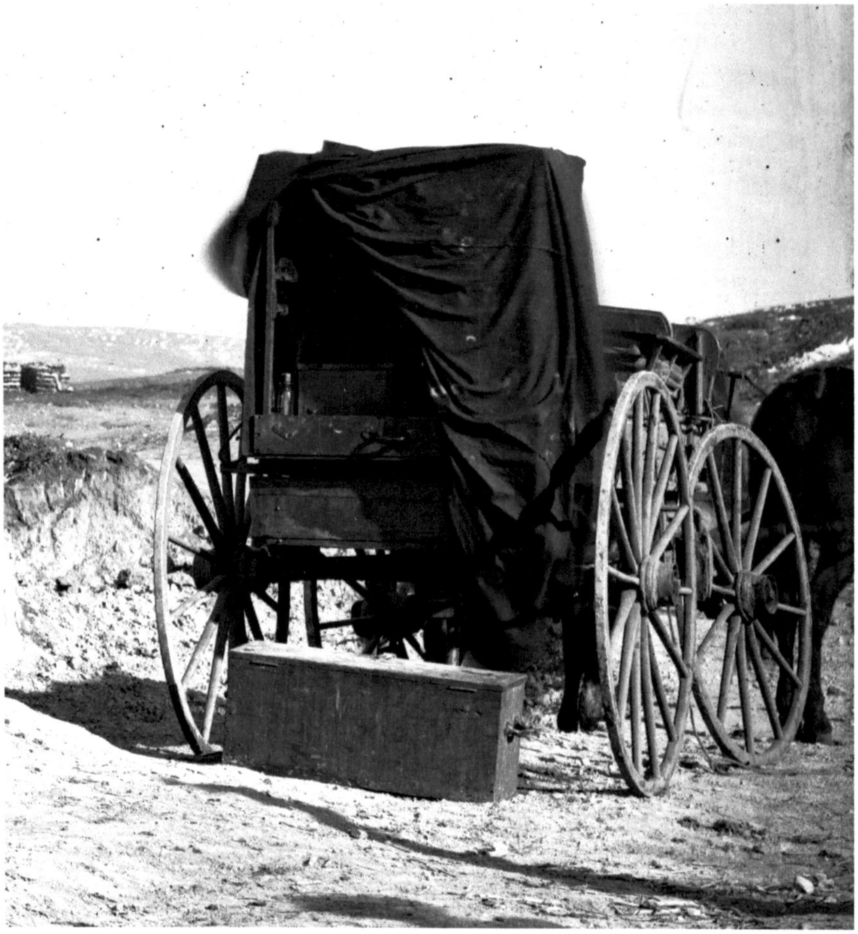

2.7. Cropped version of A. J. Russell large-format view no. 59 (Russell's developing box and his darkroom wagon). *Courtesy of the Oakland Museum of California, A. J. Russell Collection.*

were also much cheaper. Of course, with a negative (a daguerreotype is both a positive and a negative) one could print hundreds or even thousands of prints.[35] Russell began with Fawx's 6.5" x 8.5" and 8" x 10" cameras. In the spring of 1864 he constructed 10" x 13" and 8" x 11" cameras. The 10" x 13" camera (fig. 2.6) must have been durable and well made, as this was the camera he used later for his large-format railroad images. Russell found a stereo-view camera in the Orange Line storehouse and he also took stereo-view images, but whether these images were part of his official duties or to make money on the side is unknown. His Civil War stereo-views today are very rare. Perhaps because Brady had an active market in selling these views, Russell chose not to focus in this direction.[36]

To be an effective photographer Russell had to have a detachable, traveling darkroom. He used either a train or a wagon to transport this darkroom. The *Baltimore American* wrote that "General Haupt has handed over to the photographic officer a common box railroad

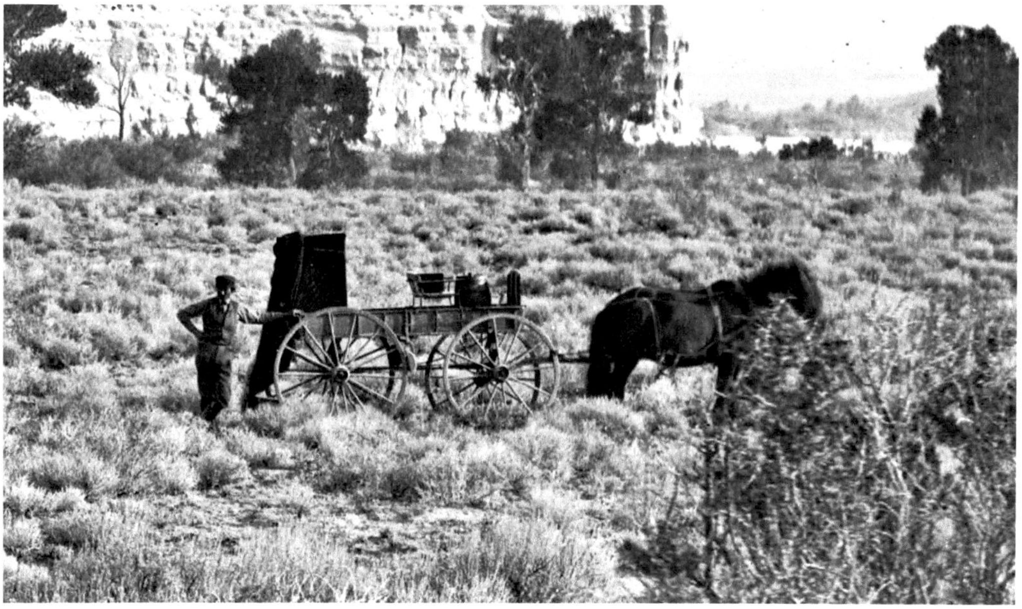

2.8. Cropped version of A. J. Russell large-format view no. 77b (Russell's darkroom wagon). *Courtesy of the Oakland Museum of California, A. J. Russell Collection.*

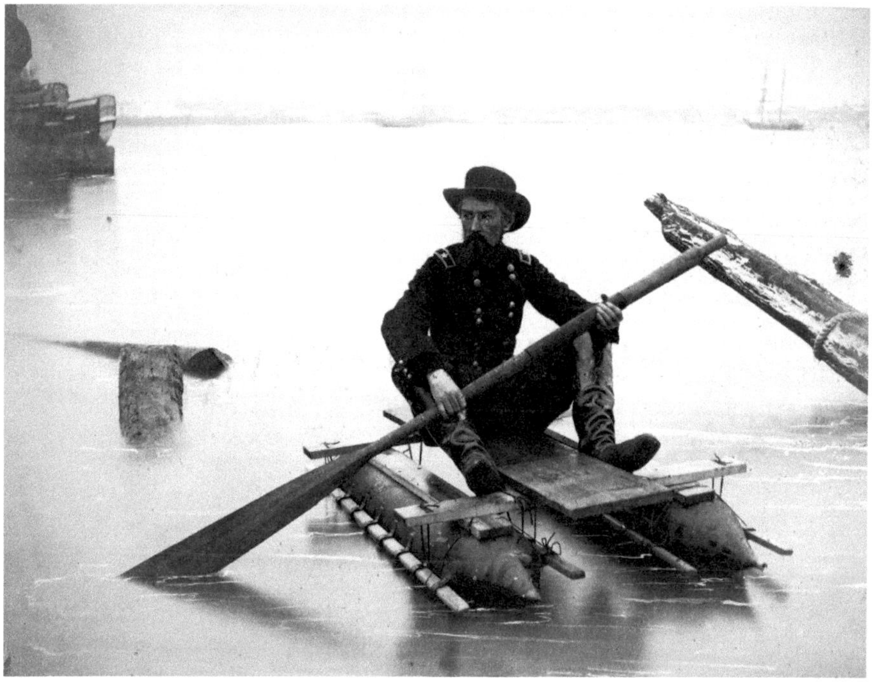

2.9. General Herman Haupt, by A. J. Russell, from Photographs Illustrative of Operations in Construction and Transportation. *Courtesy of the Library of Congress, Prints and Photographs Division.*

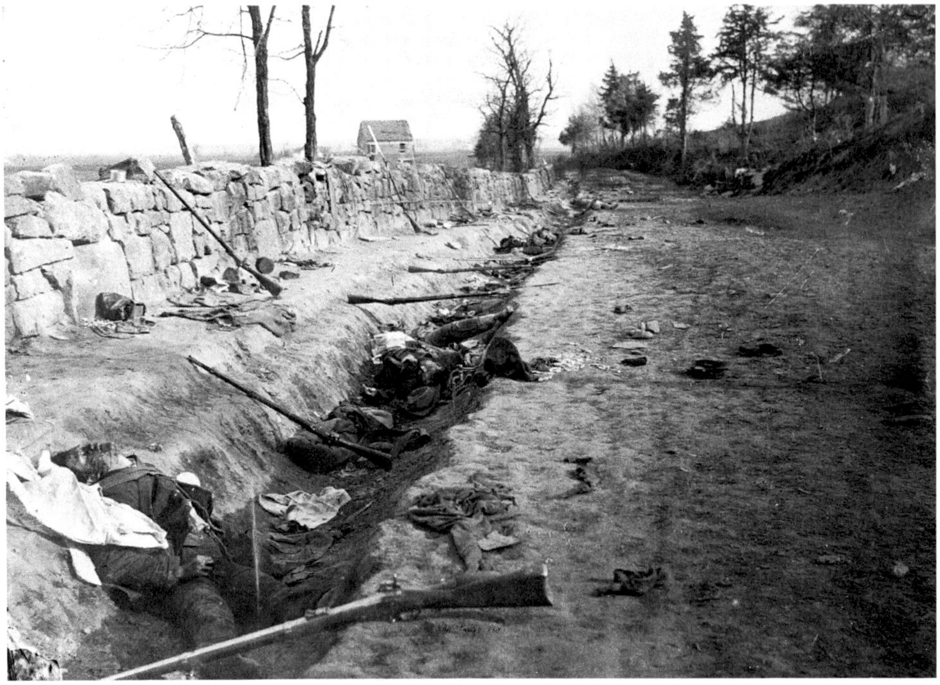

2.10. Stone wall, rear of Fredericksburg with Rebel dead, May 3, 1863, by A. J. Russell. *Courtesy of the Library of Congress, Prints and Photographs Division.*

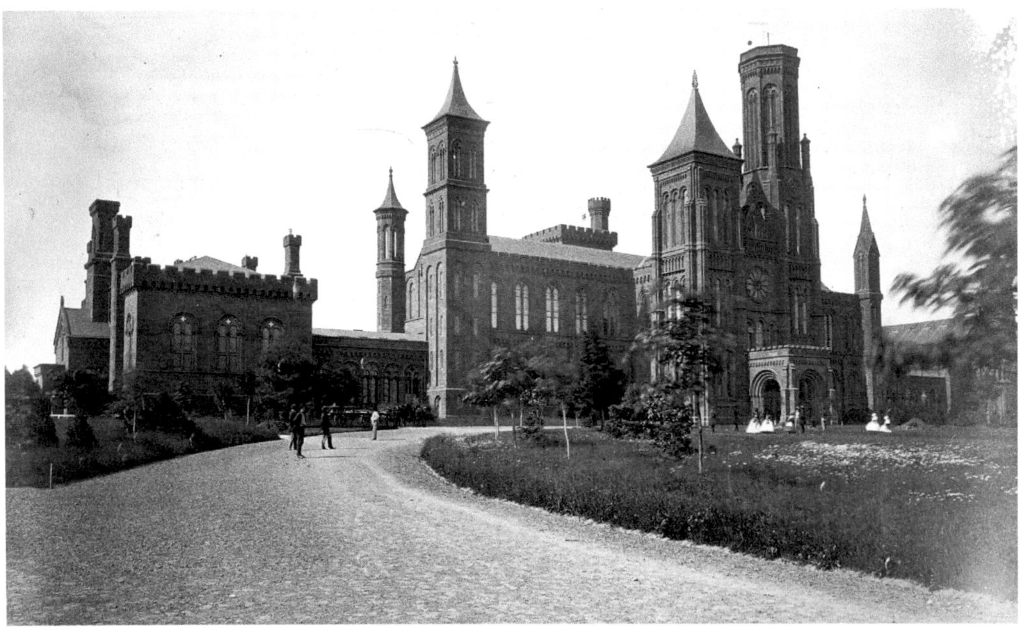

2.11. Smithsonian Institution, by A. J. Russell. *Courtesy of the Library of Congress, Prints and Photographs Division.*

car, which being the headquarters of the latter, he—as occasion serves—gets an unemployed ambulance to take his things to any point within the lines, finishing up his pictures on his return and at his leisure."[37] Later Russell obtained a standard buckboard wagon with a box attached on the rear that could act as a field darkroom. He would use this wagon in 1864 and 1865, packing it onto the railroad when needed. This was the very same vehicle that he would employ so well later over the line of the Union Pacific.[38]

Russell's superior, General Haupt was, quite simply, an American genius. He tended to solve problems using unorthodox, but effective methods. In a year and a half he completely reorganized the construction corps and, in fact, the railroads used his schema for the remainder of the war. He was as adept at wading tricky political waters as he was at organizing men to be more efficient. For instance, he would assign his workers based on their natural attributes and then have them compete against one another to increase productivity. Haupt left the army because he felt his particular genius would be wasted on merely administering the system he created. He did, however, recognize how important photography could be to help illustrate his unorthodox approaches. Haupt was developing innovative ways to construct and reconstruct bridges, railroads, and pontoon boats and Russell photographed these experiments. His photographs were a sort of visual aid in implementing Haupt's new methods. Haupt issued a report with Russell's action shots, and presented photo albums to Union military commanders, congressmen, cabinet members, and even to President Lincoln.[39]

In addition to illustrating reports, Russell photographed buildings around Washington, D.C. and Arlington, including the Capitol, the Smithsonian Institution, the Washington Aqueduct, the Treasury, and the Alexandria and Orange Railroad yard, probably as a way to learn his new craft in early 1863.[40] Soon, however, Russell would take views of the war effort. He photographed the battle of Fredericksburg in May 1863 and, in fact, he took the famous photograph (fig. 2.10) of the Rebel dead lying behind a stone wall (usually credited to O'Sullivan). Haupt wrote, "My photographer artist, Captain Russell was with me and secured several large photographic negatives—one very good one of the stone wall, with the rebel dead lying behind it."[41] The *Baltimore American* also reported on this scene, writing, "a friend informs us that after the heights of Fredericksburg were carried by Sedgwick's troops, amongst the first acquaintances he saw on the spot, and getting into position to picture the scene, was the indefatigable Captain Russell, who had previously probably been taking views as near the place as the carnage permitted."[42]

Even though Haupt retired from the army on September 14, 1863, Russell continued his role as a military photographer, which included a heavy load of printing. Throughout the fall of 1863 and winter of 1863 to 1864, Russell worked on the twenty-seven-page report *Photographs Illustrative of Operations in Construction and Transportation, as Used to Facilitate the Movements of the Armies of the Rappahannock, of Virginia, and of the Potomac, Including Experiments Made to Determine the Most Practical and Expeditious Modes to Be Resorted to in the Construction, Destruction and Reconstruction of Roads and Bridges.* By February 1864, Russell had produced at least twenty-nine copies, each with eighty-two

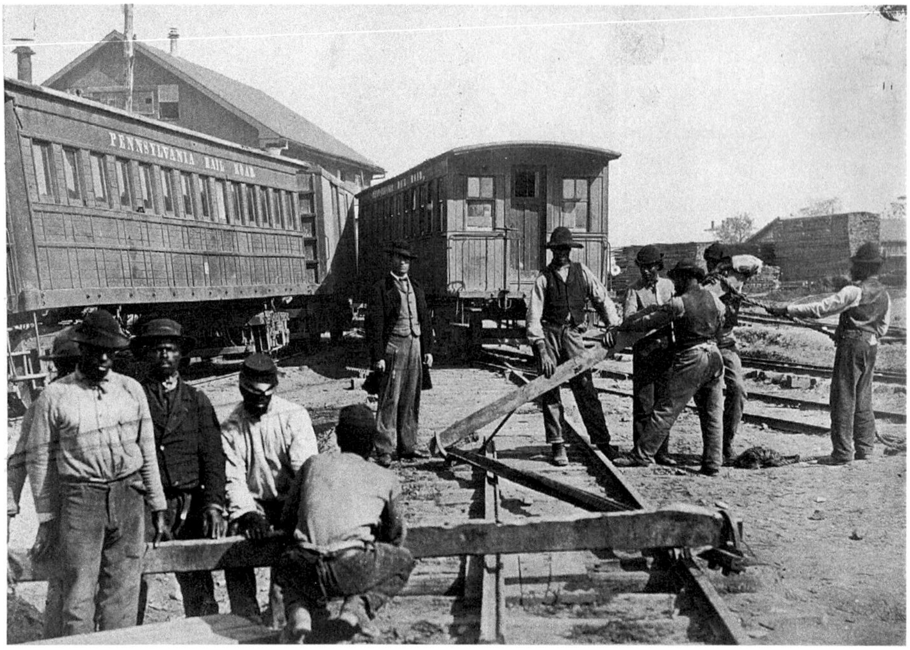

2.12. Military railroad operations in northern Virginia with men using levers for loosening rails, by A. J. Russell, from Photographs Illustrative of Operations in Construction and Transportation. *Courtesy of the Library of Congress, Prints and Photographs Division.*

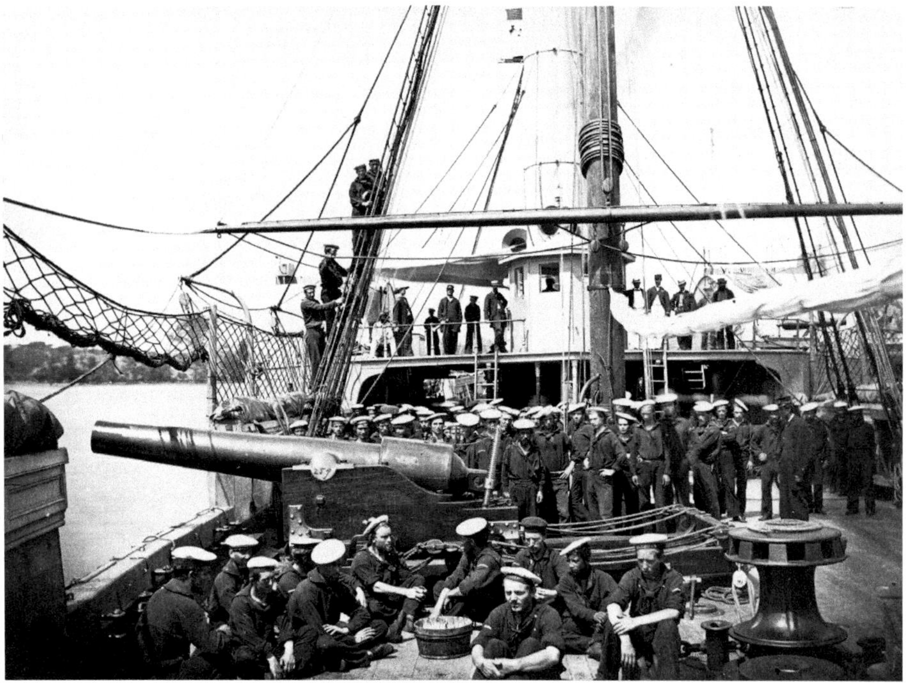

2.13. Officers and crew of the gunboat *Mendota*, James River, Virginia, July 18, 1864, by A. J. Russell. *Courtesy of the Library of Congress, Prints and Photographs Division.*

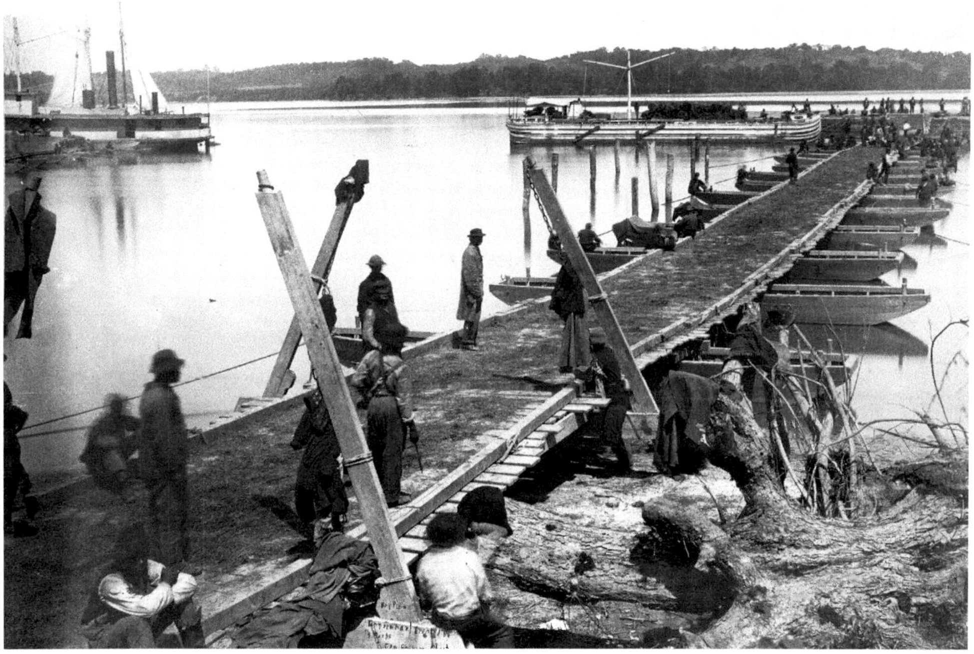

2.14. Upper wharf, Belle Plain, built by U.S. Military Railroad Construction Corps, by A. J. Russell. *Courtesy of the Library of Congress, Prints and Photographs Division.*

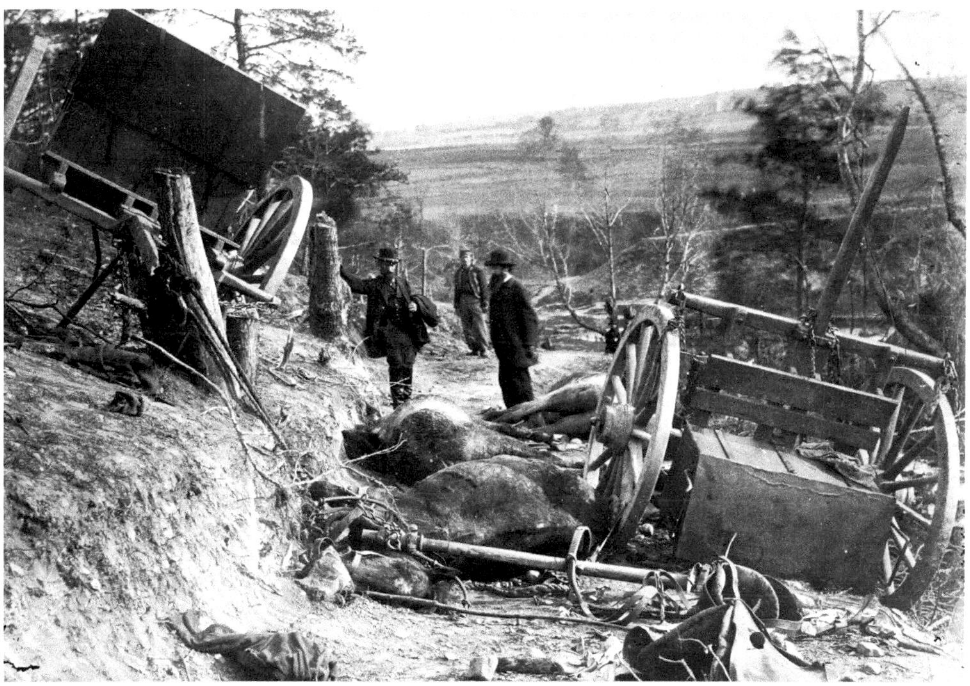

2.15. A shattered caisson, Fredericksburg, Virginia, May 3, 1863, by A. J. Russell. *Courtesy of the Library of Congress, Prints and Photographs Division.*

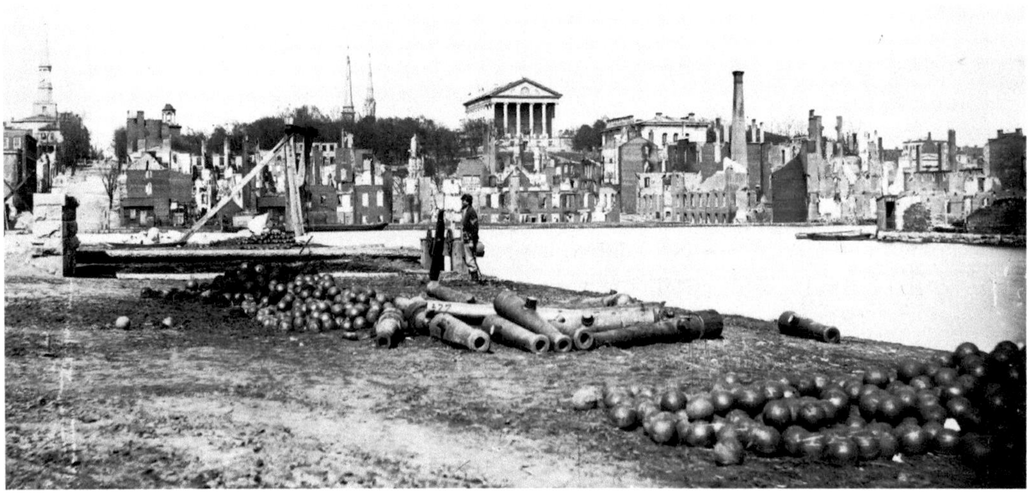

2.16. View taken from south side of canal basin, Richmond, Virginia, April 1865, by A. J. Russell. *Courtesy of the Library of Congress, Prints and Photographs Division.*

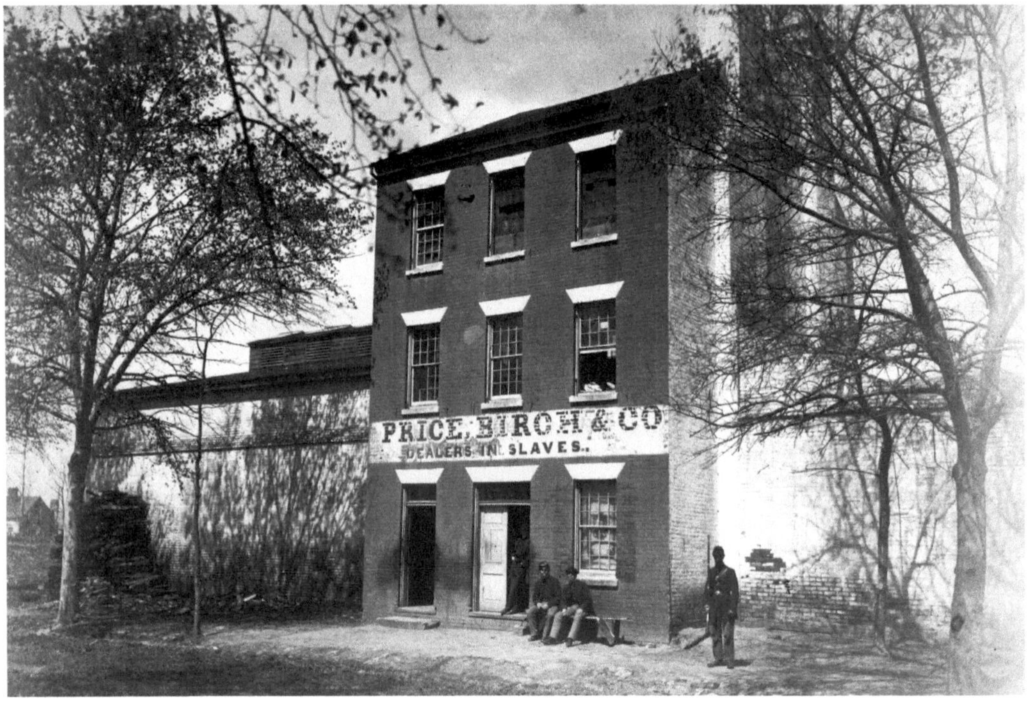

2.17. Slave pen in Alexandria, Virginia, by A. J. Russell. *Courtesy of the Library of Congress, Prints and Photographs Division.*

images. Russell also printed these photos individually or in small photo albums for the army, the War Department, politicians, and even the "Admiral of [the] Russian Fleet."[43] Images consisted of tests on truss bridges, ark boats, railroad rails being straightened and broken, the military railroad bridge across Potomac Creek, experiments with suspension trusses, the trestle bridge across Bull Run Creek, and blanket boats. Several of the images show the black freedman laborers whom Haupt effectively utilized in his work. Colonel John H. Devereaux wrote to Colonel D. C. McCallum: "The Photographic Department begins and ends with [Russell]. . . . No salaried assistant has ever been employed, and the work is done by the Captain, the Captain's servant, and a laborer. The cost pr. Month is the cost of chemicals. . . . This has provided (by Capt. Russell's estimate of ordinary trade prices) $7,000 worth of pictures, which have been distributed under Gl. Haupt's order as shown."[44]

Russell's new superior after Haupt was Major E. L. Wentz.[45] Under Wentz, Russell photographed the headquarters of General Mead and Webb and Manassas Junction before traveling with General Ulysses S. Grant in May and June of 1864, during which he shot images of Petersburg, Fredericksburg, and Belle Plain before returning to Washington, D.C., in June. In July he photographed the officers and crew of the gunboat *Mendota*, and the City Point and Army railroad.[46] In June 1864, Quartermaster General Montgomery C. Meigs (himself an avid amateur photographer) requested that Russell produce "both views and stereographs . . . showing the present condition of all buildings within . . . the new military cemetery at Arlington."[47] Russell was then assigned to work with James J. Moore on November 1, 1864, when Brigadier General Daniel C. McCallum promoted Moore to chief engineer and general superintendent of the military railroads of Virginia. McCallum obviously felt that illustrating the construction and supply activities was important for the war effort. Russell photographed the Dutch Gap Canal, pontoon bridges across the Appomattox River, and even Lincoln's presidential railroad car. In April 1865, as the war was winding down, Russell recorded the devastation of Richmond as well as Fort Mahone, Petersburg, and Fort Sedgwick. His photographs of Richmond are particularly arresting, showing a ghostly town completely destroyed by Union bombardment. After the war Russell took numerous photos in and around Washington, D.C., including Lincoln's funeral car, the cavalry depot at Giesboro Point, the arsenal yard, and the Washington waterworks. Although Russell's primary focus was on railroads and military construction, he also did not overlook the signature issue of the war, shooting images of a slave pen in Alexandria, a freedman camp in Richmond, and African-American workers building a stockade at the Orange and Alexandria Railroad yard.[48]

"THE WORLD IS INDEBTED TO THE PHOTOGRAPHIC ART"

Years later Russell would write: "The memories of our great war come down to us and will pass on to future generations with more accuracy and truth-telling illustration than that of any other previous struggle of ancient or modern times: and the world is indebted to the photographic art and a few enterprising and earnest men, who are not afraid of exposure and who could laugh

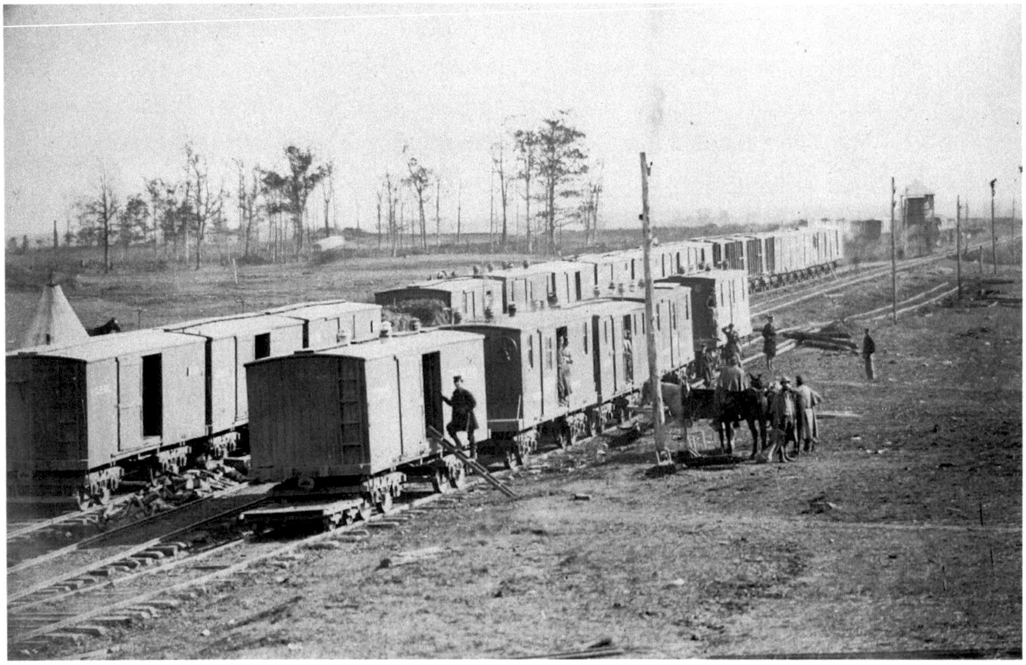

2.18. Manassas Junction, telegraph station, March 1864, by A. J. Russell. *Courtesy of the Library of Congress, Prints and Photographs Division.*

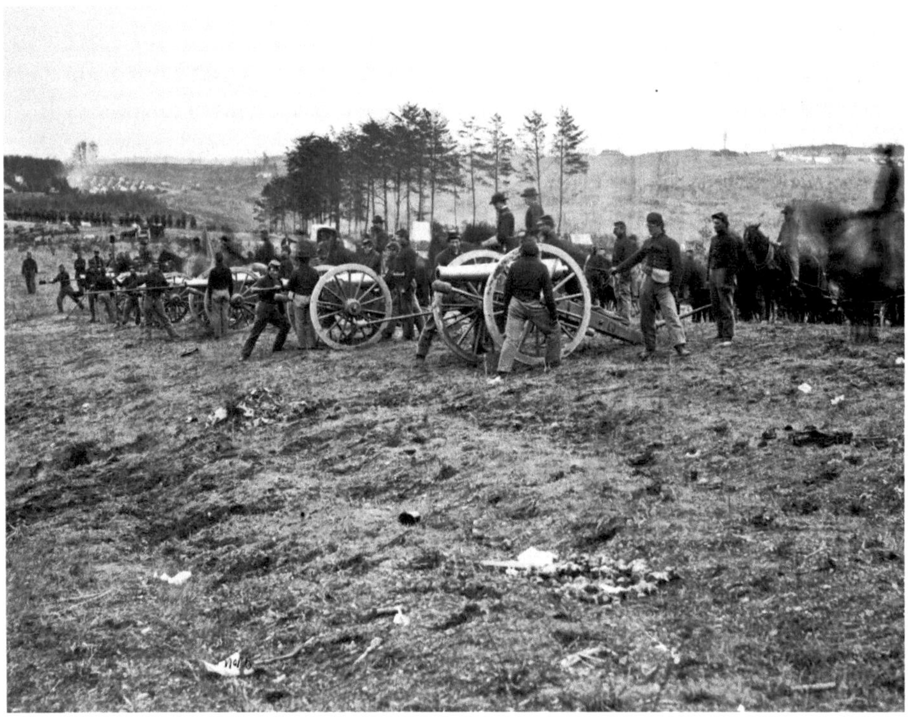

2.19. First Connecticut battery, near Fredericksburg, May 2, 1863, by A. J. Russell. *Courtesy of the Library of Congress, Prints and Photographs Division.*

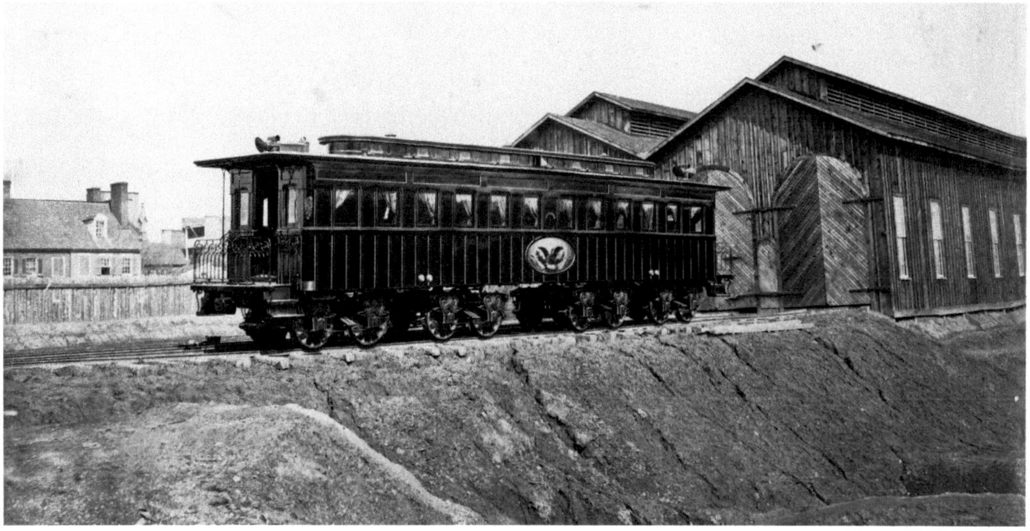

2.20. Lincoln's funeral car at Alexandria, April 1865, by A. J. Russell. *Courtesy of the Library of Congress, Prints and Photographs Division.*

at fatigue and starvation, could face danger in all shapes, and, were at all times ready to march, often between two armies, in the trenches, on the ramparts, through the swamps and forests, with the advance guard, and back again at head-quarters—not a flank movement, but the willing and indefatigable artist at his post of danger and adventure."[49] Perhaps Russell embellished his role somewhat, but he did place great emphasis on creating an accurate visual archive of the Civil War. The *Baltimore American* wrote that "photography should be employed on the battlefield in the present great conflict, by way of preserving accurate representations of scenes which will be of surpassing interest so long as the nation has a history." The newspaper went on to suggest that a historiographer should accompany Russell to write a brief sketch about each image taken, and every regiment or corps should have an official image. "Absorbed in the more pressing needs of the great conflict our people hardly appreciate the fact that they are 'making history'; a history, the minutest detail of which will be studied with intense eagerness for thousands of years to come."[50] In effect, the greater accuracy of the photographer over the illustrator would create a better record for posterity. The photograph was seen by many during this time as a higher form of art because of its greater fidelity to the actual scene. Like the railroad, photography was another nineteenth-century progressive technological solution.[51] The *Nunda News* wrote: "Until recently mankind ha[s] been mainly dependent upon the artistic painter for the best transfers of the appearances of scenes and objects to the canvas. . . . [S]till a critical and minute inspection of the perfect works of our best artists, fall far short of perfection. But the modern science of Photography overcomes this difficulty and presents the scenery and every object within the scope of the photographer's camera, true to nature—perfect."[52]

There are a number of similarities between Russell's Civil War and later Union Pacific photographic work. Russell's Civil War photos, in addition to the preservation of "more accuracy and

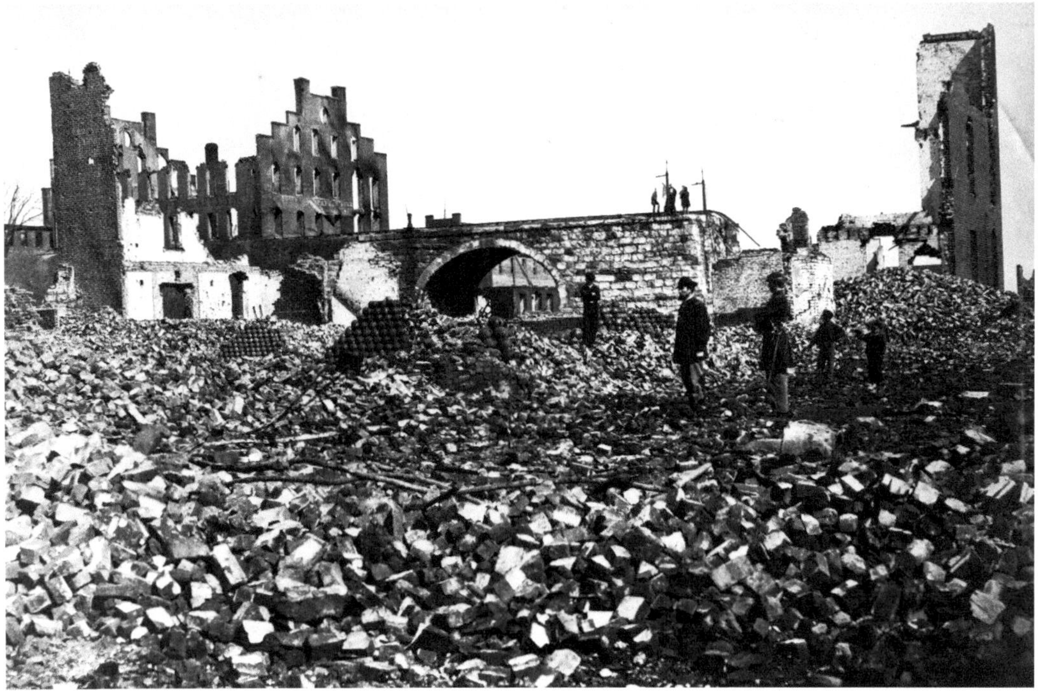

2.21. Ruins in Richmond, Virginia, April 1865, by A. J. Russell. *Courtesy of the Library of Congress, Prints and Photographs Division.*

truth-telling illustration," also became positive publicity in Washington, D.C.[53] This would also be true later for the Union Pacific not only in Washington but also with investors, the general public, and potential riders. During the Civil War, Russell photographed railroad construction, becoming familiar with using tracks, cars, engines, and the line as compositional elements. He learned how to operate a darkroom wagon and how to use a railroad to transport the wagon and photographic equipment. Russell also used both large-format and stereographic images for the same subject and he knew the limitations and strengths of each camera. He learned to command men and machines, arranging them to his liking. As well, both the Civil War images and the Union Pacific images do not show the actual events as they occur (battles and laying track). Rather, they show the before and after.

Also similar with both the Union Pacific and Civil War images was a lack of recognition for Russell's pioneering photographic work. Russell was the government's only commissioned officer whose major duties included photography; yet celebrity photographer Matthew Brady appropriated much of the credit due to Russell. Russell was not alone in this regard. Future western photographers Gardner and O'Sullivan both began working for Brady, but split off after they received little recognition for the dangerous work they did. How it happened is not clear, but somehow Brady acquired most of Russell's Civil War negatives. Some of these images Brady sold to the federal government in 1874 or 1875. These negatives

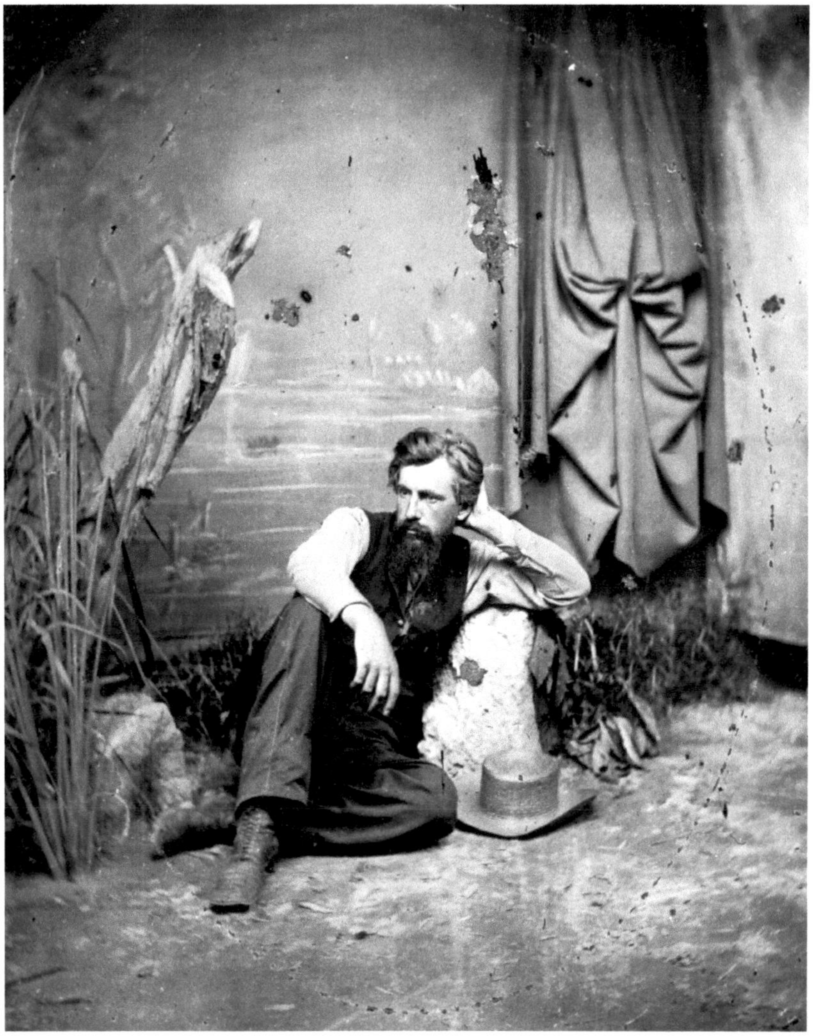

2.22. Tintype of A. J. Russell, taken around 1865. *Courtesy of the Oakland Museum of California, A. J. Russell Collection.*

(including stereo-views, as well) eventually made their way to the National Archives and the Library of Congress.[54] It was not until the 1960s and 1970s that Russell's extensive photographic activities during the Civil War were given proper appreciation. Russell's photographic snubs, however, were far in the future and at the end of the war Russell was, no doubt, thrilled to return to Nunda.[55] He was not mustered out with the 141st on June 8, 1865, and instead left the army on September 9, 1865.[56]

CHAPTER 3

The Union Pacific and Central Pacific Railroads and the Use of Photography (1862–1868)

"He had some from the Union Pacific, but they did not compare with ours."

—Edwin Bryant Crocker

By the time Russell left the army the Union Pacific Railroad Company was nearly three years old, but no rails had been laid West from its headquarters in Omaha, Nebraska. The idea for a transcontinental railroad in the minds of schemers and dreamers, however, had been around at least from the 1830s. After the United States acquired the territories of California, Oregon, and New Mexico, in the late 1840s, the issue went from abstraction to certainty. Suddenly the question was not if, but when. Actually the question was when and where to build the line and where to put the Eastern terminus. This vexing question dogged any pending legislation. The Southern slave states opposed a Northern route that would help create more free states. As well, the boom that was sure to come with the building of the line pitted state against state and even town against town. This stalemate on location, combined with serious questions of how to finance such a mammoth operation, doomed it throughout the 1850s. Out West in California a railroad connection to the rest of the country was crucial to the fledgling, but rapidly growing state. A young, talented, earnest California engineer Theodore Judah sought for years to bring the long, unproductive discussions for creating a Pacific railway to a more realistic level. Through sheer willpower, determination, and hard work, Judah did much to advance the cause in the nation's capital and in California. Completing the deal, however, would require the capital and business savvy of a Sacramento grocer Collis Potter Huntington. Huntington brought in three other California businessmen, Leland Stanford, Charles (or Charlie) Crocker, and Mark Hopkins.[1] These men were the real power behind the Central Pacific and they referred to themselves as "the Associates." They divided up their responsibilities into a remarkably efficient system. Huntington was in charge of financing and national politics, Crocker was in charge of construction, Stanford did publicity and dealt with California politics, and Hopkins was the executive accountant. The Central Pacific officially came into existence on June 27, 1861.

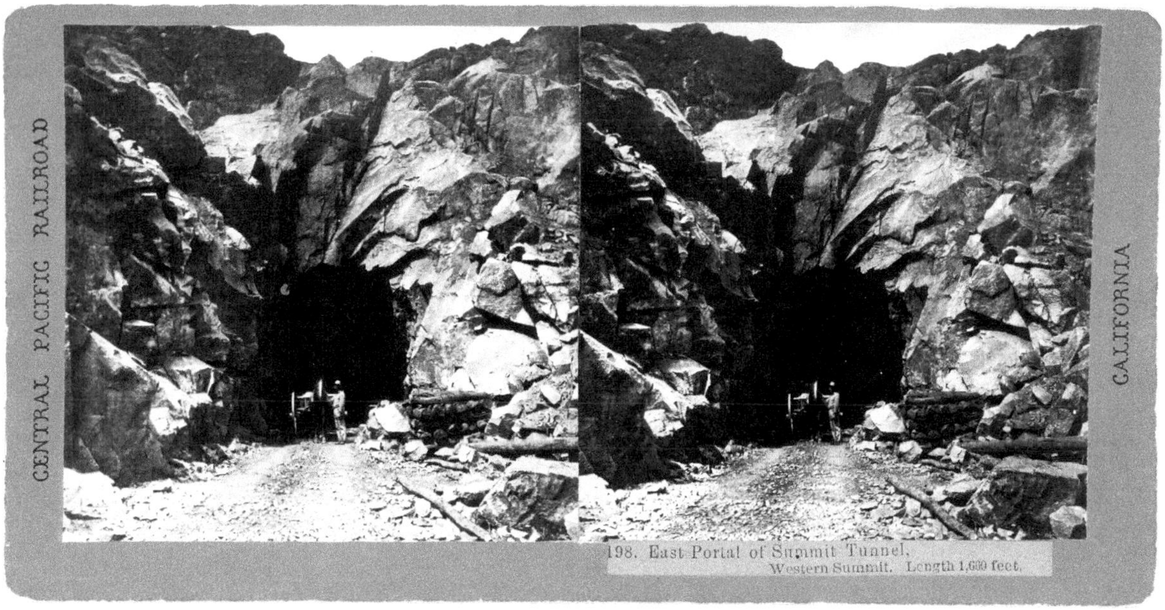

3.1. The summit of Sierra Nevada, by Alfred A. Hart, stereo-view. *Courtesy of the Library of Congress, Prints and Photographs Division.*

It was not, however, until the election of Lincoln that the sectional question could be settled and the Pacific Railway Act of 1862 passed on July 1. Lincoln, in fact, was a great proponent of the railroad and his support enabled the passage of both this legislation and the Pacific Railway Acts of 1863 and 1864. These acts gave generous subsidies in land, timber, stone, and government bonds to the Union Pacific and Central Pacific. Yet with the Civil War raging, with labor scarce and expensive, and with costs of fuel and iron very high, the Union Pacific sputtered in gaining momentum. Investors had better options elsewhere and, anyway, were skeptical of the likelihood of building a line through fifteen hundred miles of wilderness. The Pacific Railway Act of 1862 recognized the Central Pacific, but relegated it to building up to the California border where it would, presumably, meet the mighty Union Pacific.[2] Judah and the Associates, though, always assumed they could keep laying line eastward until they met the Union Pacific somewhere in Utah or Wyoming.

Meanwhile Judah would find himself pushed to the fringes of his great project. Judah did not ingratiate himself to the Associates with his estimate that the first 140 miles of the Central Pacific would cost $12 million and require eighteen tunnels, which just happened to be the first in the world through hard granite. Disgusted over the financial chicanery and engineering cost cutting by the Associates, Judah traveled to New York City in October 1863 in an attempt to find new financial partners. After traveling across the Isthmus of Panama, however, he contracted yellow fever. He passed away on November 2, 1863, in New York City.[3] The work of constructing the Central Pacific, however, continued. On January 8, 1863, ground breaking began in Sacramento and on October 26, 1863, ties were laid. By February 1864 the Central

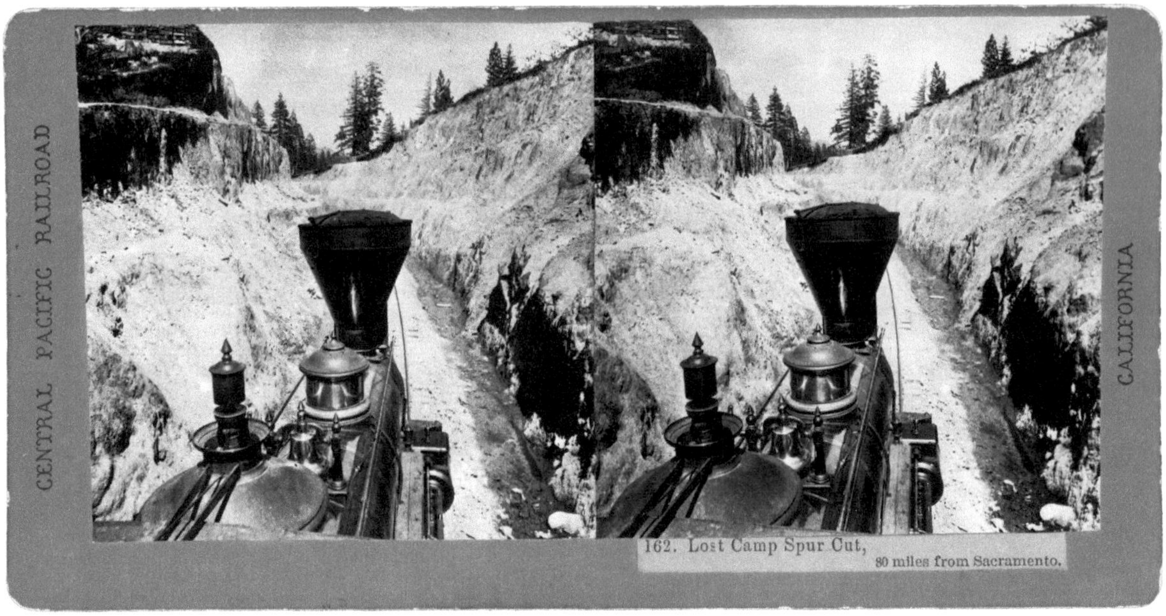

3.2. Lost Camp spur cut, eighty miles from Sacramento, by Alfred A. Hart, stereo-view. *Courtesy of the Library of Congress, Prints and Photographs Division.*

Pacific had built eighteen miles and started to make money from both freight and passengers. More importantly, Huntington got a revision of the Pacific Railway Act to place his company 150 miles into Nevada, which gave it the important mining traffic of Nevada.[4] After building into the Sierra Nevada foothills in 1864 and 1865, the Central Pacific would eventually face the hard truth of the massive tunnels needed at the summit. Huntington realized, to his chagrin, that Judah's cost estimates were conservative, if anything. The two biggest tunnels were nine hundred and sixteen hundred feet long, and for the next two years progress would be measured not in miles, or even feet, but in inches per day.[5]

In 1865 the itinerant portrait photographer Alfred A. Hart also began a daunting task: photographing the Central Pacific Railroad. There are some surprising similarities between Hart and Russell. Hart was born in Norwich, Connecticut, in 1816, but moved to New York City in 1838 and to Hartford in 1848. He worked initially as a portrait painter and then a moving panorama painter in the 1850s. In 1857 he joined up with prominent Hartford photographer Henry H. Bartlett and learned the art of the daguerreotype. In the early 1860s he moved, opening an art gallery and store in Cleveland, Ohio. He spent most of his time, however, traveling in California shooting the mining activities.[6] In January of 1866 the Central Pacific purchased thirty-two images (taken in 1865) from Hart. Thus began Hart's occupation as the Central Pacific's official photographer. As company photographer he had the authority to stop the construction of the line to take his photographs, and he could use the railroad to transport his wagon and photographic supplies.[7] Hart took hundreds of images from 1865 to

1869 and eventually the Central Pacific picked out 364 stereos to form a series documenting the entire line from Sacramento to Promontory.[8]

Both Russell and Hart described themselves as artists first and foremost, rather than photographers, but there are some important differences in their photography. For instance, Hart did not use a large-format camera and consequently his stereographic images have not been reproduced as often as Russell's detailed large-format images, made from original negatives. Hart also did not shoot unusual geography as Russell did, instead focusing on the obstacles overcome by the Central Pacific in the Sierra Nevada, such as tunnels, trestles, and cuts and fills. The Central Pacific and the Union Pacific both hoped to increase ridership through the sale of stereoscopic views, but the Central Pacific purchased at least some negatives that were independently printed, probably receiving some direct profit from their sale.[9] Hart's images contain many more trains and engines, strategically posed, including close-up views of engines (and even views from the top of engines). This may have been a result of what the Central Pacific desired from Hart, but also arose from stylistic differences with Russell. Hart's images are dramatic and celebrate the technology of the railroad as a transformational agent. Russell's images focus on people and are not as imaginative or suggestive, but instead provide a more neutral documentary record.[10] Also, Hart had more time to focus on fewer miles of track in California whereas Russell was photographing across a thousand miles from Nebraska to Utah. The quality of Russell's stereo-views in terms of the compositional elements of railroad and geography, as well as contrast of light and dark, are not as strong. Russell put more thought and effort into his large-format images and included many more, less selective images in his stereo-view series, resulting in numerous weaker samples. To the Central Pacific, Hart's images were valuable mainly for sales of the views themselves, for promotion of the line, for sale of company stocks and bonds, and to apprise Huntington, out in New York City, of the progress of the line.

Judge Edwin Bryant Crocker, the lawyer for the Central Pacific Railroad and brother of Charlie Crocker, was enthusiastic about Hart and his images. He sent packages of them to Huntington to be distributed among investors, politicians, and government officials.[11] Crocker also reproduced them as woodcuts in the *San Francisco Sunday Mercury* for promotion.[12] As the railroads built more and more line they were, of course, making money from train fares, and they wanted to promote ridership. One photographic journal of the day suggested that a photographer was instrumental in selling tickets: "The shrewd railroad men know this, and they employ no servant whose labors repay them so handsomely as the photographer. Many of them not only pay him for making these large views for them, but give him the free privilege of selling stereo and other size pictures in their cars; for see you, every gross he sells advertises their roads among the people who travel, and it pays them well."[13]

In June 1867 Crocker sent a full set of Hart's stereographic views documenting the Central Pacific's progress to Brigham Young. Crocker was currying favor with Young in the hopes that Young would provide Mormon labor for the line in Nevada and Utah. To Huntington, the most powerful man in the Central Pacific, Crocker reported of Brigham Young: "[He] was highly pleased with them. He had some from the Union Pacific, but they did not compare with ours."[14] This statement might have been a reference to the natural scenery, and the Central Pacific certainly had the Union Pacific beat in that department, but it also referred to the higher quality and quantity of Central Pacific views in 1867. In fact as 1868 began, the Union Pacific was, photographically speaking, seriously deficient. A number of photographers had already traveled along the Union Pacific, but their photographs had only wetted the public's appetite for more transcontinental railroad images, and even the floundering Kansas Pacific (also known as the Union Pacific, Eastern Division) had started photographing their hesitant progress across Kansas.

JOHN CARBUTT AND ALEXANDER GARDNER

Despite its dismal start, by 1866 the Union Pacific was picking up steam and laying track out into the Nebraska prairie at the impressive rate of one to three miles a day. The fortunes of the Union Pacific changed mostly through the efforts of one man, Dr. Thomas C. Durant. Durant was a wealthy New York City financier who took command of the project and secured the necessary financing to make the Union Pacific a viable company (and thereafter Durant would act as both a brake and engine for the project, pushing or dragging it in order to secure huge profits for himself and a small group of wealthy investors). The Union Pacific started laying track on July 10, 1865, and had forty miles by the end of 1865.[15] In 1866, with the war over, costs gradually lowered and the labor shortage eased as discharged soldiers came to Omaha looking for work. Durant also had sense enough to hire the newly retired General Jack Casement as the contractor in charge of track laying in February. Casement would push the project with relentless energy and a gift for motivating his workers.[16]

Also helping the Union Pacific's cause was the hiring of Grenville Dodge on May 1, 1866, as the Union Pacific's chief engineer.[17] Dodge may have had a talent for self-aggrandizement and he tended to claim all the credit for building the line, but as a chief engineer, he was without peer. An important, and overlooked, fact about the transcontinental railway is that when the railroads started construction from Sacramento and Omaha they were unsure where their lines would run. The Union Pacific did not know whether to run through the Rocky Mountains in Wyoming or Colorado, which canyon they would utilize through the Wasatch Mountains, and neither railroad had decided whether it would run north or south around the Great Salt Lake. By late 1867, however, Dodge and his surveyors had mapped out a line that, even today, the Union Pacific mostly follows. What is even more impressive about Dodge's route is that the maximum elevation gain is only 90 feet a mile, even though by law it was allowed 116 feet.[18]

The Union Pacific, in contrast to the Central Pacific, was working through much easier terrain in 1866, although they had to build temporary bridges across the Elkhorn, Loup Fork, and North Platte Rivers. By October 6, 1866, the Union Pacific had laid track to the 100th Meridian (near present-day Cozad) in western Nebraska. Durant, ever mindful of positive publicity and generating new stockholders, planned a grand blowout. About two hundred

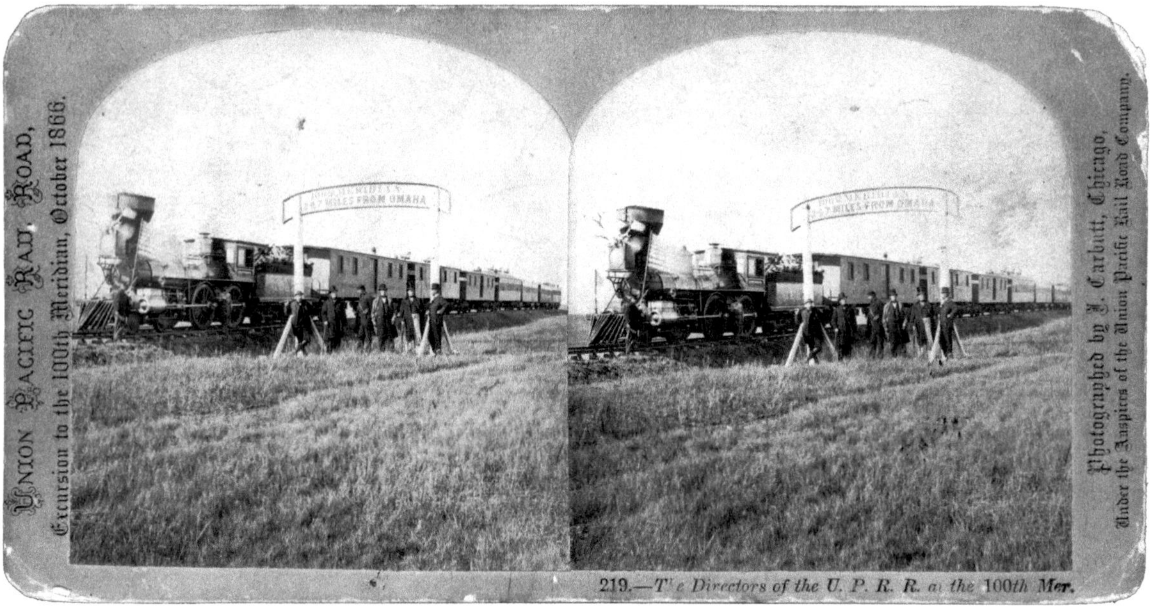

3.3. View from 100th Meridian excursion, by John Carbutt. *Courtesy of the Library of Congress, Prints and Photographs Division.*

politicians, journalists, government directors, European nobility, and titans of industry traveled to Chicago where photographer John Carbutt and his assistant Robert Hine joined them. Once they reached Nebraska, he took photographs and made prints on the spot. The excursionists witnessed sham battles staged by Pawnee scouts (who would play an important role in keeping the railroad safe from hostile Sioux and Cheyenne Indians)[19] and watched Casement and his men at work, camped out in tents, and ate sumptuous meals at every stop. Durant was heavily involved in all the details of the 100th Meridian excursion and he surely wanted a photographer to record the "historic" event. Carbutt's images, in fact, are a recording of the luminaries and what they did on this excursion. The views that Crocker denigrated in 1867 ("they did not compare with ours") may have been these photographs. Russell's images, by contrast, would systematically record the progress on the line to a particular point. Still, the precedent for using photography as a publicity tool and to record of the activities of the Union Pacific had been set.[20]

Carbutt was not the only photographer out on the line in 1866. Two men had already traveled on the Union Pacific in Nebraska, C. R. Savage (who we will meet again in 1868), and the unfortunate Ridgway Glover who was killed by Sioux Indians in Wyoming. Savage and Glover published accounts of their travels in the journal the *Philadelphia Photographer*.[21] These articles, as well as Carbutt's stereographs of the 100th Meridian excursion, surely built up interest among the public in seeing even more images of the Union Pacific. Their curiosity, however, would be mostly unsatisfied in 1867.

Dodge spent much of 1867 crisscrossing Nebraska, Wyoming, and Utah—surveying well

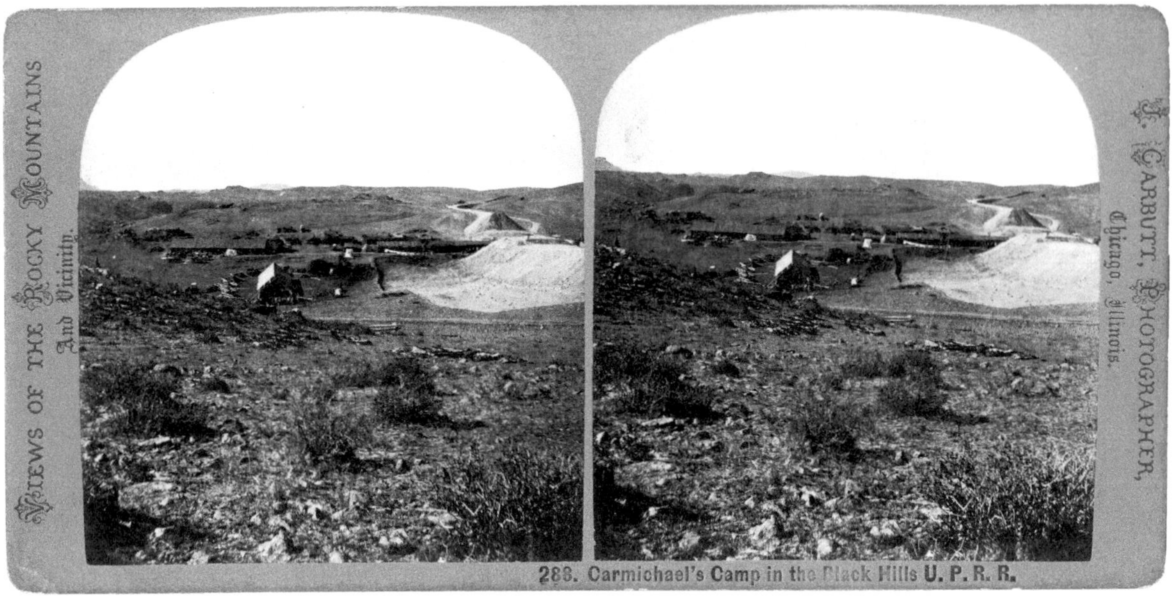

3.4. View in Laramie or Black Hills, west of Cheyenne, by John Carbutt. *Courtesy of the University of Utah, J. Willard Marriott Library, Special Collections, J. Carbutt Photograph Collection.*

ahead of the railroad as it raced along the Platte River in Nebraska—dipped quickly into Colorado at Julesburg, and then left the Platte and followed Lodgepole Creek into Wyoming. He was in Salt Lake City in September of 1867 where he viewed a series of stereo-views of the Central Pacific shown to him by an army officer at Fort Douglas. Dodge was, no doubt, curious how the Central Pacific had blasted their way through the imposing Sierra Nevada Mountains. Crocker learned about Dodge's interest and, as he had done with Brigham Young, sent him a set of his own photographs while asking the Union Pacific for a corresponding set. There was a problem, however. The Union Pacific did not have images that effectively showed their work through the Laramie Hills.[22] Carbutt would make another trip out West to Wyoming and Colorado where he photographed the Union Pacific's work on cuts and fills in the Laramie Mountains in October of 1867. He published a series of at least thirty images entitled Views of the Rocky Mountains and Vicinity. His work may not have been what the Union Pacific wanted, though, as his images of the construction in the mountains are broad overviews that do not show details very well. Dodge must have realized, despite the Union Pacific's progress across Nebraska after wintering in North Platte, that it was falling even further behind in the mini-race for images documenting their work.[23]

The Union Pacific probably also took notice of the work of the Civil War photographer Alexander Gardner with the Kansas Pacific. The Kansas Pacific officially began life as the Leavenworth, Pawnee, and Western, which became the Union Pacific, Eastern Division in 1863 and, for a time, was a viable competitor to the "real" Union Pacific. The Railway Act of 1862, in fact, established three companies, including the Kansas Pacific (which began in Kansas City).

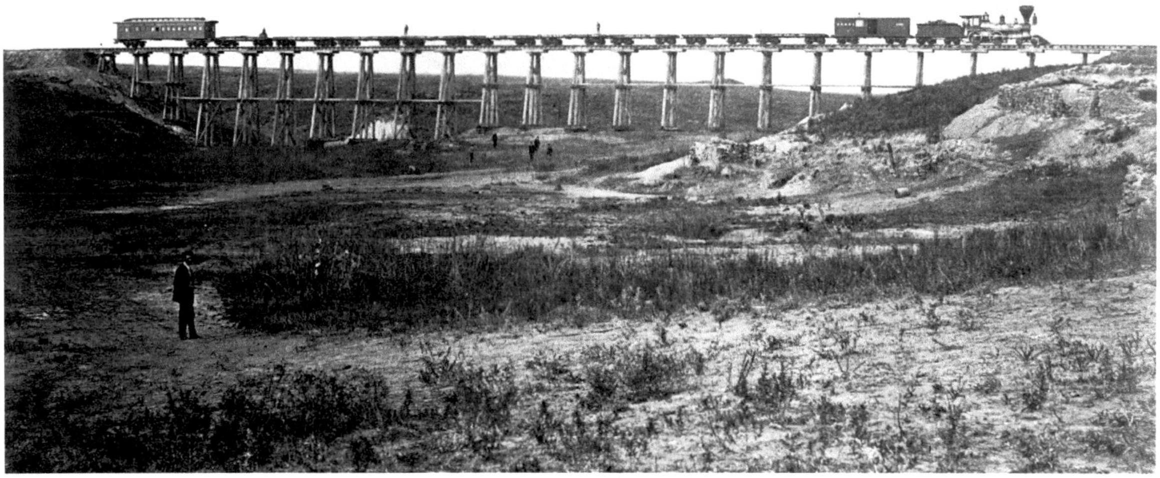

3.5. Across the continent on the Kansas Pacific Railroad, on the Great Plains, Kansas, September 1867, by Alexander Gardner. *Courtesy of the Trustees of the Boston Public Library.*

Whichever eastern railroad reached the 100th Meridian first would become the main branch of the transcontinental railroad.[24] The Kansas Pacific began laying rails before the Union Pacific, but some of the same obstacles in securing funding, labor, and high material costs hit them even harder than the Union Pacific.[25] The Kansas Pacific's photographer Alexander Gardner grew up in Glasgow, Scotland. He worked as a jeweler and editor before moving his wife and two children to America in 1855. He was the manager of the Washington, D.C. gallery for well-known "celebrity photographer" Mathew Brady. Gardner, together with Timothy O'Sullivan and George N. Barnard, photographed battlefields and Union army campaigns of the Civil War for Brady. Gardner left, however, when he was not appropriately credited for the dangerous work that he did. In the fall of 1867 and winter of 1867 to 1868, Gardner photographed the slow progress of his railroad across Kansas. Another photographer, Dr. William A. Bell, traveled all the way to California for Gardner, later publishing *New Tracks in North America.* In 1869 Gardner published an album of photographs entitled *Across the Continent on the Kansas Pacific Railroad,* and he exhibited some of these prints in April of 1868 in Philadelphia.[26] Durant, with his extensive list of spies and contacts, would have known about Gardner's work as well as the numerous sets of Central Pacific stereo-views given out by Huntington. The Civil War had increased the public's appetite for newsworthy images and the publicity-conscious Durant was, no doubt, eager to have his own photographer in the field.

Gardner's relationship to the Kansas Pacific reflects the company's preoccupation with obtaining investment and government subsidies. Gardner, for instance, was at pains to show level topography (over which a railroad could easily be built). The Kansas Pacific was also trying to sell the benefits of a more southern route as running through better agricultural land with less snow in the winter. He depicts the year-round flora and fauna, the "perpetual spring" of the southern route from Kansas to California. He also took many American Indian photographs, in part because the Kansas Pacific wanted to capitalize on the idea of the railroad as an agent of change for the Plains Indians.[27] So in early 1868 when Russell reached Omaha, he was hardly a pioneer of western railroad photography. He followed in the footsteps of two other rival railroad photographers, Hart and Gardner, as well as three other photographers who had already traveled on the Union Pacific, Carbutt, Savage, and Glover. In other words, he had some catching up to do.

"HE IS A VERY SUCCESSFUL ARTIST"

Where exactly was Russell, then, before he joined the Union Pacific in the spring of 1868? In all likelihood he returned to New York City after the war and opened an art and tintype portrait studio at 183 and 185 Eighth Avenue. Surprisingly, he did not attempt to capitalize financially on his Civil War photographs. He was certainly not in Nunda because he disappears completely from his gossipy hometown newspaper in 1866 and 1867. Russell might have been absent from railroad photography simply because he was tired of railroading after the Civil War and he was exploring other artistic options.[28] In early 1868 he reappears in his

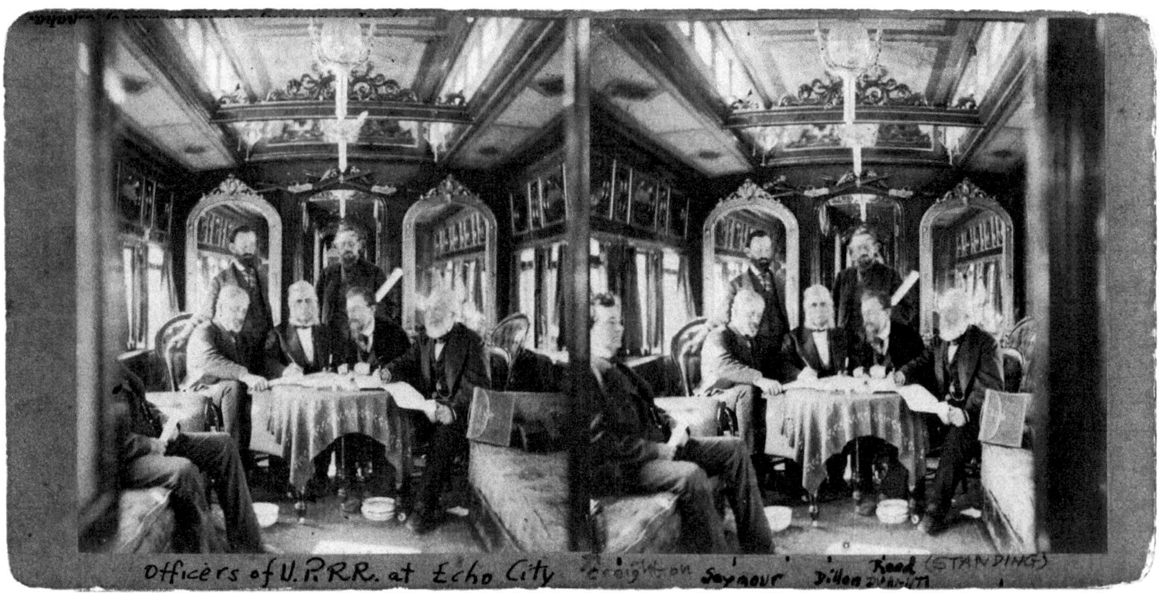

3.6. "Officers in Their Car at Echo City," by A. J. Russell, stereo-view no. 353. *Courtesy of the Union Pacific Railroad Museum, Union Pacific Collection, Photography Archives, A. J. Russell Views.*

hometown newspaper as living in New York City: "He is a very successful artist, and has made his mark in oil painting, water colors, coloring photographs; and in fact, in every department in his profession."[29] In all likelihood Russell was hired by the ever-publicity-conscious Durant in the winter of 1867 to 1868. Durant might have come to know Russell through the consulting engineer Silas Seymour. Russell had photographed the construction of the New Long Bridge during the Civil War and Seymour was the chief engineer for the project.[30] Of course nearly all of the officers and skilled labor on the Union Pacific were former Union veterans.

A central question swirling around Russell's Union Pacific photographs is: what did Durant and the Union Pacific want him to photograph or was Russell given carte blanche, photographing according to his own dictates? It seems highly unlikely that the Union Pacific had no opinion about his activities, given Durant's intense micromanagement, the high-stakes race to Utah in 1868, the control the Union Pacific would maintain over his images, and the type of photographs he took. Russell and Durant communicated throughout 1868. For instance, he photographed Durant and Union Pacific Director Cornelius S. Bushnell (fig. 3.6) in Wyoming in June and July of 1868.[31] Both railroads knew how critical 1868 would be. The race between the lines went from abstraction to reality. Both lines were eager to reach Utah to get a piece of the Salt Lake City traffic, but also to reach potential coal deposits in the Wasatch Mountains.[32]

Russell was probably not an employee of the railroad receiving a salary, although he certainly had the complete cooperation of the Union Pacific Railroad and he was clearly identified as their photographer.[33] The Union Pacific paid for his supplies and expenses, but in return it maintained control over the distribution of his photographs in 1868 and 1869, although he probably had an arrangement allowing him to sell prints in lieu of a regular salary.[34] Although there are no extant written instructions, Russell left us a huge inventory of images and we can draw some conclusions about his goals and aspirations. Today looking at Russell's images, it appears that he cast a wide net so that his views could be used for just about anything, including publicity, increasing ridership, illustrating the geology along the line, and recording the progress being made by the railroad through the mountains in Wyoming. But Russell was photographing an enormous endeavor, across a thousand miles, with a limited number of glass plates. Certainly his views represent a matter of picking and choosing what needed to be photographed and what did not.

It also might be tempting to think that Russell was hired to document the construction of this historic endeavor for the benefit of posterity. In fact, though, time and again Russell photographed what was of critical importance for the Union Pacific right then, not in the distant future. For instance, the Union Pacific knew that the Central Pacific hoped to build through Weber and Echo Canyons in Utah, and maybe even meet the Union Pacific in Wyoming. The Union Pacific, however, was hundreds of miles closer and they would have been desperate to show the federal government the work they had already done.[35] When Russell saw Durant in June 1868, did he instruct him to heavily photograph the most difficult stretch of the entire line through the Wasatch Mountains?[36] Russell ended up taking 214 stereo-views from tunnel no. 2 at the head of Echo Canyon on the Utah-Wyoming border to the mouth of Weber Canyon. Russell took far more images, mile per mile, from tunnel no. 2 on the Utah-Wyoming border to the mouth of Weber Canyon than of any other place on the 1,086 mile route from Omaha to Promontory Summit. These images focus heavily on the tunnels, bridges, cuts, and grades.

During 1868 Russell photographed, as well, all the assembly-line-like operation of railroad building, including surveying, grading, tunnel construction, cuts and fills, and finally track laying. A year later, however, he would spend much of his summer and fall photographing the finished bridges, tunnels, and cuts, especially in Weber and Echo Canyons. In late 1868 and early 1869, a controversy erupted over the shoddy construction of the Union Pacific.[37] In order to be government certified and to receive their bonds, the line had to be "first-class" or "supplied with all necessary drains, culverts, viaducts, crossings, sidings, bridges, turnouts, watering places, depots, equipments, furniture, and all other appurtenances of a first-class railroad," as well as having the necessary buildings of the Union Pacific, such as depots, roundhouses, and machine shops.[38] In response, after the "wedding of the rails" on May 10, 1869, the Union Pacific went back over the line and improved it. Many of Russell's 1868 images show the initial work of grading, digging cuts, stringing telegraph wires, constructing tunnels, and building bridges, as well as later images after the work was complete in 1869.[39] Russell's images had the same value for the Union Pacific as Hart's and Gardner's held for the Central Pacific and the Kansas Pacific. More specifically, though, Russell's work was also a tool to combat the Union Pacific's image of cutting too many corners in their race to meet up with the Central Pacific. From these two examples alone, it is apparent that Russell's images, especially the stereo-views, were essentially working documents for the Union Pacific.[40]

CHAPTER 4

Russell's First Trip out West (1868)

"He is still a gentile, although he has spent some time among the Mormon saints."

—*Nunda News*

Russell's photographic adventures did not follow a simple, linear path commencing with Omaha in the spring of 1868, then following the line through Nebraska, Wyoming, and Utah, and finishing at Promontory, Utah, on May 10, 1869. The numbering sequence of his images, which mimic an overland trip on the Union Pacific, is misleading. In fact, he returned to New York City for an extended time in the winter of 1868 to 1869, and traveled back and forth along the line. It is also important to point out that he was not alone. In today's parlance we would say that he valued collaboration. This is an important, but overlooked, facet of western nineteenth-century photography.[1] Russell was an affable fellow and he naturally sought out the advice and consultation of other photographers. He had some sort of interaction with five well-known western photographers—C. R. Savage, William Henry Jackson, Timothy O'Sullivan, Alfred Hart, and Arundel Hull—and he briefly joined two major government surveys, led by F. V. Hayden and Clarence King. As well, he worked with at least two assistants the entire time.

It is not known on what day Russell first arrived in the West, specifically in Omaha. In fact, the whole endeavor of determining Russell's whereabouts based on his images is tricky. A baseline can be established by the arrival of the line at a particular locale, which is well known. Another way to distinguish 1868 stereo-views from those of 1869 is to examine the original negatives at the Oakland Museum of California. Russell used a 4" x 8" stereo camera in 1868 and a larger 5" x 8" camera in 1869.[2] Other indicators include the presence or absence of snow, occasional dates from the stereo-view descriptions, and the transcript of O. C. Smith's diaries. In some cases, however, it is impossible to date an image because Russell could travel up and down the line as he chose, and he might photograph the same location on multiple occasions. Sometime in early April 1868 Russell arrived in Omaha, where he loaded his darkroom wagon on a Union Pacific train for the first time.[3] He may have taken some large-format photographs in Omaha, perhaps as a tune-up for later work in Wyoming and Utah, but all his Nebraska stereo-views were taken in 1869. Either way, Russell was playing catch-up, as the line was well

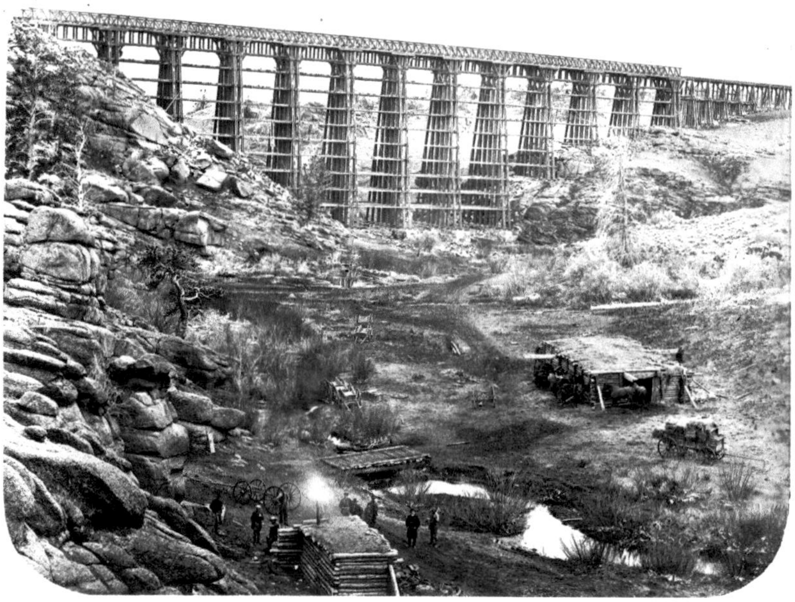

4.1. Dale Creek Trestle, view looking south, by A. J. Russell, large-format view no. 23. *Courtesy of the University of Iowa Libraries, Special Collections, Levi O. Leonard Railroadiana.*

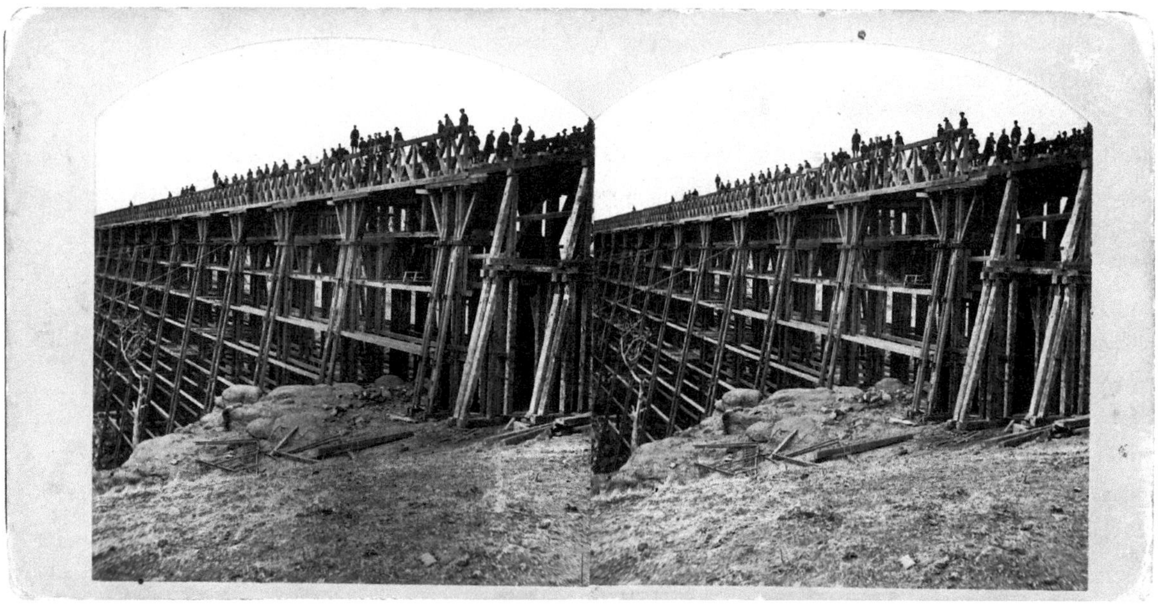

4.2. Dale Creek Trestle, after completion, by A. J. Russell, stereo-view no. 111. *Courtesy of the University of Iowa Libraries, Special Collections, Levi O. Leonard Railroadiana.*

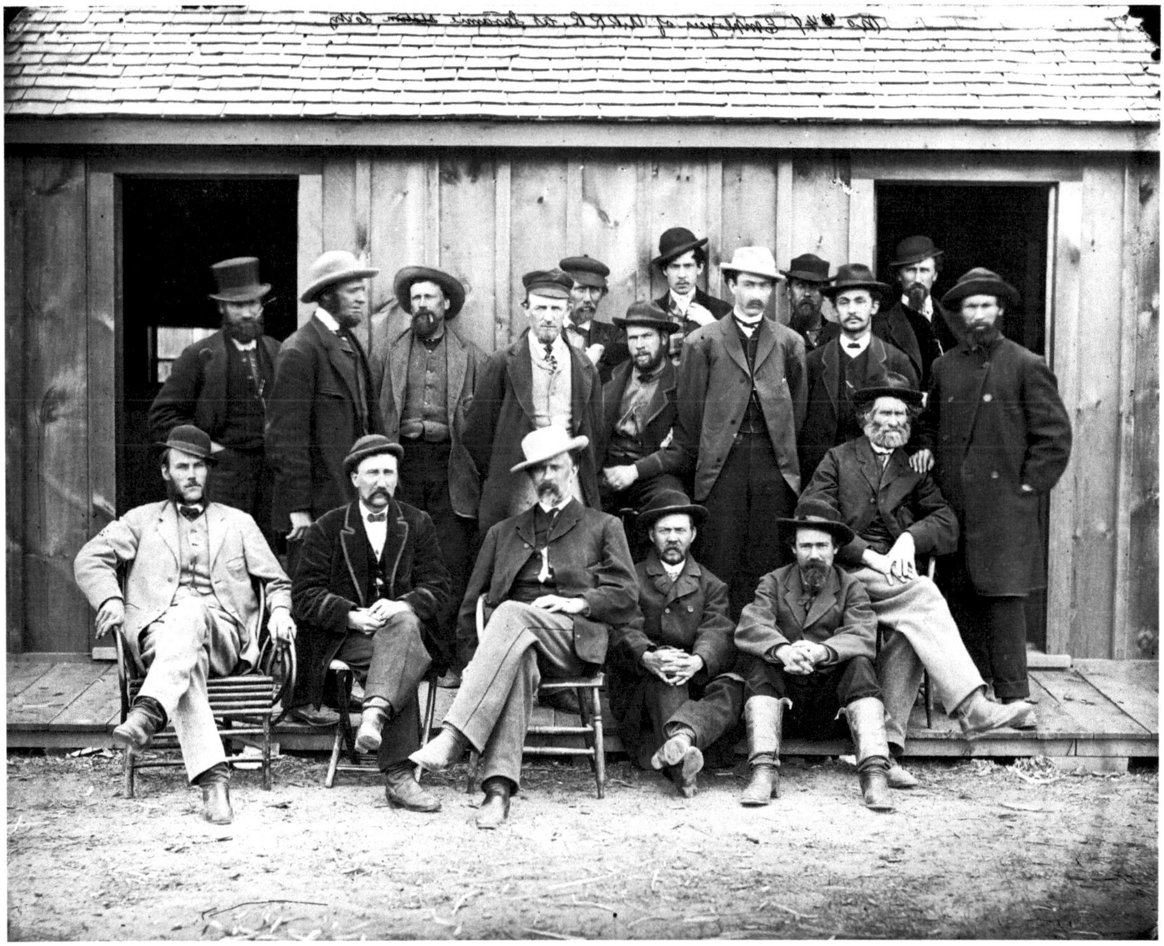

4.3. Employees of the Union Pacific in Laramie, by A. J. Russell, large-format view no. 49. *Courtesy of the Oakland Museum of California, A. J. Russell Collection.*

into Wyoming by that time. In fact, most of Russell's efforts in April and May of 1868 were directed toward the work in Wyoming through the Black (or Laramie) Mountains, which was nearly completed when Russell arrived in the early spring of 1868. Much of his work focused on the massive Dale Creek Trestle, which was completed on April 23, 1868.[4] Russell would write: "This bridge is one hundred and twenty five feet high, and five hundred feet long. Nearly all the timber of which it is built was transported from Chicago. The bridge was completed in thirty working days."[5]

At the Dale Creek Trestle, Russell was assisted by forty-two-year-old Union Pacific clerk Oliver C. Smith.[6] Smith was born in Pelham, Massachusetts, in 1825. He grew up in Massachusetts and attended the Amherst Academy. He did a variety of work in building and contracting, railroad construction, teaching, real estate, and woolen mills, living in Massachusetts, New York, Pennsylvania, and Michigan.[7] Smith was living in Amherst, Massachusetts,

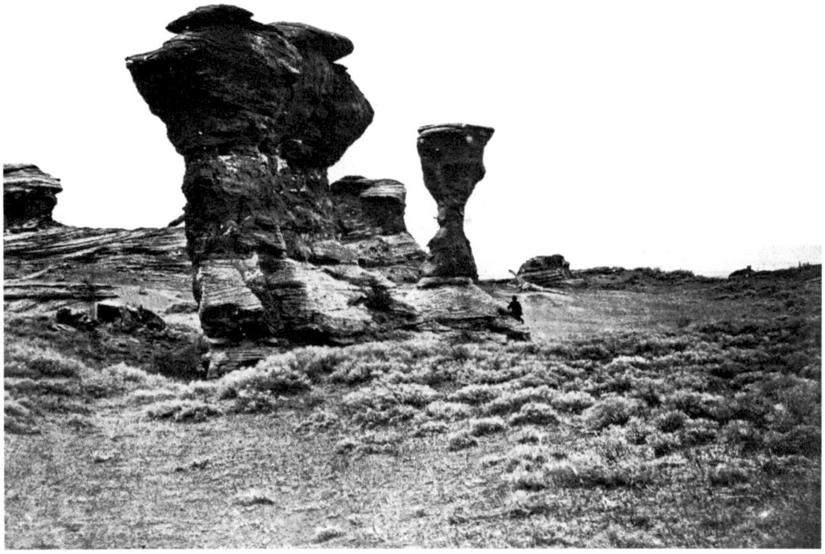

4.4. "Dial Rock, Red Buttes, Laramie Plains," by A. J. Russell, from Sun Pictures of Rocky Mountain Scenery. *Courtesy of Utah State University, Merrill-Cazier Library, Special Collections.*

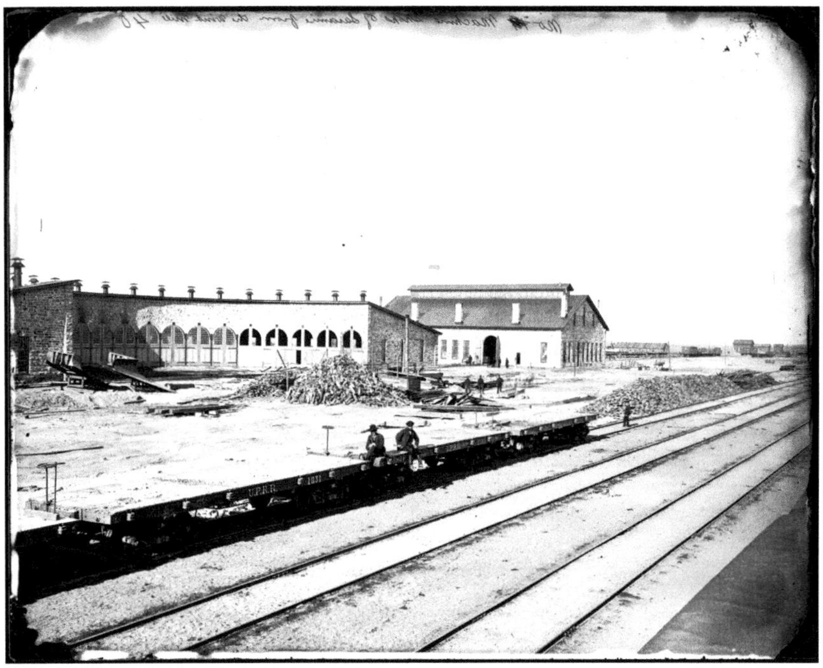

4.5. "Machine Shops of Laramie from Wind Mill," by A. J. Russell, large-format view no. 40. *Courtesy of the Oakland Museum of California, A. J. Russell Collection.*

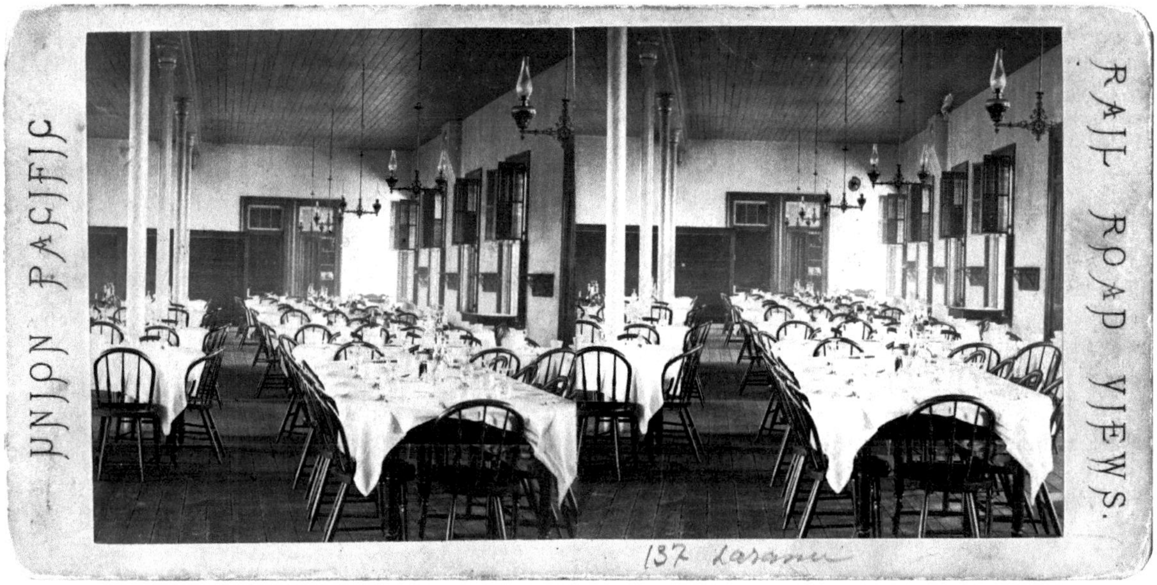

4.6. Dining area at Laramie Station, by A. J. Russell, stereo-view no. 137. *Courtesy of the Union Pacific Railroad Museum, Union Pacific Collection, Photography Archives, A. J. Russell Views.*

in January 1868 when his cousin, Union Pacific director Sidney Dillon, asked him to move west and work on the railroad. He arrived in Cheyenne on February 22.[8] Smith and Russell became friends and remained in contact as their paths crossed back and forth in Wyoming and Utah in 1868 and 1869. The two hiked and camped together, and Smith purchased numerous prints from Russell. Smith even loaned him money for printing paper. Later, in 1870, they formed a partnership to print and sell Russell's images back in New York City. Smith worked long hours and suffered from poor health, but he also maintained numerous business interests on the side. In fact, he seemed to have made as much or more money from buying and selling goods as he did from his official Union Pacific salary of twenty-five dollars a week.

In Wyoming the Union Pacific faced, for the first time, massive fills as well as difficult cuts through solid rock. Russell shot the impressive work of contractors Lewis Carmichael, Rance Hall, and John Malloy in the Black Hills.[9] The work began in the fall of 1867, but proceeded slowly because of the extreme weather at eight thousand feet, including bitter cold and deep snow.[10] The Union Pacific made the decision to work through the winter of 1867 to 1868 as long as the weather allowed, which turned out to be until January 13, when three feet of snow fell and the temperature reached thirty below.[11] In Wyoming, Russell also began a preoccupation with western geology. In addition to the practical applications of geology, and the interest of the Union Pacific in mining along the line—Russell himself invested in a copper mine in Utah—he also noted the aesthetic and esoteric interests as well.[12] He repeatedly shot unusual rock formations along the line, both in large-format and stereoscopic form. Russell's descriptions of nearly all the cuts along the Union Pacific reli-

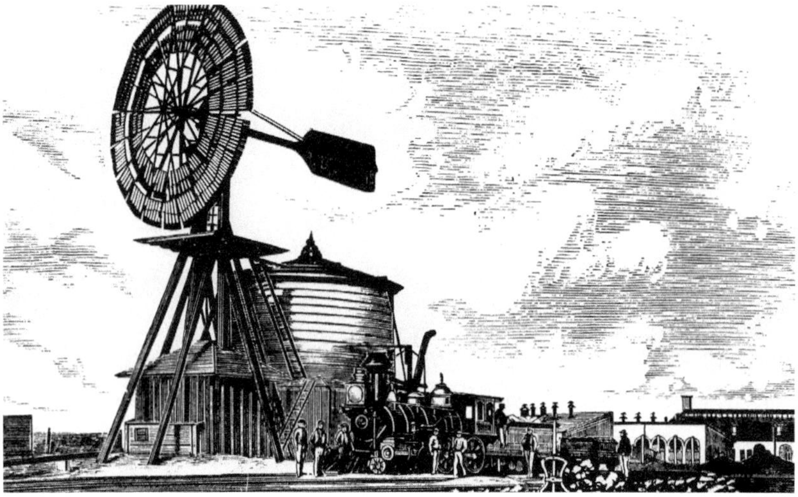

4.7. Windmill in Laramie, Wyoming (woodcut illustration made from a Russell image), appeared in *Leslie's Illustrated*, May 8, 1869.

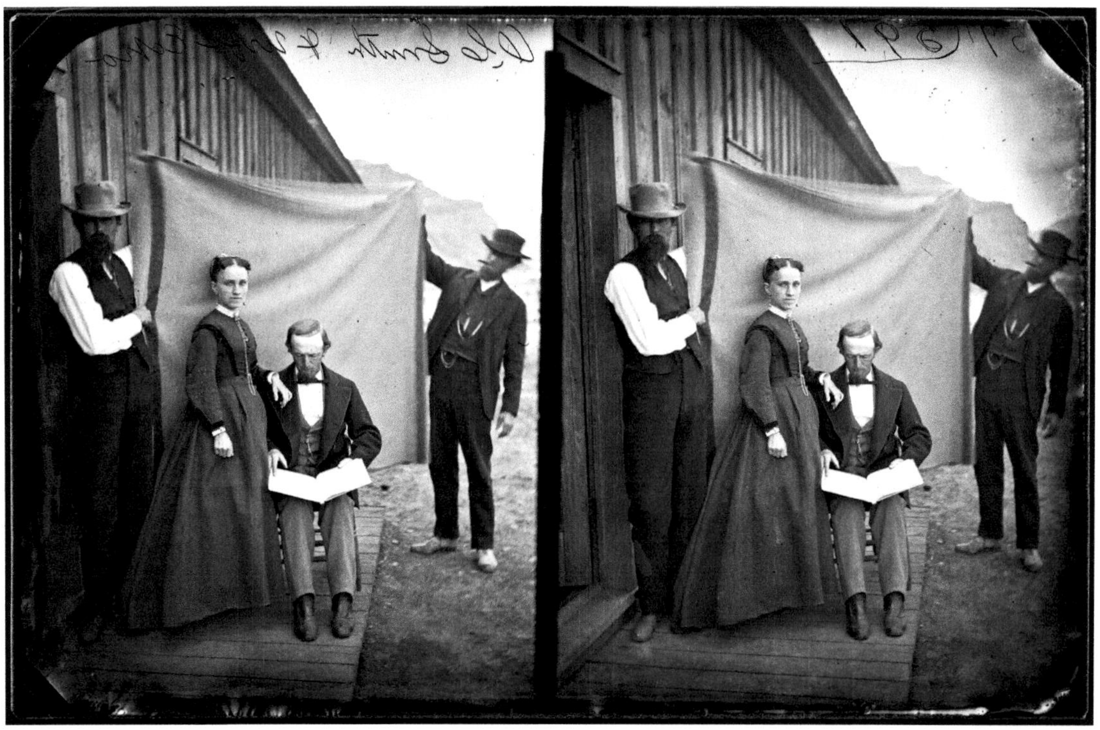

4.8. O. C. Smith and Lucy Smith, probably with Russell himself setting up "studio" portrait, taken in Echo, Utah, by A. J. Russell, stereo-view no. 591. *Courtesy of the Oakland Museum of California, A. J. Russell Collection.*

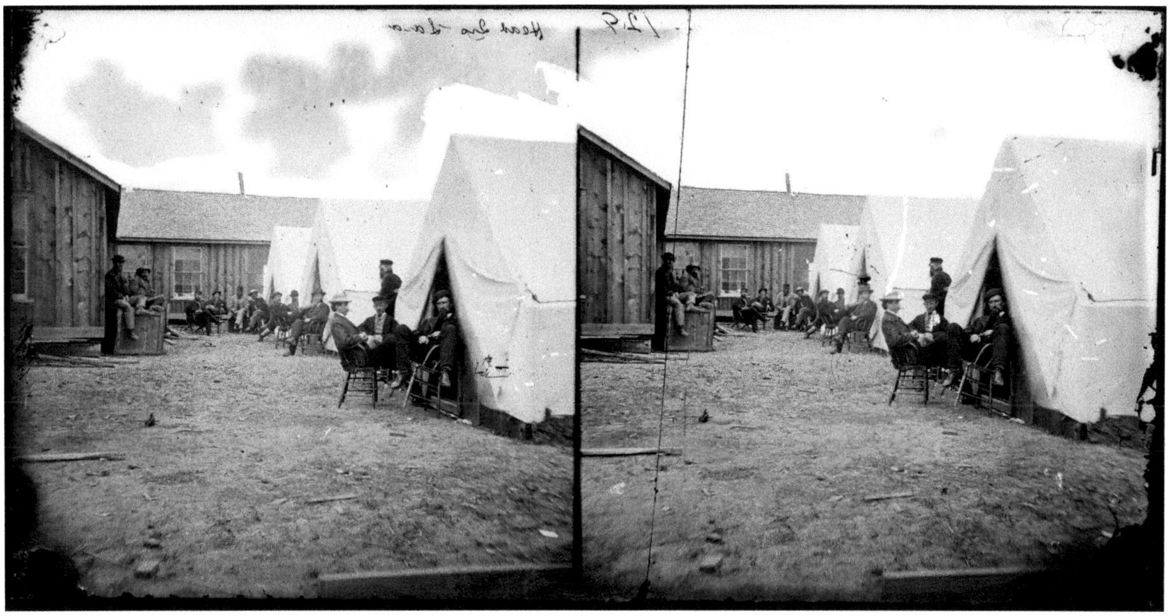

4.9. Union Pacific employee group shot in Laramie (note that many of the people from fig. 4.3. are in this photo as well), by A. J. Russell, stereo-view no. 129. *Courtesy of the Oakland Museum of California, A. J. Russell Collection.*

giously mention the type of rock and the length and depth of the cut. Laramie Mountain cuts, for example, were through hard, red granite.

Russell reached Laramie around the same time the rails arrived. He had some time on his hands as he waited for the various Union Pacific officials and dignitaries to arrive in June and July. He meticulously photographed the interior and exterior of roundhouses, dining halls, hotels, and machine shops. Russell wrote that the Laramie Hotel "was built by the Railroad Company at a cost of nearly seventy thousand dollars; its dining room will compare very favorably with those of the best buildings for like purposes in any State of the Union; it is nearly one hundred feet in length, and one thousand persons can be comfortably accommodated at table."[13] Russell also photographed the huge self-regulating windmill at Laramie, which would be used as an illustration in *Frank Leslie's Illustrated Newspaper.*[14] As well, Russell took the first of many images of Union Pacific employees both in groups and as individuals in early June. Russell shot negatives and printed photographs to sell to the Union Pacific employees throughout 1868 and 1869 (see figs. 4.8 and 4.9), probably as a way to help finance his travels.[15] In Laramie City he took many more large-format images, in fact, than with any other Union Pacific town. Unlike Russell, the railroad did not linger in Laramie but pushed northwest into the Laramie plains. In June of 1868 Russell went to the end of the line at Rock Creek, where he photographed several of the Union Pacific directors including Durant and Cornelius S. Bushnell.[16]

Around July 1 Russell traveled with the U.S. Geological Survey party under Ferdinand Vandeveer Hayden to the headwaters of the Laramie and Little Laramie Rivers.[17] That sum-

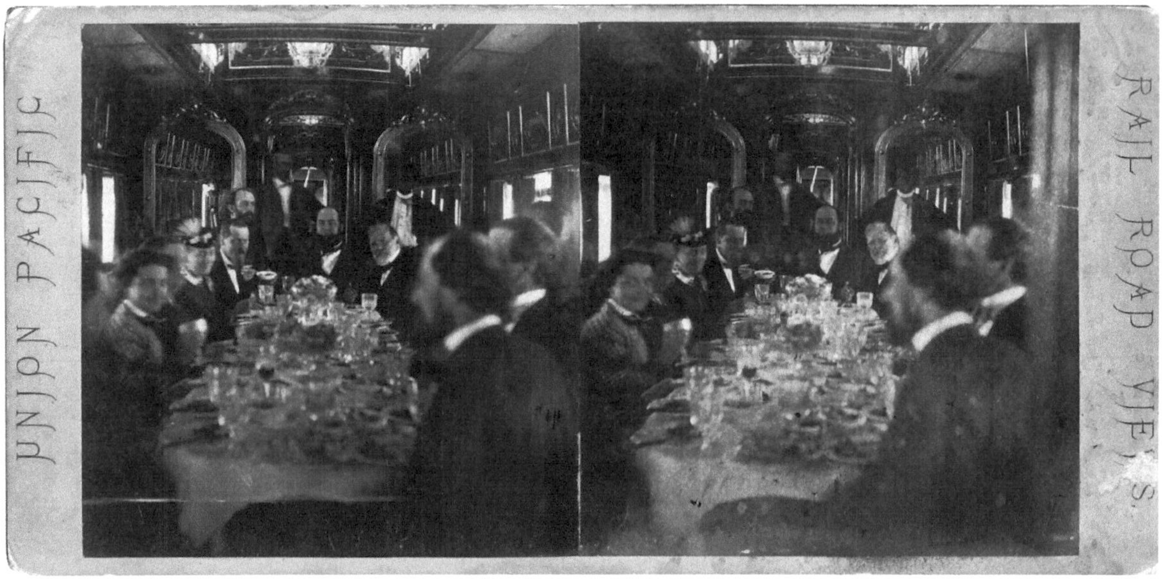

4.10. "Bushnell and Party, Rock Creek," by A. J. Russell, stereo-view no. 146. *Courtesy of the University of Iowa Libraries, Special Collections, Levi O. Leonard Railroadiana.*

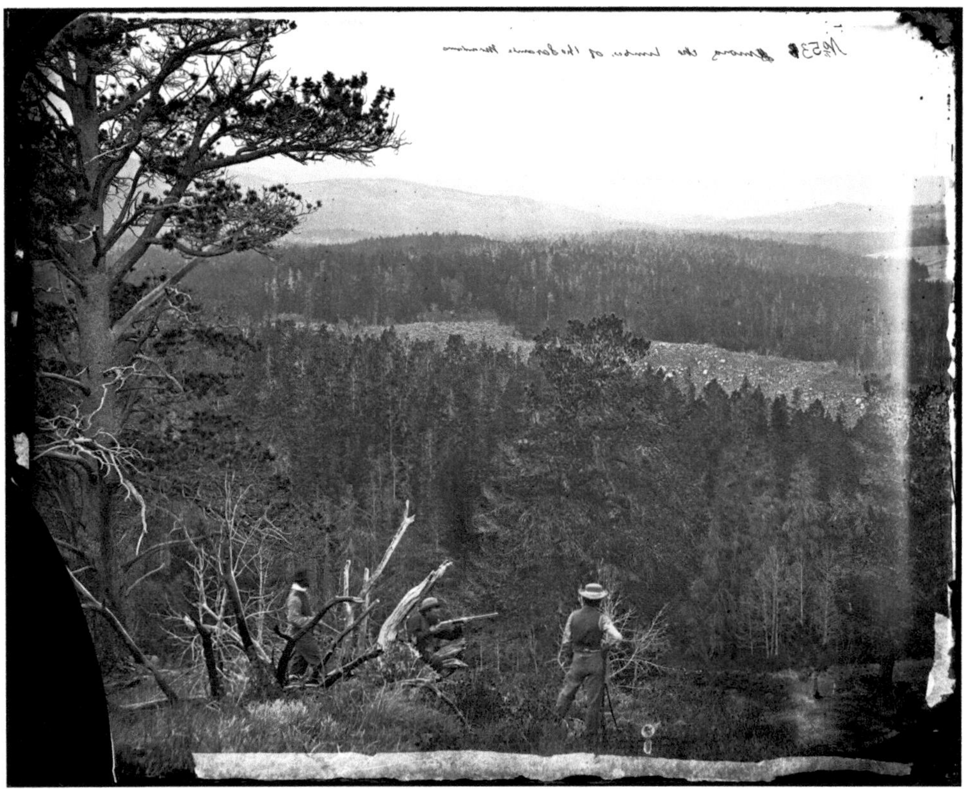

4.11. "Timber in the Medicine Bow Mountains," by A. J. Russell, large-format view no. 53. *Courtesy of the Oakland Museum of California, A. J. Russell Collection.*

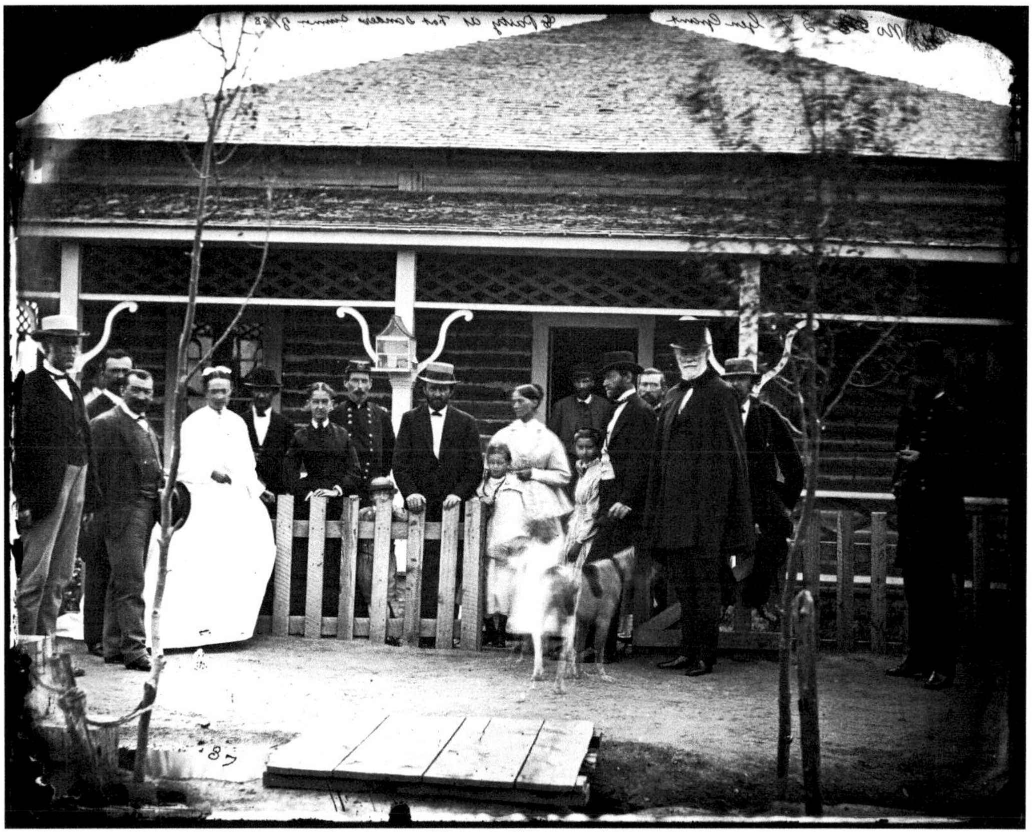

4.12. “Gen. Grant and Party at Fort Sanders Summer of ’68,” by A. J. Russell, large-format view no. 37. *Courtesy of the Oakland Museum of California, A. J. Russell Collection.*

mer there was a great deal of excitement over the supposed discovery of placer mines in the mountains.[18] Hayden wrote: “Camping with our wagons at the base of the main range of mountains, near the source of the Little Laramie, we prepared to ascend the mountains on horseback to the gold mines. We rode a distance of about ten miles before we came in view of the ‘diggings,’ and to reach them made an ascent of about two thousand feet above the bed of the creek. We were then between 10,000 and 11,000 feet above the sea, very near the elevation of perpetual snow, and where frost occurs every night of the year.”[19] Russell shot several photographs of the Little Laramie River, including one titled “Among the Timber at Head of Little Laramie River.”[20] Interestingly, Russell did not photograph the mines, instead taking several nondescript photographs of the timber of the Medicine Bow Mountains. Hayden wrote about the crucial role of these forests for ties: “Not only in the more lofty ranges, but also in the lower mountains, are large forests of pine timber, which will eventually become of great value to this country. Vast quantities of this pine in the form of railroad ties are floated down the various streams to the Union Pacific Railroad.”[21]

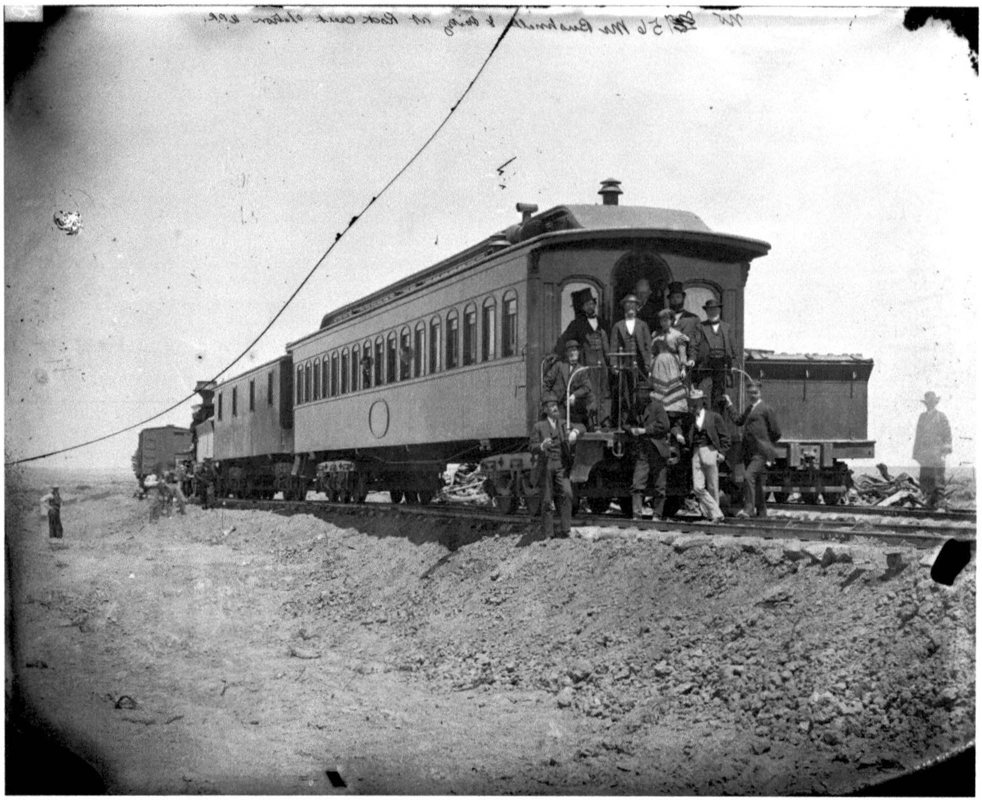

4.13. "Mr. Bushnell and Party at Rock Creek Station U.P.R.R.," by A. J. Russell, large-format view no. 56. *Courtesy of the Oakland Museum of California, A. J. Russell Collection.*

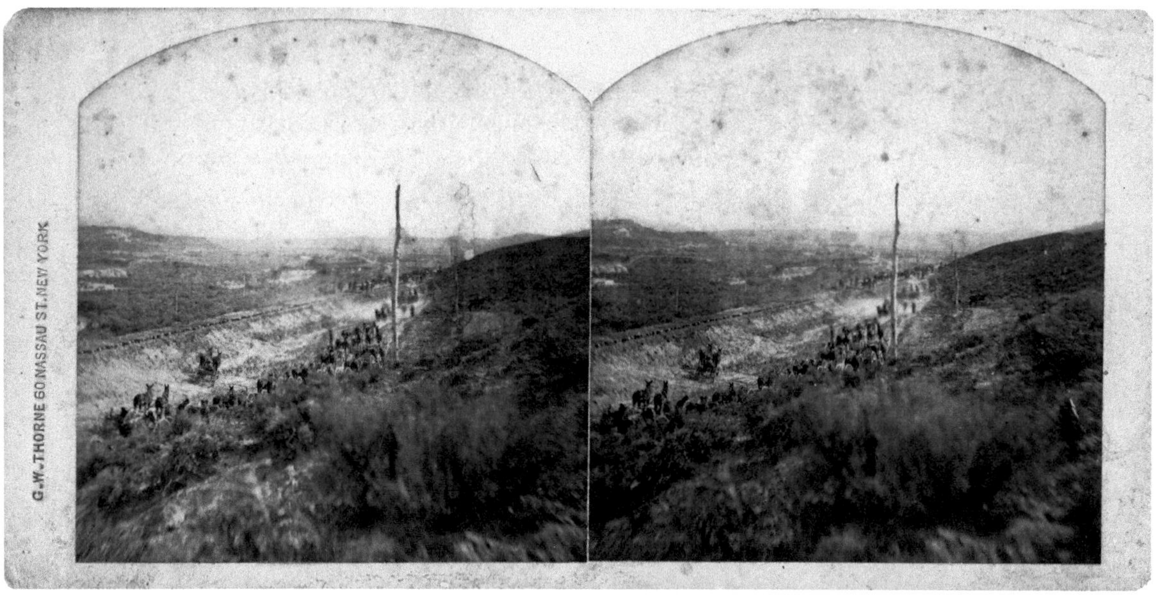

4.14. Laying track near Bitter Creek, by A. J. Russell, stereo-view no. 159. *Courtesy of Utah State University, Merrill-Cazier Library, Special Collections, Nineteenth-Century Western Stereo-Views Collection.*

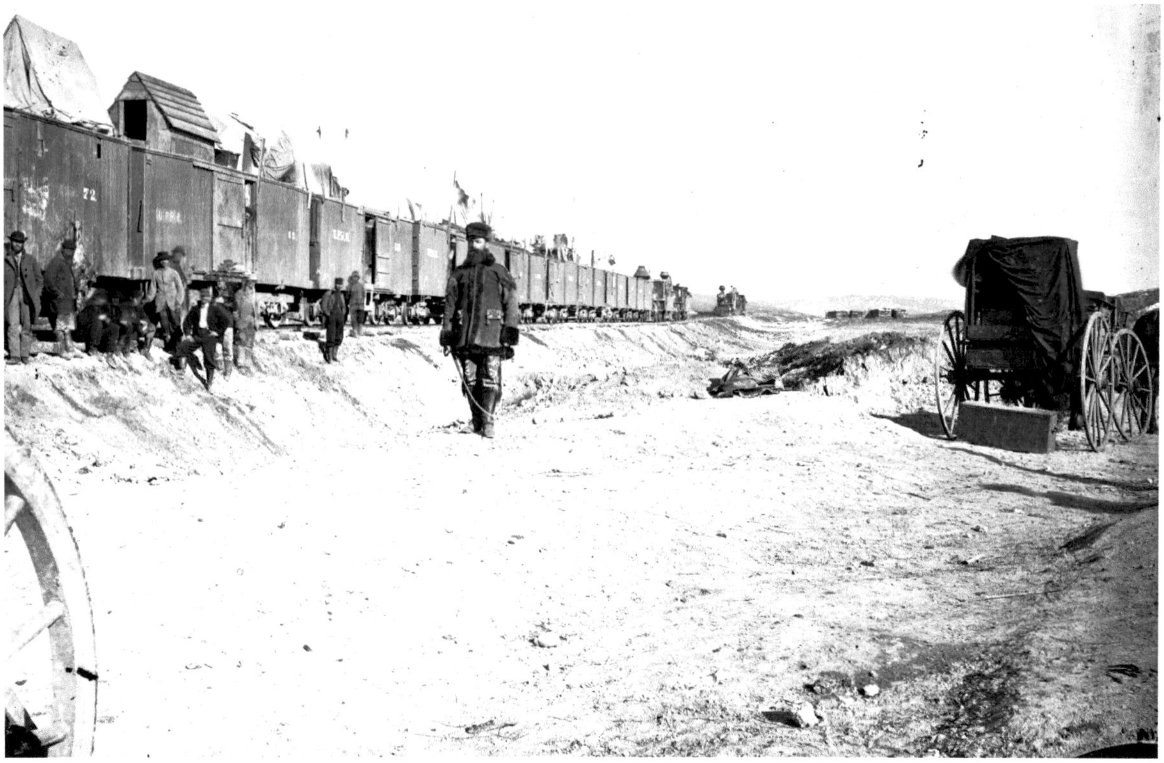

4.15. Jack Casement with whip (note Russell's wagon on the right), by A. J. Russell, large-format view no. 59. *Courtesy of the Oakland Museum of California, A. J. Russell Collection.*

Russell returned from the mountains in time to photograph the contentious meeting between Durant, Dodge, and presidential candidate Ulysses S. Grant on July 26, 1868, at Fort Saunders (located just outside of Laramie). At this meeting Grant censured and browbeat Durant for his interference with Dodge's location of the line, but also procured a promise from Dodge to stay with the Union Pacific until the line was complete. Russell took two large-format negatives and the tension in these images is almost palpable. Durant and Dodge had a running feud leading to epic boardroom battles. The Union Pacific was divided into "Durant men" and "Dodge men." Dodge and Russell had little reason to interact, and years later Dodge made a strangely cryptic reference to Russell: "A view of this gathering of officers was caught by a local photographer, who happened to be at the post [Fort Sanders]."[22]

Russell stayed in Laramie until mid-September when he finally left for the end of tracks near the Black Buttes Station located roughly halfway between Rawlins and Rock Springs.[23] About this time Russell took his iconic image of Jack Casement and his end of tracks construction crew (see fig. 4.15), which is a masterpiece of using the railroad, and all that it suggested to the 1860s public, as a dramatic backdrop to the figure of Casement as a person of power and authority.[24] In stark contrast to this image, however, Russell struggled to create effective images of the actual laying of track. From Black Buttes, he then drove his wagon to

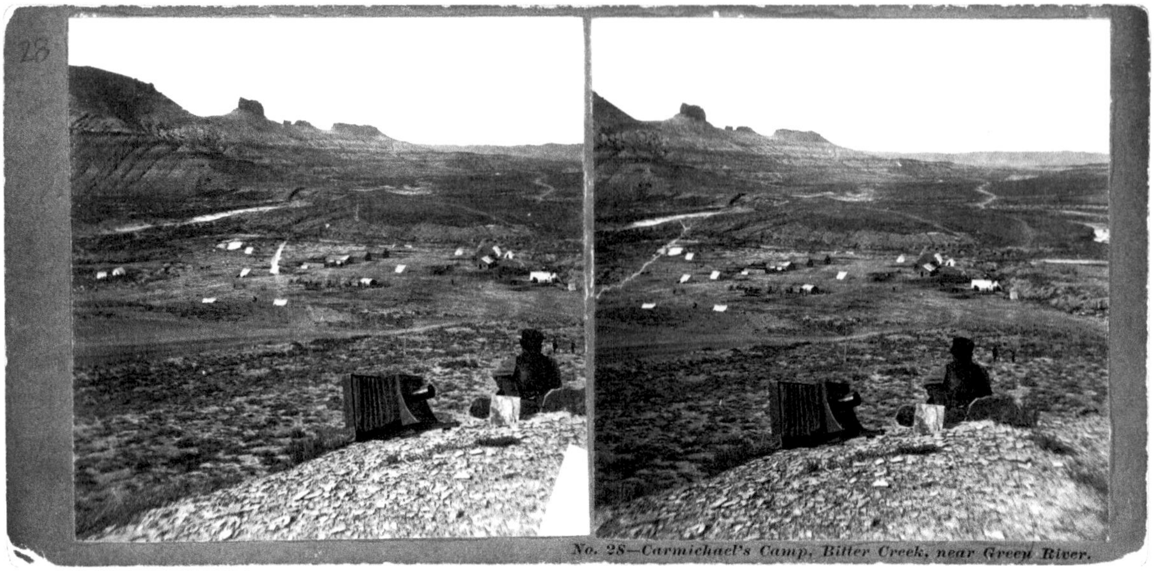

4.16. Bitter Creek Valley between Rock Springs and Green River, probably Russell himself with large-format camera, by A. J. Russell, stereo-view no. 168. (The number on the image is from Russell's earlier series Union Pacific R.R. Views across the Continent.) *Courtesy of the University of Iowa Libraries, Special Collections, Levi O. Leonard Railroadiana.*

Carmichael's encampment on Bitter Creek just east of Green River, Wyoming. Russell was now in advance of the railroad line, photographing the deep cuts that needed to be made in the Bitter Creek Valley. Russell, for the first time, also created panoramic overviews by taking three large-format negatives that could be pieced together.[25]

Smith and Russell reconnected when Smith moved to Green River with his new bride, Lucy. Smith wrote: "Myself, Lucy, Carmichael, Mr. and Mrs. Lamb, Mrs. Blair and Mr. Russell go to summit of mountain south of camp. It is a fine clear day. We name the two large piles of rocks there Smith's Buttes. Mr. Russell takes several pictures of us. We come home quite tired tonight."[26] (See fig. 4.17 for one of the pictures he mentions.) Russell also photographed the graders on the impressive cuts (thankfully made through soft shale) on the hillside west of the Green River. Russell photographed other interesting rock formations in the area along with Durant and his entourage of Union Pacific officials as the track moved through Green River in early October.

After leaving the Green River area he traveled further West, photographing the camp of contractor Michael Dowling (Russell spelled his name "Douling"), to the southeast of Evanston, Wyoming, on Aspen Summit. Amazingly, Dowling was also from Russell's hometown of Nunda, New York, but, as the story goes, neither one of them knew this fact until much later.[27] Russell also attempted to take more photographs of track laying on Muddy Creek (with no more success), as well as the wagon supply trains at the end of track, which would carry construction materials further West to Echo and Weber Canyons. Unfortunately for the modern traveler, Russell did not photograph the town of Piedmont between Bear River City and Muddy Creek

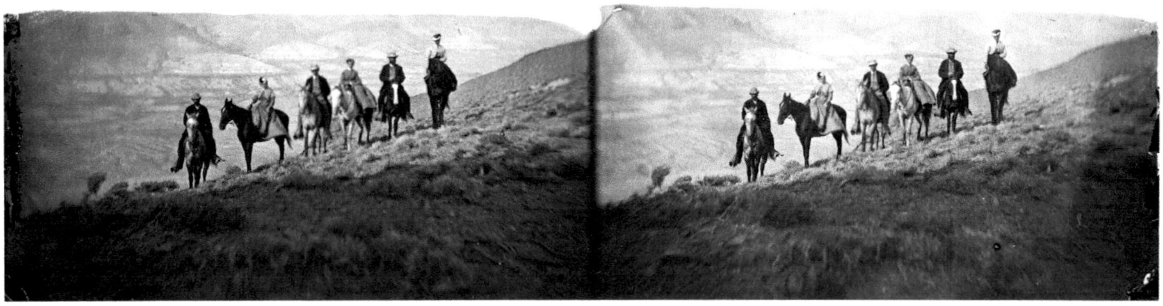

4.17. O. C. Smith, his wife Lucy, and others near Green River, by A. J. Russell, stereo-view no. 197. *Courtesy of the Oakland Museum of California, A. J. Russell Collection.*

(which today is a wonderful ghost town with several structures still intact). Many of these small stations were missed by Russell probably due to the sheer number of "towns" (often just a collection of tents) along the line.

"GUARDING THE SNOW-CLAD MOUNTAINS"

Russell heavily photographed the Union Pacific line in Utah. Utah, in fact, was hugely important to both railroads. Both companies hoped to reach coal mines in Utah, eliminating the cost of shipping it from the East, and to use Utah as a source of labor in the sparsely populated interior West. Also, as a quickly growing territory, Utah would provide riders and freight along the lines. Echo and Weber Canyons, in particular, would prove crucial to the Union Pacific in the final drama of building the transcontinental railroad. Not only was this the most difficult portion of the entire line (three tunnels through fifteen hundred feet of rock and ten bridges), but these canyons became the focus of intense, behind-the-scenes maneuvering by both companies in the fall of 1868.[28]

Brigham Young would provide the key to solving the challenges of Echo and Weber Canyons. Young was the most powerful man in Utah, and the Union Pacific had a long association with this prophet of the Mormon Church. Young was the only investor who paid full price for five shares of the Union Pacific stock in 1862 (at $1,000 each!).[29] Young eagerly followed the progress, or lack thereof, of the line after 1862. He provided encouragement, animals, and men to aid railroad surveys in Utah starting in 1864. The railroad would provide immeasurably easier passage across the plains and mountains and it would infuse some much-needed cash into the Utah economy. Whatever personal dislikes the directors of both railroads had towards Mormonism and polygamy, they recognized how crucial Utah was to their plans and they both started courting Young in 1867. For instance, as early as the fall of 1867, Union Pacific Chief Engineer Grenville Dodge spoke with Young about using Mormon laborers in Weber and Echo Canyons. Dodge would discreetly avoid the topic of where the railroad would go once it reached Ogden, south to Salt Lake City or north to Promontory. Both railroads knew that the northern route was more economical but they were hesitant to

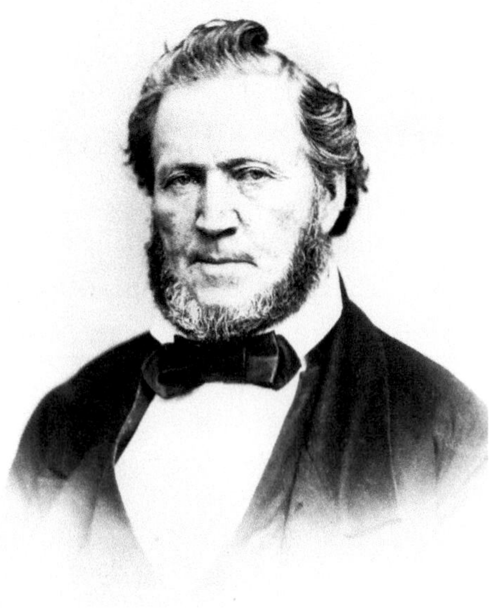

4.18. Image of Brigham Young, 1868, photographer unknown. *Courtesy of Utah State University, Merrill-Cazier Library, Special Collections.*

invoke Young's legendary temper by telling him the railroad would not be going through the city of the saints.

The Union Pacific signed the first contract with Young on May 21, 1868, at the Continental Hotel in Salt Lake City. The contract was for $2,125,000, encompassing all grading, tunneling, and bridge masonry from the head of Echo Canyon to Ogden.[30] This contract would accomplish two things. One, it would bring much-needed cash into Utah, which was still largely on a barter system, and, two, hopefully it would avoid the violence and crime of the hell-on-wheels towns that followed the Union Pacific in Nebraska and Wyoming. The *Deseret News* wrote: "Some of the public journals give interesting and graphic descriptions of the reckless characters that are gradually floating westward as they are driven from the towns of the Union Pacific railroad by vigilance committees. It is an excellent proverb that 'fore-warned is fore-armed.' There is no harm in our citizens being amply prepared, so that should a surplus of scoundrelism float this way and attempt to ply their hellish practices in this city we may be prepared to give them a proper reception."[31]

Young subcontracted out the work in smaller sections to bishops in the Mormon Church. His son Joseph A. Young and John Sharp did specialized work. Joseph F. Nounan (who was not Mormon) did much of the work under the contract. All of Young's contractors gave a 10 percent tithe to the Mormon Church.[32] As part of the agreement, "contractor's," or greatly reduced, rates on the line were given to Mormon immigrants. Work began in earnest in mid-June 1868 from the head of Echo Canyon to Devil's Gate in lower Weber Canyon. The work got off to a slow start, the major problem being a lack of proper tools. By July and August, however, the work was commencing at a favorable pace. By September, in fact, the major grading had been completed in Echo Canyon and the Mormon laborers began to focus on the Weber Narrows and Weber Canyon.[33] The accounts written for the *Deseret News* stressed the absence of alcohol, tobacco, and the use of "profane language." Adolphus H. Noon wrote to the *Deseret News* on June 28, 1868, that "we have no whiskey shebangs 'or sich' here yet, and our minds are made up that just as soon as anybody sticks them up, we will stick them down, and that too pretty deep in the creek."[34] Except for Bear River City, Russell ignored the hell-on-wheels towns, perhaps for fear of bad publicity. For instance, Hayden wrote: "The remains of these temporary cities are scattered all along the line of the railroad, and the scenes of savage barbarity, which were connected with them, have all passed away, and it were well if they could be forgotten. If we go a little way into the hills . . . we shall find a cluster of graves, every one of the inmates of which perished by violence."[35]

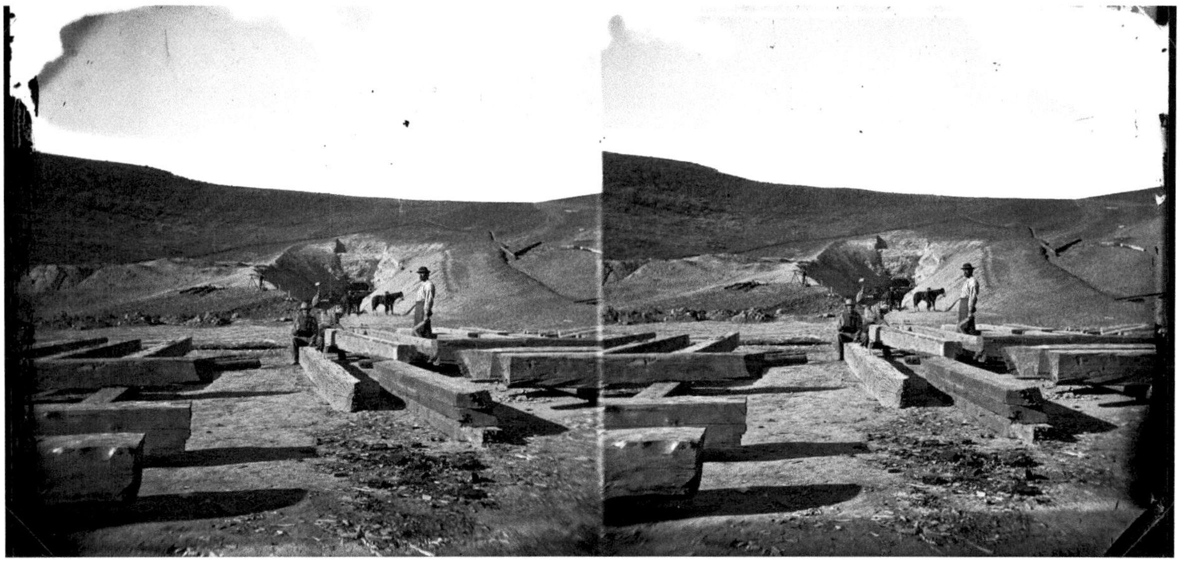

4.19. Workmen at entrance to tunnel no. 2, by A. J. Russell, stereo-view no. 267 (alternate view). *Courtesy of the Oakland Museum of California, A. J. Russell Collection.*

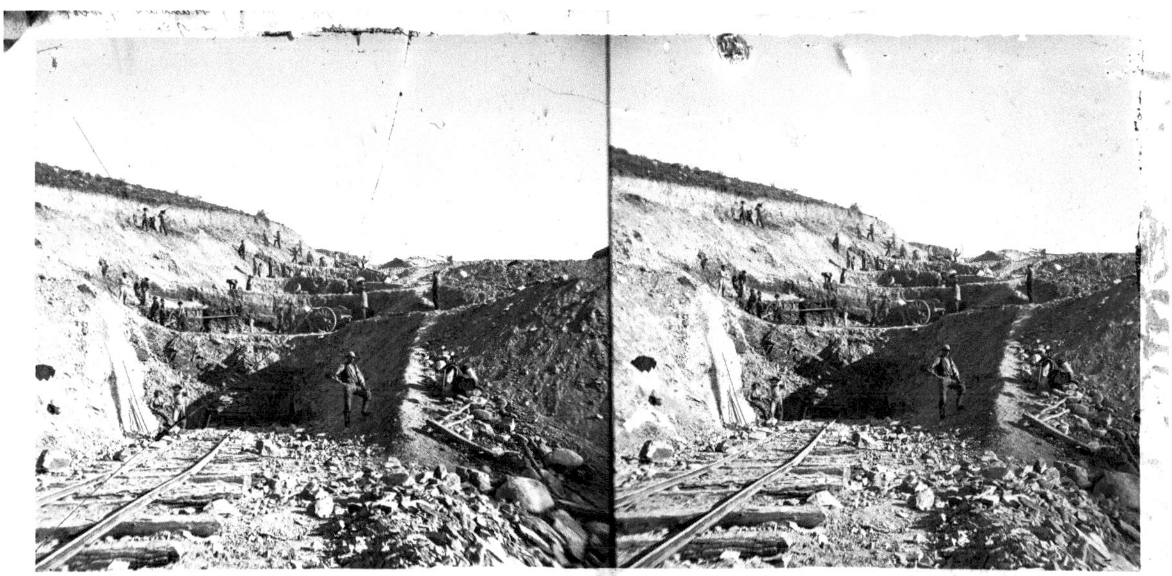

4.20. Mormon workers on a deep cut in Weber Canyon, by A. J. Russell, stereo-view no. 372. *Courtesy of the Oakland Museum of California, A. J. Russell Collection.*

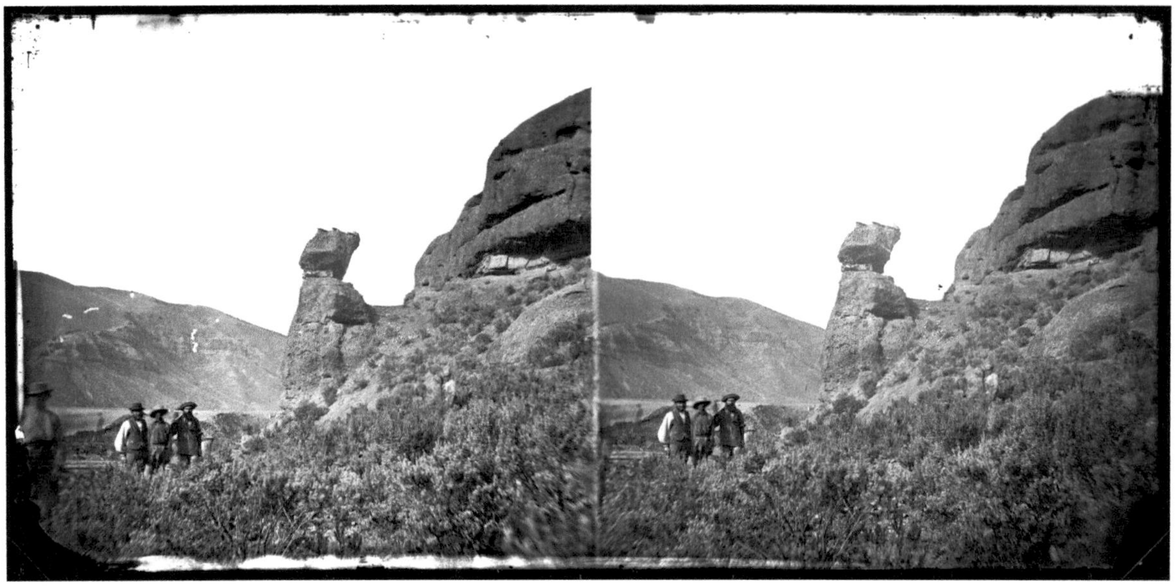

4.21. Pulpit Rock, Echo, Utah, by A. J. Russell, stereo-view no. 336. *Courtesy of the Oakland Museum of California, A. J. Russell Collection.*

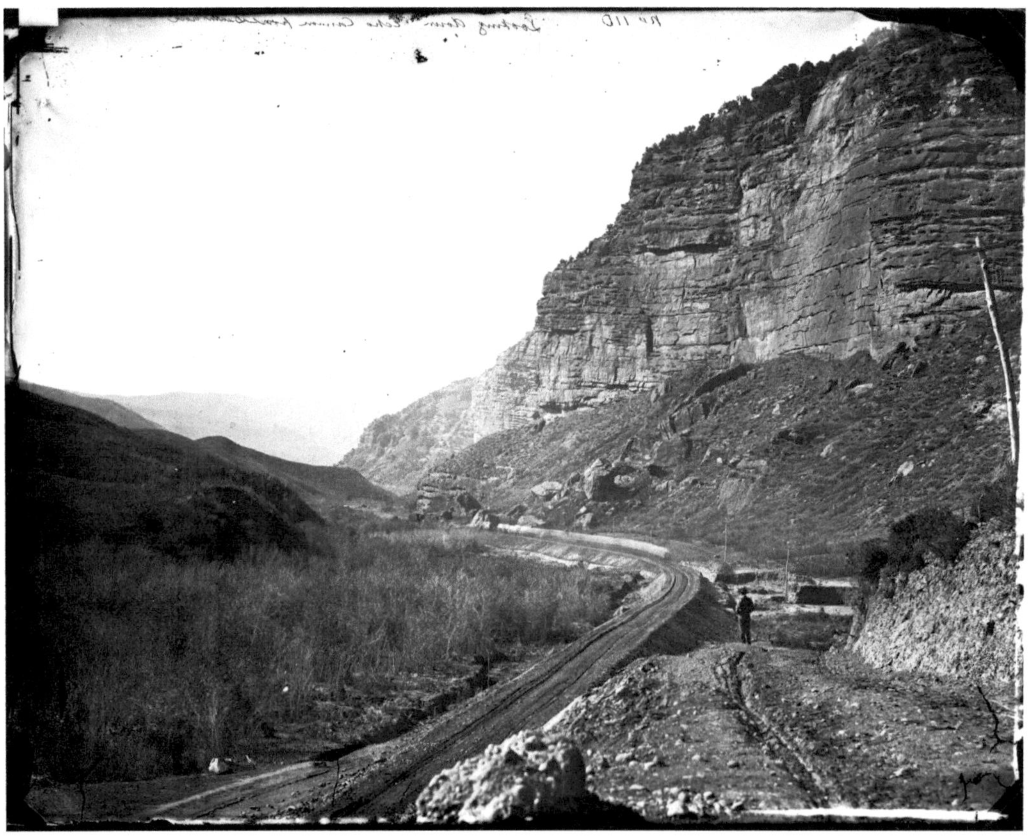

4.22. "Looking down Echo Can[y]on from Death's Rock," by A. J. Russell, large-format view no. 110. *Courtesy of the Oakland Museum of California, A. J. Russell Collection.*

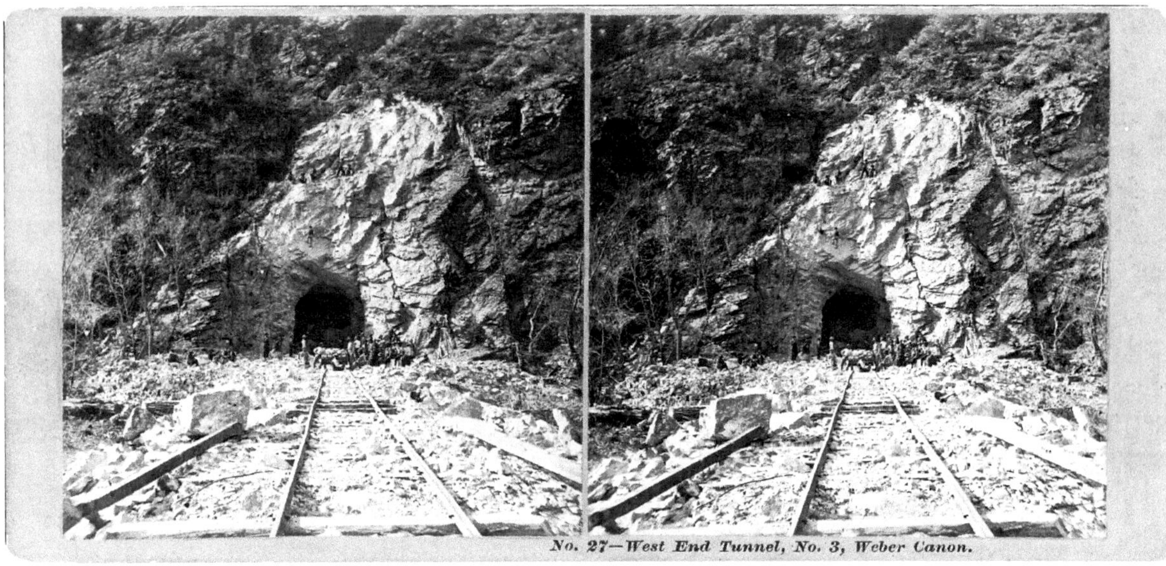

4.23. "Building Tunnel No. 3," by A. J. Russell, stereo-view no. 375. (The number on the image is from Russell's earlier series Union Pacific R.R. Views across the Continent.) *Courtesy of the University of Iowa Libraries, Special Collections, Levi O. Leonard Railroadiana.*

Russell may have ignored hell-on-wheels but he extensively photographed the work from the beginning of Echo Canyon on the Wyoming-Utah border to the mouth of Weber Canyon near Ogden. Russell's 1868 images show the more difficult aspects of the construction, such as digging tunnels and rock cuts, setting bridge foundations, and, of course, grading. This work was particularly worrisome to the board of directors of the Union Pacific, as they wanted to make sure the line was ready when the rails arrived in the spring of 1869. No doubt, as well, they were curious about the experiment with Mormon labor. Furthermore the Central Pacific had designs of building a rival line in the canyons and certainly the Union Pacific was eager to show government commissioners how much work had been completed. When looking at all his Echo and Weber Canyon images, the viewer should understand that Russell's numbering series indiscriminately mixes 1868 and 1869 images. Russell's 1869 images, after the Golden Spike Ceremony, focus on the completed tunnels and bridges, as well as his usual unusual rock formations and scenic overviews.

Given the fact that Russell was now traveling with his wagon, it is not hard to imagine that he followed a fairly linear approach to his work in October and November, methodically moving down Echo Canyon, through the Weber Narrows and into Weber Canyon (with a side trip to Coalville), only pausing occasionally for a few interesting rock formations. Russell started by taking several photographs of the workmen preparing timber supports for the uncompleted tunnel no. 2 and the "great Z." The Z allowed the engines to temporarily bypass tunnel no. 2. Trains would drive over a trestle to a Y point where they would then back under the trestle on a temporary track for over a mile to another temporary track and another Y, from which they

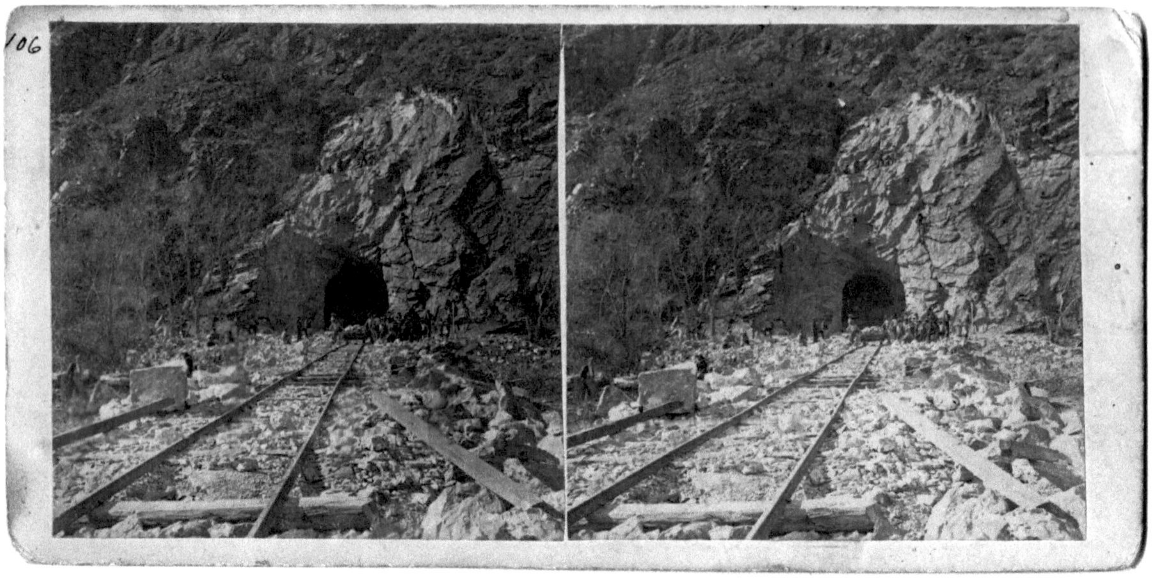

4.24. Tunnel no. 3, by C. R. Savage, stereo-view. *Courtesy of the Union Pacific Railroad Museum, Union Pacific Collection, Photography Archives.*

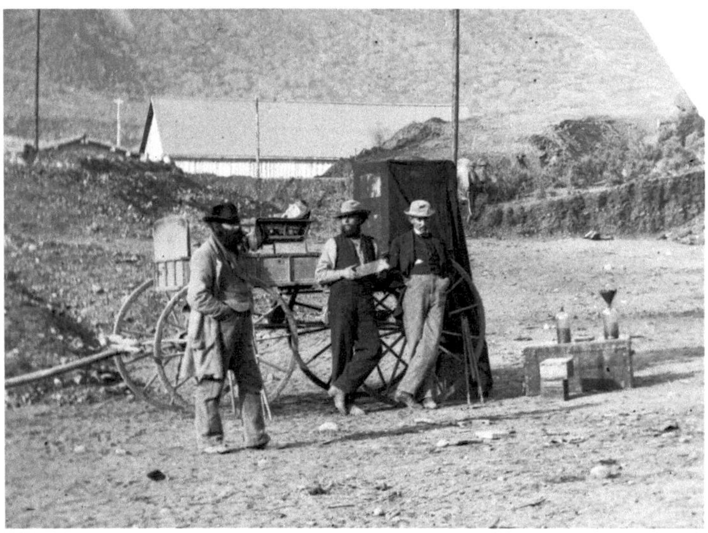

4.25. Cropped version of A. J. Russell stereo-view no. 357, "Old Stage Station, at Echo" (C. R. Savage leaning against Russell's darkroom wagon). *Courtesy of the Oakland Museum of California, A. J. Russell Collection.*

could then travel forward to rejoin the main line on the other side of the tunnel.[36] Russell shot a few of the features of Echo Canyon, including Hanging Rock, Devil's Post Office, Lion Rock, and Monument Rock, before arriving at the mouth of Echo Canyon and the junction of Echo Creek and the Weber River. At this junction he became fascinated with Pulpit Rock (so named because Young gave a sermon from the rock in 1847) and, in fact, he would eventually take eight large-format images and seven stereo-views of this unusual and arresting landmark.[37] Russell attempted to rename the rock "Sphynx of the Valley," writing, "This unique figure, bearing a strong resemblance to the Egyptian Sphynx . . . seems to be watching over the approach to the Weber Valley, and guarding the snow-clad mountains of the Wasatch range."[38] He photographed the Mormon grading crews in Echo

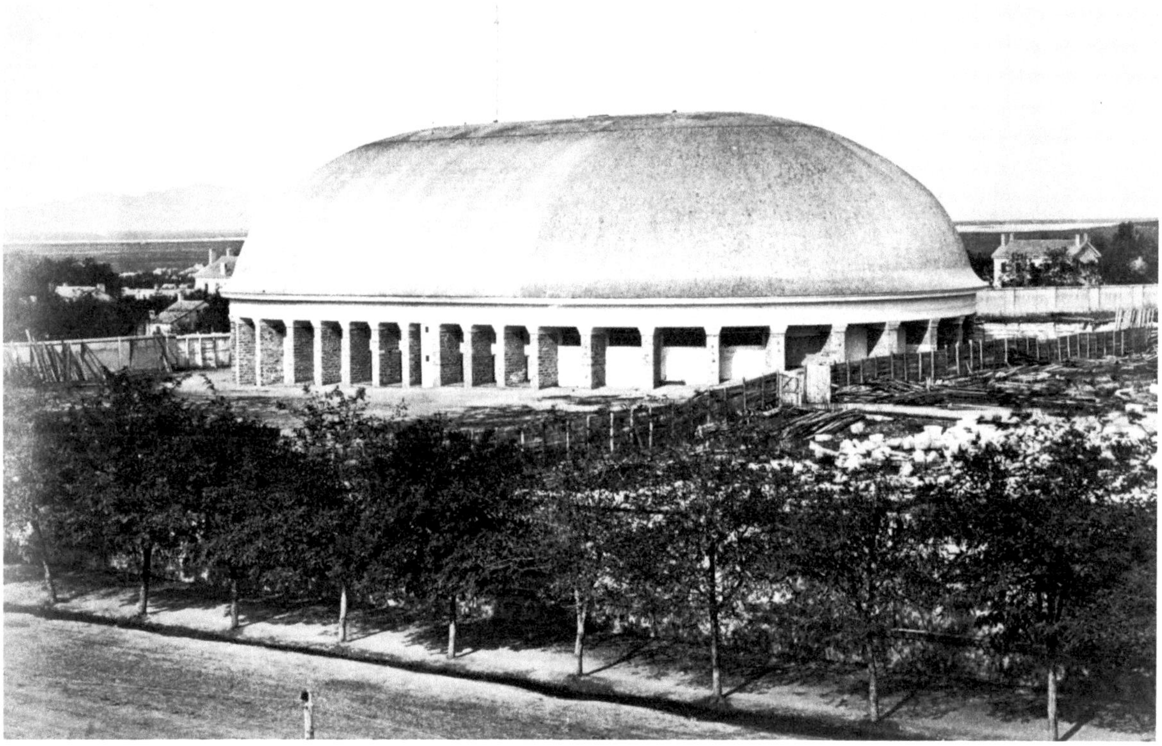

4.26. "Great Mormon Tabernacle, Salt Lake City," by A. J. Russell, from Sun Pictures of Rocky Mountain Scenery. *Courtesy of Utah State University, Merrill-Cazier Library, Special Collections.*

Canyon (and their temporary living arrangements), and the deep cuts, bridge foundations, and work on tunnel no. 3 and tunnel no. 4. Russell also took several shots of the Union Pacific's chief construction officer Samuel B. Reed in Echo. Reed and his family, in fact, would become a favorite subject in the next year.

In Echo Canyon, Russell met Salt Lake City photographer C. R. Savage. These two men, so different in many ways, would have a long and productive relationship. Charles Roscoe Savage's beginnings were modest. He grew up in England in a poor Southampton neighborhood and as the son of a gardener received very little schooling and was expected to contribute to the family finances at an early age. He did, however, have an interest in religion and in 1848, despite his family's objections, he converted to the Church of Jesus Christ of Latter-day Saints. In 1855 Savage left England for New York City. Although he was interested in photography while still in England, only when he reached New York did he begin his study in earnest. He found the trade to be very secretive and had difficulty receiving training of any kind. Eventually, through reading, experimentation, and paid lessons he became quite competent.[39] In 1860 he arrived in Council Bluffs, Iowa (then the main departure point for the Overland and Oregon Trails) where he set up a crude darkroom and gallery. He was able to earn enough

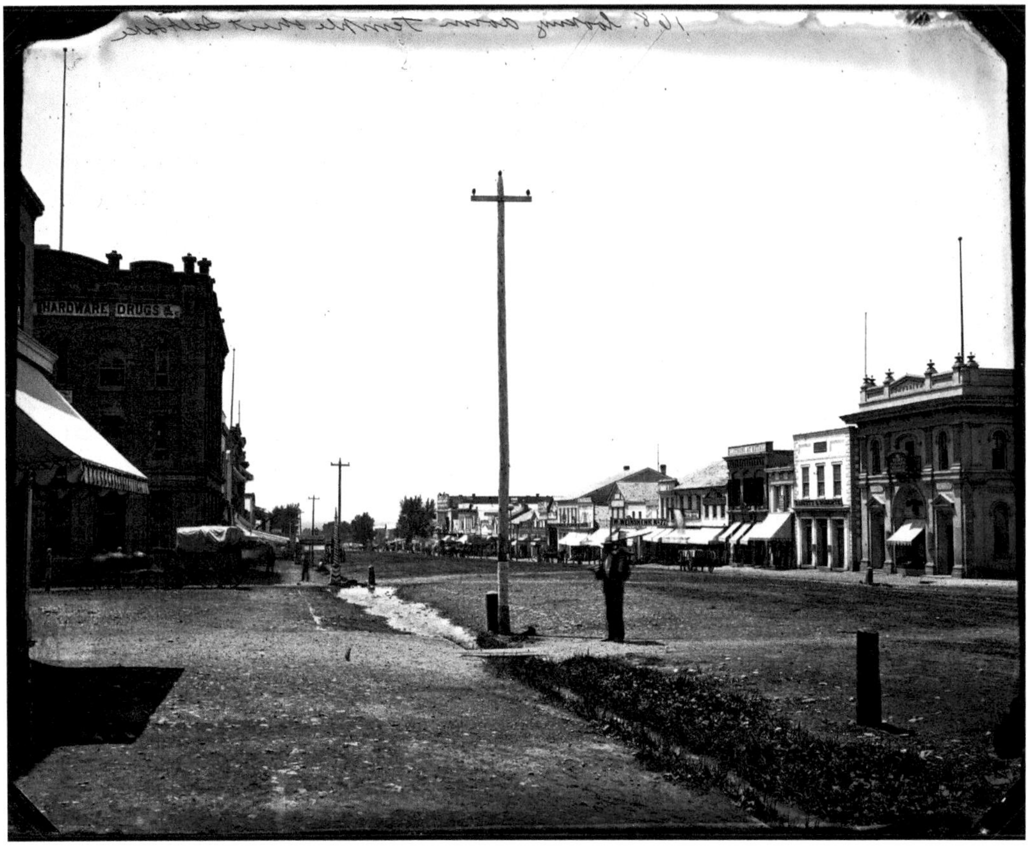

4.27. "Looking down Temple Street Salt Lake," by A. J. Russell, large-format view no. 168. *Courtesy of the Oakland Museum of California, A. J. Russell Collection.*

money to buy and outfit a wagon for his small family for the trip westward. On August 28, 1860, Savage finally reached Salt Lake City. At first his business was almost exclusively devoted to portraiture, but Savage soon went outdoors by photographing the buildings of Salt Lake City, as well as the mountains and small towns of Utah. After several years, though, Savage felt more and more isolated from other progressive photographers and from the latest developments in the art. In 1866 he came up with a daring plan to travel nine thousand miles from Salt Lake City to San Francisco to New York and then back to Utah. This trip plunged him deeply in debt, but also began his rise to national prominence as a western photographer.[40]

Savage left Salt Lake City for San Francisco by stagecoach. He visited with a number of photographers while in the city, including Carleton Watkins. He then took a steamer down to Panama, crossed the Isthmus, and took another boat north to New York City. In New York he bought photographic supplies from E. & H. T. Anthony & Co. and visited with several publishers before traveling to Philadelphia to pick up a wagon similar to the darkroom wagon used by Russell. He shipped the wagon by boat and rail to Nebraska City, Nebraska. He then traveled across the plains, into the Rocky Mountains, and back to Salt Lake City (of course photographing the more famous places on the Oregon Trail as he went). Savage made a number of contacts on this voyage and, soon after, his images started showing up as lithographs in *Harper's Weekly* and *Leslie's Illustrated* and were marketed on the East Coast through the New York firm of Fowler and Wells. Savage also subsequently published articles in *Philadelphia Photographer* and *Humphrey's Journal of Photography and the Allied Arts and Sciences*.[41]

These two men photographed together, sometimes side by side. In one view Savage is leaning against Russell's wagon (see fig. 4.25).[42] In another, they printed nearly identical stereo-views of tunnel no. 3, indicating that their camera's were side by side with the Mormon workingmen scattered all over the images.[43] As well, Russell's wagon (and perhaps Russell himself in one view) appears in several Savage stereos.[44] Russell also went to Salt Lake City to photograph the Utah territorial capital, probably in the late fall. (Several of these photographs show a thin snow high on the Wasatch mountainsides that looks like a late fall Utah snowstorm.) On at least one occasion Russell and Savage traded negatives.[45] Given their close working relationship, it is not hard to imagine that Russell came to Salt Lake City at Savage's behest. In the growing Mormon capital Russell photographed the Tabernacle, the foundations of the Salt Lake Temple, the Lion and Beehive Houses, the theater house, and Brigham Young's woolen mill at the mouth of Parley's Canyon.[46] Russell's images show Salt Lake City to be a modern, growing city, and he was clearly impressed to find such significant structures as the Tabernacle in the middle of the interior West: "This building comfortably accommodates ten thousand people and has within its dome the second largest organ in the United States."[47] With the onset of winter, Russell started home for New York around December 1, arriving in Nunda on December 9, 1868.[48] His hometown newspaper noted, "He is still a gentile, although he has spent some time among the Mormon saints."[49] For the Union Pacific, 1868 had been spectacularly successful in terms of laying track. The company started the year hoping for 350 miles and ended up laying 446. The line was just past Evanston, Wyoming, on New Year's Day and in the first few months of 1869 it would be laying tracks in Echo and Weber Canyons.[50] By this point the Union Pacific had learned that the Central Pacific had secretly received permission from the federal government to lay their own tracks in these canyons. The Union Pacific was, of course, desperate to keep them out. Part of the Central Pacific's argument was that its rival built a substandard line and they used temporary track around the yet to be completed tunnels.

What becomes obvious when examining Russell's 1868 images is not the line itself, but his preoccupation with the people of the railroad. He focused on the end product of their work, but mostly of them doing their work; the men who paused just long enough to have their image taken before resuming their backbreaking labor. Masons working on bridge foundations, freighters and their wagons, surveyors with their transits, engine crews with their engines, track layers, laborers, cooks, machinists, carpenters, graders, teamsters, and even the clerks (like O. C. Smith) pushing paper all graced his camera. Russell's job was nearly as difficult as these other workingmen on the Union Pacific. It is not hard to imagine the difficulties of hauling chemicals, cameras, glass plates, a wagon, and draft animals on and off the train, up into the mountains, and out past the end of track. His work also led him into climbing cliffs and hills for elevated views and traveling with his equipment on pack animals. But if Russell ever complained about this labor, it was not recorded.

CHAPTER 5

Russell's Second Trip West and the Golden Spike Ceremony (1869)

"The great railroad problem of the age is now solved."

—A. J. Russell

On May 10, 1869, three men—three photographers—came together in a remote corner of Utah. These men, Charles Roscoe Savage, Andrew Joseph Russell, and Alfred A. Hart, were slated to photograph what was then usually called the "wedding of the rails" or the "laying of the last rail," and what would become known as the Golden Spike Ceremony. Although the men came from very different backgrounds, they formed a friendship of sorts born from their mutual interest in photographing the construction of the transcontinental railroad. While they could have viewed themselves as competitors in a limited market, they did not. They shared photographing techniques and even a few images. Russell and Savage, of course, knew one another from the previous fall. In all likelihood, however, this was their first time meeting with Hart.

Hart had followed the progress of the Central Pacific in 1867 and 1868 in several trips from Sacramento going over Donner Summit and into the deserts of northern Nevada. He began by photographing the snowsheds built over Donner Summit, then down the Truckee River to Reno, across the Alkali Desert, through Ten Mile Canyon, and finishing at the Palisades in December 1868. In the spring of 1869 he traveled with Leland Stanford's special train that was heading to Promontory and photographed the remainder of the line in Nevada, including Carlin, Elko, and Rozel, reaching Promontory on May 7.[1]

For most of the people in the Union Pacific this was their first time fraternizing with the Central Pacific crowd: for the Union Pacific laborers the Central Pacific was a vague enemy they had rushed recklessly towards for nearly four years. If they saw beyond their preconceptions, however, they should have been impressed with the scrappy California upstart. The Central Pacific had a number of disadvantages, including not having the political clout and connections among men of power and prestige in the East, having to blast its way through the imposing Sierra Nevada Mountains, dealing with ferocious snowstorms on Donnor Summit, and finding laborers on the West Coast. Also, all the equipment aside from ties and spikes had to be shipped from the East either across the Panama Isthmus or around the Cape. In fact, the Pacific Railway Act of 1862 relegated the Central Pacific to the role of building to the California border where it would presumably meet the mighty Union

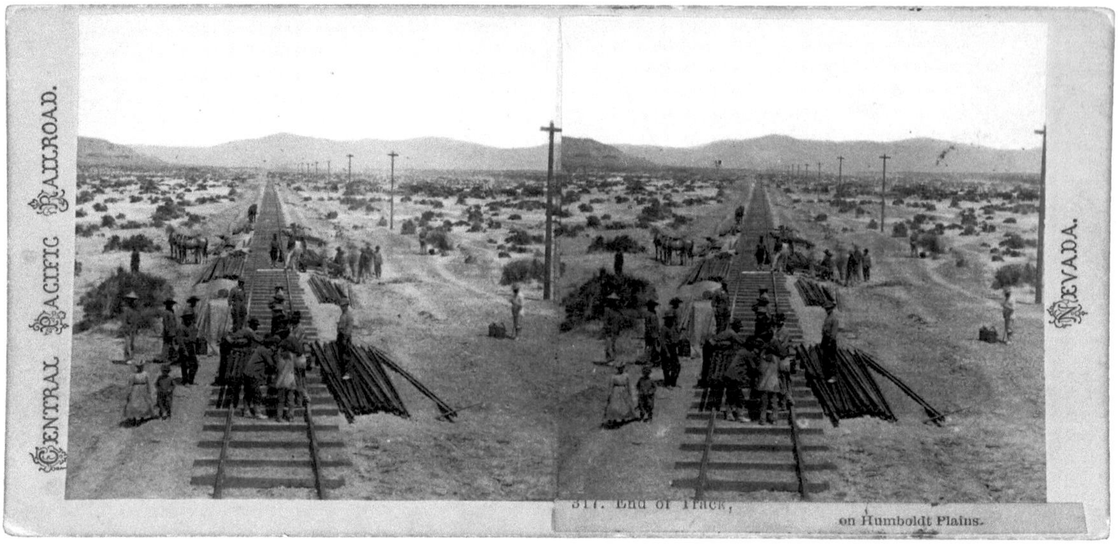

5.1. End of track on Humboldt Plains, by Alfred A. Hart, stereo-view no. 317. *Courtesy of the Library of Congress, Prints and Photographs Division.*

Pacific. The Central Pacific, however, was a better-managed, better-built line that avoided the political backlash against the Union Pacific and Durant's questionable practices. It eventually was able to remove these legal restrictions, and through pluck and determination it created a race with the Union Pacific.

Standing in its way, however, was the imposing summit of the Sierra Nevada Mountains. In 1867 and 1868 the Central Pacific built thirty-seven miles of snowsheds at great expense in a desperate attempt to keep the rails running during and after severe winter snowstorms.[2] Even before it finished a contiguous route, it started to lay line on the other side of the summit in the summer and fall of 1867. Progress was slow, however, because it had to haul materials across a stubborn seven-mile gap in the rails. On June 17, 1868, the gap (conveniently overlooked in official reports) was finally closed, and the Central Pacific now had 167 miles of continuous line.[3] Despite problems with alkali water ruining engines and shortages of supplies, the mostly Chinese crews averaged an astonishing three miles a day as they sped across the high desert country of northern Nevada.[4] By the spring of 1869, after working through the winter of 1868 to 1869, they reached Wells, where they laid rail over the grades completed by Mormon workers. In fact, the Central Pacific crews graded two hundred miles parallel to the Union Pacific, all the way from Wells, Nevada, to Ogden, Utah.

There was considerable jostling between the two companies almost to the very end. President Grant refused to release bonds to either railroad in March 1869 unless they agreed to an official meeting place. On April 8, Dodge and Huntington reached an agreement to meet at Promontory Summit. The Union Pacific, however, would sell its forty-seven and a half miles of track from Ogden to Promontory to the Central Pacific.[5] Russell took several photos of the Union Pacific cuts (although they were destined to sit unused) on the difficult ascent up from

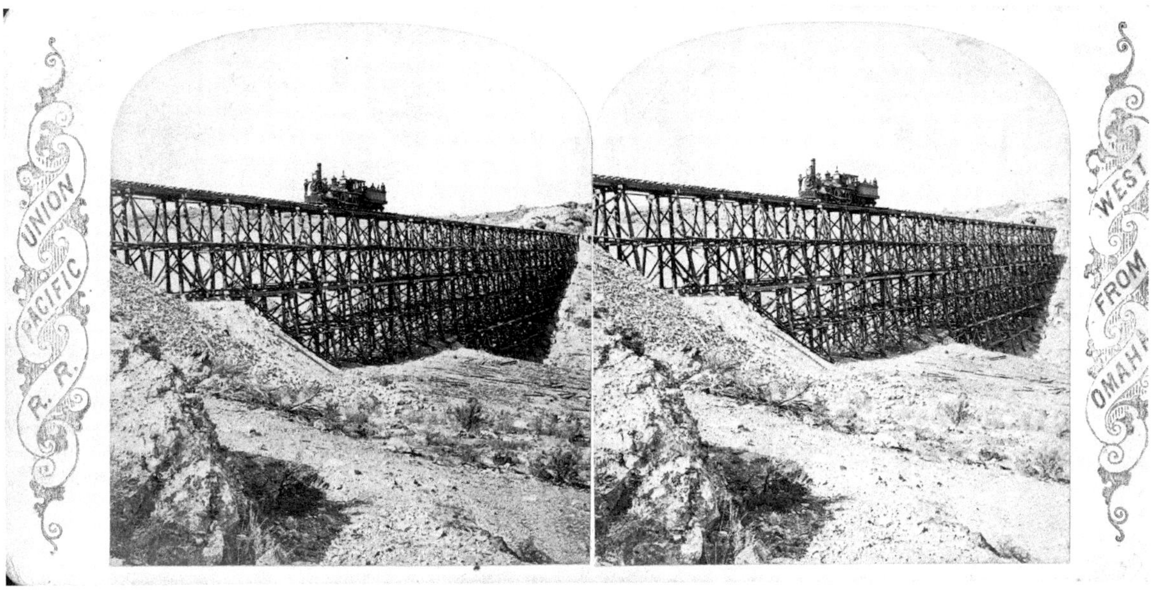

5.2. "Engine on Great Trestle, Prom[o]ntory," by A. J. Russell, stereo-view no. 531. *Courtesy of Utah State University, Merrill-Cazier Library, Special Collections. Nineteenth-Century Western Stereo-Views Collection.*

Blue Creek to the Promontory Summit. Promontory, in fact, was the meeting of the rails for passengers only until December, when Ogden became the junction.[6] Both railroads made concessions, but by the time of the wedding of the rails, the momentum had shifted to the Central Pacific and the Union Pacific was nearly bankrupt (mostly due to severe mismanagement), with a pile of unpaid bills.

Savage arrived in the area on May 7, anticipating that the ceremony would be held as originally planned on May 8. He, and the whole country, would learn that the ceremony was delayed until May 10 because the Devil's Gate Bridge in Weber Canyon had become unstable.[7] Dan Casement, the brother of track-laying superintendent Jack Casement, visited Savage's store three weeks before the Golden Spike Ceremony, but he was actually invited by consulting engineer (and Durant lackey) Silas Seymour.[8] Why Savage was invited despite the presence of Russell is not entirely clear, except that his photographs might provide extra publicity for the event and for the railroads. Either way, the images taken during the ceremony show that the two worked closely together. In fact, the *Deseret News* reported that Savage "assisted" Russell.[9] Savage spent much of his extra two days photographing Casement's workers. Like most Mormons he was appalled by the drunkenness and violence that accompanied the progress of the line. Savage wrote: "In sight of their camp were the beautiful cit[ies] of [D]eadfall and [L]ast [C]hance. I was creditably informed that 24 men had been killed in the several camps in the last 25 days. Certainly a harder set of men were never before congregated together. . . . At Blue River [Blue Creek] the returning demons . . . were being piled upon the cars in every stage of drunkenness. Every ranch or tent has whiskey for sale. Verily the men earn their money like horses and spend it like asses."[10]

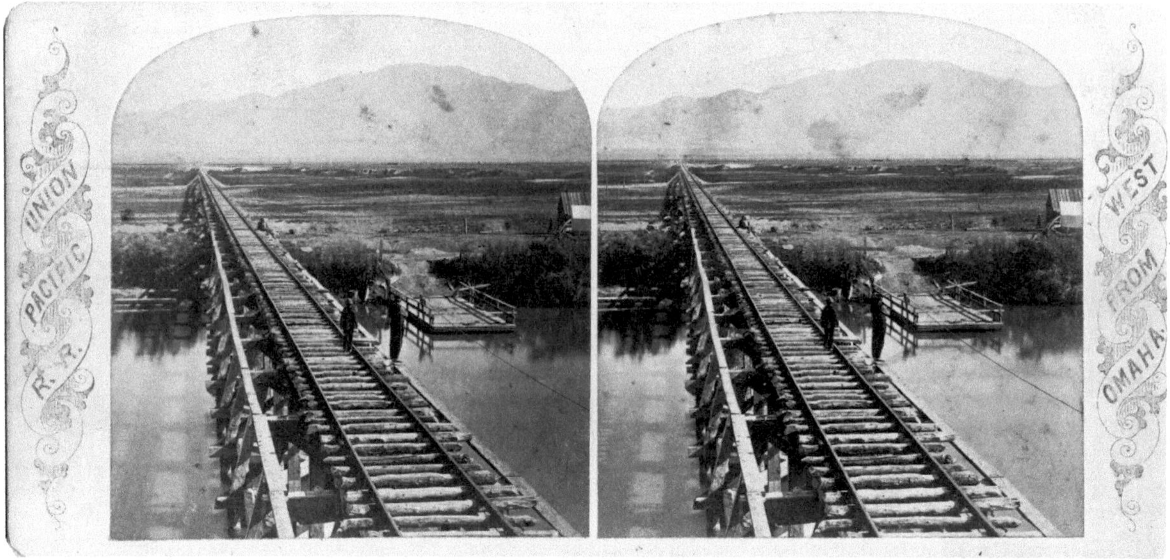

5.3. Bear River Bridge, Corinne, Utah, by A. J. Russell, stereo-view no. 505. *Courtesy of Utah State University, Merrill-Cazier Library, Special Collections, Nineteenth-Century Western Stereo-Views Collection.*

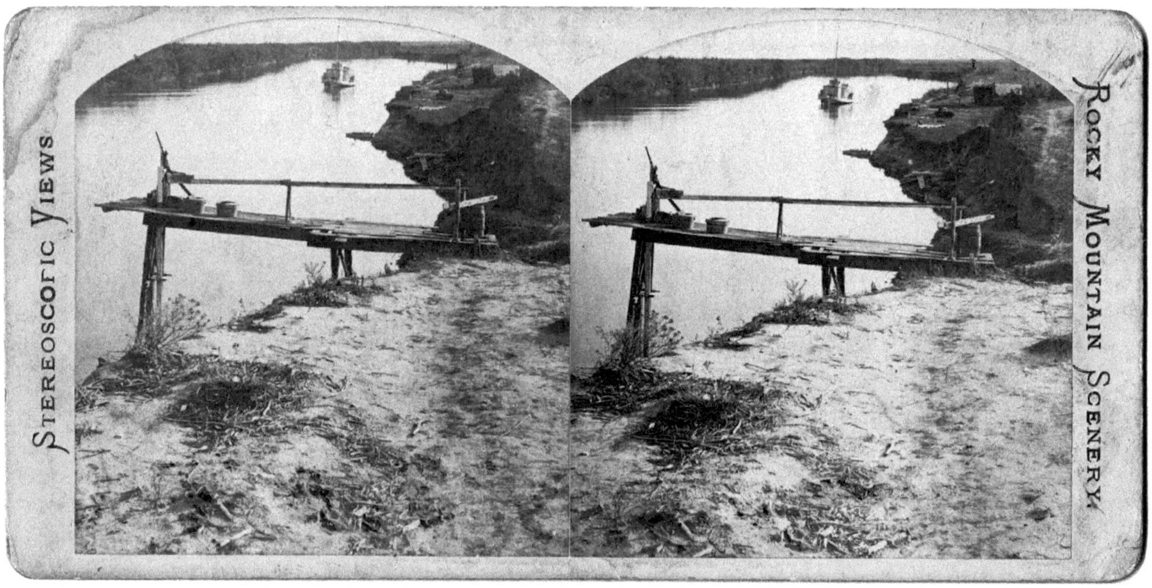

5.4. Steamer *Kate Conner* on the Bear River near Corinne, by A. J. Russell, stereo-view no. 504. *Courtesy of the Union Pacific Railroad Museum, Union Pacific Collection, Photography Archives, A. J. Russell Views.*

Meanwhile Russell reached Echo, Utah, on May 5.[11] In the spring of 1869, however, he was not in a hurry to return to Utah. The Union Pacific paid him nearly $900 for supplies and expenses, but still Durant had to scold Russell into action, writing to his attorney Henry C. Crane on April 22: "Capt Russell was to go West this week. He better not put it off if he proposes to photograph mountain scenery this spring."[12] Russell returned to Nunda on his way to Utah where he found time for a quick family portrait painting. As well, he visited with relatives in the Midwest before returning to Omaha.[13] He arrived at Blue Creek on May 6, before the Devil's Gate Bridge issue developed.[14] Between May 6 and 9 he took a series of images in the area. These images include the town of Corinne (which would later become known as the gentile capital of Utah), its businesses, the bridge and ferry over the Bear River, and the *Kate Conner*, a steamer that traveled from the mouth of the Bear River into the Great Salt Lake and south to near Salt Lake City. As well, he took photographs of the workmen waiting for their wages at Blue Creek, construction camps, and the various cuts and trestles from Blue Creek to Promontory, including the tent city of Dead Fall. He also took several images of what he called the "great trestle," which was abandoned in favor of the "big fill" soon after its completion. He might have ventured to the summit on May 7 with the first Union Pacific train. The *Alta California* wrote that "photographers are busy to-day attempting to obtain photographs at the junction of the roads, the lines of the locomotives, the scenery, appearance of the squads of laborers, etc. but it is feared that in consequence of the sultriness of the weather very good sketches will not be obtained."[15] Hart was already on the summit, but the reference to multiple photographers must have meant either Savage or Russell (or both) were there as well. What these photographers said to one another is not recorded, but surely their talk was filled with plans for the big day, the state of their chemicals and supplies, and an examination of cameras and equipment.

On May 9 Savage spent a cold night in the Union Pacific ticket office at the Promontory station, but Russell arrived from Blue Creek on May 10 at 8:20 a.m.[16] Russell was in for a very busy day. He took nearly as many images that day as Savage and Hart combined, nearly all of which were taken from different angles.[17] By this point, however, Russell was a seasoned veteran of outdoor photography and he had, in addition to Savage, one or two assistants helping him. Savage himself wrote that he "secured some nice Views . . . Saw but little of the actual driving of the gold spike and laying of the laurel tie—as I was very busy."[18] Throughout 1868 Russell traveled with at least two unnamed assistants who can be seen in many of the photographs. In 1869 "Professor" (a title he apparently gave himself) Stephen J. Sedgwick and at least one other man assisted Russell. Later, Sedgwick claimed to be part of the "Union Pacific photographic corps," but this was an effort to bolster his resume through creative word choice. For whatever reason Sedgwick was not at the ceremony, but Russell probably found another assistant. The job of the assistants would have been to carry equipment, mix chemicals, and handle the final washing and drying of glass plates. Russell's assistants might have exposed negatives, as well, after Russell did the initial setup.[19]

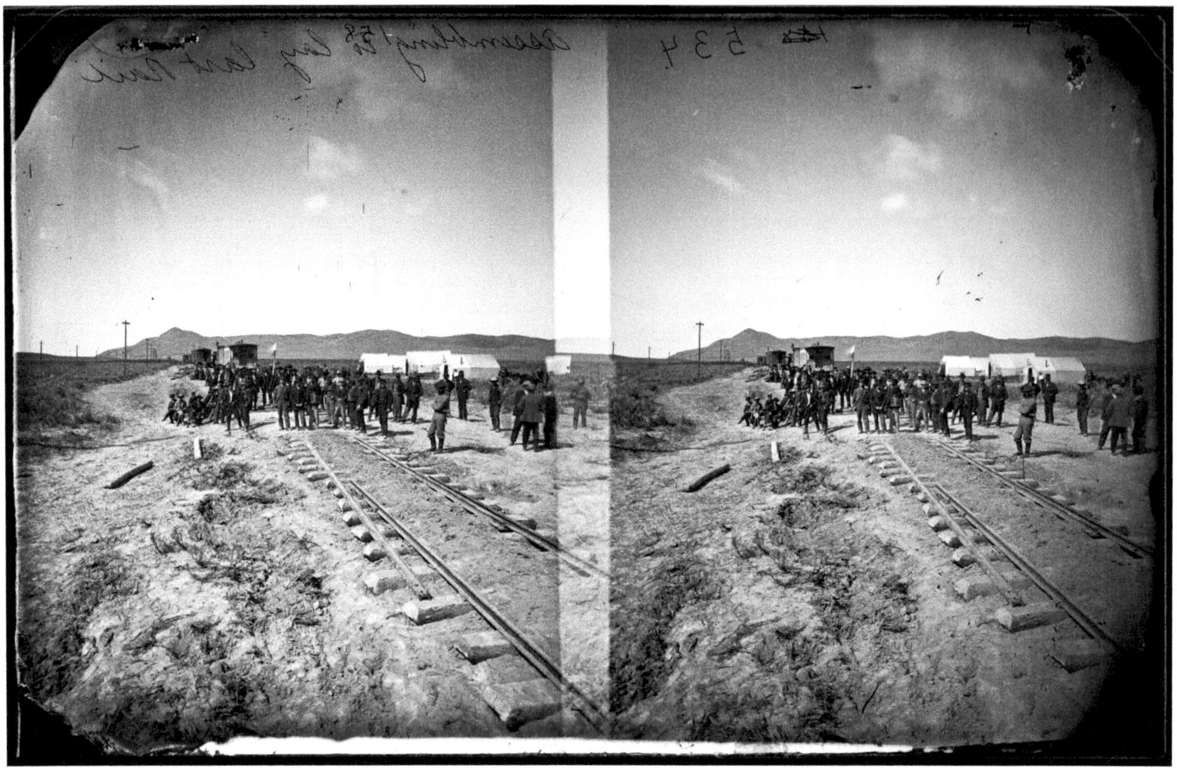

5.5. "Assembling to Lay Last Rail," by A. J. Russell, stereo-view no. 534. *Courtesy of the Oakland Museum of California, A. J. Russell Collection.*

After unloading his photographic wagon, Russell walked over to the gap and between 9:00 and 10:00 a.m. took three stereo-views (from different positions) of the small bit of open ground separating the railroads before the crowds converged, as the last bit of ballasting work, placing ties, and spiking the final rails was finished (see fig. 5.5).[20] Around 11:00 Stanford's special train arrived and Durant welcomed the Central Pacific folks into his private car.[21] Between 11:00 and noon Russell took another stereo-view as a larger crowd mingled and the work on laying the final rail and last tie commenced.[22] The two engines (Jupiter and Engine 119) were uncoupled and moved towards one another, and Russell set up his cameras further south.

Around noon Casement asked the crowd to move back, allowing the photographers to take more images (see fig. 5.6).[23] John Strobridge and Samuel B. Reed then set the last polished and inscribed tie, made from California laurel. Hart and Russell took images at nearly the same time—Hart from the tender of the Jupiter and Russell from the south. In the images several of the participants are unsure whether to look towards Hart or Russell.[24] Russell had hoped that the crowd would keep back and let him capture Stanford and Durant "driving" the last spikes (they were placed by hand into pre-drilled holes), but as the excitement grew the crowd surged towards the spot, obscuring his view (see fig. 5.7).[25] The crowd sat on horses, climbed on the engines, and used wagons as impromptu viewing platforms—anything, in

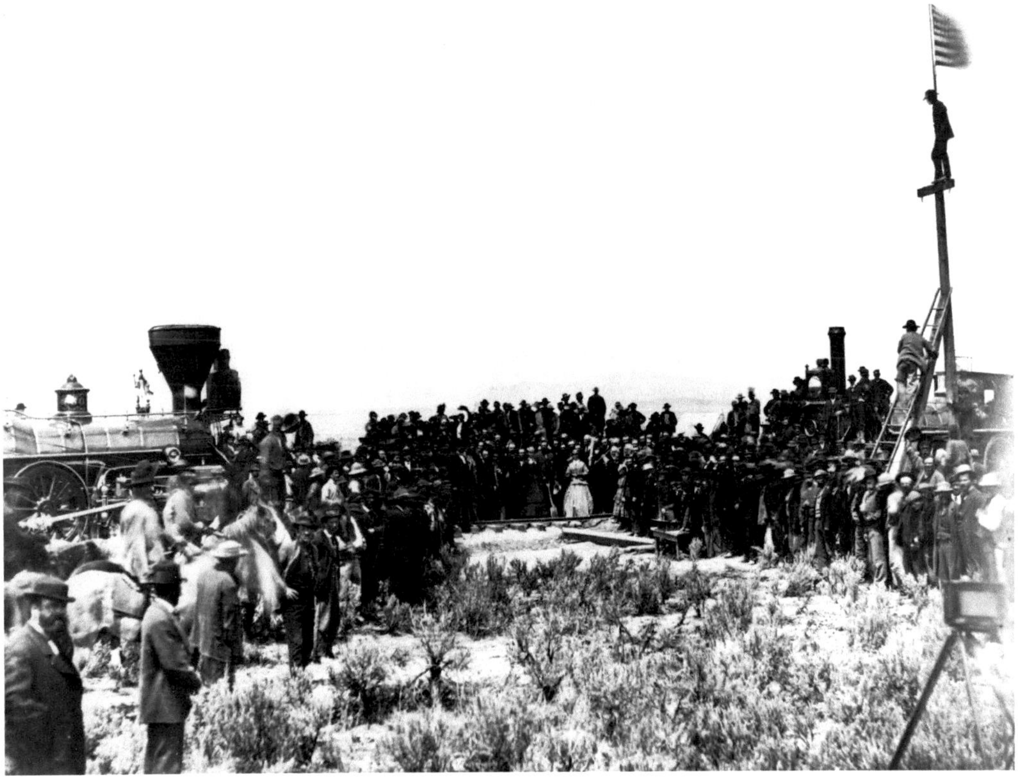

5.6. "Laying Last Rail Promontory," by A. J. Russell, large-format view no. 225. *Courtesy of Utah State University, Merrill-Cazier Library, Special Collections, Nineteenth-Century Western Stereo-Views Collection.*

short, to gain a good vantage point. The actual ceremony was fairly quick, lasting from just after noon to 12:47.[26]

The *Deseret News* noted that after the ceremony: "A half hour longer sufficed for the photographers to take views of the scenes from every available stand point. They will be much sought after."[27] Russell took the most famous photograph of the day after the ceremony when Durant and Stanford retired to their private cars for champagne and celebration.[28] The engineers moved the engines forward until they touched and the workers swarmed over and around the scene. Russell moved his large-format camera forward and Grenville Dodge and Samuel Montague shook hands.[29] This photo was, for years, attributed to C. R. Savage. Russell labeled this image "East and West Shaking Hands at Laying Last Rail," which was also used by *Leslie's Illustrated* in a woodcut illustration. *Harper's Weekly* ran a similar view based on a Savage print (see figs. 5.8 and 5.9).[30] For whatever reason, the *Harper's Weekly* illustration became better known and both *Leslie's* version and Russell's famous photograph were usually credited to Savage. This confusion persisted for years and only in the 1960s when Russell's original glass-plate negatives surfaced, including "East and West Shaking Hands," was he given definite credit.[31]

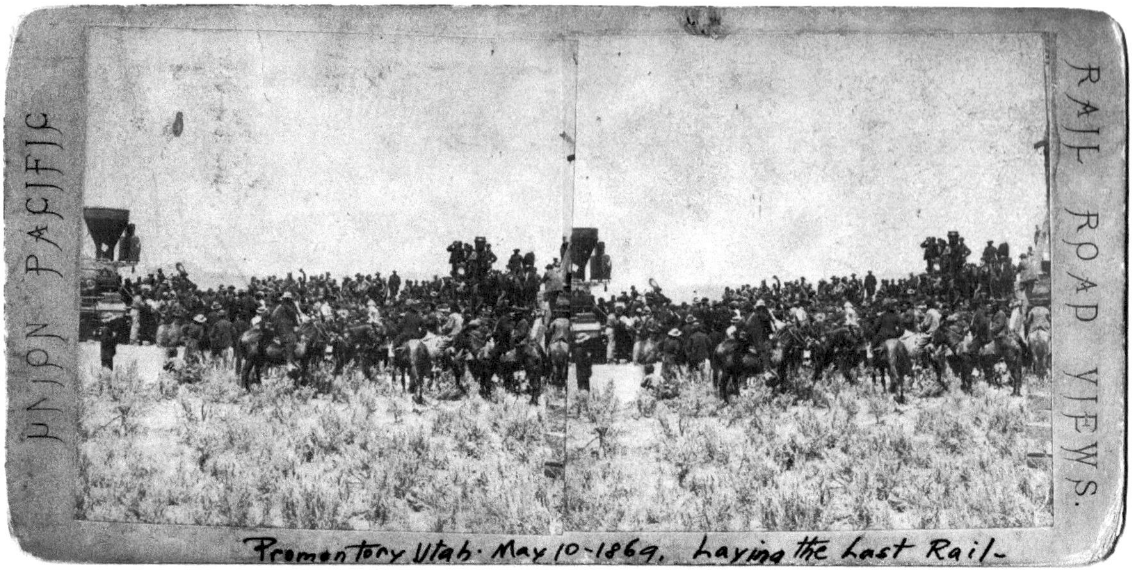

5.7. "Scene before Laying Last Rail," by A. J. Russell, stereo-view no. 541. *Courtesy of the Union Pacific Railroad Museum, Union Pacific Collection, Photography Archives, A. J. Russell Views.*

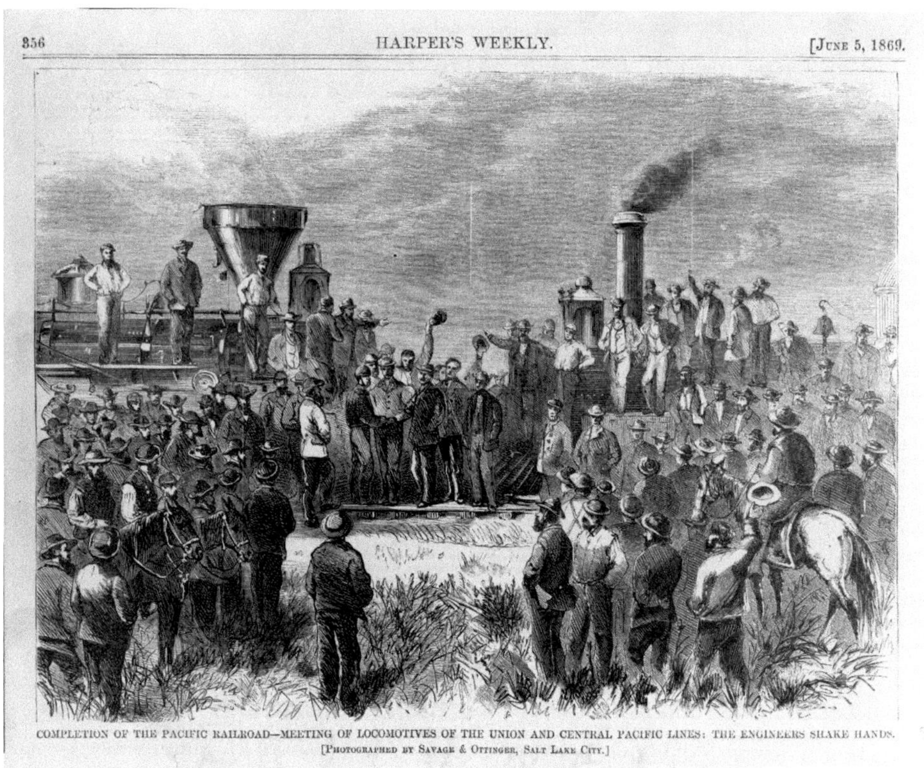

5.8. "Completion of the Pacific Railroad" (woodcut illustration made from a Savage and Ottinger image), appeared in *Harper's Weekly*, June 5, 1869. *Courtesy of the Library of Congress, Prints and Photographs Division.*

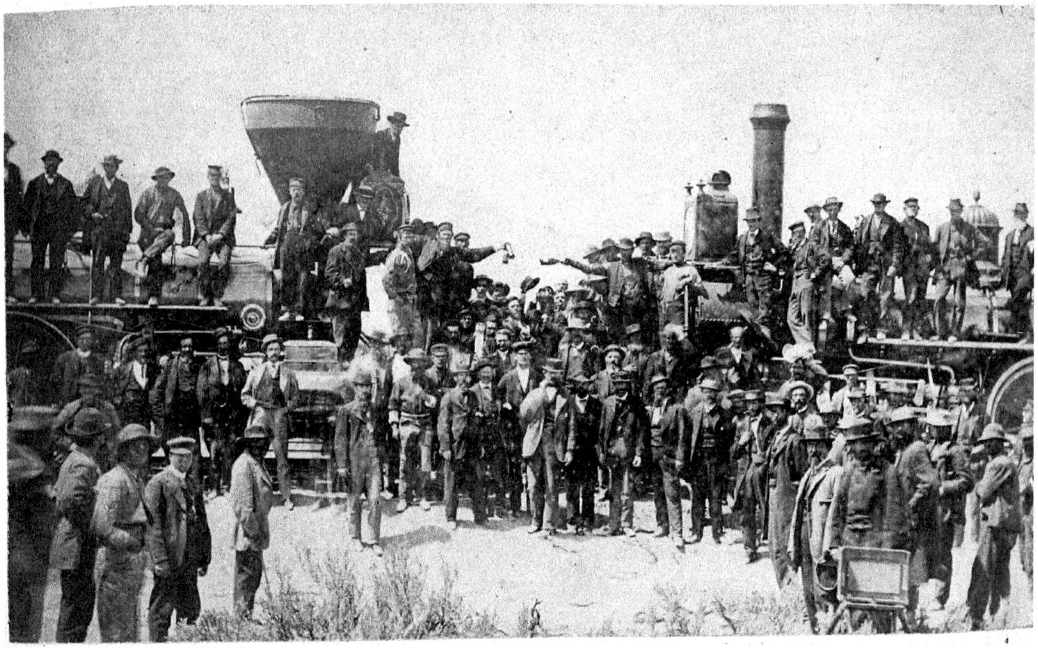

5.9. Carte de visite print at Promontory (note Russell's camera on the right), by C. R. Savage. *Courtesy of Brigham Young University, Lee Library, Special Collections, C. R. Savage Collection.*

Around 1:30, the dignitaries ambled out to the locomotives again for another round of pictures. The 21st Infantry soldiers, who arrived a bit too late for the actual ceremony, lined up, creating a semicircle around the scene as a military band played (see fig. 5.13).[32] Russell and Hart climbed aboard the opposing engines—Russell on the Jupiter and Hart on the 119—with their stereo cameras (see figs. 5.10 and 5.11).[33] Durant looked dapper and even Dodge cracked a smile as a host of Union Pacific engineers, officials, wives, and children posed for the camera. Russell took his last two images of the day as these visiting dignitaries began boarding their cars for a late lunch before leaving to their respective destinations East and West (see fig. 5.14). One of these photos consists of just the Union Pacific officials and engineers, but in the next image officers of the 21st Infantry and their wives have been added.[34] Hart took two more stereo-views of the two engines around 3:00 p.m. that, when pieced together, form a single image, but looking south, creating a mirror image of the Russell and Savage images.[35]

The idea that the Chinese workers were deliberately omitted from the ceremony photographs is one that is deeply entrenched in academia and even with the public.[36] When Chinese workers first were employed, the Central Pacific displayed the patronizing attitudes towards them that nearly all white Americans felt. For instance, that they were too frail to do hard manual labor and not intelligent enough to work as masons. Perhaps based on these attitudes, they were paid less than white laborers.[37] But the ceremony occurred before the labor conflicts of the 1870s and the Chinese workers who built the line were praised nearly as much in the press as the men who manipulated the system and reaped huge profits. It was pointed out that James Stro-

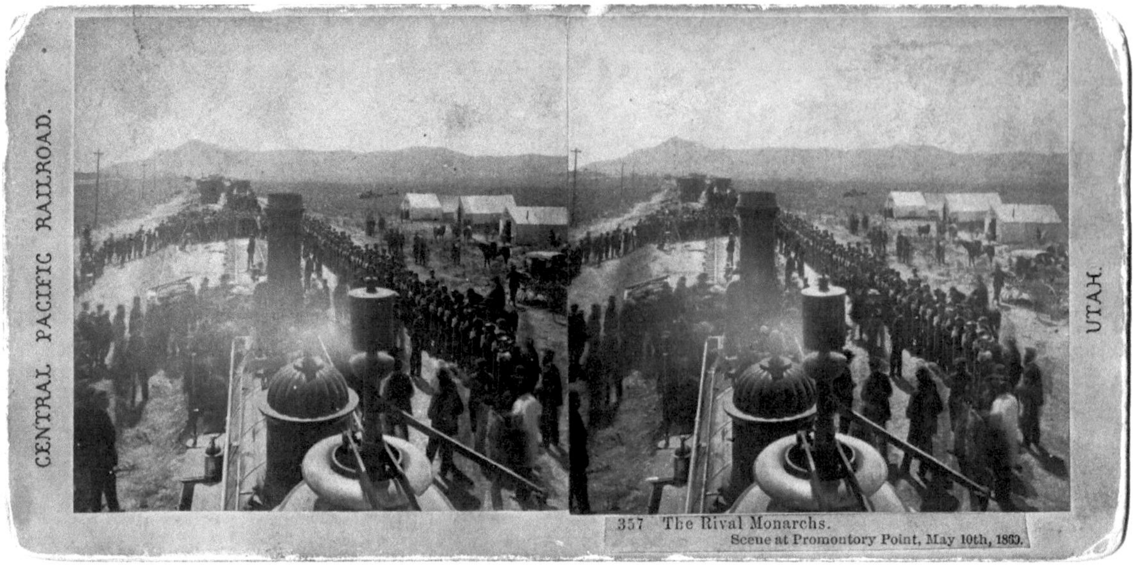

5.10. "The Rival Monarchs" (Russell on the Central Pacific engine), by Alfred A. Hart, stereo-view. *Courtesy of the Union Pacific Railroad Museum, Union Pacific Collection, Photography Archives, A. J. Russell Views.*

bridge hosted a dinner in his private car in honor of the Chinese participants at the ceremony.[38] There might be a more mundane explanation for the shortage of photographs of these Chinese workers. Union Pacific engineer James Maxwell was at the ceremony and he explained in his unpublished memoirs: "There was a photographer there from New York, and many good views were taken of the scene. There were a number of Chinese workmen engaged in tracklaying, and pictures of them were desired, but none could be had, as everyone would drop his tools and run, as soon as he knew that the lens was pointed in his direction. Persuasion was of no avail, and strategy was tried in vain. The instrument was set up behind a group of men, and made ready, but as soon as it was uncovered there was no one left in range. . . . It seemed to be their belief that if anyone had a likeness of them, they would not be free in their future state, but would be under the control of the one holding the picture. . . . At that time an exposure of at least a quarter of a minute was necessary, so that they had ample time to escape."[39]

"ILL-SHAPEN SPECIMENS OF THE 'GENTLER SEX'"

The Golden Spike Ceremony marks a subtle dividing line in content and intent with Russell's photographs. His 1868 work was mostly geared towards photographing what was vital to Durant and the Union Pacific: namely, the state of the great project and documenting the progress made in overcoming various obstacles (the rock cuts in the Black Hills, the Dale Creek Trestle, the extensive cuts in Bitter Creek Valley and around Green River, multiple bridges and tunnels in Echo and Weber Canyons, and finding suitable water and timber). Russell's 1869 photos focus on finishing the work begun in 1868, but he was also thinking

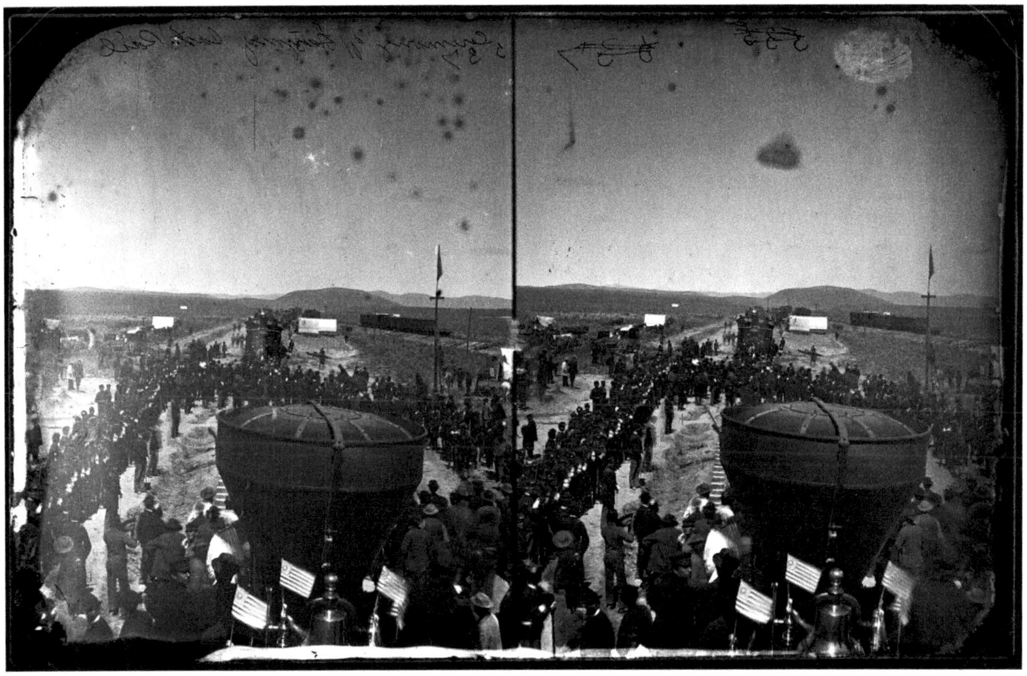

5.11. “Ceremony of Laying Last Rail” (Alfred A. Hart on the Union Pacific engine), by A. J. Russell, stereo-view no. 537. *Courtesy of the Oakland Museum of California, A. J. Russell Collection.*

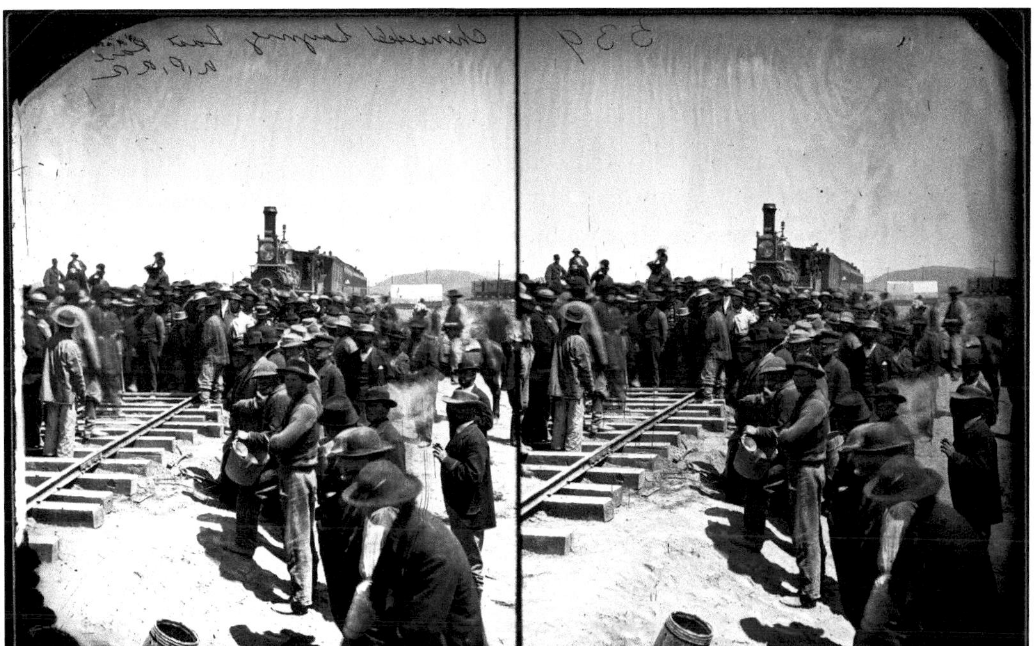

5.12. “Chinese at Laying Last Rail,” by A. J. Russell, stereo-view no. 539. *Courtesy of the Oakland Museum of California, A. J. Russell Collection.*

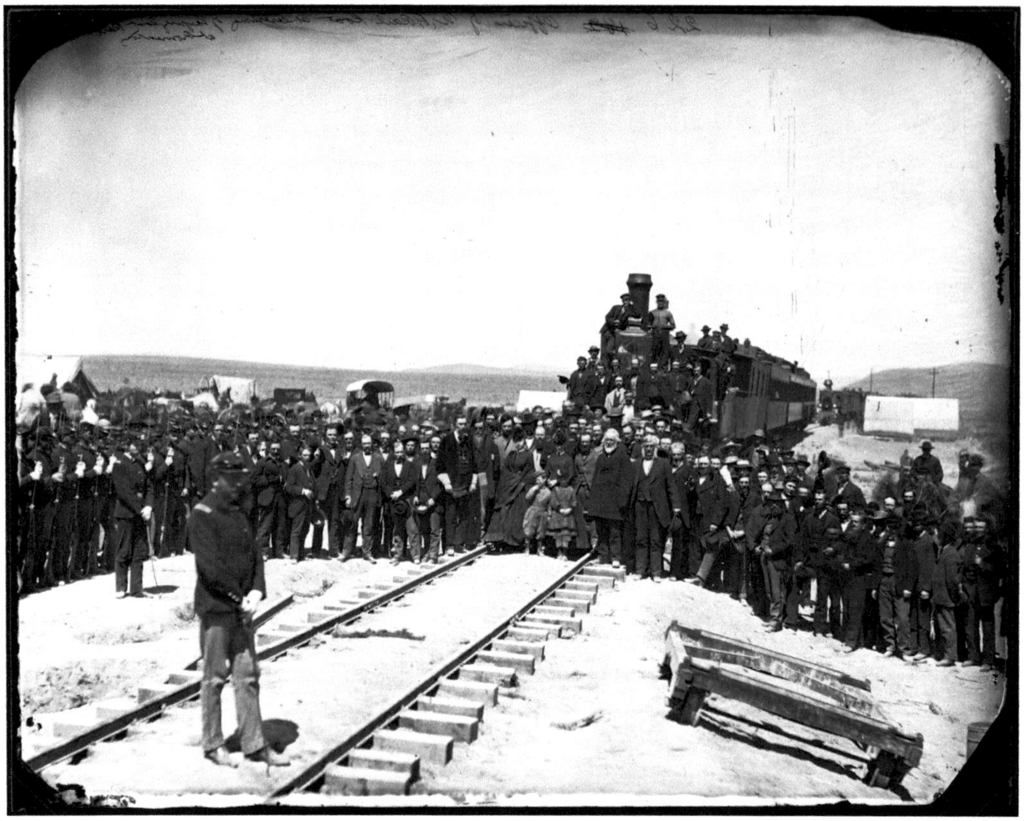

5.13. Soldiers of the 21st Infantry and officers of the Union Pacific, by A. J. Russell, large-format view no. 225b. *Courtesy of the Oakland Museum of California, A. J. Russell Collection.*

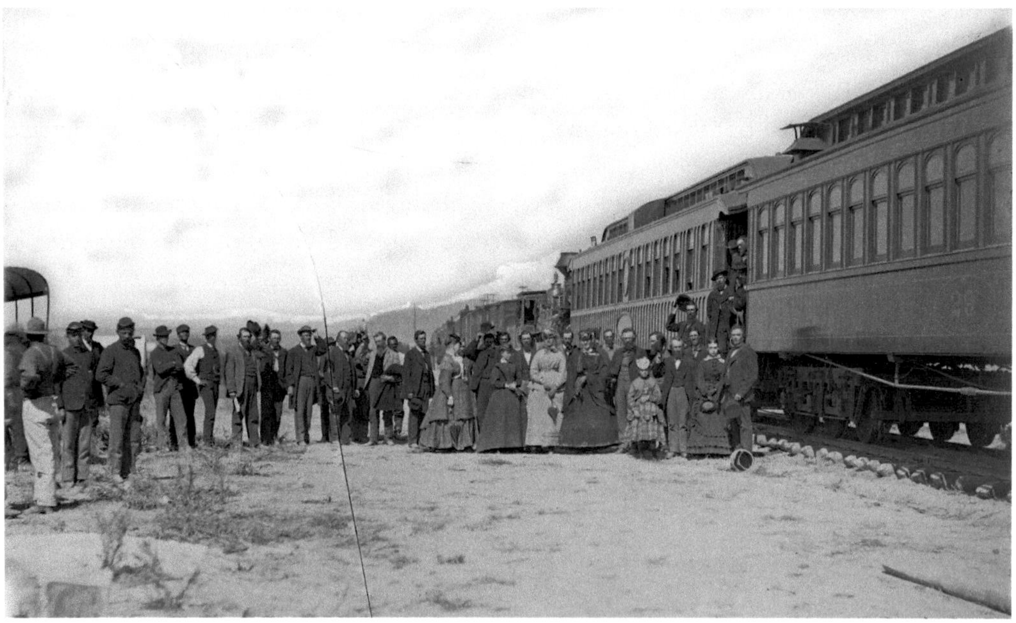

5.14. "Officers of U.P. Rail Road at Ceremony of Laying Last Rail at Promontory," by A. J. Russell, large-format view no. 226. *Courtesy of the Oakland Museum of California, A. J. Russell Collection.*

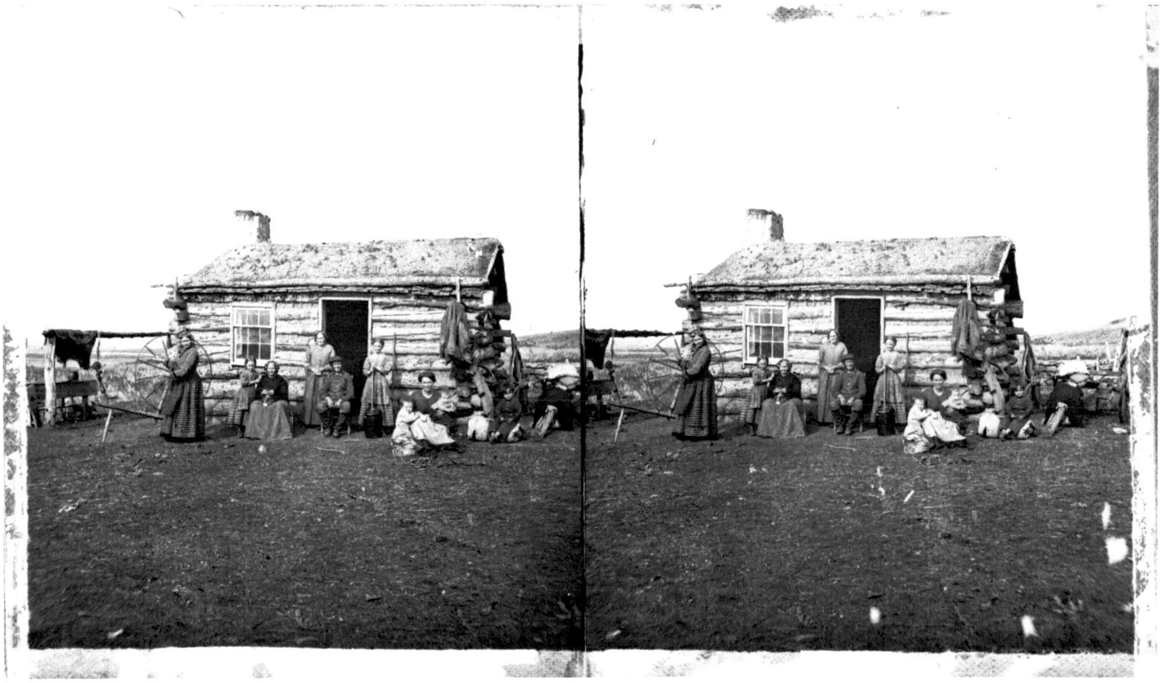

5.15. “Mormon Family, Salt Lake City,” by A. J. Russell, stereo-view no. 481. *Courtesy of the Oakland Museum of California, A. J. Russell Collection.*

long-term. The Union Pacific was in desperate circumstances, with a long list of creditors and contractors demanding payment. Photography had a role to play by encouraging tourism that would lead to increased ridership. Russell's purposes dovetailed nicely with the Union Pacific. He wanted to sell his images to encourage tourism, which meant he would profit directly from the sales, especially of his stereo-views, throughout the East. What could be better to sell than images of an event that transfixed the public's attention? In fact, he capitalized on the interest in the transcontinental railroad and of the West for years to come.

Russell sowed the seeds of his later success by appealing to a national audience. In the winter of 1868 to 1869 he published a series (Union Pacific Rail Road Views) of stereo-views for the Union Pacific.[40] He also prepared the photographs and wrote the captions for the book *Great West Illustrated*, which came out in April 1869. The book did not sell well, however, costing from fifty to seventy-five dollars at a time when the railroad workers themselves earned only three or four dollars a day. Sidney Dillon sent a copy to well-known speaker Henry Ward Beecher, hoping to promote the newly opened lands to settlement.[41] A bit earlier, on February 2, 1869, Russell presented twelve 10" x 13" prints to the photographic section of the American Institute, most likely in New York City. The correspondent for the *Philadelphia Photographer* wrote: “It is evident from these fine views that Utah is no half-way place, for among them is one of a Mormon cabin, outside of which sits the Mormon himself, having on each side two wives. Four more ugly-featured, ill-shapen specimens of the ‘gentler sex’ I never wish to see.” (See figure 5.15.)

Despite this one negative opinion of Utah's womanhood, Russell's images impressed these easterners with the sheer size of the West, how big everything seemed, and with the vast spaces: "The scenery is curious and remarkable, differing in all respects from any found upon the Atlantic coast; wild and grand as is the country, nothing is upon a small scale, the mountains are larger, and the stones appear to have attained proportions which would lead us to name them rocks."[42] Despite his natural modesty, Russell no doubt enjoyed his moment of celebrity among the elite eastern photographers. He was associated with the most famous enterprise in America, and it was happening in the most remote, wild, exotic portion of the country.

In 1869 Russell traveled with another man who would act as his assistant and later play a huge part in the distribution and marketing of his images in the 1870s. Stephen J. Sedgwick reached out to Durant through an intermediary, George Opdyke, about his desire "to make an arrangement with the Union Pacific Railroad Co. to deliver illustrated lectures on the line of the Road."[43] As this worked out, Sedgwick traveled with Russell in 1869 and then created a lecture series using Russell's images starting in 1870. Sedgwick was from Newtown, Long Island, New York. He was an educator and a gifted orator who had created a Bible composed of twenty-two bound volumes with twenty-two thousand engravings from artists all over the world.[44] Sedgwick also may have been useful as a printer. Similar to 1868, in 1869 Russell was printing images and presumably selling them as he could to employees and tourists.[45]

Also during this winter, Russell was commissioned by *Leslie's Illustrated* to send images and write articles about the completion of the great Pacific highway. The June 5 edition came out with Russell's article, as well as three of his illustrations, and for the rest of 1869 his images appeared sporadically. This progressive newspaper boasted about its progressive images, writing: "The engravings we give are a faithful reproduction of the scenes associated with the completion of the road. They are strict copies of the photographs taken expressly for *Frank Leslie's Illustrated Newspaper* at Promontory Point on that eventful 10th of May, and we can imagine no pictures more interesting to the civilized world."[46] This article may have cemented a spot for Russell as an illustrator with *Leslie's* after his western adventures were complete.[47]

"A GLORIOUS FUTURE OF PROSPERITY AND GREATNESS"

Russell's discussion of what he called the "laying of the last rail" in his hometown newspaper reveals something about his view of what the completion of the transcontinental railroad meant to the intermountain West. Russell was an adept writer, but given to rhetorical excess, and if ever there was an event that encouraged "speechifying," it was the completion of the transcontinental railroad. As with nearly everyone at the time, he used soaring rhetoric and grand statements to describe this event. Unlike most commentators, however, he was actually at the ceremony and had played a part in finishing the great project. Russell wrote: "The Continental iron band now permanently unites the distant portions of the Republic, and opens up to Commerce, Navigation and Enterprise the vast un-peopled plains and lofty mountain ranges. . . . We look forward with well founded hope to a glorious future of prosperity and greatness for the undeveloped west. . . . The next question to be solved, is what will the great interior produce, and by whom will it be peopled." Russell also acted as a publicity agent for the Union Pacific by promoting the settlement of the West through irrigation: "The casual observer in passing across the vast plains . . . will suppose that they are barren. But a closer examination will show that the soil is productive and only requires water to make them blossom as the rose." What is absent from Russell's writing, besides the American Indians who already lived on the "un-peopled" land, is the reference to divine providence and the settling of the American West. While he uses the same language of assumed economic progress, he declines to provide the usual divine stamp of approval for the railroad.[48] There is, in fact, no overtly religious reference in any of Russell's writings. This is in marked contrast to one commentator in the *Deseret News* who wrote that the train would usher in a "new era in the gathering of the Saints to Zion," and added: "Surely the Prophet Isaiah must have had reference to the speed with which they would gather the Saints from afar, by means of the great improvements of modern times. He inquires: 'Who are these that fly as a cloud, and as the doves to their window?' Is it too much to assume that he saw in vision the flying locomotive with its cloud-like smoke and its long train of cars laden with the gathering Saints?"[49] Certainly, though, the transcontinental railroad provided many benefits to the people of Utah. A three-to-six-month journey across the plains by wagon now took, for about one hundred dollars, only four days. The intermountain West was open to new settlement in a way it had never been before, and transportation for raw materials and agricultural products to markets was markedly cheaper. The difference in cost to ship materials by animal locomotion versus train was staggering. By one estimate, freighting costs on a train measured per ton per mile was one-seventeenth of the cost of freighting by wagon.[50] The *Deseret News* writer no doubt echoed the prevalent opinion in Utah that "if it brings mean, contemptible men here—bad citizens—it also carries them off with no less speed." In the final analysis: "The advantages greatly outweigh any disadvantages which it may occasion. The disadvantages we can control, and, if prudent, eventually remove."[51]

For two of our three photographers the ceremony benefited them by creating intense interest in images of the ceremony. Savage made a tidy sum of $125 in only three days from brisk sales.[52] In fact, his attendance that day was instrumental in opening doors for him with the Union Pacific to continue his photographic efforts on that line. On May 13 Russell was back in Echo.[53] After the Golden Spike Ceremony, Russell made Echo City his base of operations for at least the next four or five months. From this tiny railroad town he traveled up and down Echo and Weber Canyons, over to Salt Lake City, Bingham Canyon, and Parley's Park, and into the Wasatch and Uinta Mountains. For Hart, however, the ceremony was his last big job with the Central Pacific. Not only did the Central Pacific retain possession of his negatives, but after his patron, Judge Crocker, retired from the Central Pacific Board of Directors in late 1869, Hart was displaced by a new photographer, Carleton E. Watkins. After 1869 Hart went back to painting portraits and landscapes, but had little commercial success. He moved to New York City in 1875. Whether he and Russell ever met to relive the old days is unknown. He died back in California in 1908.[54]

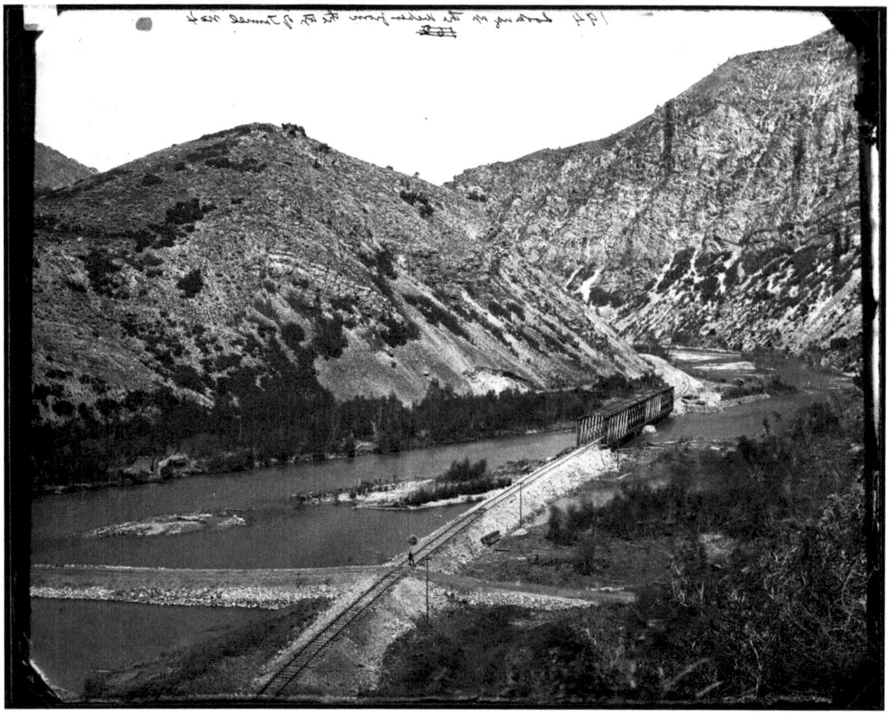

6.1. “Strawberry Ford, Weber Valley” (note that this area today is generally called the Weber Narrows), by A. J. Russell, large-format view no. 195. *Courtesy of the Oakland Museum of California, A. J. Russell Collection.*

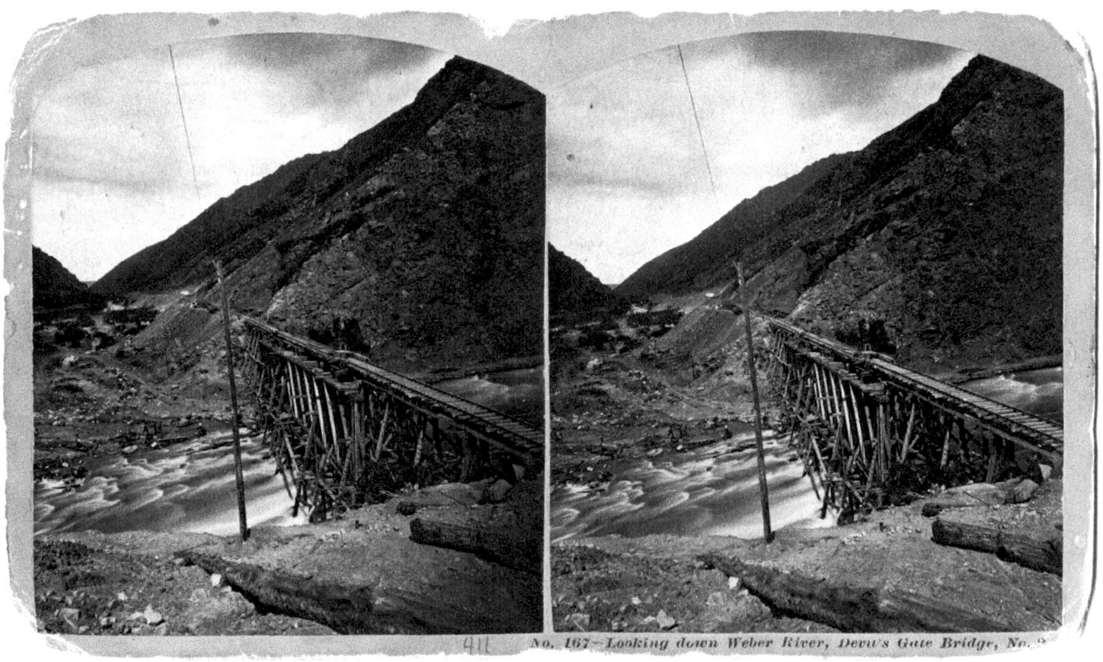

6.2. Temporary bridge at Devil’s Gate, Weber Canyon, by A. J. Russell, stereo-view no. 411. (The number on the image is from Russell’s earlier series Union Pacific R.R. Views across the Continent.) *Courtesy of the Union Pacific Railroad Museum, Union Pacific Collection, Photography Archives, A. J. Russell Views.*

CHAPTER 6
Documenting the West (Summer and Fall of 1869)

"found Russell a sociable, companionable fellow and had some very pleasant hours with him."

—William Henry Jackson

If Russell's 1868 photographs were meant to update Durant and the Union Pacific on the progress on the line first, while still being useful for public relations second, then those priorities switched in 1869. Documenting the finished product of the Union Pacific line in Weber and Echo Canyons (the tunnels and bridges) took precedence, in order to show that it was a "first class line" as required by law.[1] Furthermore, Russell would have known about the Central Pacific's schemes in late 1868 to build a rival line in these canyons. He would have been aware that critics charged the Union Pacific with building a substandard line, and he would have wanted his images to placate and assure the public as well as government inspectors, while also encouraging settlement, investment, and ridership.[2] This was the business end of what he did, but what shines through his work is that he photographed, first and foremost, the men who did the work. Russell spent months with these men and it's not hard to imagine that the likable photographer created a connection with them. After all, he was one of them. His photographs celebrate the work they did, and also by extension the building of the railroad, which Russell viewed with great pride as an important national project.

Another use of Russell's images was the sale of prints. As he had done in 1868, Russell sold images to people while he was out West in 1869.[3] Even the Union Pacific was printing and selling images back in New York City. These photographs, not surprisingly, appealed to tourists. Some of his intentions in this vein can be surmised from a series of letters he wrote to the *Nunda News* and *Anthony's Photographic Bulletin*.[4] In these letters he attempted to channel his inner Mark Twain, and Russell's narration is a mix of humor, insiderish hometown references, and colorful descriptions of then exotic peoples such as Mormons, American Indians, and the Chinese in California. Russell's descriptions are also vivid and descriptive, as if he was memorizing the physical details of the scene to take a photo or make a painting. What is lacking, unfortunately, is a discussion of his photographic rationale and methodology. Rather, Russell was much like

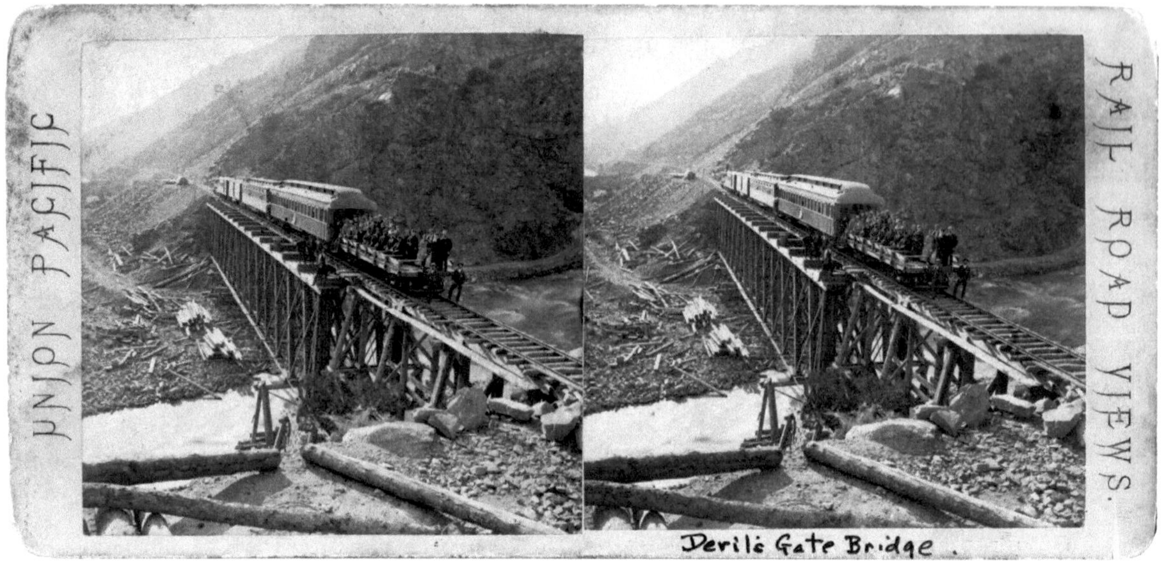

6.3. Permanent bridge at Devil's Gate, Weber Canyon, by A. J. Russell, stereo-view no. 407. *Courtesy of the Union Pacific Railroad Museum, Union Pacific Collection, Photography Archives, A. J. Russell Views.*

tourists everywhere who use their images combined with a narrative to create a more vivid portrait of their travels.[5]

Russell appealed to prospective buyers of prints in other ways as well. He included his usual unusual geology, but also added whimsical captions for rock formations (for example, Castle Rock, Temple Rock, the Sphinx of the Valley, Devil's Post Office, Witches Rock, and Druid Rock) that attributed human characteristics to the natural world. But Russell also made the railroad's features attractive in and of themselves. For instance, he described the beauty of railroad bridges: "The railroad follows the course of the Weber River between high bluffs, which are more than one thousand feet high on either side. Several of the best bridges on the road are in this vicinity, their symmetrical forms looking far more beautiful in contrast with their rugged surroundings."[6]

The completion of the permanent Devil's Gate Bridge and tunnels no. 3 and no. 4 was particularly important for the Union Pacific and its passengers. One newspaper correspondent wrote: "The Devil's gate and Strawberry Ford bridges are yet infirm, especially the former. Trains are pushed over without their engines. There is considerable delay in consequence. . . . Some of the ladies on last evening's westward bound train became frightfully nervous while the train was slowly conducted across it."[7] Devil's Gate is an impressive bit of geology where the Weber River suddenly veers seemingly straight into the mountain and then reemerges in a rushing torrent. As one might expect, Russell took several images of the newly completed structure, probably in June, including the dramatic shot "Testing Combination Bridge Devil's Gate," which showed three heavy engines sitting on the bridge.[8] He also photographed tunnel no. 3 in the Weber Narrows, writing, "The tunnel is five hundred feet in length, and was cut through trap, quartz,

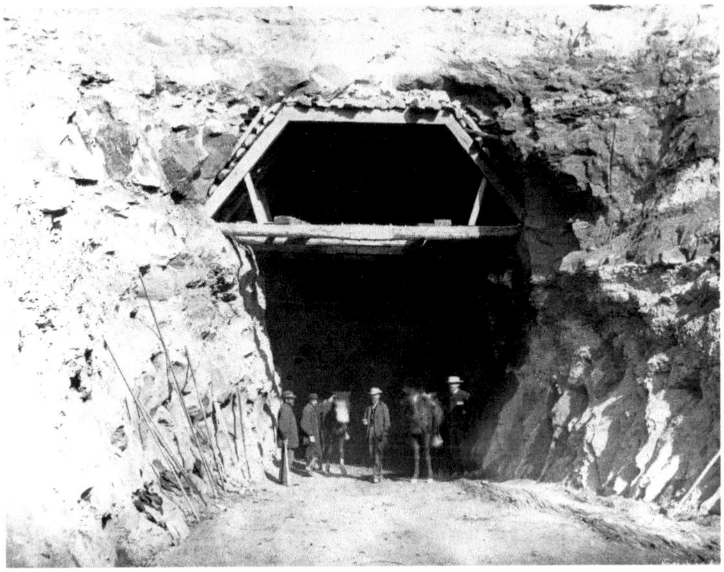

6.4. "Tunnel at Head of Echo Miller and Patterson's Work," by A. J. Russell, large-format view no. 102. *Courtesy of Utah State University, Merrill-Cazier Library, Special Collections.*

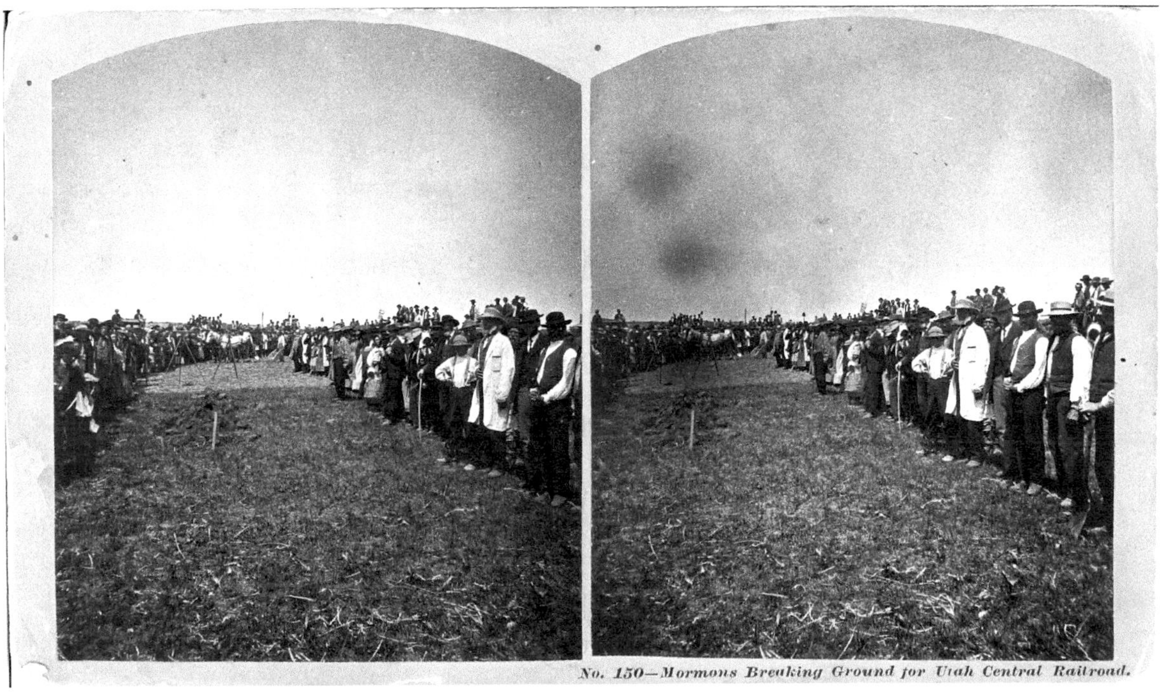

6.5. Utah Central Railroad (from Ogden to Salt Lake City) ground breaking, by A. J. Russell, stereo-view no. 483. (The number on the image is from Russell's earlier series Union Pacific R.R. Views across the Continent.) *Courtesy of the University of Iowa Libraries, Special Collections, Levi O. Leonard Railroadiana.*

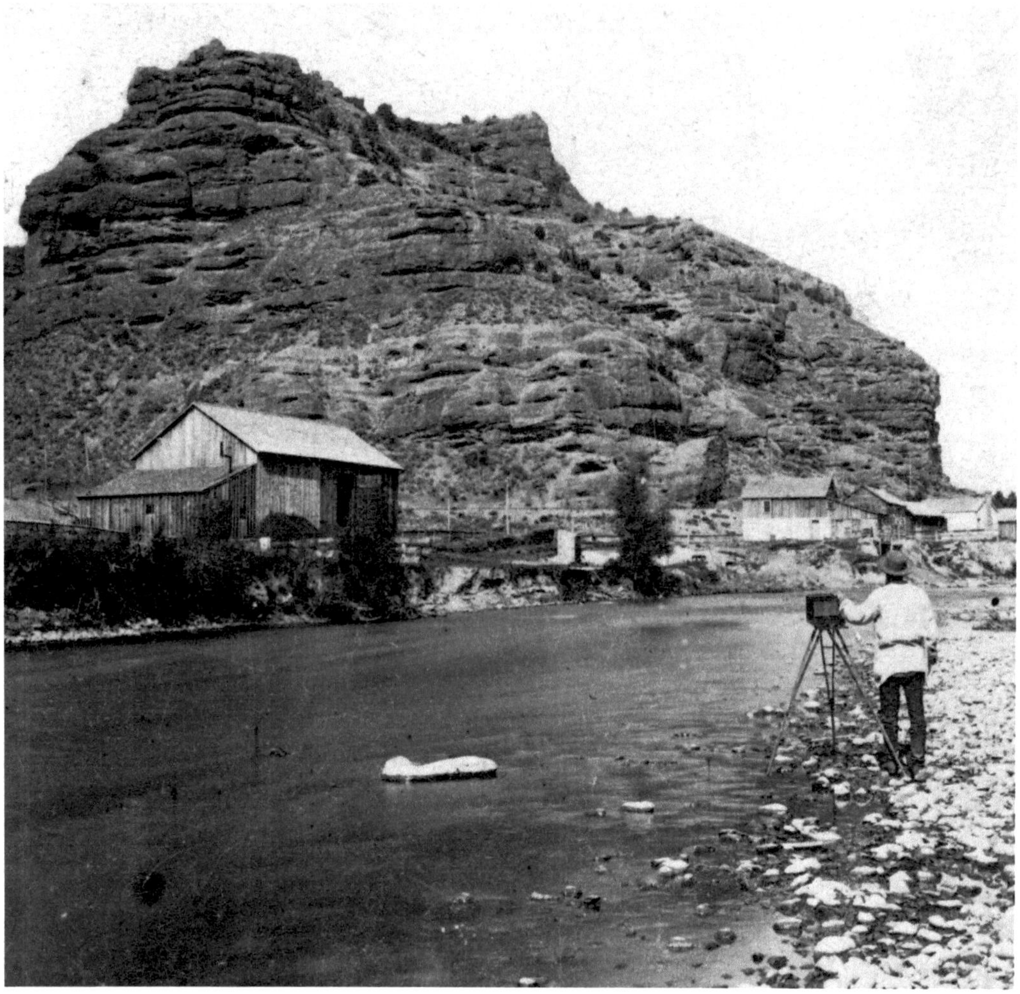

6.6. Cropped version of A. J. Russell stereo-view no. 325 (man, probably A. J. Russell, and a stereo-view camera in Echo, Utah). *Courtesy of the Union Pacific Railroad Museum, Union Pacific Collection, Photography Archives, A. J. Russell Views.*

and limestone; and the bluff is three hundred feet above the road-bed. This work was executed by Bishop Sharp and Young, and is a portion of the One Hundred Mile Job contracted for by Brigham Young."[9] As of May 26, 1869, these tunnels were not completed, and temporary tracks had to be built around them.[10]

Russell's first big job after Promontory, however, was in Ogden for the beginnings of the Utah Central Railroad. Salt Lake City photographer Savage wrote, "Major Russell sent me 1 or 2 negatives today of the [b]reaking of the sod."[11] On May 17, 1869, the Utah Central Railroad, connecting Ogden to Salt Lake City, officially began construction in Ogden. The railroad was to be an all-Utah affair built, in part, from the leftover surplus materials given to Brigham Young as a partial payment on his earlier contract. Savage could not make it to this

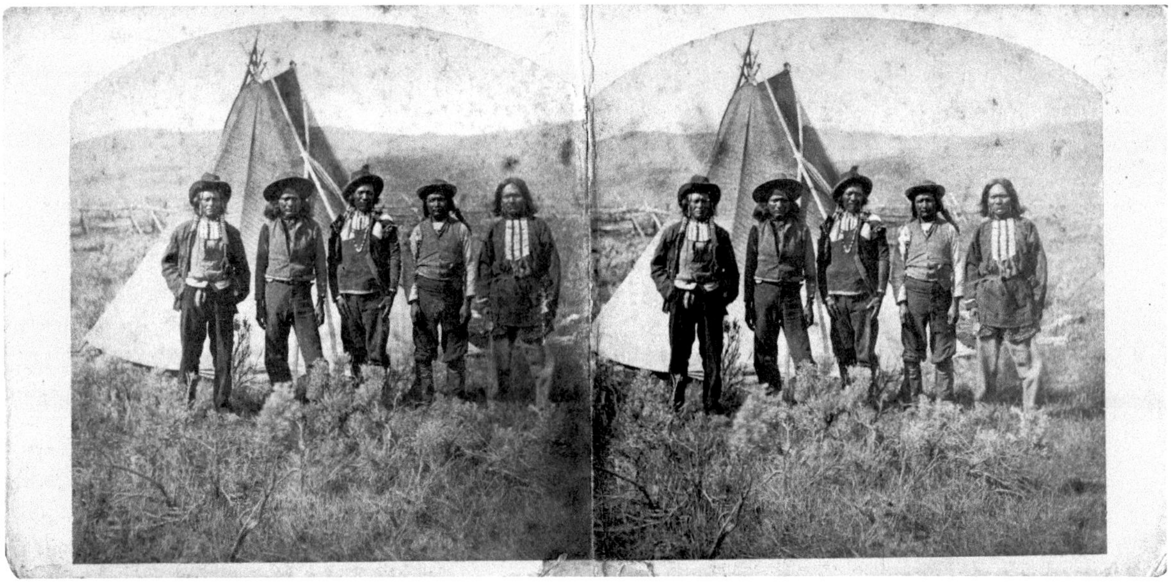

6.7. "Snake Chiefs" (Shoshone Indians), by A. J. Russell, stereo-view no. 579. *Courtesy of Utah State University, Merrill-Cazier Library, Special Collections, Nineteenth-Century Western Stereo-Views Collection.*

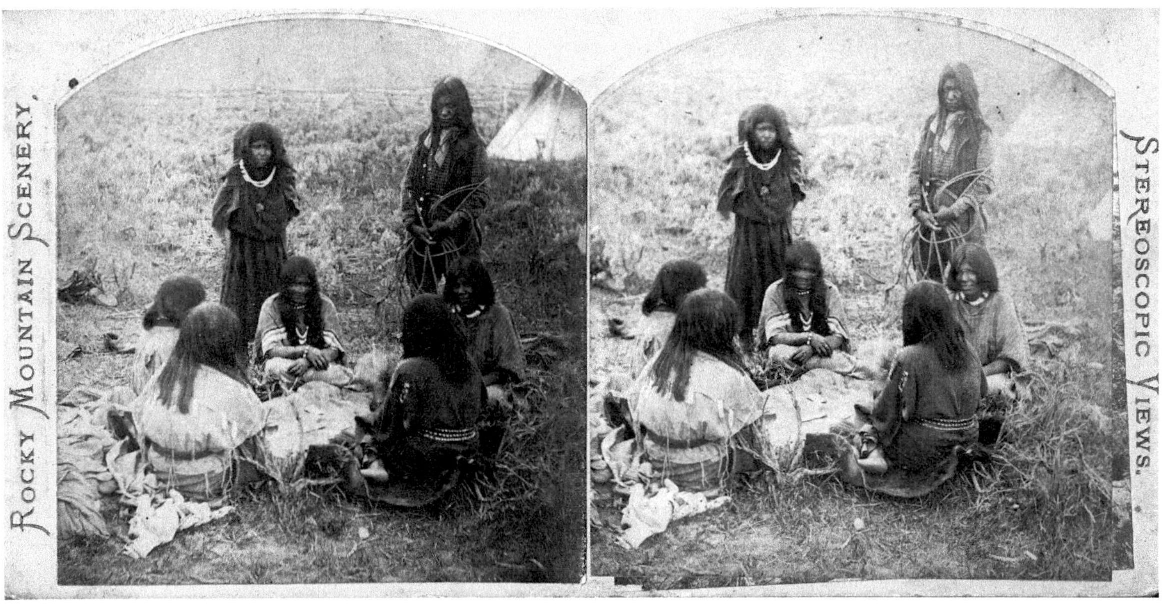

6.8. Shoshone Indian women, by A. J. Russell, stereo-view no. 582. *Courtesy of Utah State University, Merrill-Cazier Library, Special Collections, Nineteenth-Century Western Stereo-Views Collection.*

event, but soon enough he joined Russell. On May 30 and 31 Savage photographed Devil's Gate and on June 1 he met up with Russell in Echo City. Savage and Russell were in Echo at least from June 1 to June 5.[12] In fact, one image taken by Savage around this time might show Russell himself leaning against a camera tripod.[13] Russell also reunited with his old friend and collaborator Union Pacific clerk Smith in Echo.[14] Smith, Russell, and Savage all stayed in close contact throughout 1869. Smith purchased fruit and photographs from Savage and in return Savage sold items for him in Salt Lake. As well, Smith traveled with the Mormon photographer on some of his photographic excursions.[15]

On June 7, 1869, Russell took a series of images of what were probably Shoshone Indians. Russell refers to them as "Snake Indians," a name that was applied to all Shoshone and Bannock Indians of the area. They were reluctant to have their photographs taken until they were paid three dollars. Russell wrote: "I set up the instrument, took the picture, made a failure, as they supposed that I could take them whether they stood still or not. The second attempt was a success, as I made them understand I wanted them still. It made a unique group. There were no two dressed alike and no two that looked alike. . . . Most wore arms of some kind." Russell could have written a standard (for the time) mocking account of these Indians, but he shows surprising sympathy with them. He wrote, "What pleased [the women] the most was that I got the papooses they held in their arms as well as themselves, and as they crowded around me to see the pictures they would shout and laugh as they recognized each others faces."[16] Most likely these were the remnants of the northwestern band of the Shoshones who led a nomadic life in northern Utah and southeastern Idaho after the Bear River Massacre of 1863, relying mostly on handouts from the Mormon settlers. Russell's engagement with the Shoshones was probably their first time seeing a camera and having their photos taken and, as such, the situation was rife for misunderstanding. The chief of the small group asked Russell to take a photograph of a sick woman in the hopes that it would heal her and they even wanted him to help catch a thief: "They believe that when their picture is taken, that white man can see what they are doing no matter where they are. They were after me to-day to take picture of white man that stole a gun from one of the tribe. They said you take his picture, we catch um."[17]

Russell also photographed the Mormon-irrigated valleys near Echo. The images have a lyrical quality and an interesting perspective. These artistic effects could have only come from having enough time for careful thought and preparation, choosing the time and the light that was needed, and climbing hills with heavy photography equipment. Noted journalist Samuel Bowles was impressed with the industry, agriculture, and commerce of Utah, and he would write after his own western excursion to the area: "Wherever the Valley is bold enough to widen, fertile meadows gladden the eye, and Mormon thrift and Mormon polygamy begin to show their results. . . . But here we are [at Ogden] amongst the most prosperous farming settlements of Utah. . . . We see Mormon civilization in villages and farms, for forty or fifty miles or more."[18] Russell also shows his favorable view towards the industry of Utah by writing that "the valley of Salt Lake has been made a marvel of productiveness by this system of irrigation." For Russell, however, the agricultural progress in the state was not so much a testament to Mormon industry

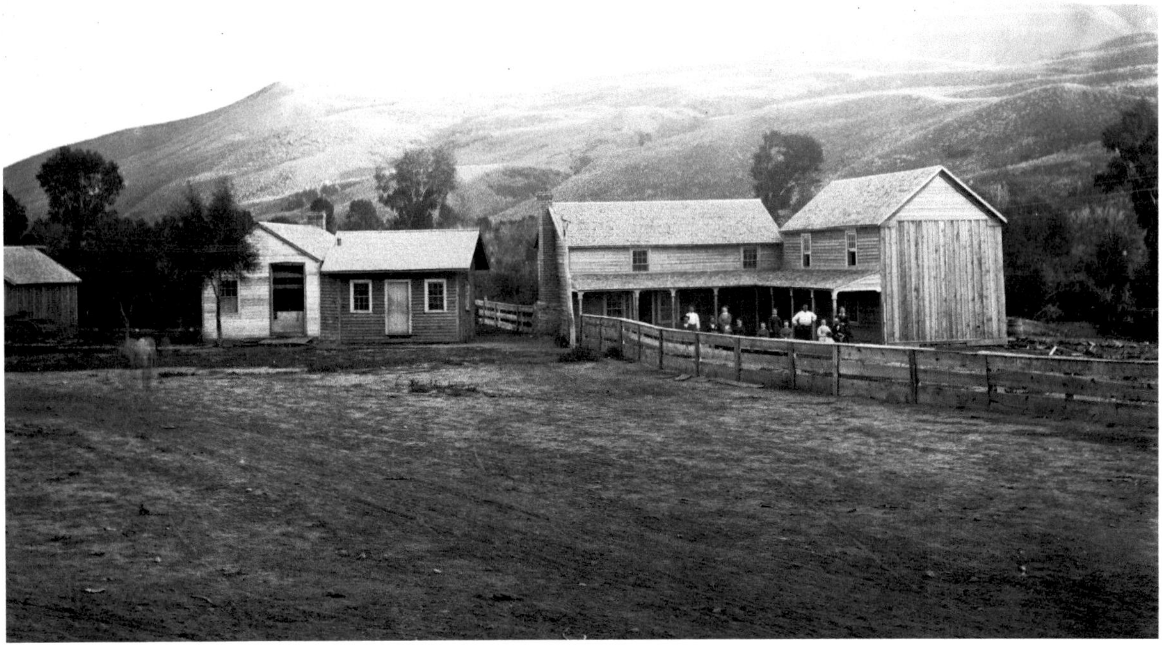

6.9. "Warner and Whitman[s] at Echo," by A. J. Russell, large-format view no. 125. *Courtesy of the Oakland Museum of California, A. J. Russell Collection.*

and cooperation, but more a result of good soil. He wrote: "This valley is no better and no different from hundreds of miles lying between Salt Lake City and Omaha. Industry has recovered the one from barrenness and desolation and can and will the other."[19] Similar to all boosters and most scientists of that era, Russell believed that the dry intermountain West was some sort of strange aberration and it soon would be "restored" with plentiful rain: "Since the settlement of that country rain has increased in proportion to the growth of the country and the spread of agriculture. Where until a few years back there was no rain, frequent showers now refresh the earth. Fresh water Springs are constantly breaking out in unthought of places, and what were barren hills and plains are now covered with luxuriant natural vegetation."[20] In these statements we can see that the earlier idea of the great American desert would, in fact, be replaced with an even greater myth. Russell also took a number of photos of mines in Utah and wrote that mining was "the foundation of a certain and permanent prosperity."[21]

In early July Russell traveled to Parley's Park (now Park City). During this trip Russell photographed two residences, those of Ephraim Hanks and Judge Snyder (or George Gideon Snyder). He also spent July 4 attempting to get a mountaintop view: "I started out this morn-

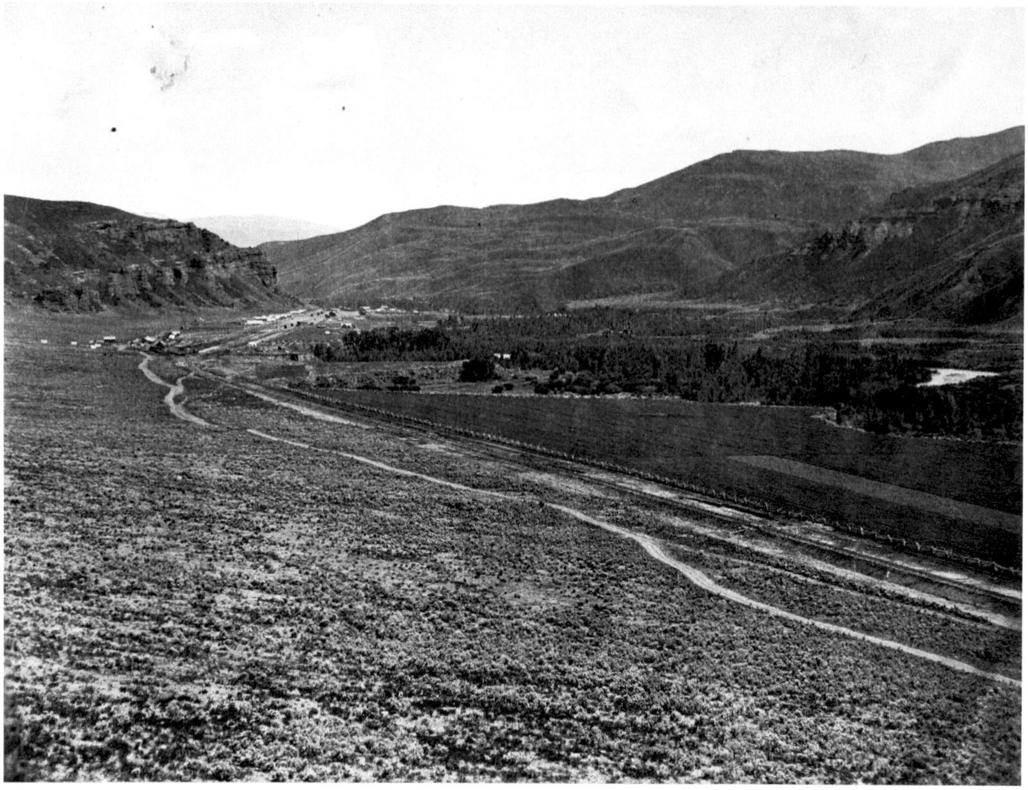

6.10. "Weber Valley from below Echo City," by A. J. Russell, large-format view no. 180. *Courtesy of the Union Pacific Railroad Museum, Union Pacific Collection, Photography Archives, A. J. Russell Views.*

ing for a trip to the top of the highest peak in this vicinity for the purpose of taking a few Photographs. In the first place my traps are heavy and cumbersome and the question came up [how]. I could not drive the wagon within three miles of the top and to carry them by hand would be an impossibility. But get the views I must. With an axe and jack knife I framed some pack saddles for my mules, tied on the app[a]ratus and with a [M]ormon friend started for our destination. The way was smooth enough until after we had passed the cottonwood and entered among the pines. Then it was up hill . . . until almost perpendicular bluffs seemed to check further progress. By picking the way along the sides we finally emerged from among the broken fragments of the rocks and found ourselves on the everlasting snow."[22]

Despite his occasional forays into scenic photography, Russell's 1869 photographs were still mostly of the people who built the transcontinental railroad. Now, however, these men had more time on their hands. The new images are at odds with the frenzied pace of the building of the Union Pacific before the Golden Spike Ceremony. Russell and his photographic subjects had found the time for rock-climbing, fishing, playing music, camping, traveling to mountaintops, and even picking flowers. Russell, in fact, had the time to take many scenic images in that summer after hiking (with his heavy equipment) to an elevated position. As

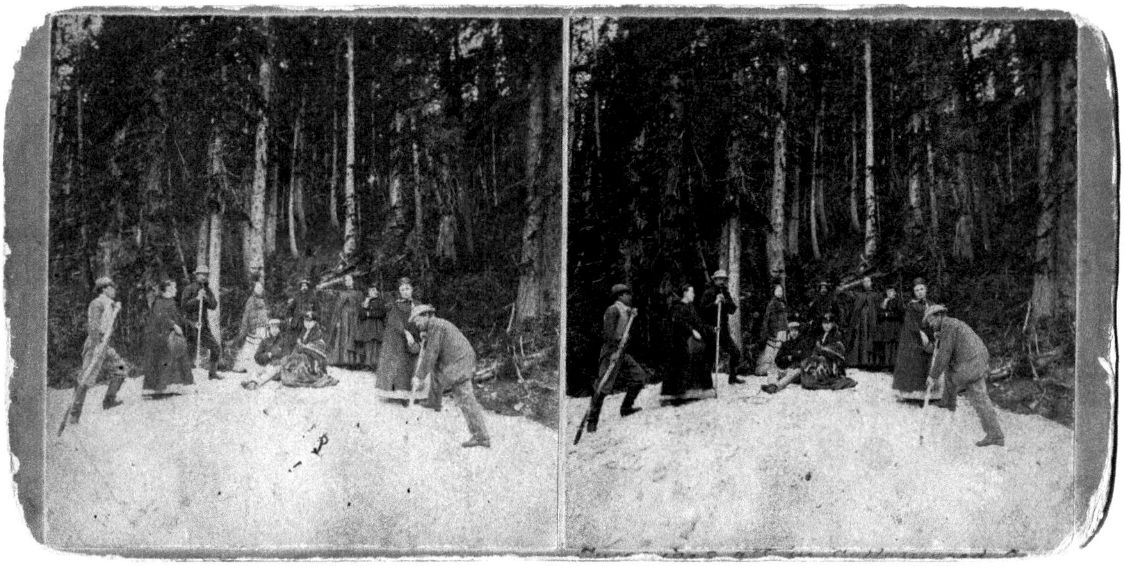

6.11. "Party on Snow White Pine [C]anyon, Aug. 1" (image from the Wasatch Mountains taken either on July 4 or in late August), by A. J. Russell, stereo-view no. 451. *Courtesy of the Union Pacific Railroad Museum, Union Pacific Collection, Photography Archives, A. J. Russell Views.*

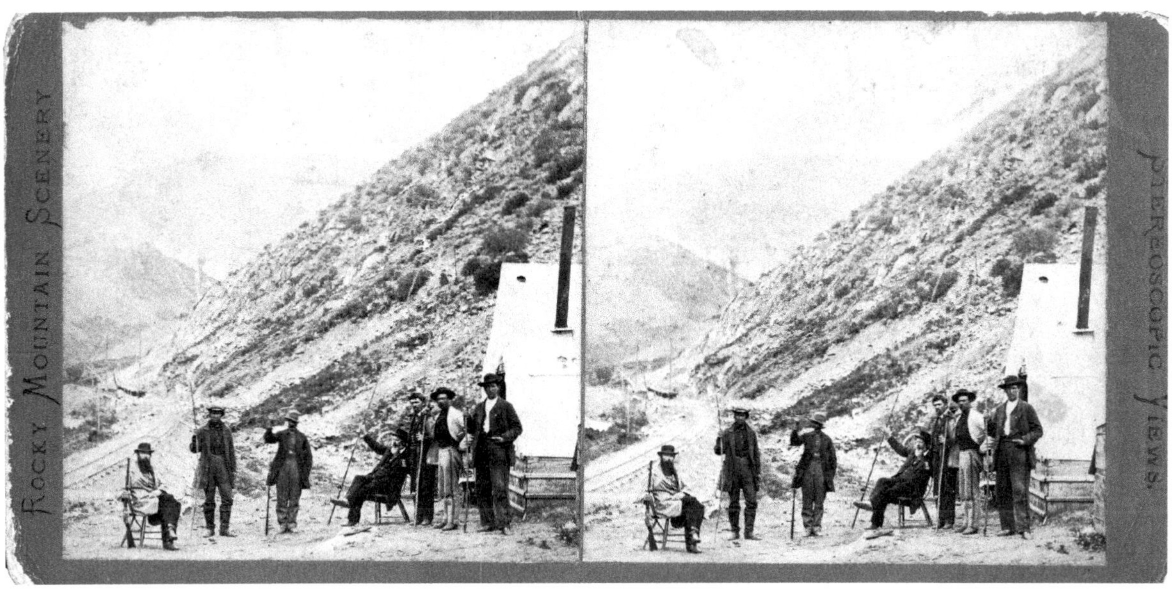

6.12. "Fishing Party, Weber [C]anyon," by A. J. Russell, stereo-view no. 371. *Courtesy of Utah State University, Merrill-Cazier Library, Special Collections, Nineteenth-Century Western Stereo-Views Collection.*

well, he sometimes put away his camera equipment and went back to sketching.[23] Many of the "white collar" Union Pacific employees had their wives with them. They continued the social activities they had known back East, and Smith on numerous occasions describes dances, card playing, and pleasure excursions in the summer and fall of 1869.

"MY MULE ENJOYED THE JOKE"

Around July 28 Russell left Echo to join the geologist Clarence King and his federal survey as they traveled to the headwaters of the Bear River. After three days of travel, he met the survey on the banks of the Bear River. The party then traveled to Christmas Meadows and transferred from wagons to mules to get into the higher country. Russell obviously felt an affinity for King, writing: "He is a young man, full of vitality and is very earnest in his pursuit after knowledge under difficulties that few men would surmount. He has ascended in the three years, over three hundred mountain peaks, taken their heights, their topographical and longitudinal bearing, notes the head and courses of the rivers, quantity and quality of the timber, &c."[24] Russell also was impressed with the skillful handling of King's wagons in the mountains: "Mr. King had two very heavy government wagons, and six mule teams. These wagons came thundering down the precipitous sides of can[y]ons, over boulders, logs and huge rocks in a manner that was enough to frighten a nervous man out of his wits."[25]

Timothy O'Sullivan was also on this trip. O'Sullivan was another Civil War photographer traveling out West.[26] Born in Ireland in 1840, his family immigrated to the United States in 1842. By the age of 18 he began working under Alexander Gardner's tutelage at Mathew Brady's Washington, D.C. gallery. In late 1861 he started taking views of the Civil War. After Gardner left Brady, O'Sullivan quickly followed suit and joined Gardner in 1863 where his work would receive more credit. After the war he joined Clarence King's survey Geological Explorations of the 40th Parallel. The 1867 and 1868 expeditions traveled in California, Nevada, and Idaho, but in 1869 O'Sullivan spent his time in Utah and Wyoming. After the 1869 season, O'Sullivan photographed with the Darien survey in the Isthmus of Panama before spending 1871 with a different survey headed by George Montague Wheeler. While 1872 saw O'Sullivan back with King, 1873 and 1874 (his last years in the West) were spent, once more, with Wheeler.[27] There is no evidence suggesting there was a professional rivalry between Russell and O'Sullivan.

During this three-week-long trip Russell made at least twenty-five large-format images and fifty-nine stereo-view images.[28] Most of the images are from a spectacular area now referred to as the Middle Basin on Stillwater Creek. Russell himself wrote: "After a ride of about 10 miles, we arrived at the head of the Bear River. It has its rise in one of the most romantic spots on earth. While on one of the mountains here I could count twenty-six lakes, the lowest of them not less than eleven thousand feet above the level of the sea, and the highest, over twelve thousand, and the snow reaching quite down to them. The greater number of these lakes are very deep; they are surrounded by a vast amphitheatre of perpendicular bluffs or mountains; a number of them rise

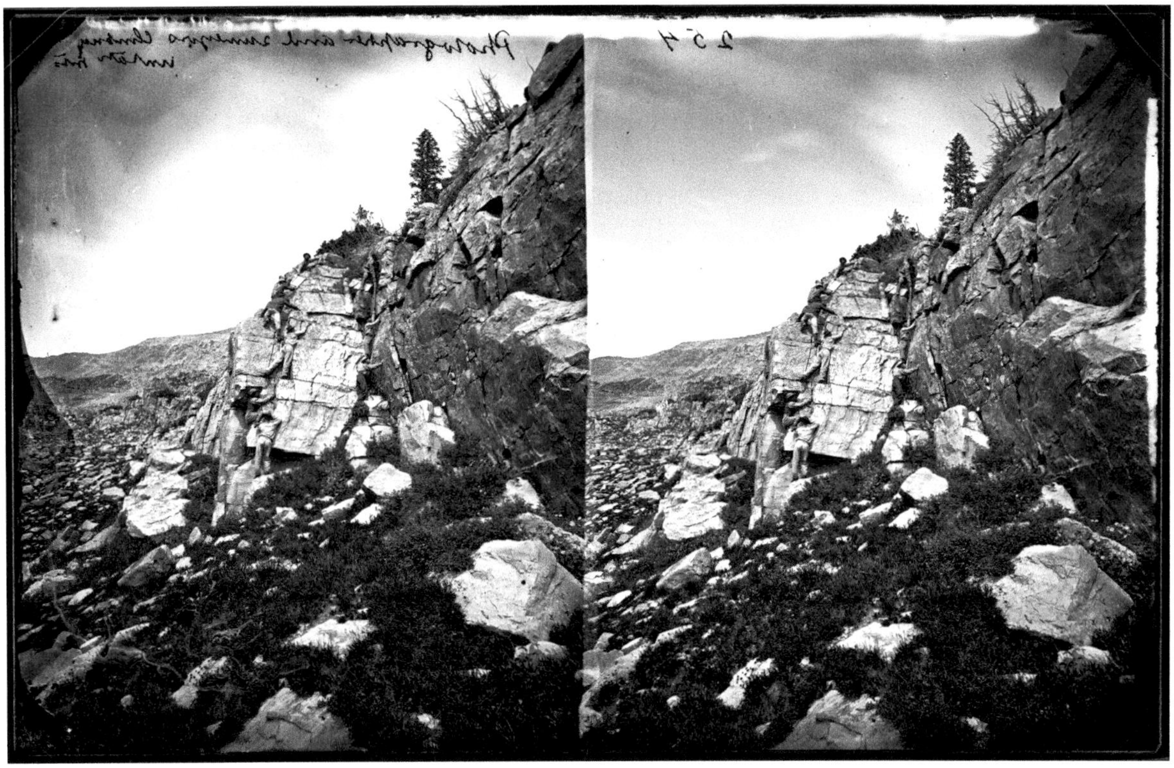

6.13. "Photographing under Difficulties" (Clarence King party in the Uinta Mountains), by A. J. Russell, stereo-view no. 254. *Courtesy of the Oakland Museum of California, A. J. Russell Collection.*

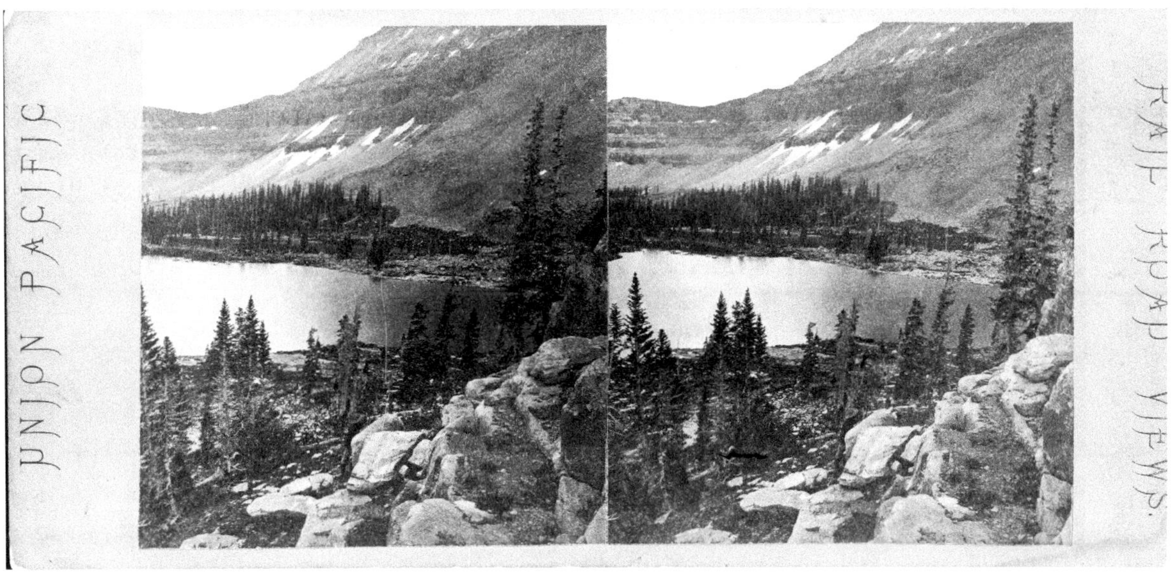

6.14. "Moore's Lake, Head of Bear River" (Ryder Lake, Uinta Mountains), by A. J. Russell, stereo-view no. 249. *Courtesy of Utah State University, Merrill-Cazier Library, Special Collections. Nineteenth-Century Western Stereo-Views Collection.*

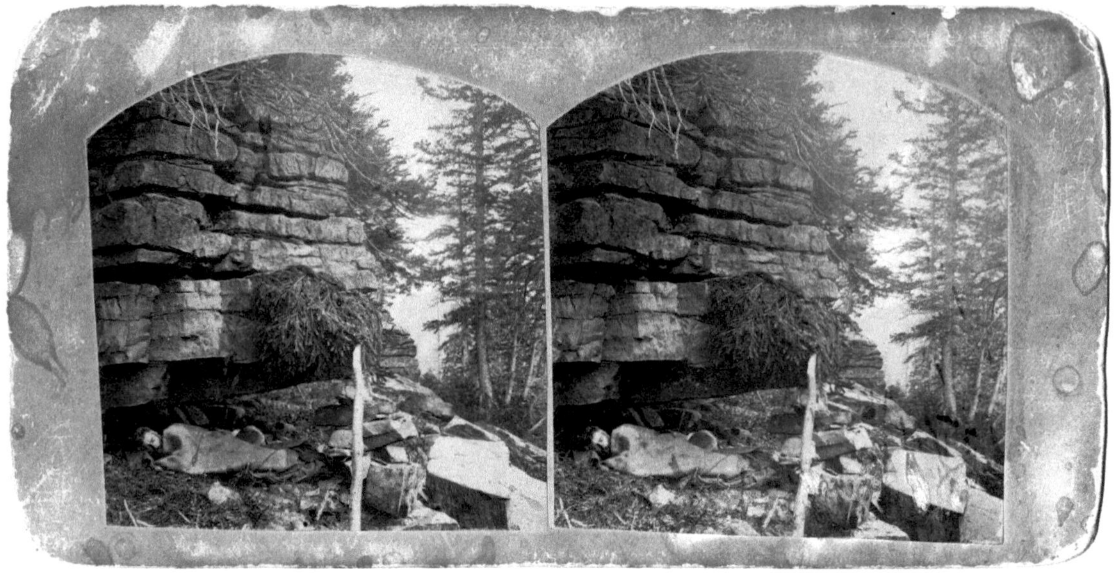

6.15. "Maj. Russell's Bedroom, Uinta[s]," by A. J. Russell, stereo-view no. 240. *Courtesy of the Union Pacific Railroad Museum, Union Pacific Collection, Photography Archives, A. J. Russell Views.*

three thousand feet higher than the lakes."[29] Russell photographed Mount Agassiz, McPheters Lake (what he called "Lake of the Sounding Shore"), and Ryder Lake (he called it "Moore's Lake"). As a former landscape painter, Russell was much more concerned with creating a lyrical, romantic scene than O'Sullivan. He frequently used water as a compositional element, using the reflection of landforms in the water. Russell's images, not surprisingly, also capture more sky and water than O'Sullivan's do, as he was mostly interested in illustrating geology.[30]

Many of these images have been erroneously, but understandably, credited to O'Sullivan, including the well-known image of Clarence King hanging perilously by a rope on a canyon wall. Fifteen of the big negatives and thirty-three of the stereos ended up with the King survey and the corresponding prints use the standard King survey mounts listing O'Sullivan as the artist. Russell kept the rest of the negatives. The O'Sullivan and Russell images can be distinguished by stylistic differences, but also because Russell's negatives are 10" x 13" instead of O'Sullivan's 9" x 12" or 10" x 12" negatives. In addition, at least three stereographic negatives in the National Archives match those published in the West from Omaha series.[31] Russell also took four panoramic negatives that, when pieced together, give an amazing overview of Salt Lake City, the valley, and the mountains. Two of these negatives were given to the King survey and two he kept as part of the Union Pacific images. The confusion over attribution with these two photographers is understandable. There were strict conventions of patronage at this time and these images were not sponsored by the Union Pacific. Russell, therefore, omitted the usual reference to the Union Pacific in the series title (the only series treated this

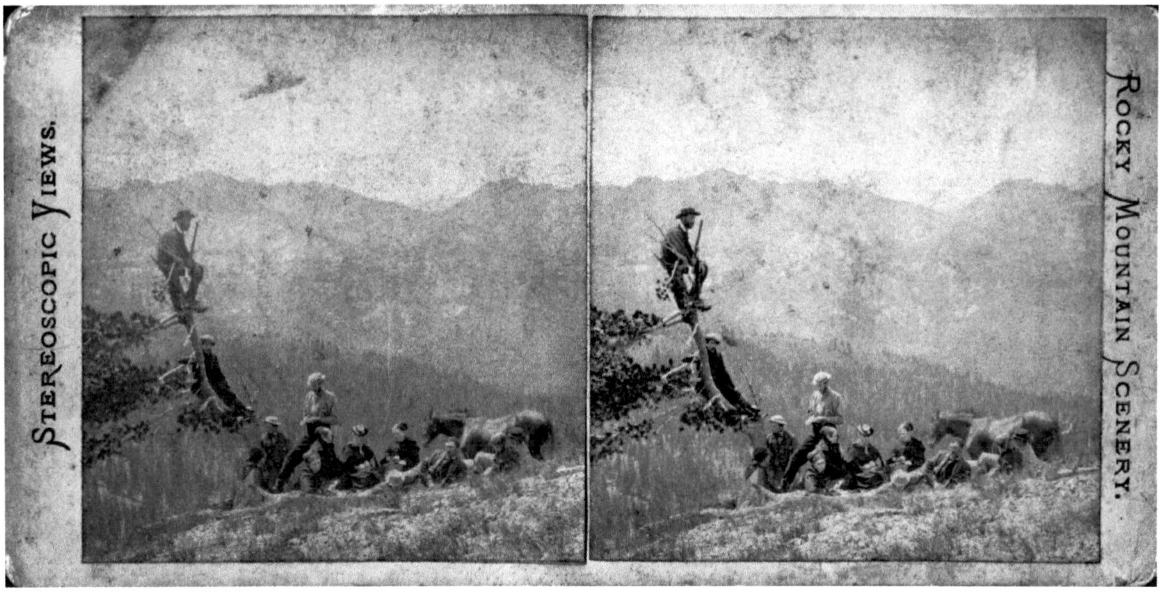

6.16. "On Wasatch Mountains" (view in Cottonwood Canyon), by A. J. Russell, stereo-view no. 465. *Courtesy of Utah State University, Merrill-Cazier Library, Special Collections, Nineteenth-Century Western Stereo-Views Collection.*

way). He accepted King's control, however, over the images that he gave to the survey.[32] When Russell wrote about his experiences in the Uinta Mountains in his hometown newspaper and in *Anthony's Photographic Bulletin*, he did not mention King in these articles.

Russell could not have taken his photo wagon to such a remote area, so all his equipment had to be packed on horses or mules. In Russell's articles he describes considerable trouble with these animals: "In going down a steep declivity my mule jumped over a tree top and I landed just back of his ears. . . . A graceful shake of the head and a musical bray from my pet and away I went on the down hill side and fetched up against a giant balsom tree. . . . Now everybody was amused at my expense, and I even think my mule enjoyed the joke as much as anybody."[33] This humorous aside reveals a key trait of Russell's personality. Much of his humor is self-deprecating, making himself the butt of the joke. As well, in his other writings, he is not providing us with moral lessons about the depravity of American Indians and Mormon polygamy, but instead views them with tolerant bemusement. Russell was a vicarious traveler in the West rather than a conqueror. Like a good journalist, he sought to describe rather than judge.

Russell returned to Bear River City on August 18, but he didn't linger long before heading back into the mountains.[34] He traveled to the Wasatch Mountains with Smith and a party made up of railroad employees and their wives in Big Cottonwood and White Pine Canyons.[35] Smith provided an unusual amount of detail in his diary for this trip: "We start after breakfast and ride about five miles over a very poor sidling road up White Pine [C]anyon to a little lake

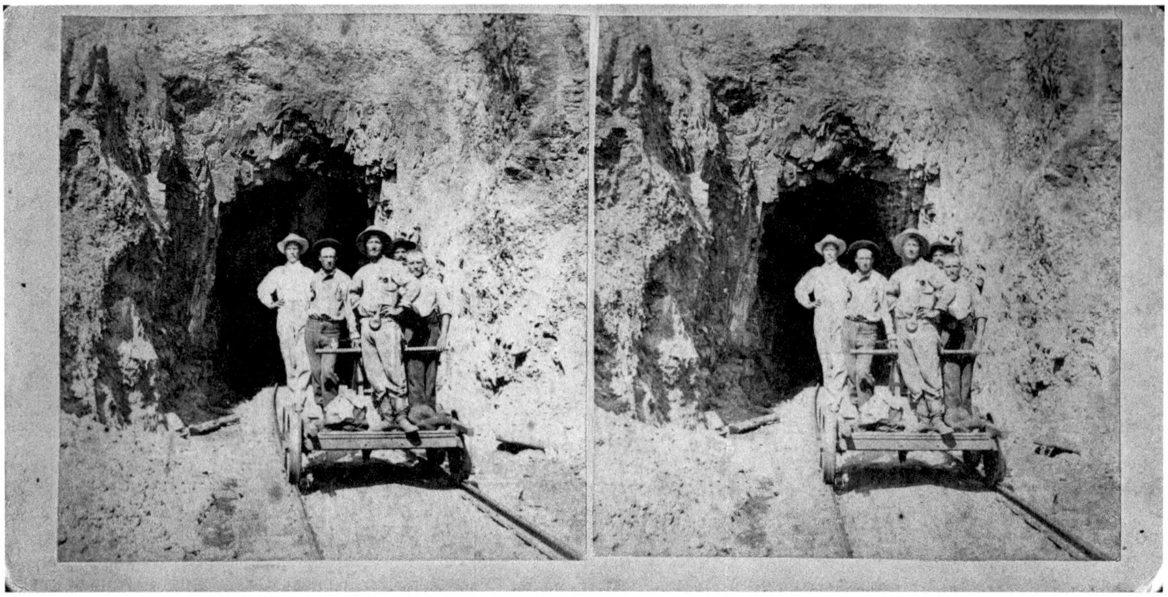

6.17. “West End Tunnel No. 4,” by William Henry Jackson, stereo-view, from Scenery of the Union Pacific R.R. series. *Courtesy of Utah State University, Merrill-Cazier Library, Special Collections, Nineteenth-Century Western Stereo-Views Collection.*

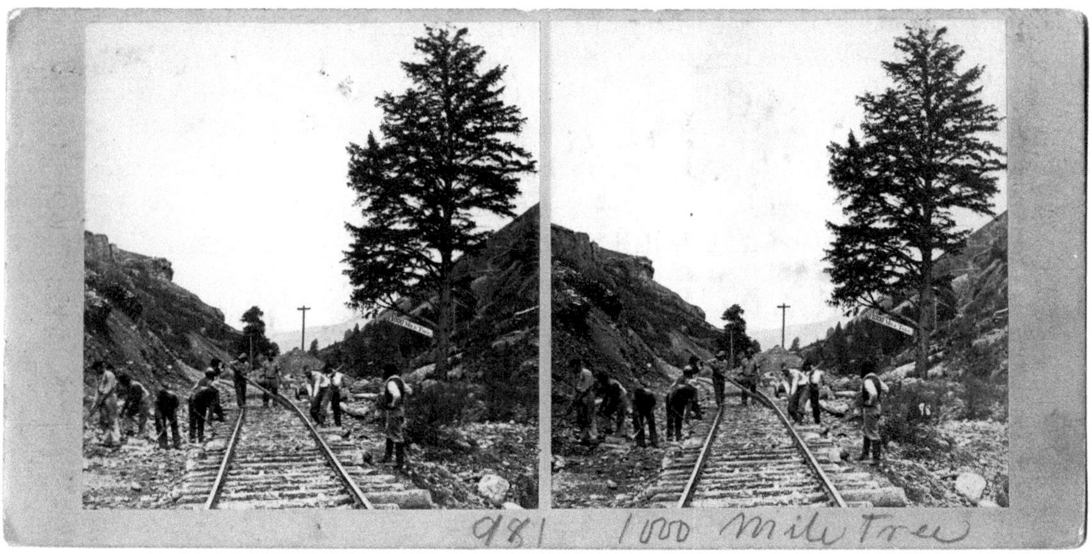

6.18. “1,000 Mile Tree, Weber Canyon,” by William Henry Jackson, stereo-view, from Scenery of the Union Pacific R.R. series. *Courtesy of Utah State University, Merrill-Cazier Library, Special Collections, Nineteenth-Century Western Stereo-Views Collection.*

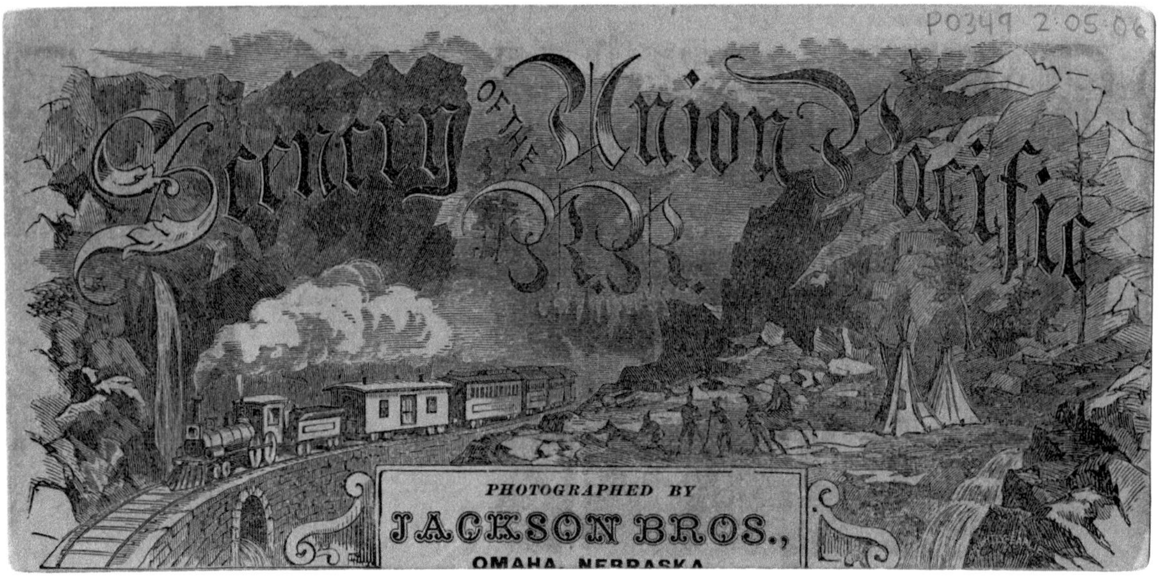

6.19. Verso of stereo-view by William Henry Jackson. *Courtesy of Utah State University, Merrill-Cazier Library, Special Collections, Nineteenth-Century Western Stereo-Views Collection.*

near the head of the [c]anyon. We name it Russells Lake. Quite a party of us go up to the top of the mountain west this morn and take up photographic operations. Mr. Russell takes some splendid views. We get down at 4 p.m. and take several more pictures of our camp and company." Smith's trip was cut short, however, and he traveled all night back to Echo to attend to his duties with the Union Pacific.[36] Russell stayed with the excursion before returning once more to Echo City.

"IT WAS A MIGHTY HARD LUG"

Interestingly, five of the best-known photographers from that era (Russell, O'Sullivan, Jackson, Hart, and Savage) were all in Utah in 1869. Jackson and another photographer Arundel C. Hull had come out to Utah slightly after the Golden Spike Ceremony where they shot stereo and 8" x 10" negatives and sold prints to people along the train route. Today Jackson is the better known of the two, but Hull was an accomplished photographer in his own right. Hull started photographing the Union Pacific towns in Nebraska in 1867 before moving on to Denver and the Colorado mining towns. In the fall of 1868 he headed north into Wyoming, photographing Cheyenne, the Dale Creek Trestle, Benton, and as far West as Green River before returning to Omaha. He was in Laramie in October where he photographed the lynching of several outlaws by a vigilante committee.[37] For Jackson this was his first trip west of Nebraska as a photographer. Jackson grew up in New York State and worked in New York and Vermont as a studio colorist. He was honorably discharged from the Union army in 1863

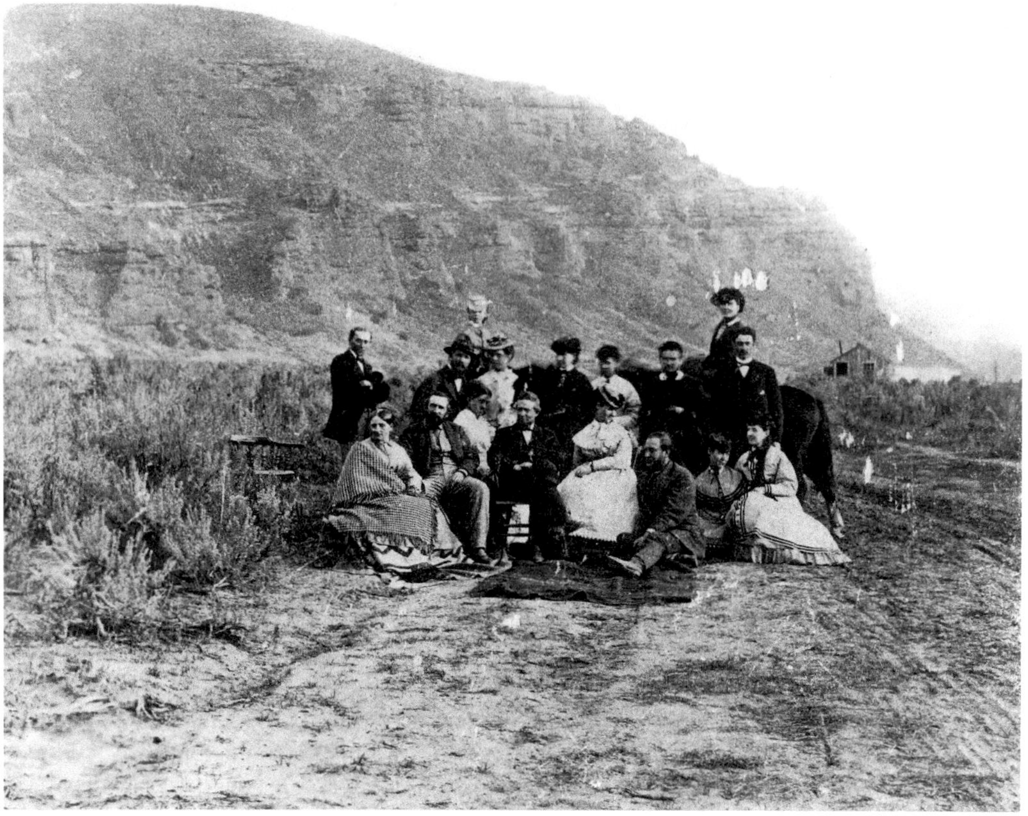

6.20. Cropped version of A. J. Russell stereo-view no. 315, "Colfax and Party, at Echo City" (Vice President Schuyler Colfax and party including Samuel Bowles). *Courtesy of the University of Iowa Libraries, Special Collections, Levi O. Leonard Railroadiana.*

and headed West, eventually making it to California with friends in 1866 and 1867. Finding adventure but little profit, he settled in Omaha in 1867, where he opened a studio with his brother. He photographed in and around Omaha and west of Omaha starting in 1867. After 1869 he would begin his monumental work with the Ferdinand V. Hayden survey, taking his best-known nineteenth-century western images from 1870 to 1878. Unlike the other western photographers, Jackson continued to photograph and promote his work well into the twentieth century, eventually assuming the status of a "living legend."[38]

Jackson, unlike Russell, kept a diary that can give us an idea of the same issues with which Russell dealt. One of the biggest problems for any photographer of that era was picking the right shot. For example, the stunning north red-rock wall of Echo Canyon just above the town of Echo can be shot from the east, west, or from the south wall, but today with the highway, Interstate 80, and private property, the options are more limited. Jackson and Russell, however, could shoot from just about any angle and as high as they could climb. If one considers the different effects of the morning and evening light reflecting on stone walls, not to mention

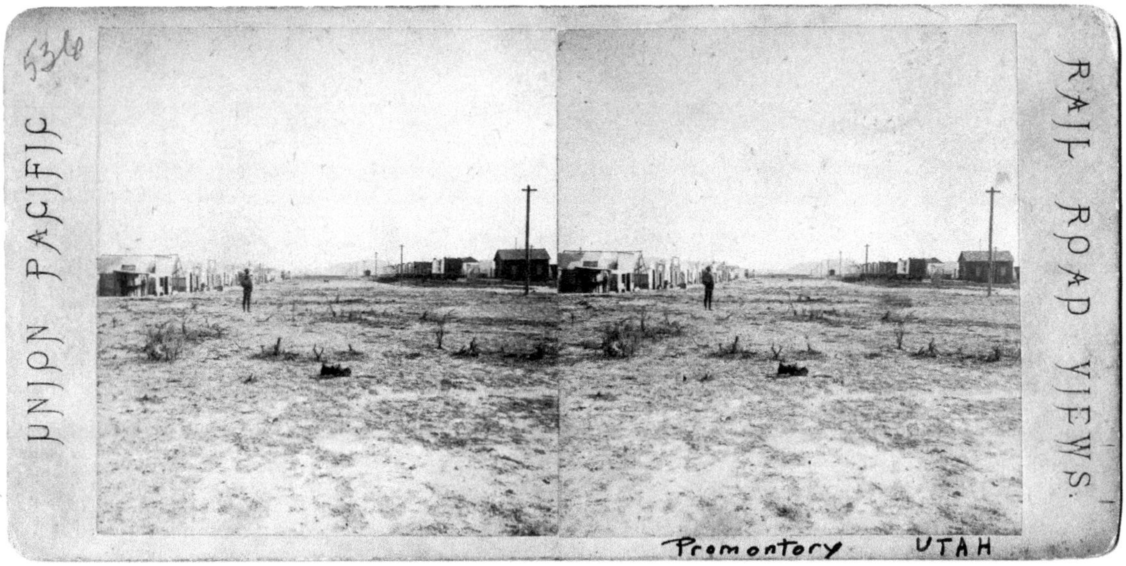

6.21. "Prom[o]ntory from West" (probably taken in November 1869), by A. J. Russell, stereo-view no. 536. *Courtesy of the Union Pacific Railroad Museum, Union Pacific Collection, Photography Archives, A. J. Russell Views.*

atmospheric effects, they had almost unlimited options for picking a shot. Jackson alludes to this when he writes, "The scenery of Echo and Weber appeared magnificent and will keep me continually perplexed when I come to select views."[39]

A wet glass-plate photographer had to be patient, sometimes waiting for days for the right conditions. Jackson discusses in detail the various effects of hazy, bright, dull, and soft light. Of course, if it is raining or too cloudy or too windy, no negatives could be taken. Jackson described shooting sixteen negatives in one day as "a good day's work."[40] Other problems included dust getting onto the negatives, finding clean water, running out of supplies, and the constant difficulties of getting the chemicals to work properly in primitive conditions. The work could be hard and physical. Hull and Jackson walked great distances at times with heavy equipment and slept on blankets or, if they were lucky, in a tent. Jackson, who was only twenty-six at the time and not unused to hard, physical labor, often complained of being tired and worn out. He wrote: "In the afternoon walked down again to where our traps were and brought up the dark box, making a picture on the way. It was a mighty hard lug and made our bones ache before we got back."[41] Russell had a couple of advantages over Jackson though. He had a wagon that could haul his heavy supplies and his finances were more solid. Jackson paid for this trip day by day, selling albumen prints to Union Pacific passengers and employees with Hull acting as an agent in soliciting customers.

Russell met Jackson in mid-September in Wasatch, Utah, located just west of the Wyoming-Utah state line. Jackson wrote: "The first of the week, Russell was here and I was with him a good bit of the time. Got the loan of his evaporating dish and boiled down our old

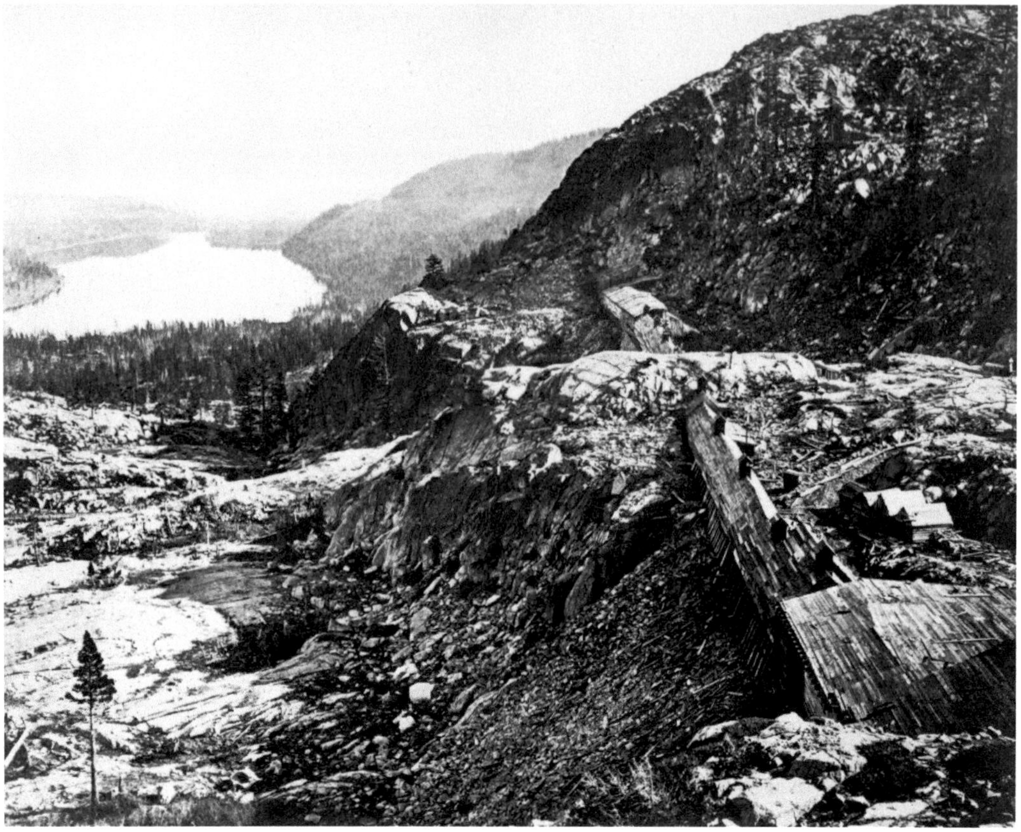

6.22. "Summit of Sierra Nevada," by A. J. Russell, from Sun Pictures of Rocky Mountain Scenery. *Courtesy of Utah State University, Merrill-Cazier Library, Special Collections.*

baths. . . . Found Russell a sociable, companionable fellow and had some very pleasant hours with him." Jackson and Russell made plans to photograph in the Uinta Mountains for the summer of 1870, but there is no evidence this was carried through.[42] Russell may have been in the area to shoot the now-finished tunnel no. 2 as well as the cuts and trestles in the area. Russell, though, once again returned to Echo where on September 12 he photographed a worship service by a group of Odd Fellows on their way to San Francisco for a national convention.[43] In early October he photographed Vice President Schuyler Colfax and journalist Samuel Bowles.[44] This was Colfax's and Bowles's second excursion on the transcontinental railroad, but this time Colfax delivered an antipolygamy speech in Salt Lake City on October 5 that was, not surprisingly, poorly received. Bowles must have been in further contact with Russell because he used two Russell images in his book *Our New West*.[45]

Russell also traveled to California in November. On his way he stopped in Promontory taking three images shortly before the town disbanded and the switching point for the two railroads became Ogden.[46] His photographs of California are sparse compared to the Union Pacific images and as Hart had worked over the line, perhaps he took a few images to provide

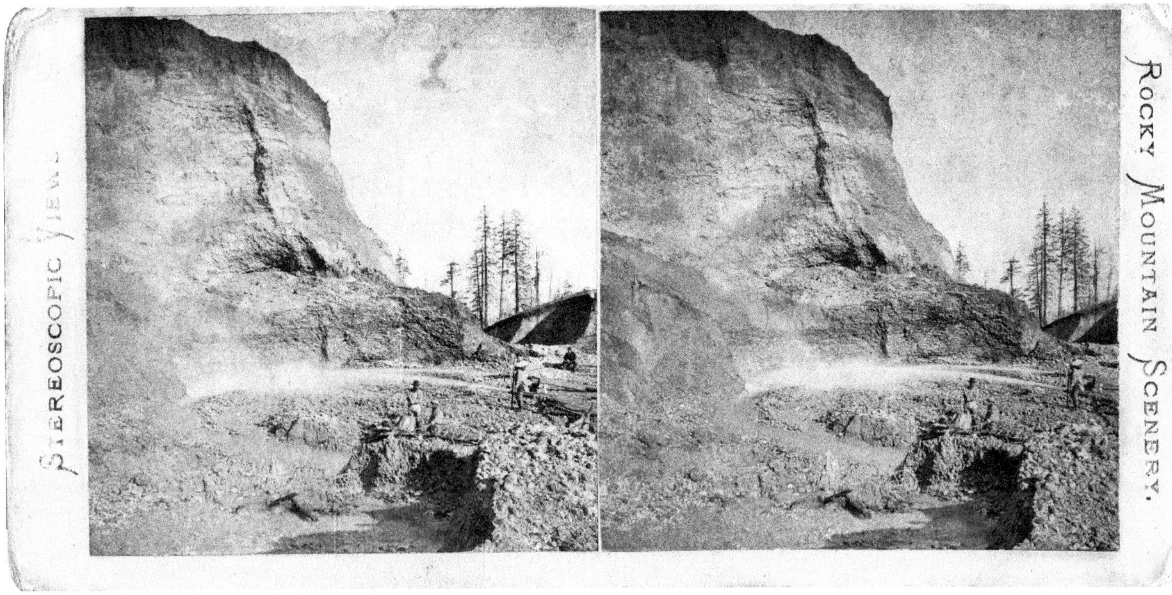

6.23. "Hydraulic Gold Mining, below Bank" (probably in the Sierra Nevada Mountains in California), by A. J. Russell, stereo-view no. 555. *Courtesy of Utah State University, Merrill-Cazier Library, Special Collections, Nineteenth-Century Western Stereo-Views Collection.*

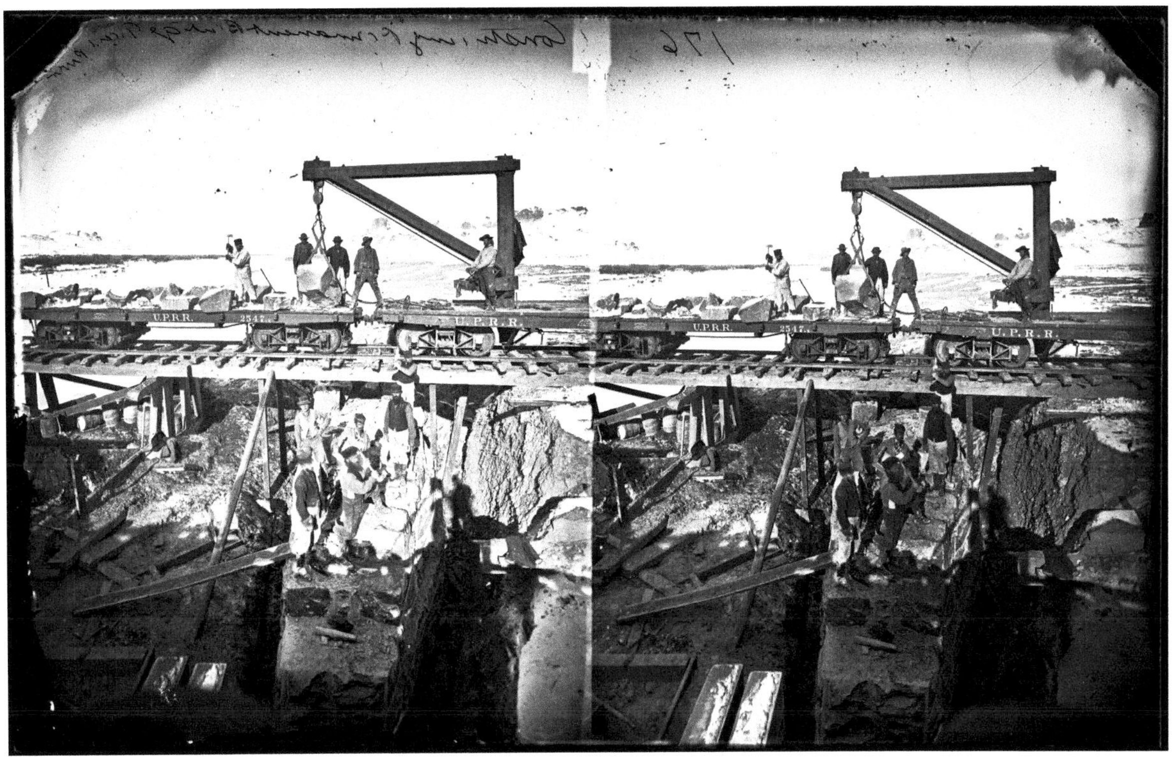

6.24. "Building Permanent Bridge, Green River" (note shadow of photographer in the lower right corner), by A. J. Russell, stereo-view no. 176. *Courtesy of the Oakland Museum of California, A. J. Russell Collection.*

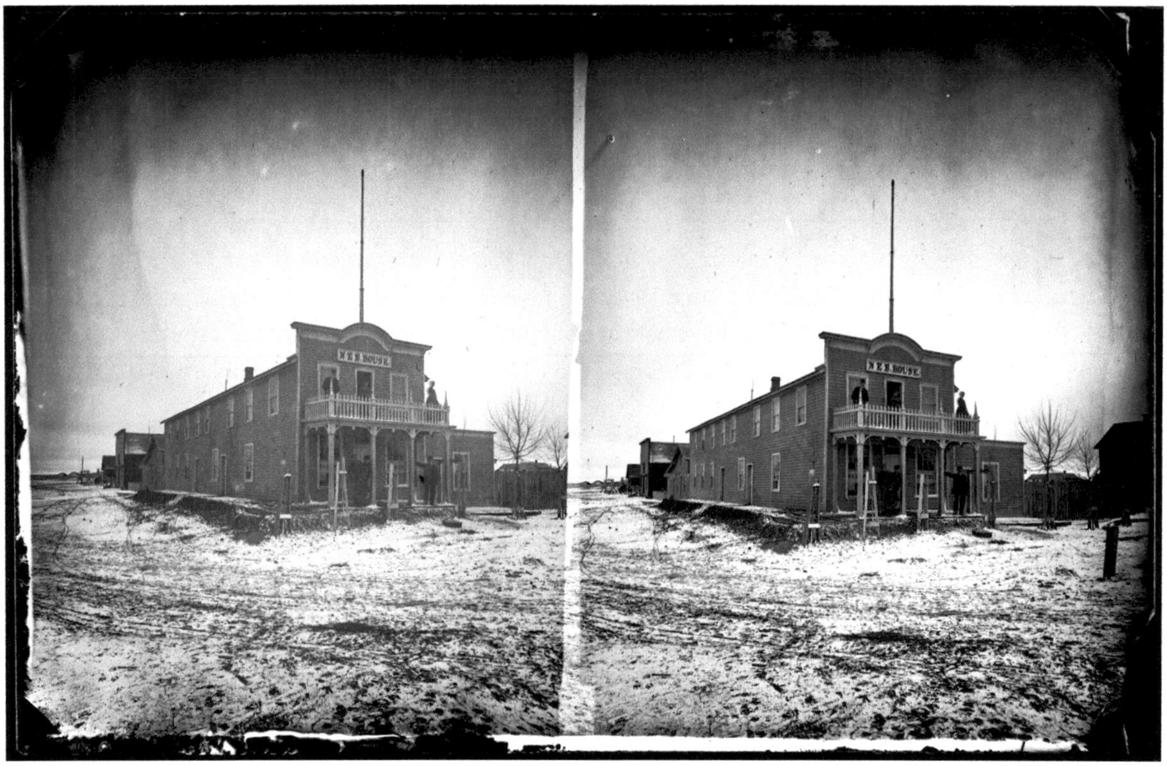

6.25. "Grand Island Hotel," by A. J. Russell, stereo-view no. 49. *Courtesy of the Oakland Museum of California, A. J. Russell Collection.*

support for the idea that he photographed the entire transcontinental railroad. Among his images are the Sierra Nevada Summit tunnel, hydraulic mining, trees, and a few images of the California towns of Colfax and Rocklin. Russell was astonished to travel over the snowy Sierra Nevada then come down to the "eternal summer" of Sacramento. While in Sacramento he clearly had an interest in the Chinese: "The peaked hat, round head, almond-shaped eyes, and the Celestial que, with the modest demeanor of John Chinaman stares us in the face at every point. They are to us a strange people, and who can tell the result of this great problem which their advent among us suggests. It is beyond the comprehension of the present age. The more we study them the less we seem to know."[47] He attended a Chinese theater that cost him 40 cents and he photographed some of their living quarters. Like many other white Americans of the time, he was both repulsed and fascinated by their ways, writing after a theater experience: "I grabbed my hat and left in disgust, and should not advise a friend to undergo the venture. . . . I can assure anyone that there is noise enough to drive ever thing else out of his head and if he is not crazy he never will be. Take a fool's advice and don't go."[48]

Russell photographed across Wyoming and Nebraska on his way home in December. He shot the machine shops and roundhouses in Rawlins (still with snow on them) before moving on to Laramie. As well, he shot Reed's Rock and Sherman Summit, and a few more scenic views in the Black Hills. In Nebraska, Russell photographed the more important towns, such as Fremont, Columbus, Grand Island, and North Platte, paying attention to dining and overnight accommodations.[49] He presented these western towns as favorably as possible, including the major structures such as churches, schools, and businesses.[50] He was providing useful, contemporary information to prospective travelers by showing depots, restaurants, and hotels. As well, he photographed the bridges over the Loup Fork and North Platte Rivers. Nebraska required little trestle and cut work, but had numerous bridges that sometimes washed out with spring flooding. Overall, however, Russell did not heavily photograph the long miles through Nebraska. There are only five large-format views and around sixty stereo-views. He was in Columbus, Nebraska, on December 19, 1869, probably with hopes of making it home to his family by Christmas.[51]

"FORCED TO SUBSIST ON GAME"

On February 1, 1870, Russell made a presentation to the photographic section of the American Institute. His talk, as one commentator put it, should have been labeled "Photographing under Difficulties." His audience of easterners was suitably impressed with his adventures: "Owing to the generally alkaline nature of the water . . . he had been forced to carry good water a distance of seventy miles . . . [and] was often absent four and five weeks, and forced to subsist upon game." The commentator went on to say: "On more than one occasion he walked some fifty miles carrying good water while he scouted for special views. Twice his horses bolted on the steep hills carrying away his prized equipment."[52] Russell's trouble with mules was mentioned. On one occasion he was swept away in a mountain stream in the Uinta Mountains and on another he fell off his mule on a steep slope, saving himself only by grabbing on to the mules ears.[53] Some hyperbole might be evident here, but suffice it to say that Russell, and all the other western railroad photographers of that era, including Jackson, Hull, Hart, Carbutt, and Savage contributed in their own ways to the Herculean effort of building the transcontinental railroad.

CHAPTER 7

Leslie's Illustrated *and the Market in Photographs after 1870*

"The railway has so abridged time and space, the continent is rapidly losing its romance and becoming prosaic."

—Thomas W. Knox

In the early part of 1870 the popular weekly *Frank Leslie's Illustrated Newspaper* ran a thirteen-part series titled Across the Continent, Overland Scenes. The articles allowed *Leslie's* to exploit interest (written as well as visual) in the new Pacific Railway. Overall the series is fairly standard fare. It discusses Salt Lake City and Mormonism, western wildlife, scenery and rock formations along the line, American Indians, and the primitive accommodations to be found in Wyoming and Utah. It also provides a few bland impressions of the railroad followed by the usual rhetoric about the line uniting the far-flung portions of the country. Thomas W. Knox, the author of these articles, however, also wrote: "The railway has so abridged time and space, the continent is rapidly losing its romance and becoming prosaic."[1] The subtext, of course, is that 1870 represented a turning point in attitudes toward the intermountain West. The exoticism of the West briefly held the public's attention but that interest slowly declined in the 1870s. Later, in the 1880s and 1890s, enthusiasm for all things western revived through the fanciful re-creations of western history found in dime novels and Wild West shows. The popularity of Russell's images reached a zenith in 1870, but thereafter quickly dropped. Russell started the decade with high hopes of cashing in on his newfound fame, but, perhaps sensing this change, gradually shifted his efforts away from his negatives.

As mentioned earlier, Russell began a relationship with *Leslie's* during the Civil War. *Leslie's* published a few of his Union Pacific images in 1868 and 1869, and it also published his written account of the Golden Spike Ceremony. Although Russell was not the author of the Across the Continent, Overland Scenes series, the newspaper used six of his large-format images.[2] The paper was well acquainted with Russell and in 1870 he became more than just a "freelance" photographer, but also a regular staff member. This work would last about ten years, until 1879, when Russell probably became a victim of corporate restructuring necessitated by Frank Leslie's large debts.[3] During these ten years (before Leslie's death on January 10, 1880) Russell became friends with the famous publisher. For instance, Russell was a wit-

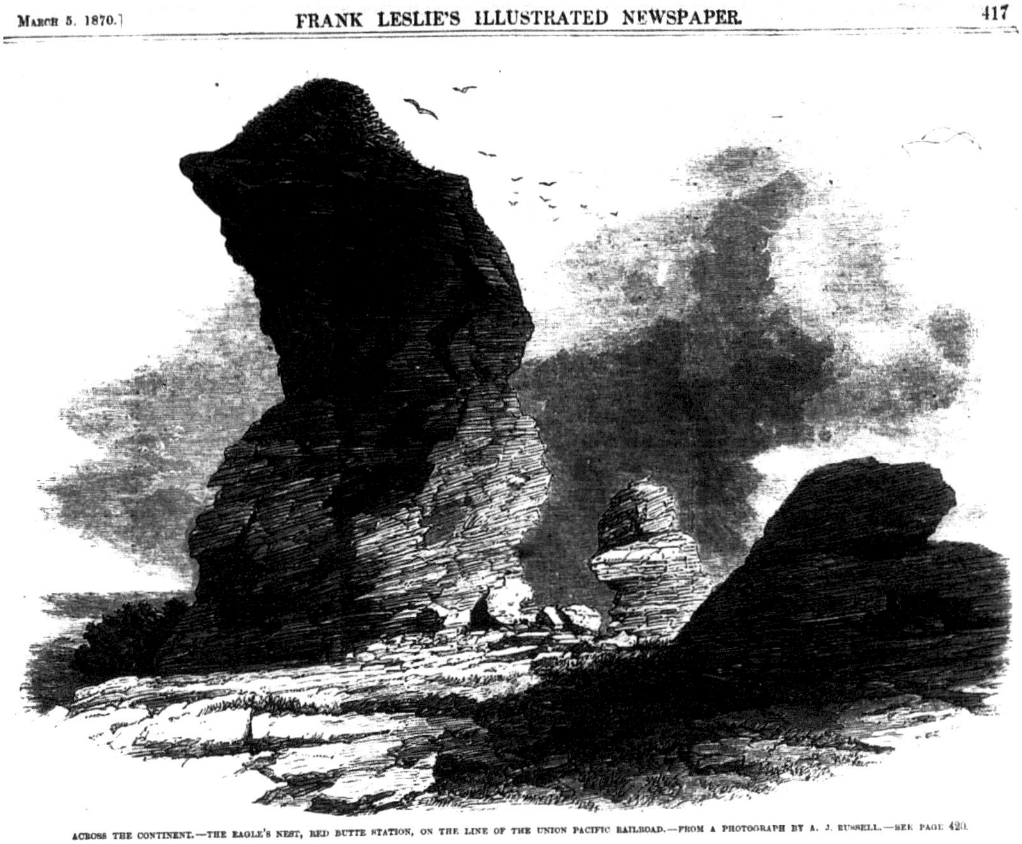

7.1. "Across the Continent" (woodcut illustration made from a Russell image), appeared in *Leslie's Illustrated*, March 5, 1870.

ness during a legal dispute over Leslie's estate. He testified that Frank Leslie was "a kind, noble and indulgent father."[4] Russell probably worked on converting photographs to the woodcut illustrations found in the paper, but he also acted as staff photographer.[5] As well, he helped to move the paper from wood engraving to photoxylography, also called photo-relief engravings. This process had begun in the Civil War for *Leslie's*, but it was not perfected until the 1870s. In this process either a photographic image is projected onto a wood block or a negative is exposed on the wood block itself, for engraving. The process was less labor intensive while producing a more detailed image than traditional woodcut engravings (which sometimes used up to eight engravers for a single image).[6]

Russell was not done with his travels, though. In June 1870, he became an itinerant photographer once again. This time he journeyed with his photographic wagon to Portage, New York, drawing sketches and taking photographs of scenes along the Erie Railroad, including the falls and the high bridge at Portage on the Genesee River. The *Nunda News* reported of his subsequent plans to visit the oil fields of Pennsylvania, as well as Cincinnati, and to end the trip in Watkins Glen, New York. It isn't clear if he completed this journey. It would have been

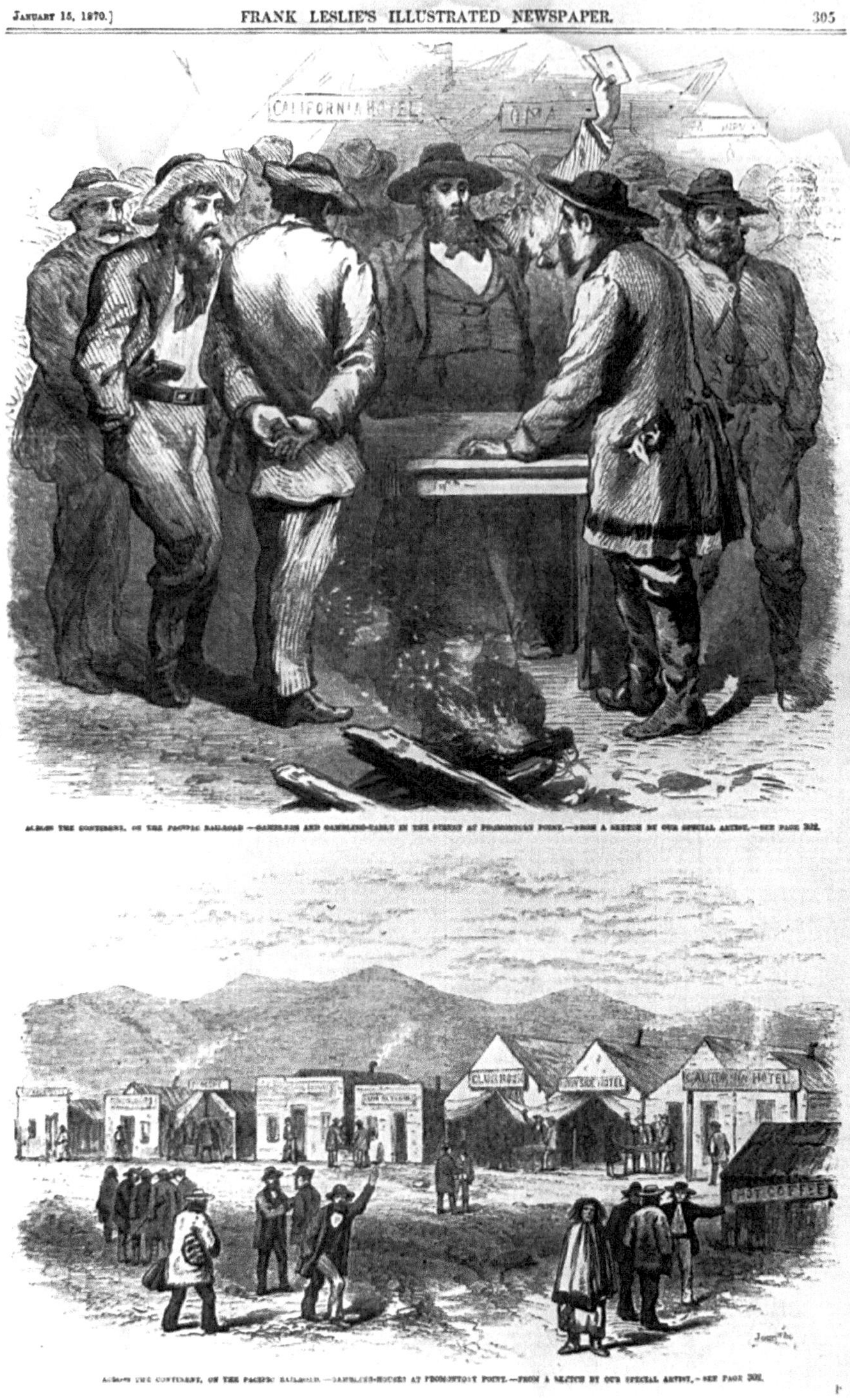

7.2. "Across the Continent" (woodcut illustration made from a sketch by an unknown artist), appeared in *Leslie's Illustrated*, January 15, 1870. *Courtesy of the Library of Congress, Prints and Photographs Division.*

a rigorous trip, but still a pale shadow of his former adventures. The sketches and photographs he took were supposed to end up as articles and images in *Leslie's Illustrated*, but they did not.[7] In 1873 he may have traveled to New Mexico. He wrote a remarkably detailed article and created an illustration for *Moore's Rural New-Yorker* on the subject of sheepherding.[8] Later, in 1875, he was in Philadelphia experimenting with the American Optical Company's 4" x 5" pocket camera.[9] There is no evidence, however, that Russell traveled with Frank Leslie and his second wife, Miriam Squier, on their well-publicized western excursions in 1877 and 1878.

In addition to his work with *Leslie's*, Russell used his railroad images to earn money elsewhere. In 1868 and 1869 the Union Pacific made a strong claim to Russell's images. In fact, in 1869 Durant used another man, Robert Pittman, to print Russell's 1868 images. Curiously, though, by 1870 the Union Pacific had relinquished this control.[10] This may have been because Durant resigned from his position in the Union Pacific after the Golden Spike Ceremony, but the Union Pacific also had a different set of problems in the 1870s.[11] Either way, Russell set to work on the monumental task of organizing his 900+ negative collection into series. He created a new stereoscopic series titled Rocky Mountain Scenery. Russell was trying to reach a wider audience and it must have worked: judging by the number of extant copies today, Rocky Mountain Scenery was the best-selling of all the various stereographic series. Russell was no longer a corporate photographer and this set was not directed towards Union Pacific directors, government officials, or potential investors, but instead provided a vicarious trip along the transcontinental railroad, starting in Omaha and finishing in California. This concept of a vicarious journey was not unfamiliar to Russell, as his panorama paintings from ten years earlier followed the same method.

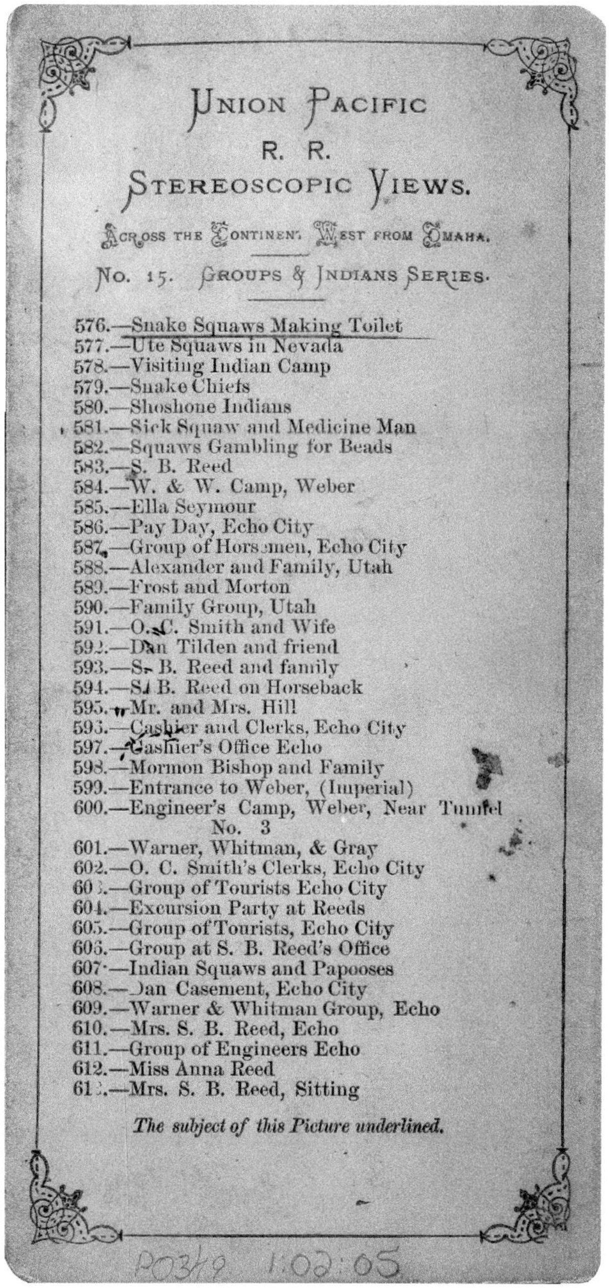
UNION PACIFIC
R. R.
STEREOSCOPIC VIEWS.
ACROSS THE CONTINENT WEST FROM OMAHA.
NO. 15. GROUPS & INDIANS SERIES.

576.—Snake Squaws Making Toilet
577.—Ute Squaws in Nevada
578.—Visiting Indian Camp
579.—Snake Chiefs
580.—Shoshone Indians
581.—Sick Squaw and Medicine Man
582.—Squaws Gambling for Beads
583.—S. B. Reed
584.—W. & W. Camp, Weber
585.—Ella Seymour
586.—Pay Day, Echo City
587.—Group of Horsemen, Echo City
588.—Alexander and Family, Utah
589.—Frost and Morton
590.—Family Group, Utah
591.—O. C. Smith and Wife
592.—Dan Tilden and friend
593.—S. B. Reed and family
594.—S. B. Reed on Horseback
595.—Mr. and Mrs. Hill
596.—Cashier and Clerks, Echo City
597.—Cashier's Office Echo
598.—Mormon Bishop and Family
599.—Entrance to Weber, (Imperial)
600.—Engineer's Camp, Weber, Near Tunnel No. 3
601.—Warner, Whitman, & Gray
602.—O. C. Smith's Clerks, Echo City
603.—Group of Tourists Echo City
604.—Excursion Party at Reeds
605.—Group of Tourists, Echo City
606.—Group at S. B. Reed's Office
607.—Indian Squaws and Papooses
608.—Dan Casement, Echo City
609.—Warner & Whitman Group, Echo
610.—Mrs. S. B. Reed, Echo
611.—Group of Engineers Echo
612.—Miss Anna Reed
613.—Mrs. S. B. Reed, Sitting

The subject of this Picture underlined.

P0349 1:02:05

7.3. Verso of stereo-view no. 576 by A. J. Russell. *Courtesy of Utah State University, Merrill-Cazier Library, Special Collections, Nineteenth-Century Western Stereo-Views Collection.*

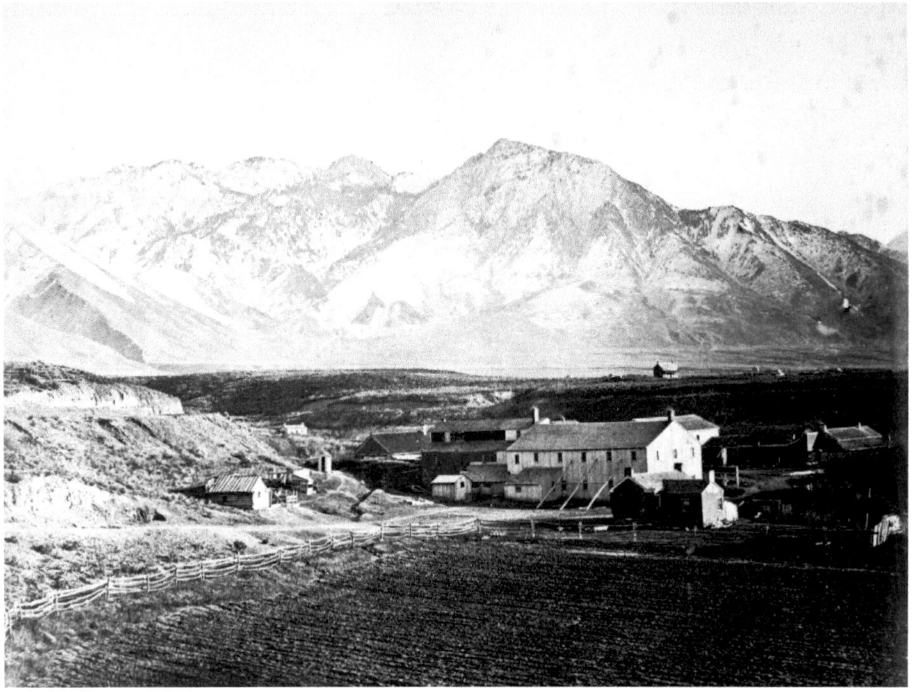

7.4. "Wasatch Range of Rocky Mountains: From Brigham Young's Woolen Mills, Utah," by A. J. Russell, from Sun Pictures of Rocky Mountain Scenery. *Courtesy of Utah State University, Merrill-Cazier Library, Special Collections.*

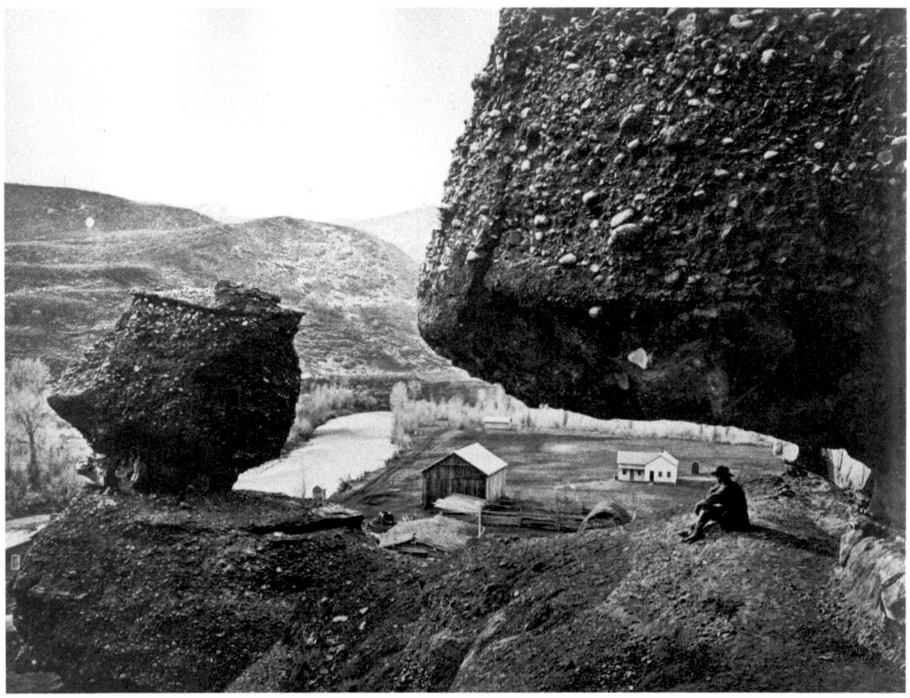

7.5. "Hanging Rock: Echo City, Utah," by A. J. Russell, from *Sun Pictures of Rocky Mountain Scenery. Courtesy of Utah State University, Merrill-Cazier Library, Special Collections.*

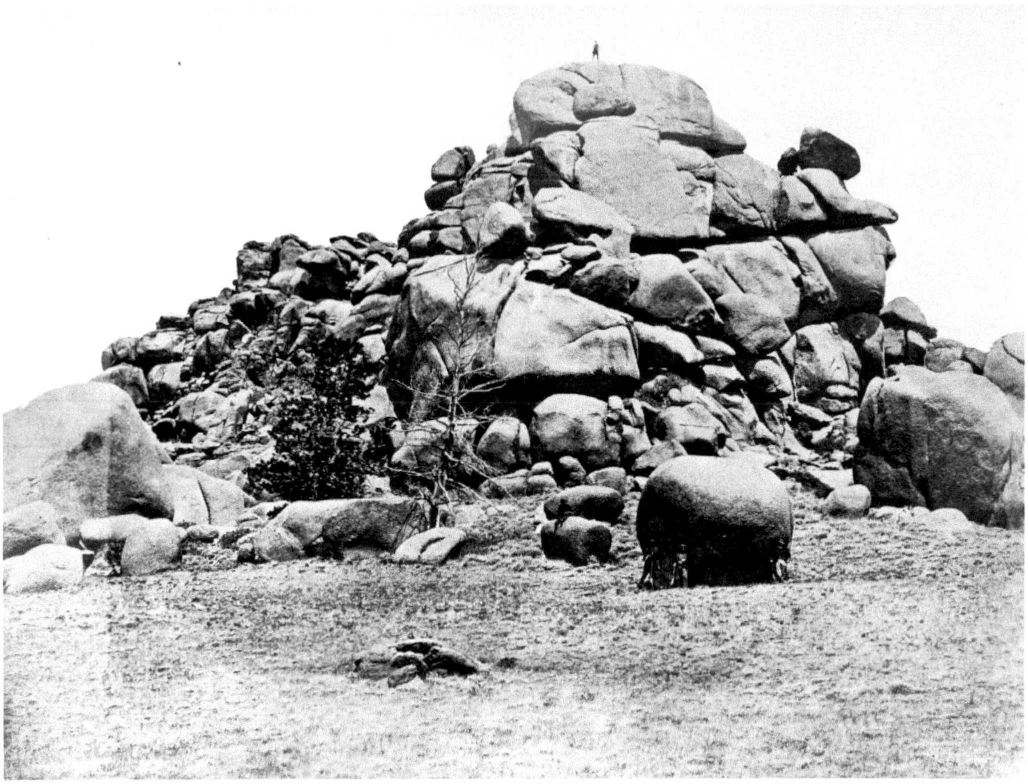

7.6. "Skull Rock (Granite): Sherman Station, Laramie Mountains, Wyoming," by A. J. Russell, from *Sun Pictures of Rocky Mountain Scenery. Courtesy of Utah State University, Merrill-Cazier Library, Special Collections.*

Russell undertook yet another project in early 1870, participating in Ferdinand V. Hayden's publication with the long-winded title *Sun Pictures of Rocky Mountain Scenery, with a Description of the Geographical and Geological Features, and Some Account of the Resources of the Great West: Containing Thirty Photographic Views along the Line of the Pacific Railroad, from Omaha to Sacramento.*[12] This volume sold for twenty-five dollars, but unlike *The Great West Illustrated*, it sold well.[13] Hayden was in charge of the U.S. Geographical and Geological Survey and he wanted to capitalize on the interest in visual images of the West and to promote the study of geology. Hayden explains in the book, "The Pictures have been arranged so as to commence with the first range of mountains west of Cheyenne, and to continue thence to the Salt Lake Valley with the view that the book may be used as a guide by those who will avail themselves of the grand opportunities for geological study."[14] Russell's albumen images tipped in to this book show not only geological, but also manmade structures in Wyoming, Utah, and California. Hayden obviously placed a high value on photographs as illustrative tools. When describing the formations of Echo Canyon in Utah he wrote: "Our illustrations serve well to show the variety of this wonderful scenery and as, 'Rock Studies' they are unsurpassed. To the intelligent eye they speak for themselves better than pages of description."[15]

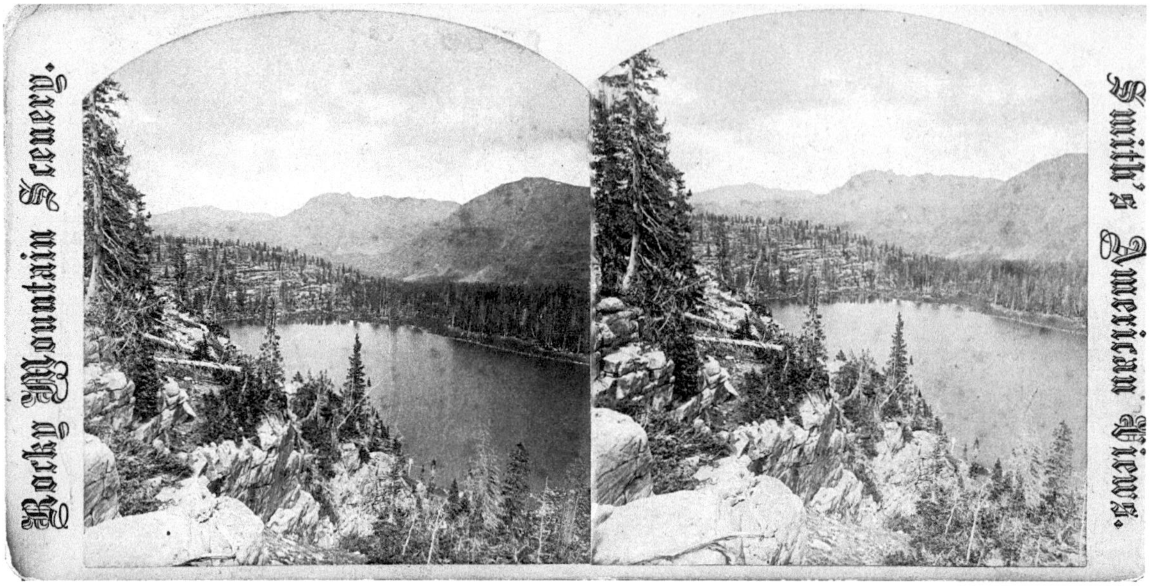

7.7. “Moore’s Lake, from South West” (Ryder Lake in the Uinta Mountains), by A. J. Russell, stereo-view no. 250. *Courtesy of Utah State University, Merrill-Cazier Library, Special Collections, Nineteenth-Century Western Stereo-Views Collection.*

It is obvious when reading *Sun Pictures of Rocky Mountain Scenery* that geology for Hayden was no mere academic enterprise. He is at pains to use his knowledge of geography and geology to point out coal to be mined, timber to be cut, minerals to be extracted, granite to be quarried, and rich soil to be sown. Words like “abundant” and “inexhaustible,” and, of course, “limitless,” are used liberally in the book. Indeed Hayden, in his giddiness, writes, “The habit of using superlatives will grow upon us so that they will form the greater part of our forms of speech, and common language will prove altogether too tame for our purposes.”[16] Hayden and Russell did not see an inherent tension between the beauty of western scenery and the rapid economic development they both predicted. Take, for instance, Hayden’s description of the Medicine Bow Mountains: “Indeed the pine groves and grassy openings are so arranged and proportioned, that the whole scene appears as if it might have been partially the work of art.” Hayden then points out that “these openings and grassy slopes will make excellent pasture ground,” and further that “even now the mountain sides are full of tie cutters, who cut and float hundreds of thousands of ties down the mountain streams 50 to 100 miles to the Union Pacific Railroad.”[17] Hayden commented upon the importance of coal as well: “In the vicinity of the Rocky Mountains, in Wyoming and Colorado, coal in immense quantities has been hidden away for ages, and the Union Pacific Railroad has now brought it near the door of every man’s dwelling.”[18] Twenty-six of the thirty images in the book focus on geologic and rock formations in Wyoming, Utah, and California; one is of the Union Pacific Trestle at Promontory Summit; and three are of Mormon structures in Utah, including one of the Salt

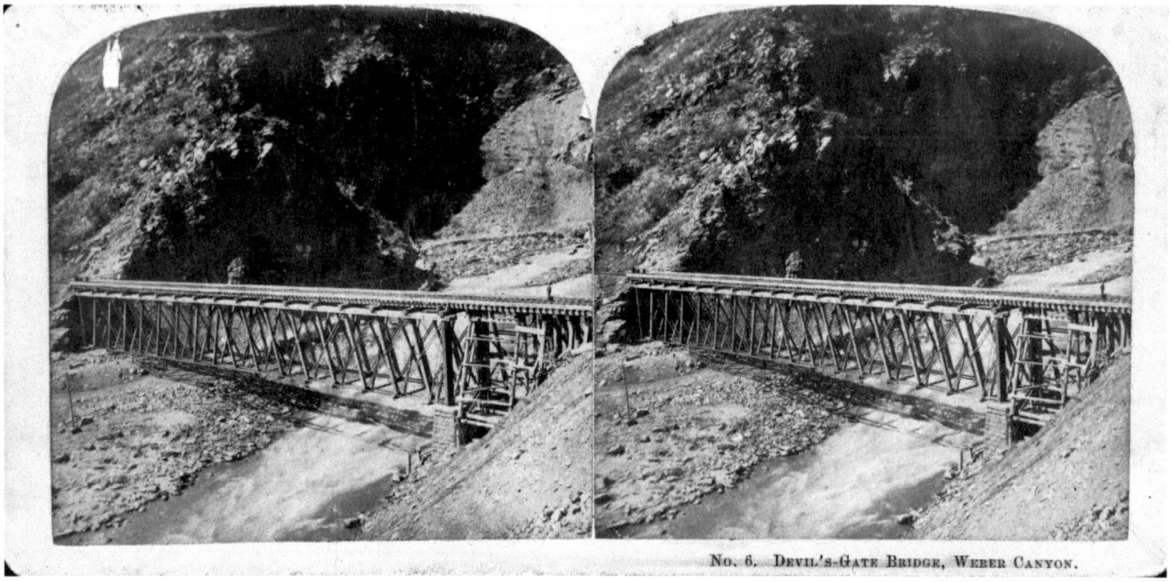

7.8. "Devil's Gate Bridge, Weber Canyon," by C. W. Carter, stereo-view. *Courtesy of Utah State University, Merrill-Cazier Library, Special Collections, Nineteenth-Century Western Stereo-Views Collection.*

Lake City Tabernacle, an overview of Salt Lake City with the foundations of the Salt Lake City Temple, and an image of Brigham Young's woolen mills (which serves to illustrate the Wasatch Mountains in the background). The photographs in *Sun Pictures of Rocky Mountain Scenery* are of geologic interest, not dramatic scenes that document the construction of the Union Pacific Railroad. Here Russell shows his flexibility as an artist. Most of these images were taken after the joining of the rails when Russell had more time to pick and choose his subjects. In these photographs nature is not an obstacle to be overcome, but a source of interest for the prospective traveler. Russell, it turns out, had at least a rudimentary understanding of geology and this book may explain his preoccupation with geologic formations.[19] Hayden refers to the possibility (which would be unfulfilled) of an additional book published about the geography of the Sierra Nevada Mountains "if this work meets with favor from the public."[20] Despite the success of *Sun Pictures of Rocky Mountain Scenery,* though, Russell's large-format images were still not nearly as popular as his stereo-views.

"OBJECTS MOST ATTRACTIVE AND WONDERFUL"

In early 1870 Russell and his friend from the Union Pacific, O. C. Smith, continued the financial arrangement begun in 1869 and now both worked out of a gallery at 390 Bowery Street.[21] Together they printed and sold Russell's images, including both stereo-views and large format. They sold the stereo-views through their store and also through distributors such as George W. Thorne.[22] The nature of this relationship is not entirely clear, but, for instance, from July to

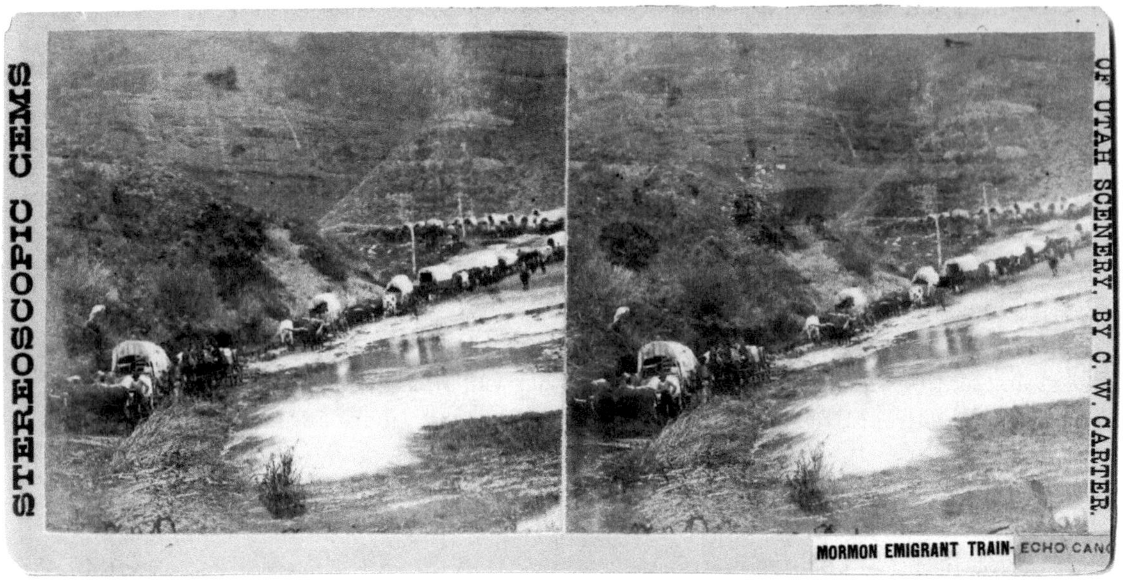

7.9. "Mormon Emigrant Train: Echo Canyon," by C. W. Carter, stereo-view. *Courtesy of Utah State University, Merrill-Cazier Library, Special Collections, Nineteenth-Century Western Stereo-Views Collection.*

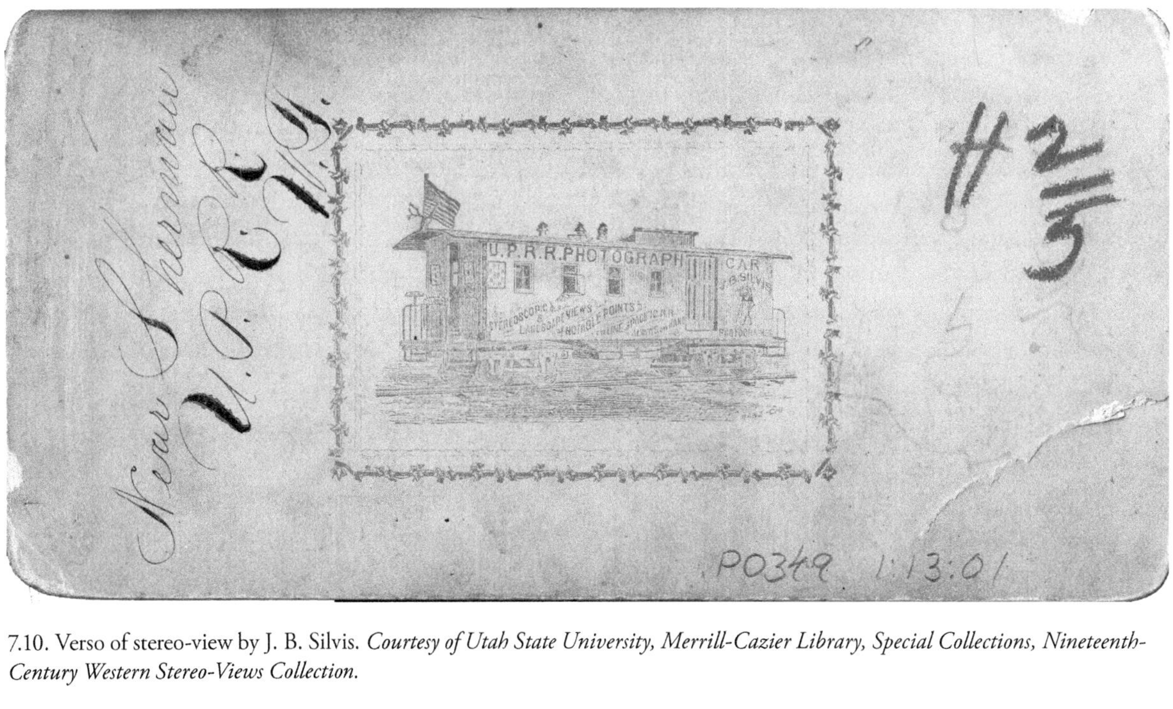

7.10. Verso of stereo-view by J. B. Silvis. *Courtesy of Utah State University, Merrill-Cazier Library, Special Collections, Nineteenth-Century Western Stereo-Views Collection.*

November, 1869, Smith's diary details how he purchased large numbers of images from Russell and loaned him money when needed for printing paper and shipping costs. It is probable that Smith purchased large numbers of prints for later resale, in effect, acting as a sales agent for Russell. Smith and Russell's cozy financial relationship in 1869 even extended to Russell helping Smith with a profitable side business of selling corn.[23]

Sometime in 1870, however, Smith took charge of Russell's negatives, buying them from Russell for one thousand dollars.[24] He moved to Brooklyn with the negatives, opening a gallery at 314 Washington with his Uncle Asa, who acted as a printer.[25] The arrangement was apparently amicable, however, as Smith and Russell continued to work together. Smith published the Rocky Mountain Scenery series under the new label Smith's American Views, and Smith worked hard to market and sell the views in 1871 and 1872. In fact, both series were probably produced simultaneously, but Russell's active partnership with Smith was over by 1871. Smith traveled West again from Chicago to Salt Lake City in July and August 1871, selling views along the route.[26] As well, he began lecturing in Massachusetts, using magic glass-lantern slides. Smith was not satisfied with the profits from these lectures and he started working as an agent and paymaster for the Whitestone branch of the Long Island Railroad.[27] In late 1872 Smith began a three-year stint with the Canada Southern Railway as a wood agent. In 1875 he moved to Rock Springs, Wyoming, where he lived for the remainder of his life.[28]

Russell might have moved away from transcontinental railroad photography simply because the market was getting crowded. In addition to Savage, another Utah photographer C. W. Carter started photographing the Union Pacific route in 1867 or 1868 and continued his efforts into the 1870s. William Henry Jackson, T. C. Roche (whom Russell knew from the Civil War and who photographed anonymously for E. & H. T. Anthony & Co.), and J. B. Silvis were also taking images in 1869 and 1870.[29] Silvis, in particular, would fill the niche that Russell occupied. Silvis started photographing the stage stations along the overland route in Wyoming and Utah even before the construction of the Union Pacific. In 1869 he mostly took portraits of Union Pacific employees, but in the fall of 1870 he created a photography railroad car that was a mobile studio and darkroom. This arrangement was much more convenient than using a darkroom wagon, as Silvis would travel the length of Union Pacific several times a year and during all seasons. Silvis continued this arrangement until 1882 when competition from local photographers forced him to sell the photograph car.[30] As well, Carleton Watkins, the most critically acclaimed of the western photographers at that point, created a series of more expensive, high-quality stereo-views in 1873, which sold well on the West Coast.[31]

Stephen Sedgwick obtained Russell's original negatives from Smith around 1873 and he published a catalog of the stereographic images in 1873, 1874, and 1879. These lists reproduce Russell's original verso lists not just in terms of image descriptions, but also with the same font and graphics. The only difference is that Russell's name has been omitted. Sedgwick returned to New York City from his work with Russell out West in October, 1869, and started lecturing again in 1870, presumably using Russell's images.[32] Still, the arrangement between Russell and Sedgwick must have been satisfactory as the two maintained a friendly relation-

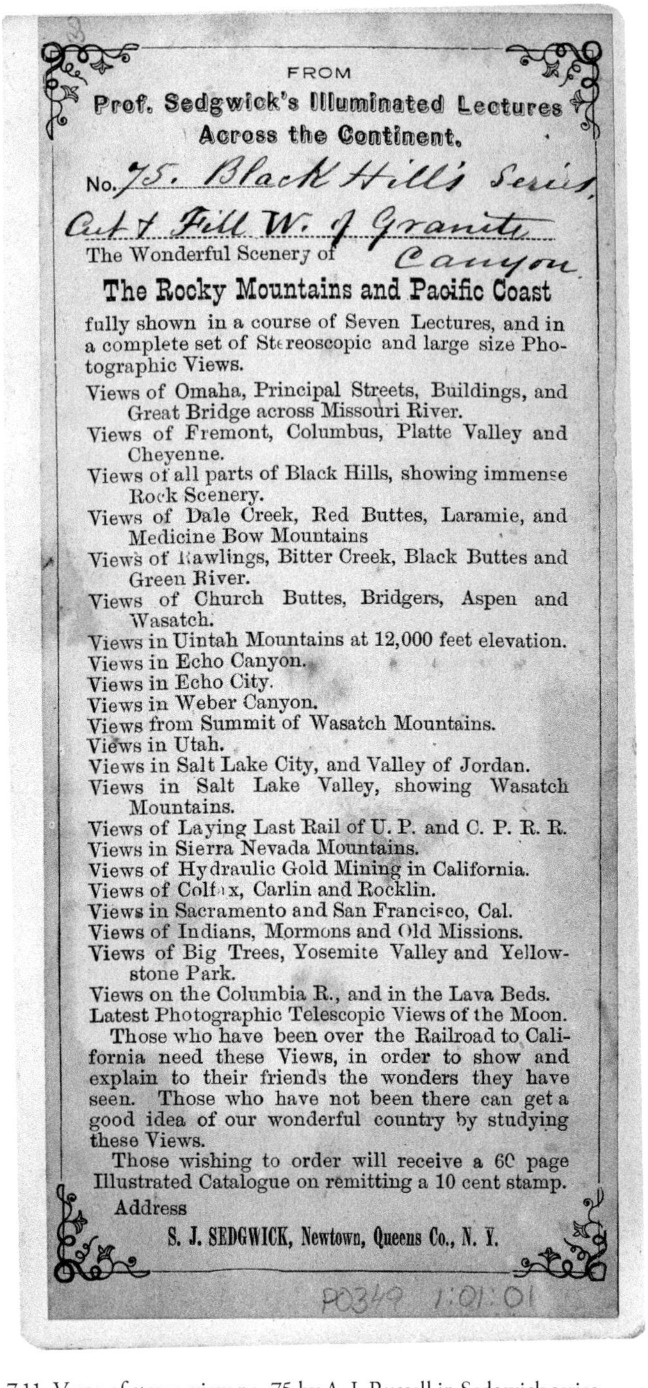

FROM

Prof. Sedgwick's Illuminated Lectures Across the Continent.

No. 75. Black Hill's Series

Cut & Fill W. of Granite Canyon

The Wonderful Scenery of

The Rocky Mountains and Pacific Coast

fully shown in a course of Seven Lectures, and in a complete set of Stereoscopic and large size Photographic Views.

Views of Omaha, Principal Streets, Buildings, and Great Bridge across Missouri River.
Views of Fremont, Columbus, Platte Valley and Cheyenne.
Views of all parts of Black Hills, showing immense Rock Scenery.
Views of Dale Creek, Red Buttes, Laramie, and Medicine Bow Mountains
Views of Rawlings, Bitter Creek, Black Buttes and Green River.
Views of Church Buttes, Bridgers, Aspen and Wasatch.
Views in Uintah Mountains at 12,000 feet elevation.
Views in Echo Canyon.
Views in Echo City.
Views in Weber Canyon.
Views from Summit of Wasatch Mountains.
Views in Utah.
Views in Salt Lake City, and Valley of Jordan.
Views in Salt Lake Valley, showing Wasatch Mountains.
Views of Laying Last Rail of U. P. and C. P. R. R.
Views in Sierra Nevada Mountains.
Views of Hydraulic Gold Mining in California.
Views of Colfax, Carlin and Rocklin.
Views in Sacramento and San Francisco, Cal.
Views of Indians, Mormons and Old Missions.
Views of Big Trees, Yosemite Valley and Yellowstone Park.
Views on the Columbia R., and in the Lava Beds.
Latest Photographic Telescopic Views of the Moon.

Those who have been over the Railroad to California need these Views, in order to show and explain to their friends the wonders they have seen. Those who have not been there can get a good idea of our wonderful country by studying these Views.

Those wishing to order will receive a 60 page Illustrated Catalogue on remitting a 10 cent stamp.

Address

S. J. SEDGWICK, Newtown, Queens Co., N. Y.

7.11. Verso of stereo-view no. 75 by A. J. Russell in Sedgwick series. *Courtesy of Utah State University, Merrill-Cazier Library, Special Collections, Nineteenth-Century Western Stereo-Views Collection.*

ship. Sedgwick was a natural promoter and Russell was not, so perhaps this relationship benefited both men.[33]

In the 1870s, glass-lantern slideshows replaced the moving panorama paintings in popularity. Sedgwick traveled throughout New England, New York, and Pennsylvania, giving his lectures using glass-lantern slides made from Russell's images. In his 1874 catalogue Sedgwick printed "testimonials" from satisfied lecture attendees. One such testimonial reflects the glossy rhetoric of the day but probably also reflects Sedgwick's skillful oration:

> Then came the Great West—the former State House, at Omaha, and following this a succession of scenes, true to nature and to art, of the Plains, the Rocky Mountains, suspension bridges, trestle bridges, tunnels (seeing the landscape through them), station houses, engine houses, cars of famous lengths, sleeping cars (views exterior and interior), rivers, a Mormon village, Vice-President Colfax and party, and a multitude of other objects most attractive and wonderful. His audience was transported to distant wilds, to terrific heights, translucent lakes, and natural scenes of the most disordered kind and others of peerless sublimity. The fearful sweep of the railroad grade and the self-poised rocks overhead. Yet, despite the dangers and the vast distance, we were made to feel eager to journey over the route to witness the scenes so charmingly presented. It will not surprise us

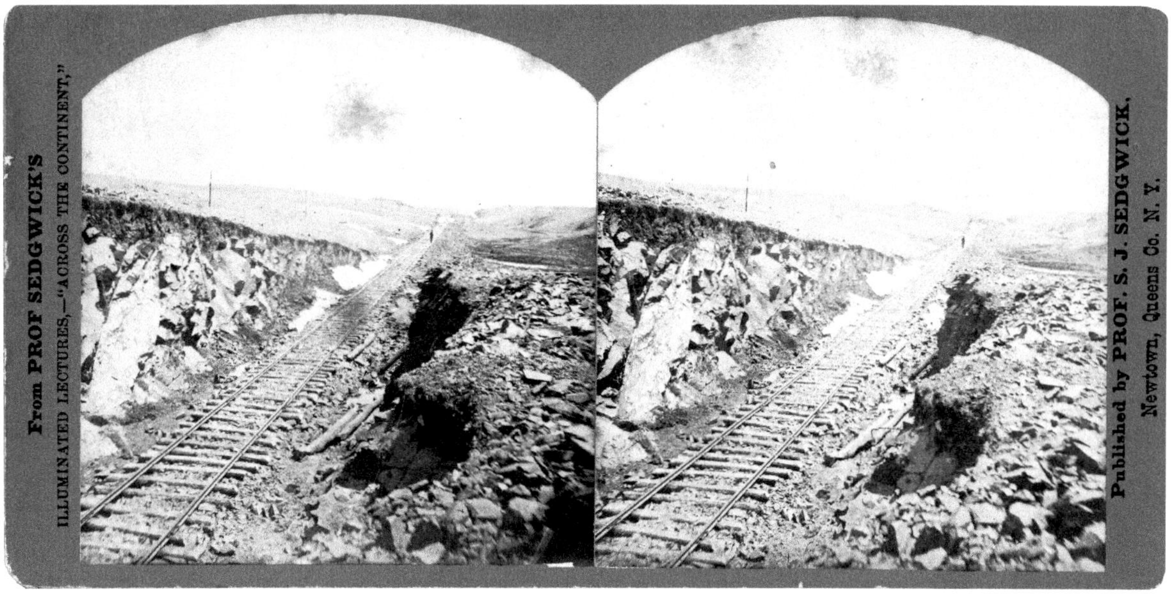

7.12. "Cut and Fill West of Granite [C]anyon" (front of stereo-view no. 75 by A. J. Russell in Sedgwick series). *Courtesy of Utah State University, Merrill-Cazier Library, Special Collections, Nineteenth-Century Western Stereo-Views Collection.*

> to learn that the great Pacific Railroad has gained a much larger passenger list by the Professor's ta[l]king exhibitions.[34]

Even if Russell did not control his negatives, he still had to earn a living. In addition to his work at *Leslie's*, Russell also maintained an art studio where he had a design and decorating business, painted large canvases from his western sketches, and did fresco work in hotels.[35] In 1872 he returned to Utah and then later sold a painting of Echo Canyon.[36] In other words, the remarkable flexibility he showed as an artist before his years with the Union Pacific was still very evident afterwards. This studio, and Russell's myopic art projects, probably became Russell's primary source of revenue after 1879. Despite his considerable talent with a camera, Russell, in contemporary credits, nearly always listed himself as an artist rather than photographer.

CHAPTER 8

Russell's Images and the Rise and Decline of Western Photography

"The construction of our railroads has so revolutionized the West, that at the present time we can see or realize very little of its former condition."

—Ferdinand V. Hayden

Russell died in obscurity on September 22, 1902. His wife followed not long after, on September 27, 1903.[1] What Russell did with his life after 1880 is still something of a mystery. In 1882 he applied unsuccessfully for the position of chief photographer in the Supervising Architects Office of the Treasury Department.[2] In 1891 he applied for a disability pension from the military. At that point he suffered from senility and failing eyesight.[3] In 1895 he was living with his daughter Cora in Saint Cloud, Minnesota, but he must have returned to Brooklyn at some point, because he is buried in the Cypress Hill cemetery.[4]

What is not a mystery is Russell's status in what is often referred to as the golden age of western photography.[5] This era was defined by high demand in the East for western views, the creation of high-quality artistic images, and a technological switch from daguerreotypes to collodion wet-plate glass negatives. If one had to put a start and a finish on this period, it begins with Carleton Watkins shooting what would become Yosemite National Park in 1861 on mammoth plate negatives and ends with William Henry Jackson leaving Hayden's U.S. Geological Survey in 1878. Despite the difficulties and expense of collodion wet-plate photography, all the western federal surveys as well as the major railroad companies employed a professional photographer. The best-known of this time include Russell, Watkins, and Jackson, as well as C. R. Savage, Timothy O'Sullivan, Edweard Muybridge, Alexander Gardner, and Alfred Hart. Lesser-known photographers include William Bell, Jack Hillers, Arundel C. Hull, and John Carbutt. These western photographers were adventurers, artists, scientists, and salesmen, and they scoured the West—on horseback, by wagon, on the railroads, and even by boat—to gain photographic "firsts."

When Russell began working for the Union Pacific in 1868, images of the West, especially stereo-views, were in high demand. Eastern audiences eagerly sought images of what was considered an inaccessible and romantic place, a place only a handful of people had seen firsthand. The completion of the transcontinental railroad created an unprecedented public interest in the West, along with the very real possibility that one could visit this exotic place. The Union Pacific, of course, benefited from this interest and used it to encourage ridership. For example, in *Sun Pictures of Rocky Mountain Scenery,* Hayden urged travelers to use the new railroad to study the geology of the West. He wrote, "I shall ask the reader to travel with me along the line of the Union Pacific Railroad . . . to cull a flower or examine an Indian village or read some wonderful legend which attaches to almost every portion of this country. . . . In many a locality we shall find the poet's utterance no fiction, that there are 'sermons in stones' . . . Scenes more wonderful than any related in the far-famed Arabian Nights."[6] *Leslie's Illustrated* predicted that Europeans would come to America to see the marvels of the West similar to Americans traveling to see the cultural marvels of Europe.[7]

The quality of these western images both artistically and technically was very high. Western photographers were usually conventional artists who turned to the medium for economic reasons. These men put a great deal of time and thought into their images, and they used large negatives—some as big as 20" x 24"—which provided remarkable clarity of detail. They went to extraordinary lengths to visit the hard-to-reach places of the West, so naturally they sought to create the highest-quality images possible. They knew their photography was, more likely than not, a one-time opportunity. After 1875, the demand for expensive high-quality images diminished as cheaper versions of traditional tourist destinations became more popular.[8]

Most important, however, is that during this golden age, with the help of new photographic technology, western photographers helped to shape the discussion of the importance of the West to the rest of the nation. In order to understand this influence one has to understand how people in the 1860s and 1870s viewed the images, both literally and symbolically. For example, we must understand that the public typically viewed different images in different formats than we do today. Today the large-format views of Russell are frequently used in exhibits, books, and online; the whole body of Russell's work has been mostly ignored in favor of a few dramatic photographs. In these images he portrayed the builders of the railroad in heroic terms as masters of an impossibly forbidding landscape. In the 1860s, however, the East enjoyed the visual spectacle of the West mostly through moving panoramas, woodcut illustrations in popular magazines, glass-lantern slide presentations, and stereo-views. Remarkably, Russell had his hand in all four mediums in one way or another. Historians, though, have typically neglected the influence of these other mediums, stereo-views in particular.[9]

In the late 1850s and early 1860s, Americans first viewed commercially produced photographs through the stereographic card, which boomed in popularity. Stereo-views revolutionized photography by providing affordable images of exotic locations for the average American. In the 1860s no respectable home was complete without a stereographic viewer and baskets of stereo-views which cost about two dollars per dozen. *Scientific American* commented: "The remarkable success which has attended the introduction of stereoscopes affords a theme for reflection. . . . The stereoscope is one of the means destined to advance our national taste for art. It affords amusement and instruction to children and pleasure to old age. It costs so little that we can calculate on its penetrating the homes of the humblest men."[10] Unlike daguerreotypes, ambrotypes, and tintypes (which are, technically, one-of-a-kind negatives) a stereographic image could be printed by the thousands from an original collodion wet-plate glass negative. The mass production of stereo-views opened up a vast new market for western photographers.[11]

Interest and popularity in the West by happy coincidence corresponded with the equal interest and popularity in the stereo-view. In fact, selling western stereo-views could be quite lucrative. It was rumored that John Wesley Powell paid off the mortgage for his Washington, D.C. home through the sale of stereo-views taken by his photographer John K. (Jack) Hillers.[12] The numerous western surveys used the popularity of stereo-views to help pay for their photographers and perhaps even for their expeditions by providing free copies to members of Congress who voted on yearly appropriation bills.[13] Russell's railroad images, not surprisingly, were among the most popular. It is hard to gauge this popularity because publication numbers are not available, but based on the number of extent copies today, they had to have been brisk sellers.[14] In 1870 *Leslie's Illustrated* noted: "Photographers have been busy, and already the stereoscopic views of the great overland route of American are for sale in the principal European cities. Everywhere they are exciting wonder and admiration."[15]

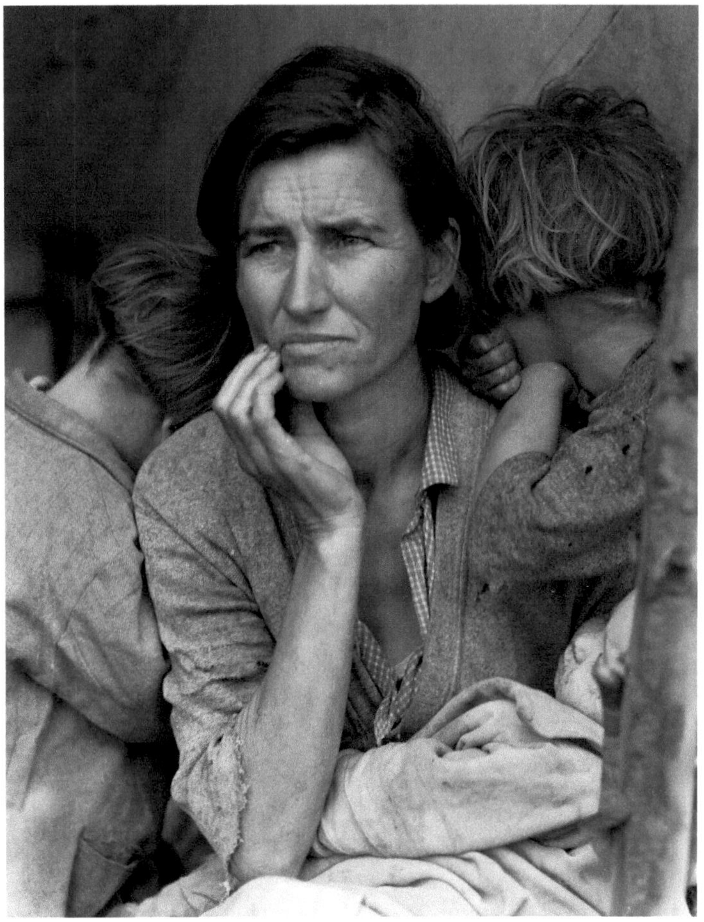

8.1. "Migrant Mother," by Dorothea Lange, 1936. *Courtesy of the Library of Congress, Prints and Photographs Division.*

In order to understand the importance to the public of these popular stereo-views one needs to think about narration. Images need commentary, even if it is only an internal dialogue, to explain their significance. This is true whether you are looking at your uncle's vacation to Mount Rushmore on Facebook or if you are selling stereo-views in the 1860s.[16] Russell's earlier moving panorama paintings and Sedgwick's glass-lantern slide lectures used a narrator who explained the significance of what the audience was seeing. Images in weekly illustrated newspapers were linked to stories or a caption—or both. Russell's stereo-view captions are short and not particularly descriptive, but there was an internal dialogue for people in the 1860s when looking at a stereo-view. The symbolic cultural significance of the transcontinental railroad, which might not be readily apparent today, was a major contributor to this internal dialogue. Members of every generation, in fact, will have images that carry a unique meaning whether it is Dorothy Lange's depression-era migrant mother, or Joe Rosenthal's flag-raising at Iwo Jima, or Nick Ut's photo of Phan Thi Kim Phuc as a child in Vietnam, burned and naked after a Napalm attack. For instance a railroad photographer used symbolism that provided an easy metaphor in 1869 not readily apparent today. The visual impact of a railroad line receding into the distant wilderness was a metaphor for the railroad bringing civilization to the West, and, frequently, for the "vanishing" Indian. Russell counted on his viewers connecting the imagery of the railroad and the idea of riding the transcontinental railroad with triumphant westward expansion.[17] The unspoken narration in Russell's stereo-views was that these photos fit within the larger narrative of the railroad bringing American institutions westward. In his writings and in his images, Russell did not, of course, challenge the idea that settlement of the West was anything other than a fulfillment of America's destiny, a necessary and desirable step in the progress of American institutions and American liberty. Russell's images fit within a narrative of an expansionist, progressive nation with the railroad acting as the essential agent in transforming the wilderness and uniting the county through economic growth.[18] Any other interpretation would have undercut the market for Russell's images and alienated his Union Pacific employers. Russell was, first and foremost, a capitalist with an artistic bent. He was a man who spied an economic opportunity and took it.

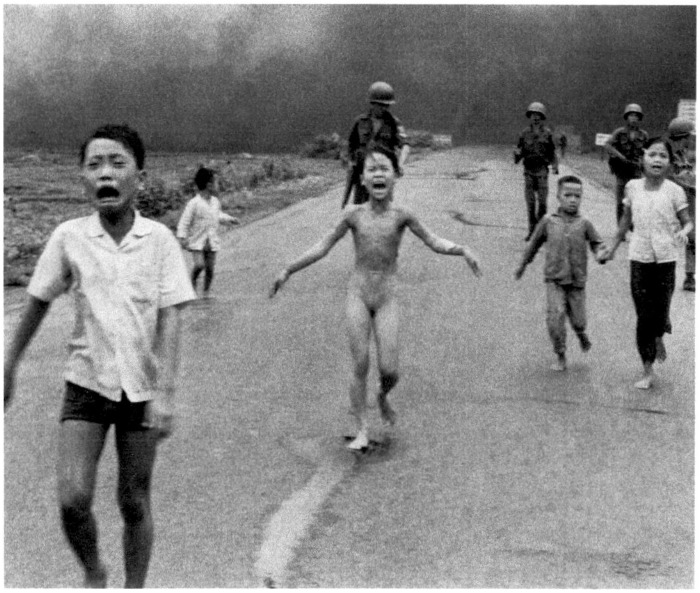

8.2. "Napalm Girl," by Huynh Cong "Nick" Ut, 1972. *From the Associated Press, AP Photo/Nick Ut.*

Russell's stereo-views were so popular because they fit within this patriotic narrative of the railroad. The prevailing public opinion was that if the Civil War represented a major problem for the idea of American exceptionalism, the completion of the Pacific Railway redeemed the county and proved that unity lay not only on a north to south axis, but also East to West. These ideas were so ingrained in the American consciousness that even newspaper editors struggled to describe the meaning of the Golden Spike Ceremony: "Human language," wrote the *Cheyenne*

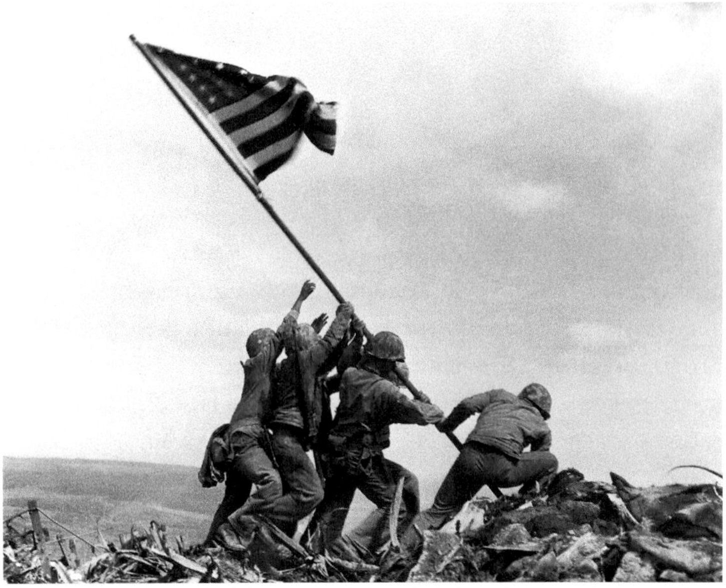

8.3. "Raising the Flag on Iwo Jima," by Joe Rosenthal, 1945. *From Associated Press, AP Photo/Joe Rosenthal.*

Daily Leader, "is inadequate to portray, in proper shape, the magnitude and importance of the work just completed. Even imagination is weak in its conceptions of the grandeur of results which shall unfold, in full and immediate realization of untold benefits to humanity."[19] Other commentators, however, found the words necessary to reflect on the importance of the completion of the Pacific Railroad. Nearly every politician, and every newspaper, in fact, used remarkably similar rhetoric. Themes that arise over and over were the binding of the East with the West, that the national destiny lay in the West, and that the rapid settlement of the West was crucial to the economic well being of the nation. As an added bonus, of course, the Pacific Railway paved the way to the supposed riches of Asia.[20]

Public perception of the intermountain West before the completion of the railroad, however, was decidedly mixed.[21] Some of the earliest narratives of the land west of the 100th Meridian were strongly negative. For instance, Edwin James, the botanist and geologist for Stephen Long's 1819 exploration party, which followed the Platte River from the Missouri River to the Rocky Mountains, wrote: "I do not hesitate in giving the opinion, that it is almost wholly unfit for cultivation, and of course, uninhabitable by a people depending upon agriculture for their subsistence. Although tracts of fertile land considerably extensive are occasionally to be met with, yet the scarcity of wood and water, almost uniformly prevalent, will prove an insuperable obstacle in the way of settling the country."[22] Numerous commentators, in fact, disparaged the habitability of the intermountain West from the 1820s and 1860s.[23] In 1868 Captain William Raynolds (who had spent the better part of 1859 and 1860 exploring the upper Missouri and Yellowstone Rivers in Montana and Wyoming) noted the issues that would be associated with a lack of water and wood: "I have no hesitation in asserting, that the greater portion of the whole country embraced within my line is unsusceptible of profitable settlement."[24] Although the idea of a great western desert was eventually dispelled, the notion that this area was mostly unsuitable for American settlement remained very much alive. *Leslie's Illustrated* wrote, "The American Desert, as it used to be marked on our school[day] maps, existed more in imagination than in reality;

there are no seas of sand utterly barren and desolate, though for practical purposes there is a great deal of land that is utterly worthless."[25] Even when politicians and boosters ramped up the rhetoric in the late 1860s, what Wallace Stegner referred to as "an age of the wildest emotionalism and nationalist fervor,"[26] there was still a recognition that the intermountain West would never be settled to the same extent as the rest of the nation. As late as 1873, popular author J. H. Beadle wrote: "In the West are regions of utter desert so vast that a New England State might be hidden in them, and only pass for a respectable oasis. Any route across the continent must traverse a complete desert from five hundred to a thousand miles wide. The Union Pacific enters upon it about Laramie, and with the exception of Salt Lake Valley, and perhaps two or three others, continues in all the way to the Sierras."[27]

Beyond the problems with inhospitable terrain, though, western travelers found a lack of amenities. Contrary to the popular perception of rugged nineteenth-century Americans who enjoyed sleeping under the stars, most travelers were highly concerned with comfort and the dearth of it out West. The crude conditions along the Union Pacific were a major theme for *Leslie's Illustrated* in 1870: "The proprietor of a genuine hotel on the plains is a dilapidated individual. . . . His establishment is a hastily-built affair, with sides of logs or rough boards, and a roof of canvas not always impervious to water. But the landlord is monarch of all he surveys, and will brook no insult, as his ready revolver will tell you."[28] A more serious problem was that the West was not entirely safe even for photographers. Ridgway Glover was an enthusiastic but reckless young man desperate to photograph in the West. He underestimated the danger that Sioux Indians posed at that time and he was killed and scalped in northern Wyoming on September 16, 1866.[29] Although some of the numerous reports of Indian attacks reported in popular periodicals were doubtlessly false or greatly exaggerated, in the mind of the public they must have created extreme unease.[30]

This is the background against which Russell photographed. By comparison his images paint the intermountain West much differently.[31] The directors of the Union and Central Pacific Railroads were eager to dispel any notions that the West was not safe for travelers or that the West could hold anything less than a glorious economic future. The railroad, in fact, would create a new destiny in the West, and the railroad's photographers would be crucial components in creating this new destiny. The photographs taken by Russell and others ultimately point to the future of the West rather than the past.[32] A viewer of Russell's images was shown that Salt Lake City was not the center of a dangerous and un-American religious sect, but a prosperous, progressive city with new stone and brick buildings as well as modern conveniences. Wyoming was not a wasteland fit neither for man nor beast, but was home to geological fascinations and vast coal deposits. Russell's photos of Mormon irrigated fields, for instance, showed that the land only needed a bit of irrigation to be fertile. His images of timber and rivers and lakes proved that the West was not a treeless and waterless wasteland. His stereo-views of coal and gold mining operations "proved" that mining as well held a bright future. Finally, his depiction of the towns, stone and brick structures, and even hotels

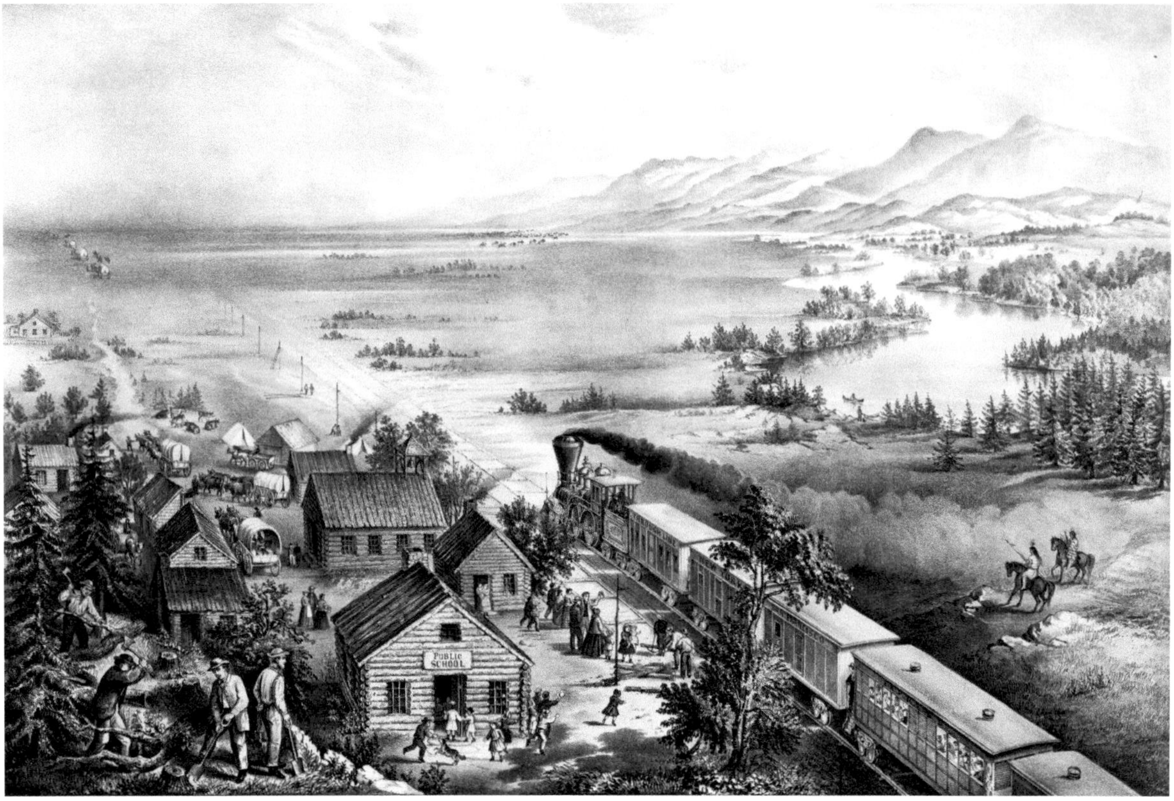

8.4. "Across the Continent: Westward the Course of Empire Takes Its Way," by Francis Palmer, 1868. *Courtesy of Utah State University, Merrill-Cazier Library, Special Collections.*

and restaurants "proved" that the West had the amenities necessary for eastern travelers. For example, a seemingly simple image of a hotel or restaurant in Grand Island, Nebraska, reassured a traveler that comfortable accommodations really existed. Stereo-views of churches and stone buildings in Laramie, Wyoming, dispelled the notion that all Union Pacific towns were rowdy hell-on-wheels affairs consisting of only canvas structures. Russell, perhaps unwittingly, emphasized the possibilities of a prosperous, but also safer and more comfortable West. This West was not a dangerous place fit only for (as it was commonly expressed in popular literature) "wild beasts and savages." Although there were vast spaces in the West, there was also industry, railroads, mining, and modern cities. This "new West" was a safe place to travel through, and maybe even to relocate and begin a new life. The railroad was, of course, the primary agent of this transformation. Hayden, who, like Russell, vigorously promoted the rapid settlement of the West wrote that "the construction of our railroads has so revolutionized the West, that at the present time we can see or realize very little of its former condition."[33] The well-known travel journalist Samuel Bowles would expand on this idea: "So completely is the Pacific Railroad henceforth the key to all our New West; so thoroughly must all knowledge of the characteristics of the latter radiate out from the former as a central line, that its story should be told almost at the outset, even to the anticipation of earlier experiences."[34] As a railroad photographer Russell had a unique role among western photographers in helping to shape this national narrative of a new West. His photographs were important in showing a railroad that not only linked Omaha with Sacramento, but that also opened up the previously undeveloped western interior to settlement. This West was a land of limitless economic potential tamed by the transcontinental railroad.[35]

A NEW VISION OF THE OLD WEST

One might suggest that Russell was the same as peddlers of Wild West imagery who would come later in the 1880s. Did he not oversell the possibilities of western settlement and undersell the inherent drawbacks of western aridity? Did he not romanticize the work of the Union Pacific and the land it traversed through images such as "East and West Shaking Hands"? As well, Russell ignored the harsh realities of the building of the Pacific Railroad. Workers were killed and maimed to enrich a small band of already wealthy easterners who manipulated markets to reap huge profits, and the dispossession of Native American Indians from their land and culture was hastened. The key, however, is that one must examine the totality of what he did, including the stereo-views, rather than the few, mostly large-format images frequently reproduced for coffee table books. It is true that Russell's large-format views were more romanticized and distorted, ignoring the underlying issues of the building of the transcontinental railroad. But remember that his stereo-views, along with other formats, had a much wider audience and these views are remarkably ordinary. As the public eagerly followed the progress of the transcontinental railroad in their hometown newspapers, they yearned for images that illustrated what seems mundane in the twenty-first century, but that fit within their understanding of why the railroad was so important. In effect, Russell was creating a visual catalog of the railroad. Most notably, he consciously included the employees who actually built the line, but also the towns and stations, the overnight accommodations, the roundhouses, the bridges, tunnels, cuts, and even geologic wonders.[36] Although he had economic reasons for what he did, and his images were infused with capitalist symbolism, Russell showed in his stereo-views the West as it was, more or less. He did not need to create a romantic vision of the West in order to get people to purchase his photographs.

Similar to all artists, western photographers had their own biases and created their own distortions. Yet they also offered a much more realistic depiction of the American West than later evocative re-creations found in dime novels, Wild West shows, rodeos, movies, and popular TV shows. In his stereo-views Russell offered a straightforward visual experience, and he did not need to manipulate his images into an alternate vision in order to maintain the public's interest. If anything his images always looked forward to a new future (not a nostalgia for the "old West") created by the transcontinental railroad. The West, accompanied with a triumphant capitalistic narrative, but mostly unadorned, was enough for the public in the 1860s and 1870s. This unique opportunity to make high-quality realistic images would only last for a few years. Russell and Gardner left the West, O'Sullivan passed away, Watkins got too old, Savage focused on his art store, and Muybridge, in his pursuit of motion pictures, lost interest. The demand for unique high-quality images waned as the public looked for cheaper copies of familiar tourist destinations. The West did not appear as romantic, exotic, and adventurous as earlier and a "freshening" of the subject was needed to hold the public's attention.[37] Thus the realism of the photograph gradually became surpassed for a far more romanticized vision. Long before Buffalo Bill Cody popularized the Wild West, these photographers, however briefly, created a new vision of the old West.

EPILOGUE

The Forgotten Photographs of the Union Pacific, from Obscurity to Rediscovery

"The genius lies with whoever moved the earth and set the grade."

—Weston J. Naef and James N. Wood

One gets the sense that Russell was a quiet, modest, thoughtful man who just got caught up in the big events of his time. His relative obscurity was, in part, caused by his lack of self-promotion. Russell did not do much "horn tooting" and thereby was relegated to a footnote (as the author of the famous Golden Spike Ceremony image) in the story of American photography, whereas he really deserves his own chapter. For example, the popular 1919 book *Building the Pacific Railway* by Edwin L. Sabin does not even mention Russell nor does it mention his attendance at the Golden Spike Ceremony. Russell's legacy was obscured for a number of reasons. He did not maintain control of his Civil War and Union Pacific images and subsequently others (usually Mathew Brady and Stephen Sedgwick) received the credit. As well, the more realistic depiction of the interior West that he and the other western photographers created in the 1860s and 1870s was largely overshadowed by popular Wild West imagery. And finally, his biography was just not seen as relevant. Even when his photographs were used and he was credited, Andrew J. Russell was just a name with no backstory. Accordingly his images were not placed within the context of their creation or analyzed as art, and the stereo-views were nearly completely neglected.[1] A photographer, however, can live a second life. The layers of obscurity have slowly been peeled back.

Russell's large-format photographs from *Sun Pictures of Rocky Mountain Scenery* and *The Great West Illustrated* were still used, despite his biographical obscurity, and from the 1910s to the 1950s several of these images were featured in popular historical publications. Books such as *Trails, Rails, and War: The Life of General G. M. Dodge* and *Hear the Train Blow* reproduced numerous Russell photographs.[2] Even then, however, photography was not the principle method that the public used to visually conceptualize the West. Photographs are stuck to a single time and place and just cannot be manipulated to the extent of other mediums in order to re-create a colorful, romantic vision of the old West. More popular from the 1920s to the 1960s were western movies and television shows.

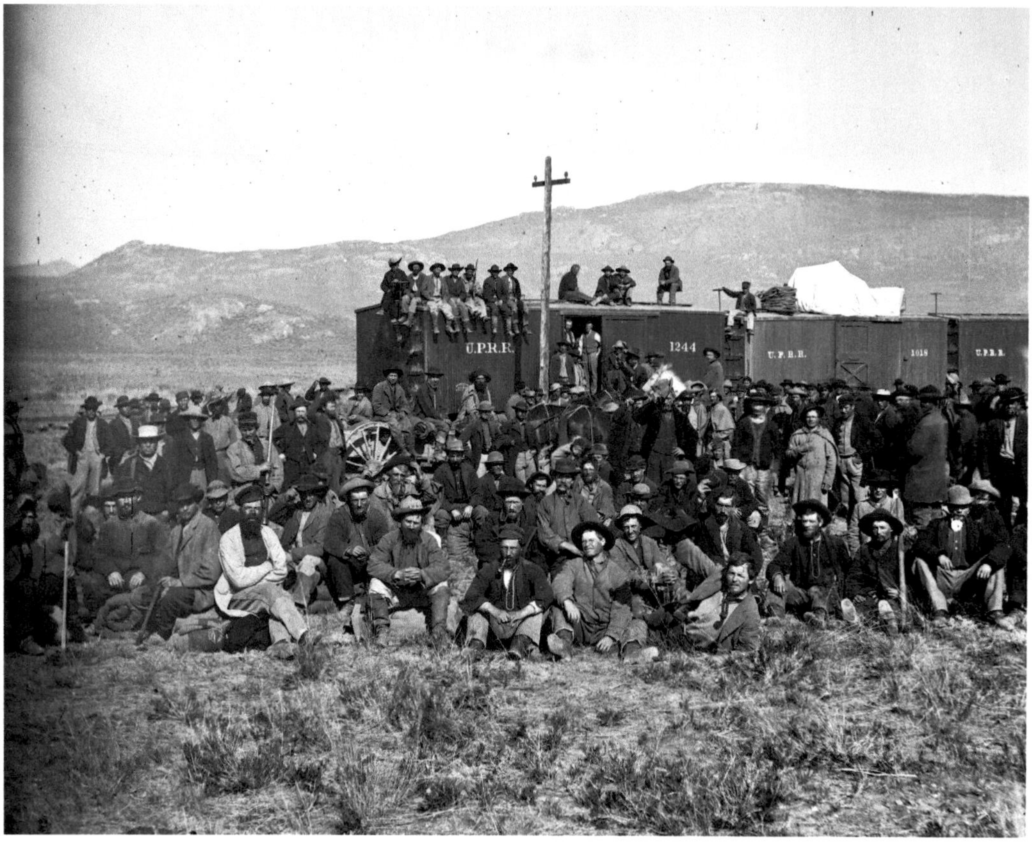

9.1. Cropped version of A. J. Russell stereo-view no. 513, "Paymaster's Car, Blue Creek." *Courtesy of the Oakland Museum of California, A. J. Russell Collection.*

In the 1960s, however, through the work of William Pattison (a professor of geology at the University of California, Los Angeles) details of Russell's life emerged. Russell was definitively acknowledged as the author of not only the famous Golden Spike image, but also numerous other well-known western photographs.[3] In the late 1950s, Pattison conducted research on Stephen Sedgwick's lectures of the 1870s and came across a large cache of original wet-plate negatives housed at the New York Geographical Society. These negatives, of course, were the result of Russell's labor in 1868 and 1869. Stephen Sedgwick possessed the negatives and his daughter inherited them in 1920. She gave them to her family doctor Abbott C. Combes, who donated them to the New York Geographical Society in 1940, still in their original slotted wooden cases. At that time they were thought to have been taken by Sedgwick.[4] Pattison realized that images attributed to Russell in *Sun Pictures of Rocky Mountain Scenery* and *The Great West Illustrated*, as well as numerous others, matched up with the negatives in the New York Geographical Society collection.[5]

Now the basic biographical details were known, and a large cache of original negatives was identified.[6] As the hundredth anniversary of the Golden Spike Ceremony neared, authors used Russell's images as part of a patriotic, self-congratulatory rhetoric.[7] Although these writers acknowledged Russell's authorship, who took the photographs was not important, rather that they reinforced a certain viewpoint about the West. It was not until the 1970s when artistic analysis and academic rigor began to be applied to the golden age of western photography. An entire chapter of *Era of Exploration* was devoted to Russell. This chapter added further biographical detail and placed Russell's images within the context of artistic developments of the day, comparing his work with that of other western photographers.[8] This interest in new interpretations of western photography came from a number of sources with a much wider acknowledgement of photography as an art form and from the rise of a healthy collector's market. If western landscape photography was art, then biographical details and historical background were obviously important in establishing context. In the 1980s and 1990s this interest in the historic and artistic influences on Russell's work continued with the work of Susan Danly Walther and Susan Williams. Walther, as an art historian, placed Russell's photographs (along with those of Alexander Gardner) within the context of artistic conventions of the time. Williams added a great deal of biographical information and data about individual images, and she started to create a chronology of his Union Pacific photographs.[9] Most recently Glenn Willumson's book *Iron Muse* synthesized the work of earlier authors and created a new understanding (using the conceptual framework of Martha Sandweiss's *Print the Legend*) of the railroad photographs by both Russell and Alfred Hart. Willumson emphasized that Russell's work should be considered as part of a larger corporate archive. As such his images need to be placed within the story of the creation of this archive. As well, as a corporate photographer, Russell had much less artistic license than commentators had assumed.[10] Willumson also analyzed how Russell's work fit within other visual media of the time, such as printed illustrations.

But even as Russell has emerged from the shadows of historical obscurity, there are still other layers of mystery that await further investigation. It is my hope that *Across the Continent* will lead the way to a greater use of Russell's entire body of work. In particular the stereo-views still remain underutilized in comparison to the large-format images. This is somewhat understandable because the large-format images provide a stunning amount of detail. We can, however, now get quality images by scanning the smaller stereographic negatives. The images that once were so hard to track down are freely available online from numerous institutions, such as the New York Public Library, the University of Iowa Special Collections, Utah State University Special Collections, the Library of Congress, and the Oakland Museum of California.[11] As well, stereo-views are available for sale from numerous online sources and rare book and antique dealers.[12] While these stereo-views do not have the visual drama of the large-format views, they could be the illustrative basis for filling in the details needed to create a new kind of history of the Union Pacific Railroad.

The Union Pacific Railroad laborers fall in a kind of historical donut hole; a no-man's-land situated somewhere between old West, labor, business, and popular history. Labor historians have ignored the transcontinental railroad because of a dearth of primary sources and a lack of conflict with management. Even the new West historians with their emphasis on gender, race, class, and the environment have stayed away. In the 1980s and 1990s these historians set the tone for questioning the standard narratives of the American western experience; but in a rush to condemn the excesses of a capitalist system and the government that supported this system, they avoided even the appearance of endorsing those who helped build this system. Richard White's thought-provoking and exhaustively researched book *Railroaded* does not mention the irony of western laborers who were part of the dominant culture, but who occupied a subordinate role.[13] Perhaps White is just not comfortable with the story of laborers who created something that, in his eyes, should not have been created at that time.[14] Surely, though, we can find a middle ground. The Union Pacific Railroad is worthy of in-depth study because it was one of the first modern, large corporations in the United States, and it is nearly impossible to overstate its importance in the minds of Americans desperately seeking a symbol of national unity. We can still be awed by the fact that it was a staggering achievement while acknowledging that not everyone reaped its benefits.

The 150th anniversary of the completion of the transcontinental railroad in 2019 will be celebrated with numerous exhibits, proclamations, and probably as much "speechifying" as the original ceremony of 1869. From an engineering, finance, and construction standpoint these celebrations are justified. The building of this railroad was truly an amazing accomplishment. In 1865 the conventional wisdom was that it would take at least ten years, and maybe twenty, to get it done. There was nothing but a few small forts for over five hundred miles between eastern Nebraska and the Mormon settlements in Utah. With the railroad, a trip that had taken as much as three months now took three days and separated family members who could not endure the harsh trip across the prairies could now be reunited. Also, the overall economic benefits to the interior mountain West were undeniable. California boomed with access to eastern markets. Western products, such as silver, beef, coal, wheat, and wool, could be shipped back East at a fraction of the previous cost. That said, we also should remember that it was a messy, ugly business. Employees risked their lives just by working on the Union Pacific. In addition to death by industrial accident, murder by criminals, and exposure to inclement weather, they were also sometimes killed by hostile Sioux and Cheyenne Indians. Corruption, already rampant in government and finance, became even worse. Corrupt politicians were bribed for favorable legislation, corrupt government officials were bribed to write favorable reports, and even journalists were bribed to write favorable newsprint. The displacement of Native Americans from their lands continued at an even faster pace. Violent hell-on-wheels towns sprang up across Nebraska, Wyoming, and even Utah, and a few already wealthy men made huge amounts of money through sleight-of-hand fiscal machinations while workers were sometimes denied their wages. Instead of writing about the same five or six men and using the same five or six images over and over again that mythologize the railroad, maybe we could also focus on the engineers, surveyors, graders, spikers, clerks, cooks, teamsters, and everyone else who lived and died to get the thing done. Maybe, in a small way, the stereo-views that focus on these engineers, surveyors, graders, spikers, clerks, cooks, and teamsters can be a start to creating a more well-rounded, complete, in-depth—almost three dimensional—vision of the railroad. A new history of the Union Pacific based on the story of its laborers would illuminate how these laborers did not come West as discoverers, to trap furs, to fight Native Americans, or to settle the land. Like Russell they traveled to and through the West, gained a small measure of fame, and returned, no doubt, changed as a result.

The iconic photograph of the Golden Spike Ceremony that you knew about even before you read this book is one of the best-known images in American history. Yet a photograph is only an accurate representative of a single time and place, a tiny fragment, easily manipulated, of the larger truth. In the end, the Golden Spike image captures just one small moment in what was the building of the transcontinental railroad. If we are to fixate on one image, a better one is figure 9.1 of Union Pacific laborers waiting for their paychecks. My attempt to recover the life of just one man among thousands who worked for the Union Pacific can serve as a small example for other historians. Let us start by focusing on the thing that is right before our eyes in the famous photograph and in my alternate image, the people who made it happen. The key to a better understanding of the construction and meaning of the first transcontinental railroad is staring back at us in the faces of the people in the image, most of whom still remain anonymous.

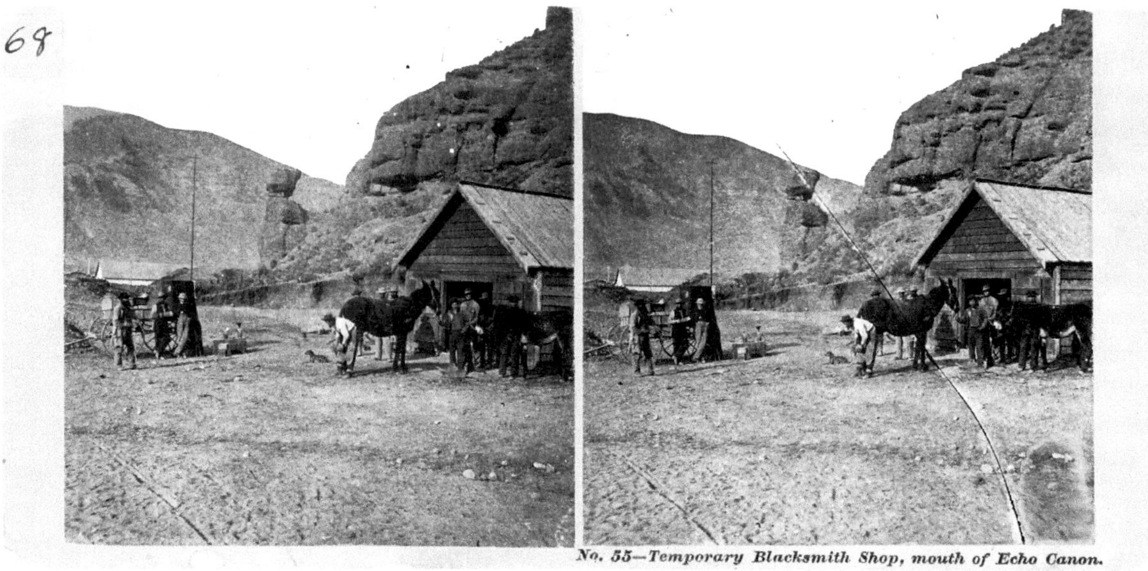

Catalog 1 Front of Union Pacific R.R. Across the Continent series, with A. J. Russell stereo-view no. 357. (This series used Russell's earlier numbering system.) *Courtesy of the University of Iowa Libraries, Special Collections, Levi O. Leonard Railroadiana.*

CATALOG OF RUSSELL'S UNION PACIFIC PHOTOGRAPHS

Introduction to the Catalog

During the summer of 2010 I explored the Union Pacific Railroad line in Utah, Wyoming, and Nebraska. This adventure led me from the May 10 celebration at Promontory Summit, to modern downtown Omaha, to scrambling along cliff faces, to a ten-mile hike into the High Uinta Wilderness area. The insight gained from actually seeing the line and then looking at copies of Russell's images and thinking about how he created them was invaluable. I could not have created this catalog had I not traveled along the route. During this summer, however, I discovered the need for a single catalog of Russell's work that includes both stereo-views and large-format images. Although it seems a simple concept to create a catalog of Russell's Union Pacific photographs (after all, he numbered his views and placed the stereo-views in series, putting captions on the verso side), the task is deceptively tricky.

There is an almost bewildering number of stereo-view styles printed by Russell himself, and some later by O. C. Smith and Stephen Sedgwick (see figs. Catalog.1 through Catalog.9 for examples) who, in fact, did not credit Russell. Causing further confusion, verso styling might be consistent with the front of the sterio-view, but in many cases the front might be plain with no verbiage. Russell actually employed two numbering systems (in this catalog I am using the more expansive system found in the Rocky Mountain Scenery series). As well, some stereo-views have no identifying information at all, but based on the subject, camera position, placement of figures, and numbering, they are clearly by Russell. Also, later, cheaper lower-quality versions were used in the American Views series (see fig. Catalog.3). There are even unlabeled stereo-views that have handwritten numbers and descriptions on the verso (see fig. Catalog.4).[1]

Russell sometimes did not describe his own images accurately. For instance, he clearly was confused about which cut is which at Promontory. As well, some of the stereo-views have no identifying information on the verso or, in some cases, have the wrong identification on the verso. Rocky Mountain Scenery was the final set of stereographic images Russell sold, and considering he was describing over six hundred images, it is not surprising that with this series, in particular, he blundered a few times.

Another problem in identifying Russell's stereo-views is that both Russell and Mormon photographer Charles Roscoe Savage sold identical images. The two photographed, sometimes side by side, in Echo Canyon and the Weber Narrows, and even traded negatives. We should also be wary of crediting Russell for every Union Pacific view in the late 1860s and early 1870s because there were several others, in addition to Savage—John C. Carbutt, Arundal C. Hull, C. W. Carter, and William Henry Jackson—who also took very early views of the Union Pacific. I hope this catalog with clear up some of the confusion about who took which photograph.

The final, but most vexing problem is that of Russell's odd numbering system. For instance, for the stereo-views he has numerous "alternate" views, which are different but similar views given the same number. Sometimes that number has an added letter listed on the negative or image and sometimes not. These alternate views are not listed in the Rocky Mountain Scenery series although for stereo-view no. 71 there is a 71A and a 71B. The problem is that it is not always clear what is the definitive image, versus which is the alternate. The further one looks, in fact, the more alternate versions come out of the woodwork. It is impossible to say with certainty that this catalog has captured all of Russell's alternate images. One can make an argument that with the stereo-views, he was creating two sets of negatives, one for himself and one for Union Pacific. I should also point out that large-format images do not fare much better. There are no alternate images, but sometimes he added 1/2 to a number for two similar views and sometimes, for mysterious reasons, he added a letter instead.

Inevitably some judgment calls had to be made. I came to the conclusion that Russell himself (or his assistant) was inconsistent and sometimes incorrect with his numbering system. The most definitive sources are the numbers that Russell himself wrote on the original negatives housed at the Oakland Museum of California. Although even then, he wrote the number and description as much as a year and a half after he took the photo.[2] The second best source is an original stereo-view with a verso description. Yet one has to be careful here, as well, because sometimes these numbers do not match numbers from the original negatives, and at times the wrong series list is used on the verso. The list in this book comes from the titles listed on original stereo-views on the verso of the Rocky Mountain Scenery series, Russell's numbering on the negatives themselves, the content of the image matched to a description, and viewing firsthand the locations on the Union Pacific line from Omaha to Promontory.

In May of 1863 the *Baltimore American* included an article about Russell's Civil War photographs and asked a question: "Why should not the Government have a good photographic officer and the needful staff or assistants with each division of the army in active service? . . . The pictures thus procured, and the records, descriptions, accompanying them, might be deposited in the Government archives, to be considered invaluable hereafter in making up the details of this great conflict of the age."[3] Thus the idea of creating a publicly accessible archive of Russell's work has its origins back to the Civil War, but this idea has never been fully realized for his Civil War images.[4] Even a publicly accessible archive of his Union Pacific negatives at the Oakland Museum of California did not open until 1969. It is my hope that I can lead researchers to an institution that houses an original, whether this is the Oakland Museum of California, the Union Pacific Railroad Museum, or somewhere else, to get the best-quality reproduction.[5] I think, as well, that this catalog will aid local communities along the route of the Union Pacific in seeking out Russell's images. These communities are located within a transportation corri-

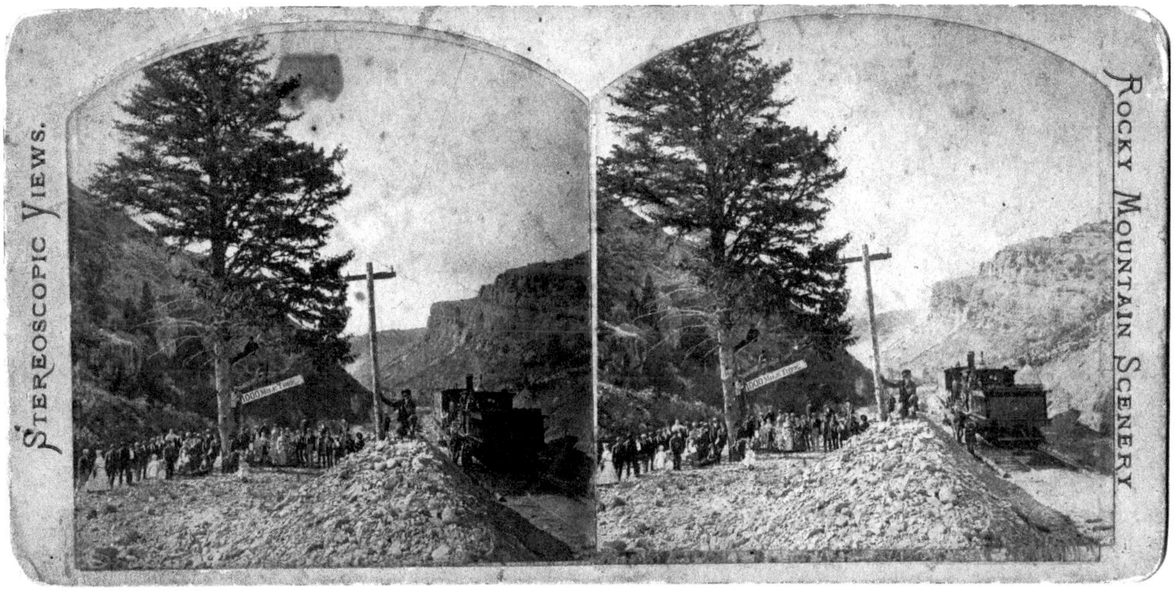

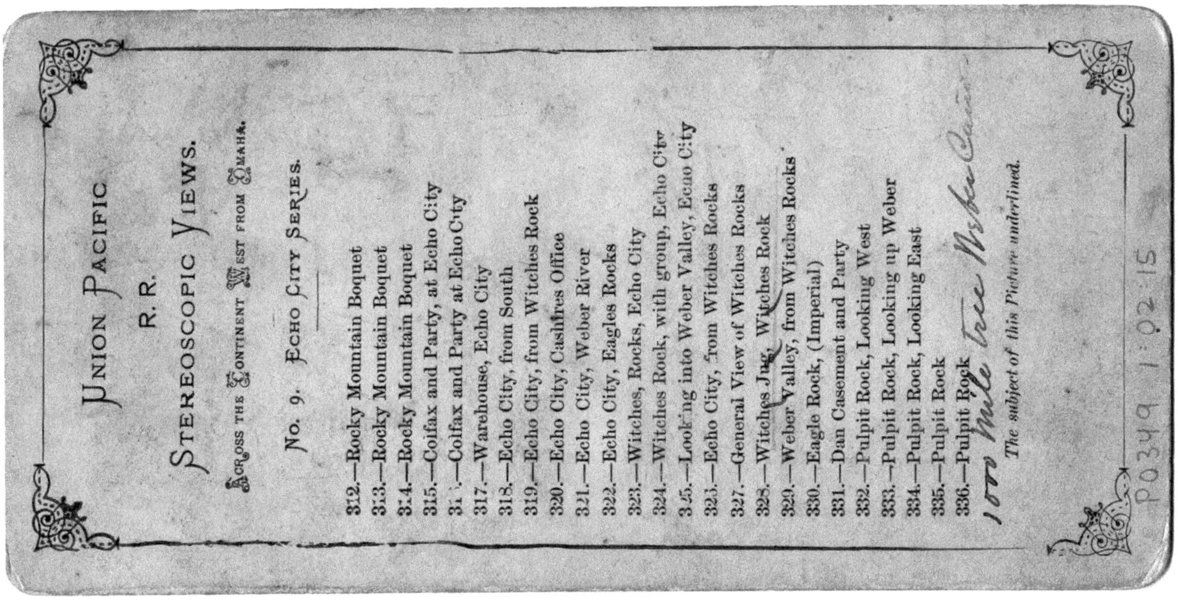

Catalog 2 Front and verso of Russell's Rocky Mountain Scenery, Stereoscopic Views series, with A. J. Russell stereoview no. 369. *Courtesy of Utah State University, Merrill-Cazier Library, Special Collections, Nineteenth-Century Western Stereo-Views Collection.*

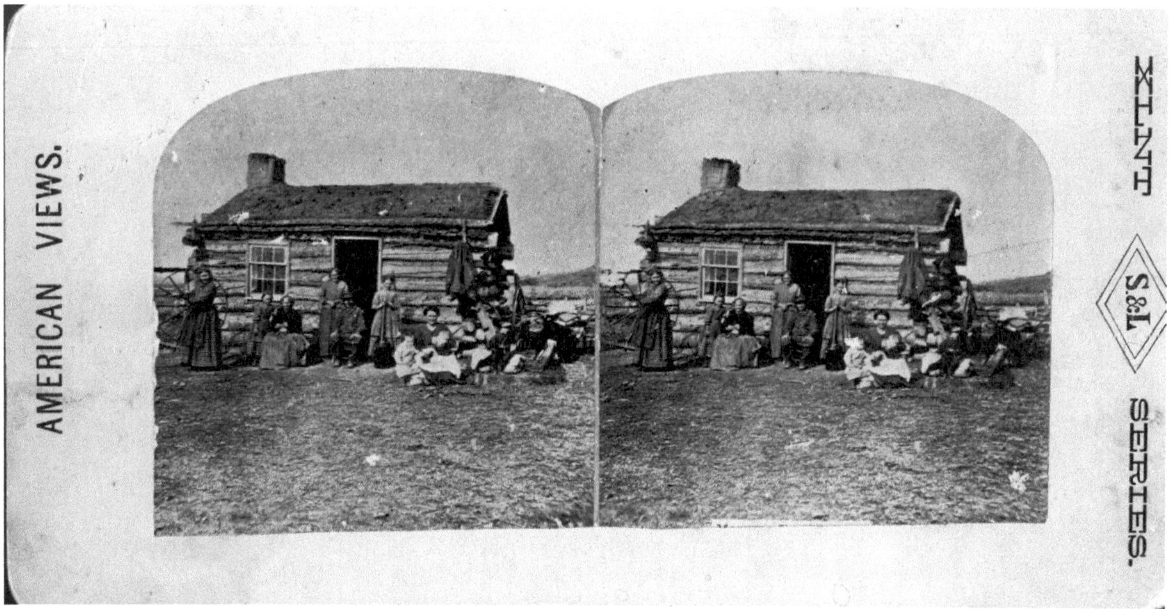

Catalog 3 Front of American Views series (note image is lower quality than earlier Russell, Smith, and Sedgwick printings), with A. J. Russell stereo-view no. 481. *Courtesy of Utah State University, Merrill-Cazier Library, Special Collections, Nineteenth-Century Western Stereo-Views Collection.*

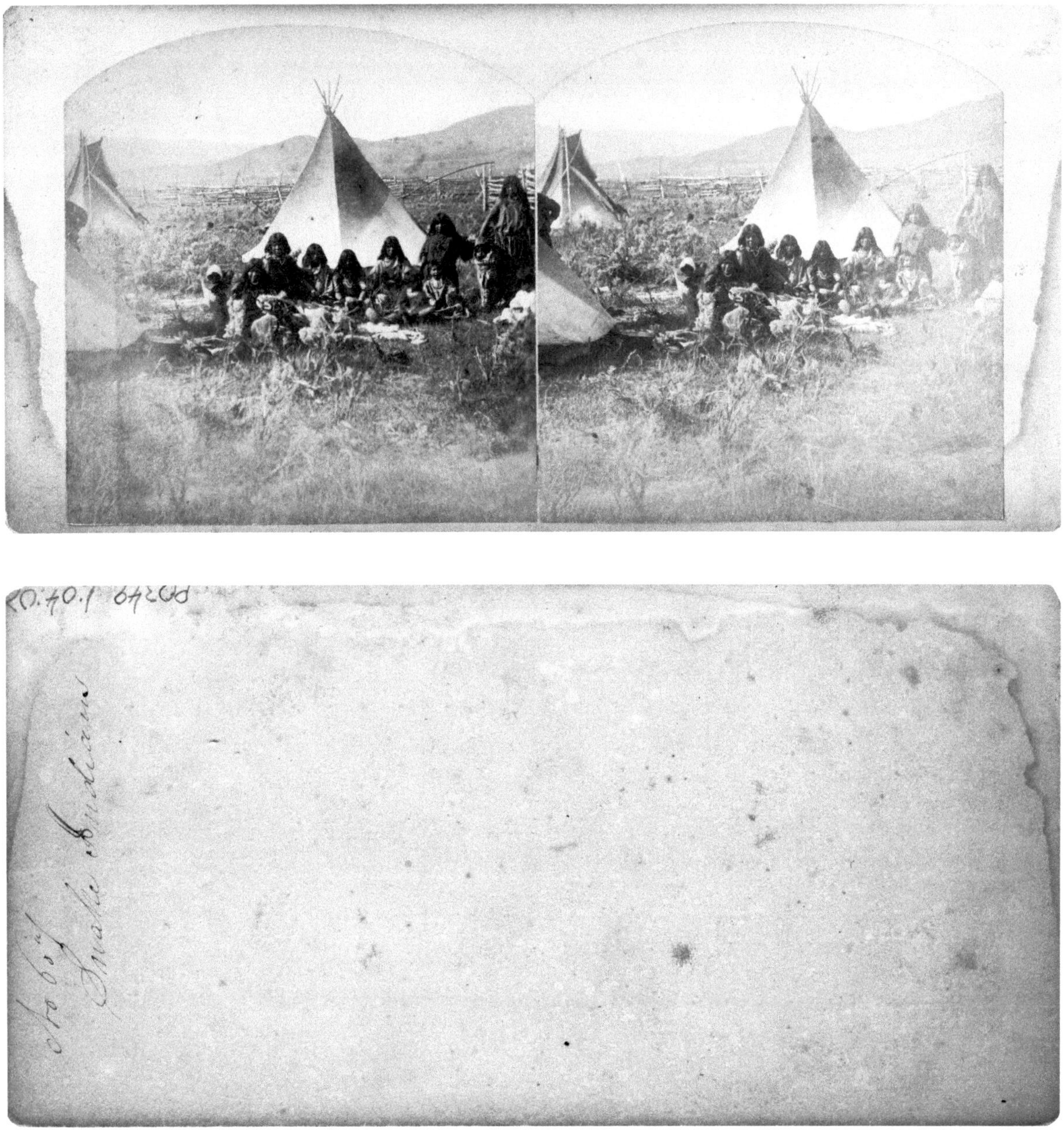

Catalog 4 Front and verso of untitled printing with handwritten description, with A. J. Russell stereo-view no. 607. *Courtesy of Utah State University, Merrill-Cazier Library, Special Collections, Nineteenth-Century Western Stereo-Views Collection.*

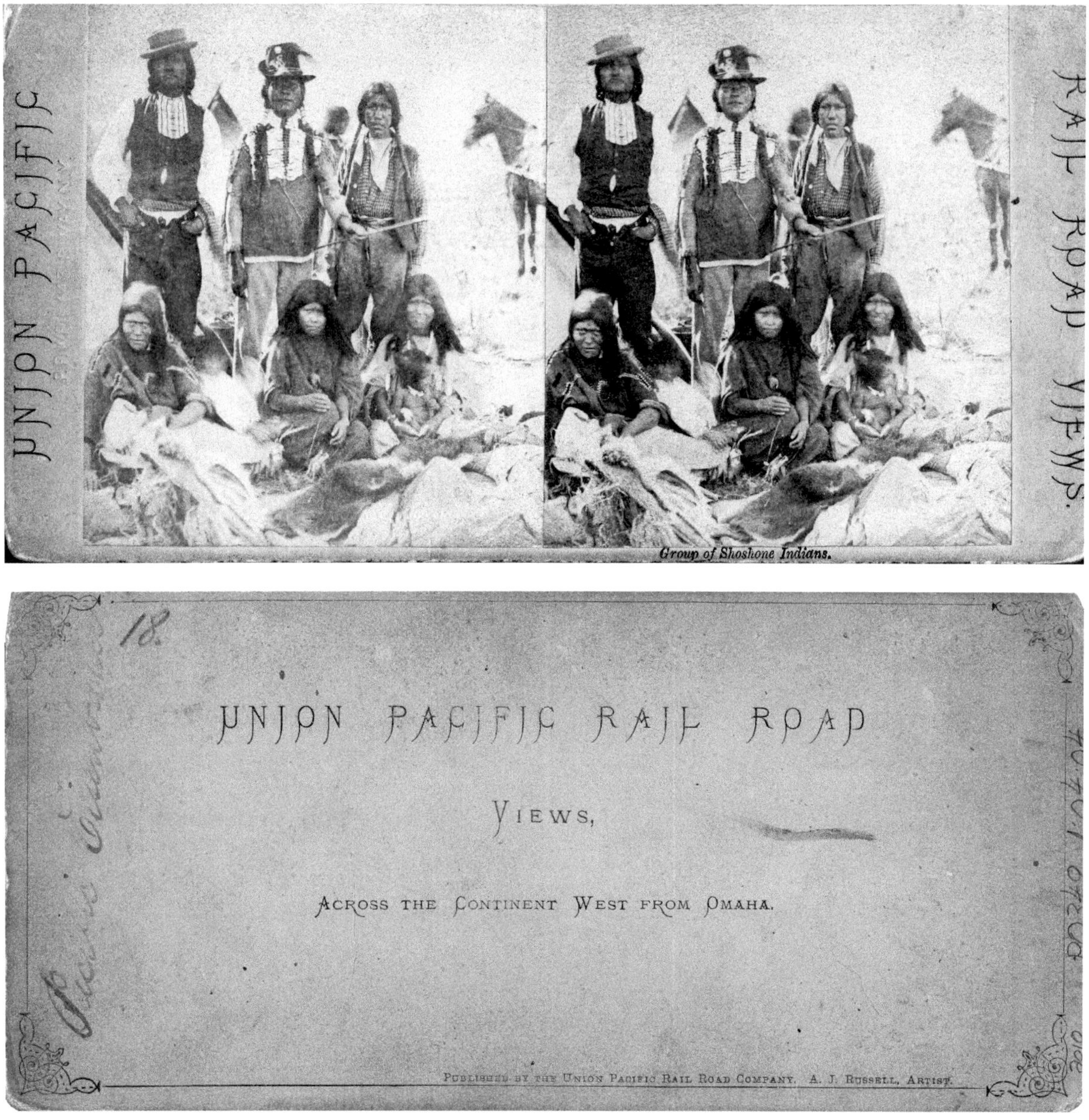

CATALOG 5 Front and verso of West from Omaha series (note that this is the only series "published by the Union Pacific Rail Road Company"), with A. J. Russell stereo-view no. 580. *Courtesy of Utah State University, Merrill-Cazier Library, Special Collections, Nineteenth-Century Western Stereo-Views Collection.*

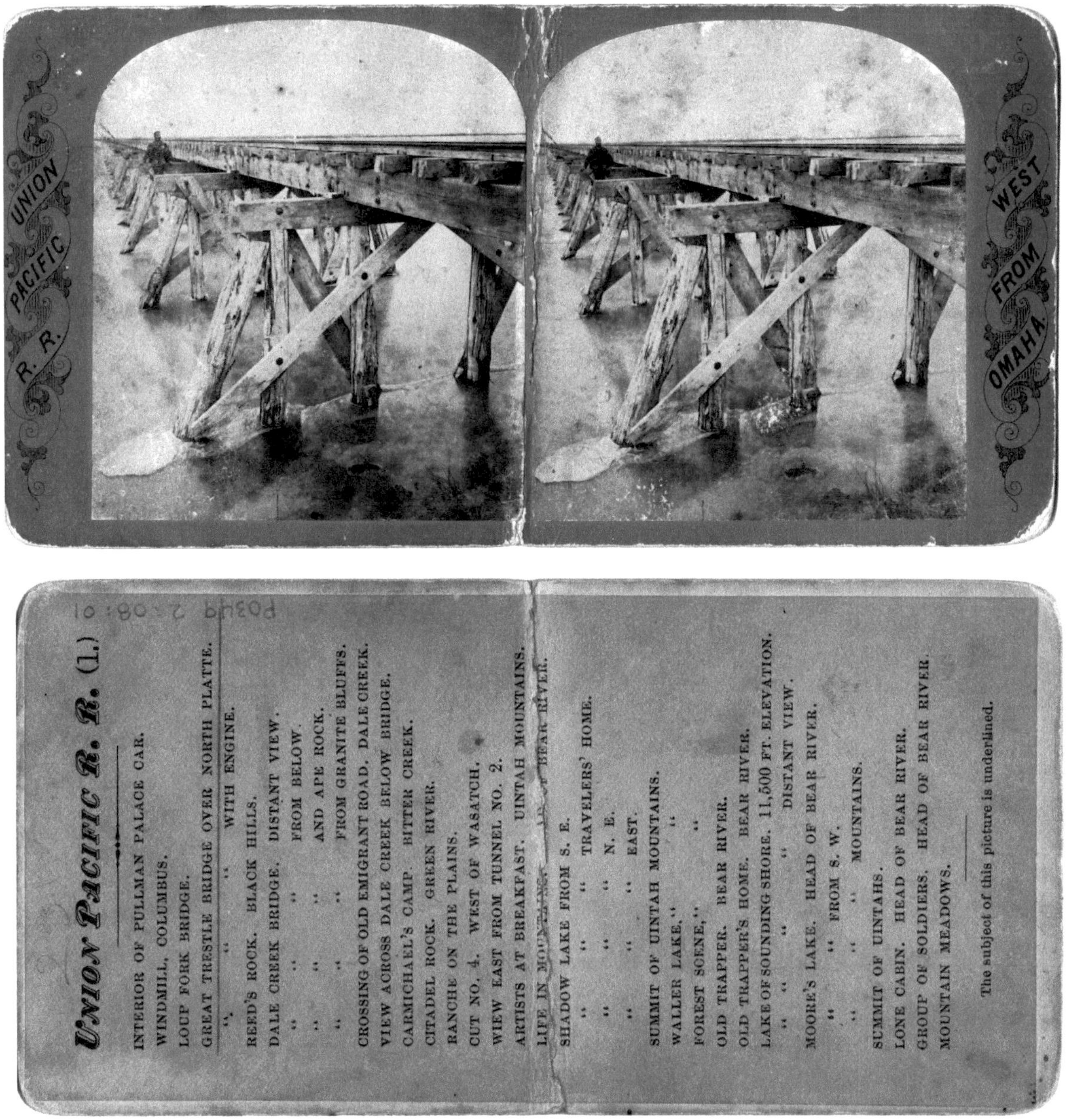

UNION PACIFIC R. R. (1.)

INTERIOR OF PULLMAN PALACE CAR.
WINDMILL, COLUMBUS.
LOUP FORK BRIDGE.
GREAT TRESTLE BRIDGE OVER NORTH PLATTE.
" " WITH ENGINE.
REED'S ROCK. BLACK HILLS.
DALE CREEK BRIDGE. DISTANT VIEW.
" " " FROM BELOW.
" " " AND APE ROCK.
" " " FROM GRANITE BLUFFS.
CROSSING OF OLD EMIGRANT ROAD, DALE CREEK.
VIEW ACROSS DALE CREEK BELOW BRIDGE.
CARMICHAEL'S CAMP. BITTER CREEK.
CITADEL ROCK. GREEN RIVER.
RANCHE ON THE PLAINS.
CUT NO. 4. WEST OF WASATCH.
WIEW EAST FROM TUNNEL NO. 2.
ARTISTS AT BREAKFAST. UINTAH MOUNTAINS.
LIFE IN MOUNTAINS. HEAD OF BEAR RIVER.
SHADOW LAKE FROM S. E.
" " TRAVELERS' HOME.
" " " N. E.
" " " EAST.
SUMMIT OF UINTAH MOUNTAINS.
WALLER LAKE. "
FOREST SCENE. " "
OLD TRAPPER. BEAR RIVER.
OLD TRAPPER'S HOME. BEAR RIVER.
LAKE OF SOUNDING SHORE. 11,500 FT. ELEVATION.
" " " DISTANT VIEW.
MOORE'S LAKE. HEAD OF BEAR RIVER.
" " FROM S. W.
" " " MOUNTAINS.
SUMMIT OF UINTAHS.
LONE CABIN. HEAD OF BEAR RIVER.
GROUP OF SOLDIERS. HEAD OF BEAR RIVER.
MOUNTAIN MEADOWS.

The subject of this picture is underlined.

CATALOG 6 Front and verso of Union Pacific R.R., West from Omaha series, with A. J. Russell stereo-view no. 51. *Courtesy of Utah State University, Merrill-Cazier Library, Special Collections, Nineteenth-Century Western Stereo-Views Collection.*

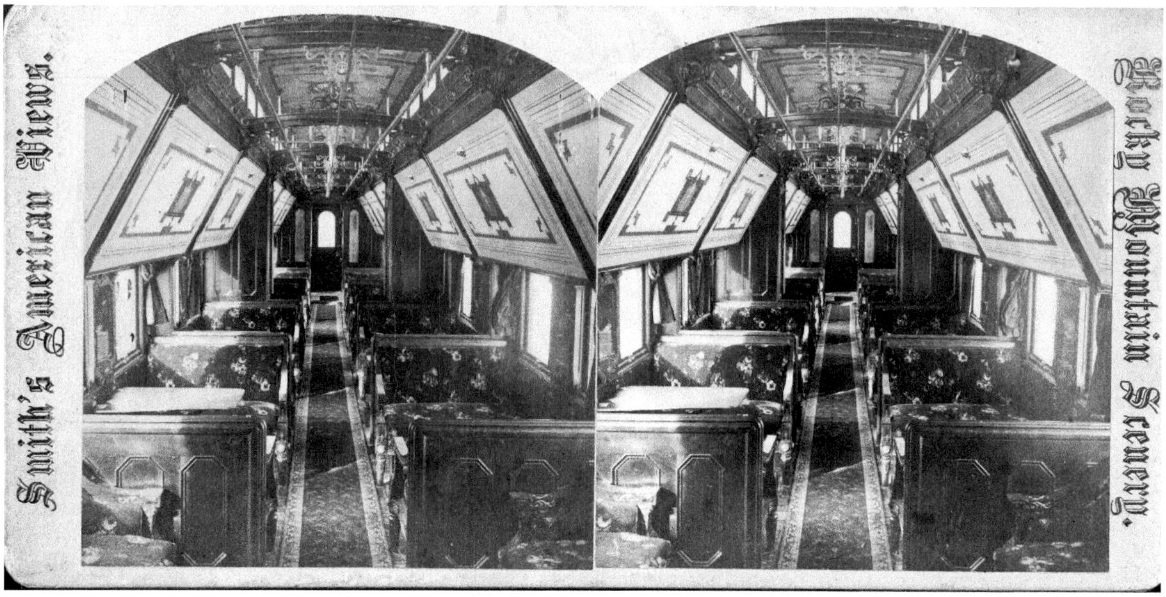

Catalog 7 Front of Smith's American Views, Rocky Mountain Scenery, with A. J. Russell stereo-view no. 20. *Courtesy of Utah State University, Merrill-Cazier Library, Special Collections, Nineteenth-Century Western Stereo-Views Collection.*

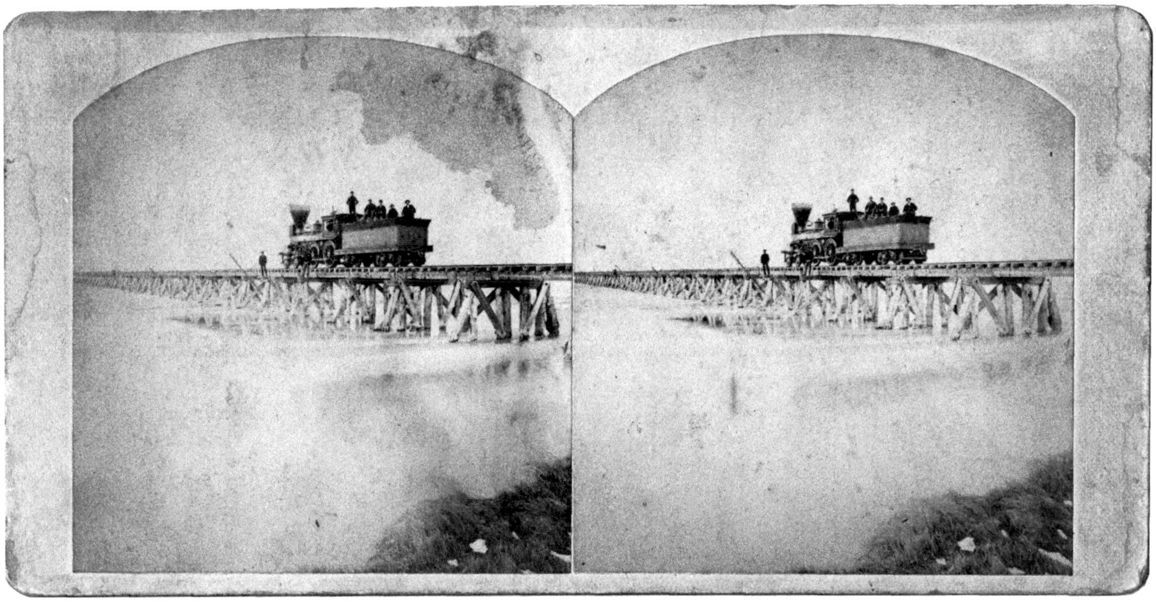

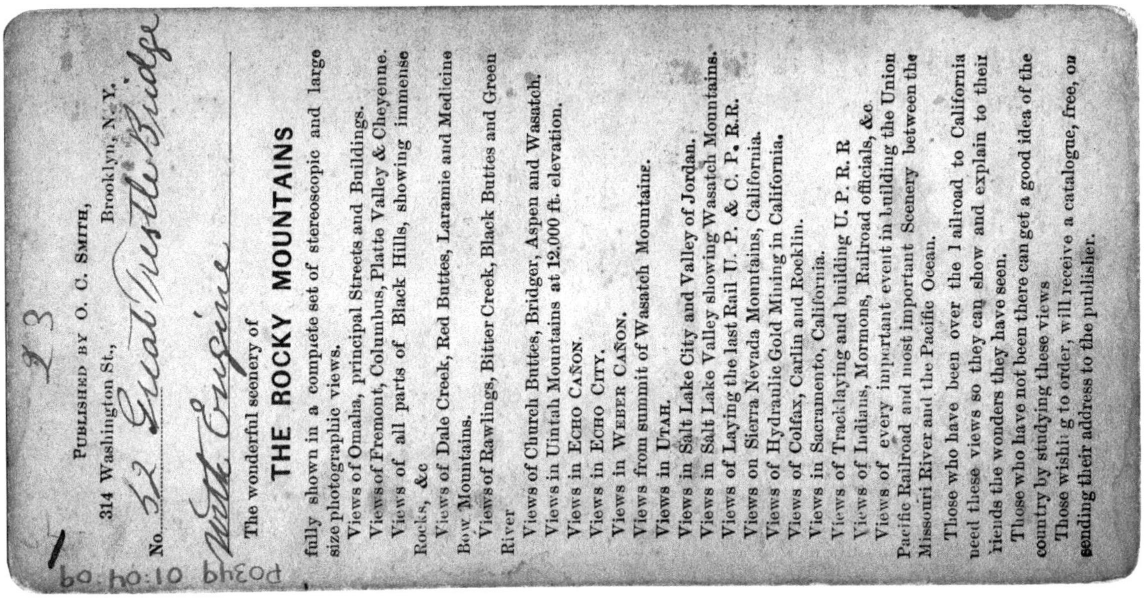

PUBLISHED BY O. C. SMITH,
314 Washington St., Brooklyn, N. Y.
No. 52 Great Trestle Bridge with Engine

The wonderful scenery of
THE ROCKY MOUNTAINS
fully shown in a complete set of stereoscopic and large size photographic views.
Views of Omaha, principal Streets and Buildings.
Views of Fremont, Columbus, Platte Valley & Cheyenne.
Views of all parts of Black Hills, showing immense Rocks, &c
Views of Dale Creek, Red Buttes, Laramie and Medicine Bow Mountains.
Views of Rawlings, Bitter Creek, Black Buttes and Green River
Views of Church Buttes, Bridger, Aspen and Wasatch.
Views in Uintah Mountains at 12,000 ft. elevation.
Views in ECHO CAÑON.
Views in ECHO CITY.
Views in WEBER CAÑON.
Views from summit of Wasatch Mountains.
Views in UTAH.
Views in Salt Lake City and Valley of Jordan.
Views in Salt Lake Valley showing Wasatch Mountains.
Views of Laying the last Rail U. P. & C. P. R.R.
Views on Sierra Nevada Mountains, California.
Views of Hydraulic Gold Mining in California.
Views of Colfax, Carlin and Rocklin.
Views in Sacramento, California.
Views of Tracklaying and building U. P. R. R
Views of Indians, Mormons, Railroad officials, &c.
Views of every important event in building the Union Pacific Railroad and most important Scenery between the Missouri River and the Pacific Ocean.
Those who have been over the railroad to California need these views so they can show and explain to their friends the wonders they have seen.
Those who have not been there can get a good idea of the country by studying these views
Those wishing to order, will receive a catalogue, free, on sending their address to the publisher.

CATALOG 8 Front and verso of Smith's Wonderful Scenery of the Rocky Mountains series, with A. J. Russell stereo-view no. 52. *Courtesy of Utah State University, Merrill-Cazier Library, Special Collections, Nineteenth-Century Western Stereo-Views Collection.*

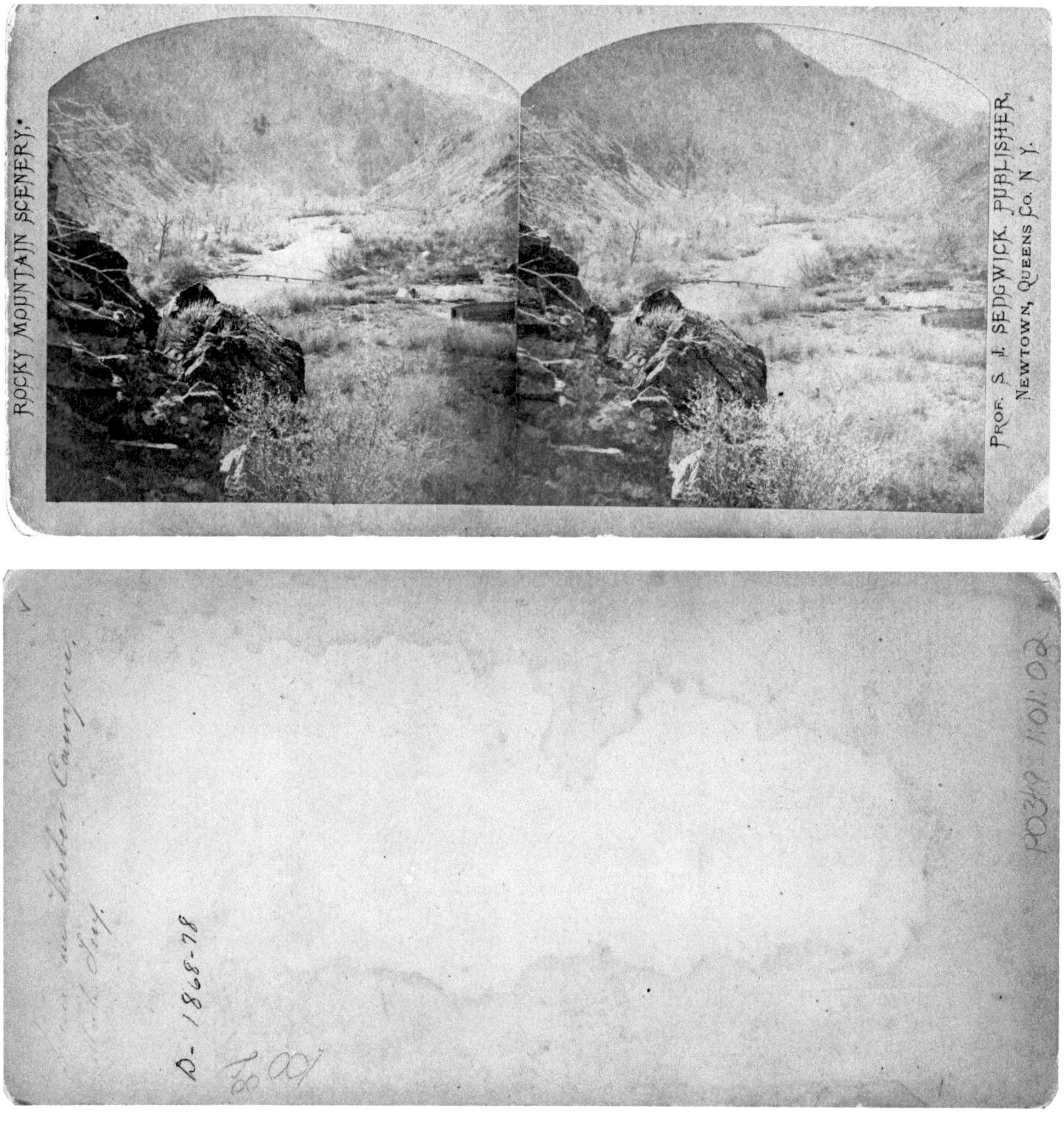

CATALOG 9 Front and verso of Sedgwick's Rocky Mountain Scenery series, with A. J. Russell stereo-view no. 376. *Courtesy of Utah State University, Merrill-Cazier Library, Special Collections, Nineteenth-Century Western Stereo-Views Collection.*

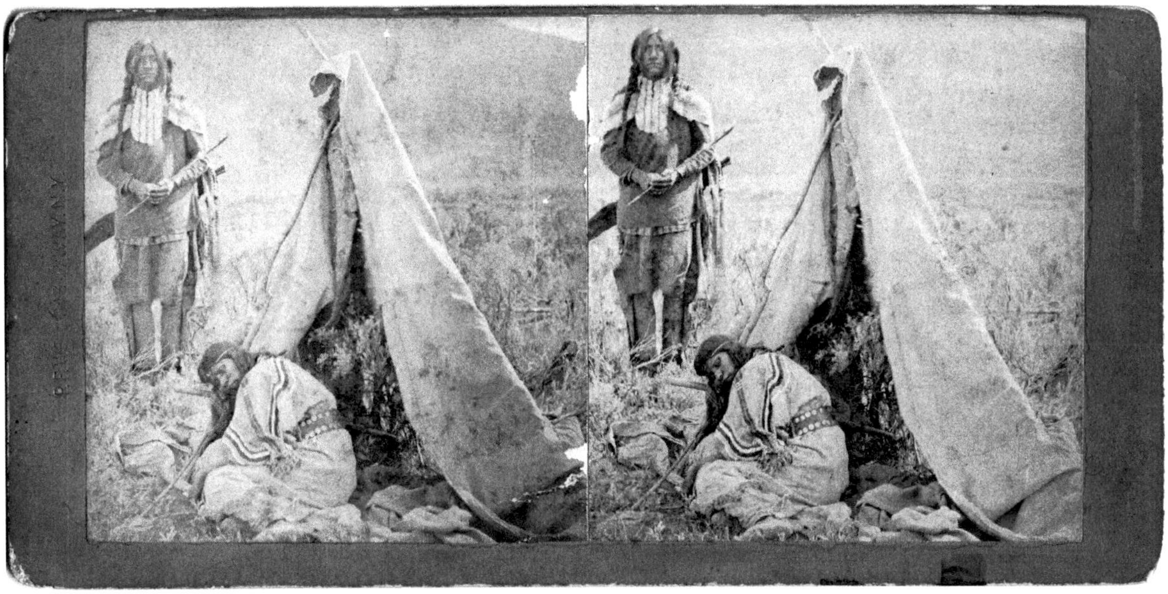

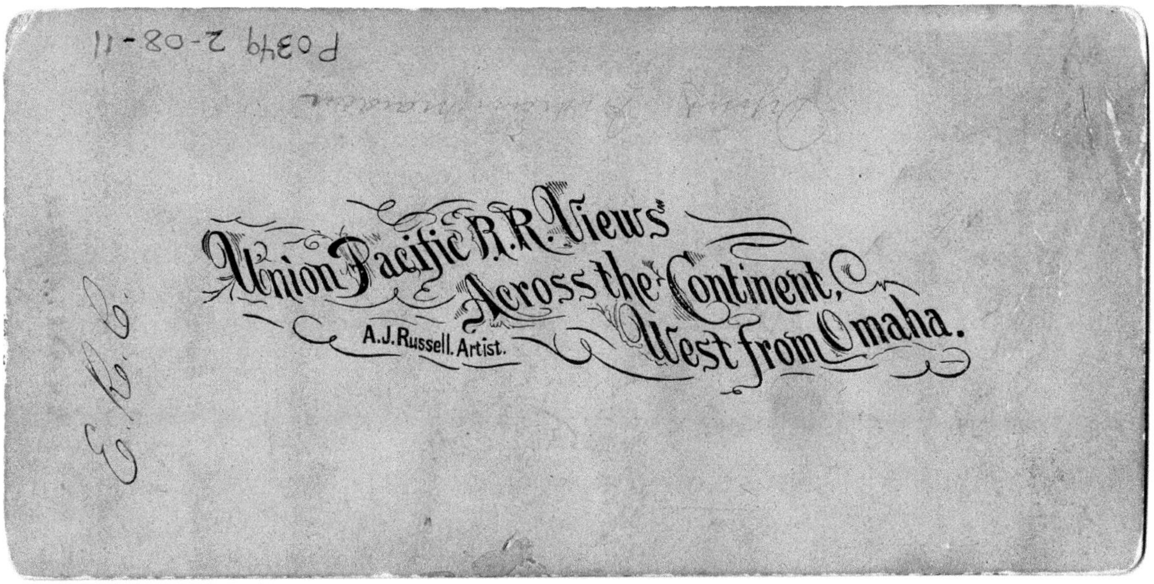

Catalog 10 Front and verso of Union Pacific R.R. Views across the Continent series (note this series consists of 1868 images and is usually numbered), with A. J. Russell stereo-view no. 581. *Courtesy of Utah State University, Merrill-Cazier Library, Special Collections, Nineteenth-Century Western Stereo-Views Collection.*

dor that started with Native American migrations and continued with wagon trails, the pony express, the transcontinental railroad, the Lincoln Highway, and finally, the interstate highways. The lives of the people along the old Union Pacific line are shaped by the building of the transcontinental railroad in ways they might not even realize. I would also encourage adventure seekers to use the catalog to travel along the route of the Union Pacific for themselves, to complete their own then-and-now re-photography projects.

The individual stereo-view titles are taken directly from the titles listed on the verso of the Rocky Mountain Scenery series. Obvious misspellings were corrected and are indicated with brackets. For whatever reason, sometimes locations were included and sometimes not. As well, for some images I could not find a copy at any institution and these are indicated as "not available" in parentheses. Luckily in only one case did Russell double-number an image in the Rocky Mountain Scenery series (no. 31 in his stereo-views), and only once did a specific image from the Oakland Museum of California not match up with the corresponding image at the Union Pacific Railroad Museum (no. 232 in his stereo-views). An imperial view (not to be confused with a large-format view) is one image, instead of dual images, eight inches wide, taken with one lens of a stereo-view camera. The large-format view descriptions are from Russell's descriptions on the original negatives, or from the descriptions in Russell's *Great West Illustrated*.

Finally, this catalog could only be complete if I could examine every Russell stereo-view held in private or public hands in the United States, Canada, and Europe. Because I cannot, it is inevitable that this catalog does not contain every Russell stereo-view and all the alternate versions that were published in the various sets of Russell stereos. I believe, however, that this catalog captures 98 to 99 percent of all Russell images published.

ABBREVIATIONS

UPRM refers to the Union Pacific Railroad Museum, Union Pacific Collection, Photography Archives, A. J. Russell Views.

OMCA refers to the Oakland Museum of California, A. J. Russell Collection of original negatives.

USU refers to Utah State University, Merrill-Cazier Library, Special Collections and Archives, Nineteenth-Century Western Stereo-Views Collection.

ROCKY MOUNTAIN SCENERY (ROCKY MOUNTAINS) STEREOSCOPIC VIEWS

No. 1. Omaha Series[6]

1. "U.P.R.R. Offices" (UPRM)
2. "Catholic Church and Cozens Hotel" (UPRM and OMCA)
3. "Looking down Douglas Street" (UPRM and OMCA)
4. "View of Churches, Omaha" (Not Available)
5. "Block on Douglas Street" (UPRM and OMCA)
6. "Street Scene, Thirteenth Street, Omaha" (UPRM)
7. "Block on Farn[h]am Street" (UPRM and OMCA)
8. "Omaha from Old Capitol" (UPRM, which has an alternate view, and OMCA)
9. "Looking down Farn[h]am Street, Omaha" (UPRM)
10. "Omaha from Height" (UPRM and OMCA)
11. "U.P.R.R. Offices" (Not Available)
12. "Farn[h]am Street from Height" (UPRM)
13. "Block on Farn[h]am Street" (UPRM)
14. "General View of Omaha" (UPRM)
15. "Churches No. 2" (UPRM)
16. "Street View of Machine Shop" (UPRM)
17. "Interior of Passenger Coach, Omaha" (UPRM)
18. "Interior of Passenger Coach, Omaha" (Not Available)
19. "Passenger Coach, U.P.R.R." (UPRM)
20. "Interior of Pul[l]man Palace Car" (USU)
21. "Machine Shops from Bluffs" (UPRM and OMCA)
22. "Machine Shops, Omaha" (UPRM and OMCA)
23. "Turn Table and Machine Shops" (UPRM and OMCA)
24. "Tank and Machine Shops" (UPRM and OMCA)
25. "Distant View Machine Shops" (UPRM and OMCA)
26. "Interior of Carpenters' Shops" (UPRM and OMCA)
27. "Omaha Machine Shops from West" (UPRM and OMCA)
28. "Machine Shops Looking West" (UPRM and OMCA)
29. "Machine Shops from Lumber Yard" (UPRM and OMCA)
30. "Bird's Eye View of Omaha" (Not Available)
31. "Old Capitol, Omaha" (OMCA, which lists "Old Capitol of Omaha" as 30)

No. 2. Platte Series

31. "Fremont Hotel" (UPRM and OMCA, which has an alternate view)[7]
32. "Main Street, Fremont" (UPRM and OMCA)
33. "Fremont Hotel, Near View" (OMCA)
34. "Grain Elevator, Fremont" (UPRM and OMCA)
35. "Seminary, Fremont" (UPRM and OMCA)
36. "Columbus, from Tank" (UPRM and OMCA)
37. "Columbus, (New Town), Street View" (UPRM and OMCA)
38. "Windmill, Columbus" (UPRM)
39. "Front Street, Columbus" (UPRM and OMCA)
40. "Clother's Hotel, Columbus" (UPRM)
41. "Loup Fork Bridge, Interior View" (UPRM and OMCA)
42. "Loup Fork Bridge, Exterior View" (UPRM and USU)
43. "Second Street, Grand Island" (UPRM)
44. "Gristmil[l], Grand Island" (UPRM and OMCA)
45. "Turn Table, Grand Island" (OMCA)
46. "Distant View of Grand Island" (UPRM and OMCA)
47. "R.R. Eating House, Grand Island" (UPRM and OMCA)
48. "Round House, Grand Island" (UPRM and OMCA)
49. "Grand Island Hotel" (UPRM and OMCA)
50. "Grand Prairie View near Grand Island" (UPRM and OMCA)
51. "Great Trestle Bridge over North Platte" (UPRM and USU)
52. "Great Trestle Bridge, with Engine" (UPRM and USU)
53. "North Platt[e] Station, from the East" (UPRM and OMCA)
54. "Front Street, North Platt[e] Station" (UPRM and OMCA)
55. "Hotel at North Platte" (UPRM and OMCA)
56. "U.S. Barracks, North Platte" (UPRM and OMCA)
57. "Machine Shops, from South West, N.P." (UPRM and OMCA)
58. "Front of Hotel, North Platt[e] Station" (UPRM and OMCA)
59. "Machine Shops, from N.W., North Platte" (UPRM and OMCA)
60. "Hotel, Cheyenne" (UPRM and OMCA)
61. "Looking West from Hotel, Cheyenne" (UPRM and OMCA)
62. "R.R. Hotel Dining Room, Cheyenne" (UPRM and OMCA)
63. "Passenger Train and Hotel, Cheyenne" (UPRM)
64. "Bird's Eye View of Cheyenne" (UPRM and OMCA)
65. "View on Sixteenth Street Cheyenne" (UPRM and OMCA)
66. "View on Sixteenth St., Looking North, Cheyenne" (UPRM and OMCA)
67. "Young Antelope, Cheyenne" (Not Available)
68. "Round House, Cheyenne" (UPRM and OMCA)

69. "Legislative Halls, Cheyenne" (UPRM)
70. "Distant View of Cheyenne" (UPRM)
71. "Churches, Cheyenne" (UPRM)
71A. "Fremont, from Verandah of Hotel" (UPRM)[8]
71B. "North Platte Machine Shops" (UPRM)

No 3. Black Hills Series

72. "Lime Kiln Cut, Granite [C]anyon" (UPRM and OMCA)
73. "Lime Kiln Cut, Granite [C]anyon" (UPRM and OMCA)
74. "Lime Kiln Cut, Granite [C]anyon" (UPRM)
75. "Cut and Fill West of Granite [C]anyon" (UPRM, OMCA, and USU)
76. "Fill No. 2 West of Granite [C]anyon" (UPRM and OMCA)
77. "Bowman's Cut, East of Sherman" (UPRM and OMCA)
78. "Bowman's Cut, East of Sherman, No. 2" (UPRM and OMCA)
79. "Mulloy's Cut, East of Sherman" (UPRM)
80. "Hall's Fill near Sherman" (UPRM and OMCA)
81. "Sherman Vale" (UPRM)
82. "High Rocks, near Sherman Station" (UPRM and OMCA)
83. "Reed's Rock, Near View" (UPRM and USU)
84. "Reed's Rock, from Buffalo Bills" (OMCA)
85. "Sherman, Front Street" (UPRM)
86. "Reed's Rock" (UPRM and OMCA)
87. "Back Bone of Black Hills" (Not Available)
88. "Boulders and Timber, Black Hills" (UPRM and OMCA)
89. "Gri[zz]ly Bear Peak, Black Hills" (UPRM, which has an alternative view)
90. "Rifted Rock, Black Hills" (OMCA)
91. "Look-Out Peak, Black Hills" (UPRM and OMCA)
92. "Timber Scene, Black Hills" (UPRM and OMCA)
93. "Summit, Black Hills" (UPRM)
94. "Sherman, Looking West, Black Hills" (UPRM and OMCA)
95. "Windmill at Sherman Station" (UPRM and OMCA)
96. "Valley of Shadow, Black Hills" (UPRM and OMCA)
97. "Rocky Way, Black Hills" (UPRM and OMCA)
98. "Timber Line, Black Hills" (UPRM)
99. "Specimen of Scrub Pine, Black Hills" (UPRM)
100. "Chugwater Peaks, Black Hills" (Not Available)
101. "Hermit's Glen, Black Hills" (UPRM and OMCA)

No 4. Dale Creek and Laramie Series

102. "Dale Creek Bridge, Snow Scene" (UPRM and USU)
103. "Dale Creek Bridge, from Above" (UPRM, OMCA, and USU)
104. "Dale Creek Bridge, from Ape Rock" (UPRM)
105. "Dale Creek Bridge, Distant View" (UPRM and OMCA)
106. "Dale Creek Bridge, Approach from West" (UPRM, which has an alternative view, and OMCA)
107. "Dale Creek Bridge, from Above" (UPRM and OMCA)
108. "Dale Creek Bridge, Distant View, Snow Scene" (UPRM)
109. "Dale Creek Bridge, from Druid's Rock" (UPRM, OMCA, and USU)
110. "Dale Creek Bridge, from Ape Rock" (UPRM, which has an alternate view)
111. "Dale Creek Bridge, Perspective View" (UPRM, OMCA, and USU)
112. "Dale Creek Bridge from Below" (UPRM)
113. "Dale Creek Bridge from Above" (Not Available)
114. "Dale Creek Bridge from Granite Bluffs" (UPRM)
115. "Dale Creek Bridge, from above Bridge" (OMCA)
116. "High Bluffs, Dale Creek" (UPRM and OMCA)
117. "Devil's Gate, Dale Creek [C]anyon" (UPRM and OMCA)
118. "Looking down from Bridge" (Not Available)
119. "Crossing of Old Emigrant Road" (UPRM)
120. "Looking across Dale Creek, below Bridge" (OMCA)
121. "Turban Rock, Dale Creek [C]anyon" (OMCA)
122. "High Rocks, Dale Creek" (OMCA)
123. "Eagle Gap, Dale Creek" (OMCA)
124. "Cut No. 3 West of Dale Creek" (UPRM and OMCA)
125. "Cut No. 3 West of Dale Creek" (UPRM and OMCA)
126. "Cut No. 5 West of Dale Creek" (Not Available)
127. "Cut No. 4 West of Dale Creek" (OMCA)
128. "Commissioners, Fort Saunders" (UPRM and OMCA)
129. "Head Quarters, Laramie" (UPRM and OMCA)
130. "Front of Hotel, Laramie" (UPRM, which has an alternate view)
131. "Round House, Laramie" (Not Available)
132. "Second Street, Laramie" (UPRM)
133. "B. Street Looking East, Laramie" (UPRM)
134. "Skating Pond, Laramie" (UPRM)
135. "R.R. Hotel, Laramie" (UPRM)
136. "Hospital, Looking over Plains" (UPRM)
137. "Dining Room, Hotel, Laramie" (UPRM)
138. "Machine Shots, Laramie" (UPRM)

139. “Cinnamon Bear, Laramie” (UPRM and OMCA)
140. “Rear View of Machine Shops, Laramie” (UPRM)
141. “Episcopal Church, Laramie” (UPRM)
142. “Laramie” (Imperial View, Not Available)
143. “Laramie Vall[e]y, 75 Miles South of R.R.” (UPRM, which has an alternate view)
144. “Snow and Timber Line, Medicine Bow Mts.” (UPRM and OMCA)
145. “Rock Cut, Red Buttes” (UPRM, which has an alternate view, and OMCA)

No 5. Bitter Creek Series

146. “Bushnell and Party, Rock Creek” (OMCA, which has two alternate views)
147. “Machine Shops, Rawlins Springs” (UPRM and OMCA)
148. “Round House, Rawlins Springs” (OMCA)
149. “Machine Shops, Rawlins Springs, from W” (UPRM, which has an alternate view, and OMCA)
150. “Engines in Round House, Rawlins Springs” (UPRM and OMCA)
151. “Engines in Round House, Rawlins Springs” (OMCA)
152. “Distant View Round House, Rawlins Sp[ring]s” (OMCA)
153. “Black Buttes Station” (UPRM and OMCA)
154. “Hermit’s Grotto, Black Buttes” (UPRM and OMCA)
155. “Amphitheatre, Black Buttes” (UPRM and OMCA)
156. “Fairy Grotto, Black Buttes” (UPRM and OMCA)
157. “Caves in Mountain, Point of Rocks” (UPRM and OMCA)
158. “Black Buttes from Mountains” (UPRM and OMCA)
159. “Gen. Casements Laying Track” (OMCA and USU)
160. “Laying Track, Instantaneous” (UPRM)
161. “Long Cut, Bitter Creek” (UPRM and OMCA)
162. “Unloading Ties, Bitter Creek” (UPRM and OMCA)
163. “Mummy Rock, Black Buttes” (UPRM and OMCA)
164. “Carmichael’s Camp, Bitter Creek” (UPRM and OMCA)
165. “Carmichael’s Camp, Bitter Creek” (UPRM and OMCA)
166. “Carmichael’s Cut, Bitter Creek” (UPRM, which has an alternate view, and OMCA)
167. “Carmichael’s Cut, Bitter Creek” (UPRM and OMCA)
168. “Carmichael’s Camp, in Distance” (UPRM and OMCA)
169. “Carmichael’s Cut, Bitter Creek” (UPRM and OMCA)
170. “Carmichael’s Cut, Bitter Creek” (UPRM and OMCA)
171. “On Mountains, Green River” (UPRM and OMCA)
172. “On Mountains, Green River” (OMCA)
173. “Cut near Green River” (UPRM and OMCA)
174. “Cut Horses at Work, Green River” (UPRM and OMCA)

175. “Giant’s Club, Green River” (UPRM and OMCA)
176. “Building Permanent Bridge, Green River” (UPRM and OMCA)
177. “Cit[a]d[e]l Rock, Green River” (UPRM)
178. “Citadel Rock Elevation, Green River” (OMCA)
179. “Temporary Bridge, Green River” (UPRM and OMCA)
180. “Station, Green River” (OMCA)
181. “Temporary Bridge, from below, Green R.” (OMCA)
182. “Station and Engine, Green River” (UPRM and OMCA)
183. “Side Cutting, Green River” (UPRM and OMCA)
184. “Side Cutting, with Engine, Green River” (UPRM and OMCA)
185. “Cribwork Bridge, Green River” (UPRM and OMCA)
186. “Rock Cut Where Fish Were Found” (OMCA)
187. “Teapot Rock, Green River” (UPRM and OMCA)
188. “Teapot Rock, (Distant), Green River” (UPRM and OMCA)
189. “Giants Head Stone” (Not Available)
190. “Side Cut, Green River” (OMCA)
191. “Side Cut, Green River” (UPRM and OMCA, which has an alternate view)
192. “Side Cut, Green River” (OMCA)
193. “Looking up Valley, Green River” (OMCA)
194. “On Mountains, Green River” (Not Available)
195. “Count[le]ss and Party, Green River” (OMCA)
196. “Side Cut, Green River” (UPRM and OMCA)
197. “Above the Valley, Green River” (OMCA)
198. “At Work on Rock Cut, Green River” (Not Available)
199. “Laying Track near Green River” (OMCA)

No 6. Bridger Series

200. “Granger Station” (UPRM and OMCA)
201. “Old Tower Church Buttes” (UPRM and OMCA)
202. “Pillars of Hercules, Buttes” (UPRM and OMCA)
203. “Church Buttes” (UPRM)
204. “Church Buttes Station” (UPRM and OMCA)
205. “Ranch on the Plains” (UPRM and OMCA)
206. “General Casement” (UPRM and OMCA)
207. “Reynolds and Douling’s Camp, Aspen” (UPRM and OMCA, which has an alternate view)
208. “Grader’s Camp, Aspen” (UPRM, which has an alternate view, and OMCA)
209. “Grader’s Cabins, Aspen” (UPRM and OMCA)
210. “Laying Track on Muddy” (OMCA, which has an alternate view)
211. “Casement’s Cars, Aspen” (UPRM and OMCA)

212. “Engine Blowing Off Steam, Wasatch” (UPRM and OMCA)
213. “Wasatch Station” (UPRM and OMCA)
214. “Wasatch Eating House” (UPRM and OMCA)
215. “Wasatch Passenger Train” (UPRM and OMCA)
216. “Wasatch Temporary Round House” (UPRM and OMCA)
217. “Wasatch, Distant View” (UPRM and OMCA)
218. “Wasatch, from West” (OMCA)
219. “Trestl[e] Great Z Temporary” (UPRM and OMCA)
220. “Looking West from Wasatch”’ (UPRM and OMCA)
221. “Looking down Great Z” (UPRM and OMCA)
222. “Cut No. 2, West of Wasatch” (UPRM and OMCA)
223. “Trestle Great Z” (UPRM and OMCA)
224. “Cut No. 4 West of Wasatch” (UPRM)
225. “Cut No. 5 West of Wasatch” (UPRM, OMCA, and USU)
226. “Cut No. 5 West of Wasatch” (UPRM and OMCA)
227. “Looking East from Tunnel No. 2” (UPRM and USU)
228. “Great Trestle, near Tunnel No. 2” (UPRM and OMCA)
229. “Tunnel No. 2. Looking Down” (UPRM)
230. “Camp at Tunnel No. 2” (UPRM and OMCA)
231. “Dining Room of Camp” (UPRM and OMCA)

No. 7. Uinta[h] Series

232. “Artists at Breakfast, Uinta[s]” (UPRM, which has an alternative view, and OMCA, which has a different image and a different description than UPRM, “Men, Women and Children in front of a Brush Shelter”)[9]
233. “Life in Mountains, Head of Bear River” (UPRM)
234. “Shadow Lake, Uinta[s]” (UPRM)
235. “Shadow Lake from South East” (UPRM)
236. “Shadow Lake from Traveler’s Home” (UPRM)
237. “Shadow Lake from North East” (UPRM and USU)
238. “Shadow Lake from North” (Not Available)
239. “Shadow Lake from East” (UPRM)
240. “Maj. Russell’s Bedroom, Uinta[s]” (UPRM and OMCA)
241. “Summit of Uinta Mountains” (UPRM)
242. “Waller Lake, Uinta Mountains” (UPRM)
243. “Forest View, Uinta Mountains” (OMCA)
244. “Old Trapper, Bear River” (UPRM)
245. “Old Trapper’s Home, Bear River” (UPRM)
246. “Lake of Sounding Shore, 11,500 Feet High” (UPRM)

247. “Spectre Lake, Looking West” (Not Available)
248. “Lake of Sounding Shore, Distant View” (Not Available)
249. “Moore’s Lake, Head of Bear River” (USU)
250. “Moore’s Lake, from South West” (UPRM and USU)
251. “Moore’s Lake, No. 2” (Not Available)
252. “Moore’s Lake, View from Mountains” (UPRM)
253. “Large Spruce Pine, Uinta[s]” (Not Available)
254. “Photographing under Difficulties” (UPRM and OMCA, which has a different description, “Photographer and Surveyors Climbing Uinta Mts.”)
255. “Spectre Lake, Uinta Mountains” (UPRM)
256. “Summit of Uinta[s]” (UPRM)
257. “Rain Storm on Spectre Lake” (UPRM and OMCA)
258. “Serge[a]nt Swark, the Guide” (UPRM and OMCA)
259. “Lone Cabin, Head of Bear River” (UPRM)
260. “Carter’s Lake. The Highest Body of Fresh Water in Uinta[s]” (UPRM)
261. “Veg[e]tation at 11,000 Feet Elevation” (UPRM)
262. “Group of Soldiers, Head of Bear River” (Not Available)
263. “Mountain Meadows” (UPRM and USU)
264. “Looking down Bear River” (UPRM and OMCA)

No. 8. Echo [C]anyon Series

265. “Tunnel No. 2 Head of Echo” (OMCA)
266. “Tunnel No. 2 Head of Echo” (UPRM and OMCA)
267. “Chimney Rock, Head of Echo” (UPRM and OMCA, which has two alternate views)
268. “Castle Rock, Head of Echo” (UPRM and OMCA)
269. “Castle Rock, Old Watch Tower” (UPRM and USU)
270. “Castle Rock, No. 2” (UPRM and OMCA, which has an alternate view)
271. “Castle Rock Station” (UPRM and OMCA)
272. “Castle Rock, Distant View” (UPRM and OMCA)
273. “Castle Rock, Old Watch Tower” (Not Available)
274. “Eastern Portal Tunnel No. 2” (UPRM)
275. “Castle Rock Station, from Mountains” (OMCA)
276. “Temple Rock, Looking East” (UPRM and OMCA)
277. “Temple Rock [C]anyon” (UPRM and OMCA)
278. “Echo [C]anyon, from Scorpion Hill” (UPRM)
279. “Stage Station, Hanging Rock” (UPRM, which has an alternate view, and OMCA)
280. “Devil’s Post Office, Echo [C]anyon” (UPRM and OMCA)
281. “Castle on Mountains” (UPRM and OMCA)
282. “Lion Rock, Echo [C]anyon” (UPRM)

283. “Rocky Mountain Hotel” (UPRM and OMCA, which has a different description, “Rocky Mountain Hotel Rooms to Let on Ground Floor”)
284. “Chimney Rock, Echo [C]anyon” (UPRM and OMCA)
285. “Castle on Mountain, Echo [C]anyon” (UPRM, USU, and OMCA, which has a different description, “Brigham’s Monument Echo Canyon”)
286. “Mormon Camp, Echo [C]anyon” (UPRM, which has an alternate view, and OMCA, which has an alternate view)
287. “Chimney Rock, Echo [C]anyon” (OMCA)
288. “Western Portal Tunnel, No. 2” (Not Available)
289. “Depot at Wasatch” (UPRM)
290. “Steam Shovel Loading, Echo [C]anyon” (UPRM and OMCA)
291. “Steam Shovel Unloading Echo [C]anyon” (UPRM and OMCA)
292. “Looking Down from Death’s Rock Echo [C]anyon” (UPRM, OMCA, and USU)
293. “Echo [C]anyon, Looking East” (UPRM and OMCA)
294. “Stage Station, Hanging Rock” (UPRM and OMCA)
295. “Looking East, Morman Fort, Echo [C]anyon” (Not Available)
296. “Supply Train, Going Down” (UPRM, which has a different description, “Mormons Transporting Supplies, Echo Canyon”)
297. “Looking up the Bluffs, Echo [C]anyon” (UPRM and OMCA)
298. “Looking down Grade, Echo [C]anyon” (OMCA)
299. “Looking up Echo [C]anyon” (UPRM and OMCA)
300. “Looking down Echo [C]anyon” (UPRM and OMCA)
301. “Capt[ain] Clanzton Echo [C]anyon” (OMCA, which has a different description, “Mr. Clayton on Horseback”)
302. “Stage Ranch at Head of Echo [C]anyon” (UPRM, which has a different description, “Stage Station, Hanging Rock, Echo Canyon,” and OMCA, which has a different description, “Echo Station, Head of Echo Can[y]on”)
303. “Odd Fellows Holding Service, Echo [C]anyon” (UPRM)
304. “Face of Temple Rock, Echo [C]anyon” (UPRM and OMCA)
305. “Steamboat Rocks, Echo [C]anyon” (OMCA)
306. “Echo from Temple Rock, Echo [C]anyon” (UPRM and OMCA)
307. “Monument Rock, Echo [C]anyon” (Not Available)
308. “Monument Rock, No. 2, Echo [C]anyon” (UPRM and OMCA)
309. “Monument Rock, No. 3, Echo [C]anyon” (OMCA)
310. “Monument Rock, Echo [C]anyon” (OMCA)
311. “Looking up from Great Eastern, Echo [C]anyon” (UPRM and OMCA)

No. 9. Echo City Series

312. “Rocky Mountain Bo[u]quet” (UPRM and OMCA)

313. "Rocky Mountain Bo[u]quet" (OMCA)
314. "Rocky Mountain Bo[u]quet" (OMCA)
315. "Colfax and Party, at Echo City" (UPRM and OMCA)
316. "Colfax and Party, Echo City" (UPRM and OMCA)
317. "Warehouse, Echo City" (UPRM and OMCA)
318. "Echo City, from South" (OMCA)
319. "Echo City, from Witches Rock" (UPRM and OMCA)
320. "Echo City, Cashi[er]s Office" (UPRM, which has an alternate view, and OMCA)
321. "Echo City, Weber River" (UPRM and OMCA)
322. "Echo City, Eagles Rocks" (OMCA)
323. "Witches, Rocks, Echo City" (OMCA)
324. "Witches Rock, with Group, Echo City" (OMCA)
325. "Looking into Weber Valley, Echo City" (UPRM)
326. "Echo City, from Witches Rocks" (OMCA)
327. "General View of Witches Rocks" (Not Available)
328. "Witches Jug, Witches Rock" (OMCA)
329. "Weber Valley, from Witches Rocks" (UPRM and OMCA, which has an alternate view)
330. "Eagle Rock" (Imperial View, OMCA)
331. "Dan Casement and Party" (UPRM and OMCA)
332. "Pulpit Rock, Looking West" (UPRM and OMCA)
333. "Pulpit Rock, Looking up Weber" (UPRM and OMCA)
334. "Pulpit Rock, Looking East" (UPRM and OMCA)
335. "Pulpit Rock" (UPRM)
336. "Pulpit Rock" (OMCA)
337. "Hanging Rock, Echo City" (UPRM, which has an alternate view, and OMCA)
338. "Snake Head Rock, Echo City" (USU)
339. "Mouth of Echo [C]anyon" (UPRM, which has an alternate view, and OMCA)
340. "Warehouse, Rear View" (UPRM and OMCA)
341. "Hanging Rock, Echo City" (Not Available)
342. "Echo, from Conglomerate Peaks" (UPRM and OMCA)
343. "Eagle Rocks, No. 2" (UPRM and OMCA)
344. "Bromley House, Echo City" (UPRM and OMCA)
345. "S. B. Reed and Captain Davis" (OMCA)
346. "Weber Valley, from Eagle Gap" (UPRM, which has an alternate view, but not 346 itself, and OMCA)
347. "Distant View of Echo City" (USU)
348. "Sentinel Rock, Echo City" (Not Available)
349. "Lady on Horseback, Echo City" (UPRM and OMCA, which has an alternate view)
350. "Giants Graveyard, Echo City" (UPRM and OMCA)
351. "Weber River, at Echo [C]anyon" (UPRM and OMCA, which has an alternate view)

352. “Conglomerate Peaks” (Imperial View, OMCA)
353. “Officers in Their Car at Echo City” (UPRM)
354. “Needle Group, Witches’ Rocks” (UPRM)
355. “Witches’ Rocks” (UPRM)
356. “Odd Fellows Group at Echo” (OMCA)
357. “Old Stage Station, at Echo” (UPRM and OMCA)
358. “Pulpit Rock, at Echo” (UPRM, which only has a copy negative)

No. 10. Weber [C]anyon Series

359. “Wilhelmina Pass” (UPRM and OMCA)
360. “Wilhelmina Pass” (Not Available)
361. “Wilhelmina Pass” (Not Available)
362. “Wilhelmina Pass, Distant View” (Not Available)
363. “Wilhelmina Pass, from Echo City” (UPRM)
364. “Wilhelmina Pass, from Tank” (Not Available)
365. “Wilhelmina Pass, from East” (UPRM)
366. “Wilhelmina Pass, from Stone Quarry” (UPRM and OMCA)
367. “1,000 Mile Tree, Looking South” (UPRM and OMCA)
368. “1,000 Mile Tree Gorge” (UPRM)
369. “1,000 Mile Tree, Excursion Party” (UPRM and USU)
370. “1,000 Mile Tree, Eastern Portal” (Not Available)
371. “Fishing Party, Weber [C]anyon” (OMCA and USU)
372. “West End Tunnel No. 3” (UPRM, which has a different description, “Mormons Worked on a Tiered Cut,” and OMCA)
373. “Camp at Tunnel No. 3” (Not Available)
374. “Building Tunnel No. 3” (UPRM)
375. “Building Tunnel No. 3” (UPRM)
376. “Foot Bridge at No. 3” (UPRM, which has an alternate view)
377. “Mormon Camp at Tunnel No. 3” (UPRM)
378. “Devil’s Shoot” (Not Available)
379. “Engineers Head Quarters at Tunnel No. 3” (UPRM and OMCA)
380. “Building First Bridge over Weber” (UPRM and OMCA)
381. “Looking down Weber, from Stone Quarry” (UPRM and OMCA)
382. “From Slate Point, Looking Down” (UPRM and OMCA)
383. “From Slate Point, Looking Down” (OMCA)
384. “Tunnel No. 4” (UPRM and OMCA)
385. “Tunnel No. 3, from Mountains” (UPRM, which has an alternate view)
386. “Bridge No. 30, above Tunnel No. 3” (UPRM)
387. “Looking up Weber, from Tunnel No. 3” (UPRM and OMCA)

388. “Eastern Portal of Tunnel No. 3” (UPRM and OMCA)
389. “Devil’s Shoot, Distant View” (UPRM, which has an alternate view, but not 389 itself)
390. “Finger Rock, Weber [C]anyon” (UPRM, which has an alternate view, but not 390 itself, and OMCA)
391. “Bridge above Tunnel No. 4” (UPRM)
392. “Tunnel No. 3 from 1,000 Ft. Above” (UPRM)
393. “Looking West from Strawberry Ford” (OMCA)
394. “Distant View of Strawberry Ford” (UPRM and OMCA)
395. “Entrance to Tunnel No. 4” (OMCA)
396. “Devil’s Shoot, Perspective” (UPRM)
397. “Weber River, Bridge No. 32” (Not Available)
398. “Telegraphic Corps, Weber [C]anyon” (UPRM and OMCA)
399. “Strawberry Ford, Weber [C]anyon” (UPRM and OMCA)

No. [11]. Devil’s Gate Series[10]

400. “Devil’s Gate Bridge, General View” (UPRM and OMCA)
401. “Devil’s Gate Bridge, Testing Combination” (UPRM)
402. “Devil’s Gate Bridge, Temporary” (UPRM and OMCA)
403. “Devil’s Gate, from Bluffs Opposite” (UPRM and OMCA)
404. “Devil’s Gate Bridge, Distant View” (UPRM and OMCA)
405. “Devil’s Gate, Side Cut” (UPRM and OMCA)
406. “Devil’s Gate, Looking Up” (OMCA)
407. “Devil’s Gate, Group of Tourists” (UPRM)
408. “Devil’s Gate Bridge, Perspective” (UPRM and OMCA)
409. “Devil’s Gate Bridge, Perspective” (UPRM and OMCA)
410. “Devil’s Gate Bridge, Showing River” (OMCA and USU)
411. “Devil’s Gate Bridge from Below” (UPRM and OMCA)
412. “Rapids of Weber, Instantaneous” (OMCA)
413. “North’s Camp, from Above” (UPRM and OMCA)
414. “North’s Camp, Foot of Mountains” (UPRM and OMCA)
415. “North’s Camp, from Mouth of Weber” (Not Available)
416. “Road at Mouth of [C]anyon” (UPRM and OMCA)
417. “Looking up Weber, from Mouth” (UPRM and OMCA)
418. “North’s Camp” (UPRM and OMCA)
419. “Looking into Devil’s Gate” (UPRM and OMCA)
420. “Mouth of Weber, from Uintah Station” (UPRM, which has an alternate view, and OMCA)
421. “Looking up the Weber” (UPRM and OMCA)
422. “Looking into Weber, from Rocks” (UPRM, which has an alternate view, and OMCA)

423. "Rapids of Weber, Instantaneous" (OMCA)
424. "Weber, from Cavern" (OMCA and USU)
425. "Salt Lake, from Wasatch Mountains" (UPRM and OMCA)
426. "Salt Lake, Bird's Eye View" (Not Available)
427. "Salt Lake Valley, from 2,000 Ft. Elevation" (UPRM and OMCA)
428. "Looking up Weber, from Side of Mountain" (UPRM)
429. "On Wasatch Mountains, Looking East" (UPRM and USU)
430. "Distant View of Prom[o]ntory and Salt Lake" (OMCA)
431. "Looking across from Summit of Mountains" (OMCA)
432. "U.P.R.R. from 3,000 Ft. Elevation" (UPRM and OMCA)
433. "Bird's Eye View of Weber" (UPRM, which has an alternate view, and OMCA)
434. "Salt Lake, from Summit of Wasatch" (UPRM and OMCA)
435. "Turnpike Road, Weber [C]anyon" (UPRM and OMCA, which has an alternate view)
436. "Mountain Mahogany" (UPRM and OMCA, which has an alternate view)
437. "Distant View of Salt Lake" (UPRM and OMCA)
438. "Salt Lake Valley from Mouth of Weber" (UPRM)
439. "Looking down into Weber from Lookout" (OMCA)
440. "Looking across Weber at 3,000 Feet Elevation" (UPRM and OMCA)
441. "Looking down on Morgan Valley" (OMCA)
442. "Looking from 2,000 Feet Elevation into Valley" (UPRM and OMCA)
443. "Bird's Eye View of Weber [C]anyon" (OMCA)
444. "Weber River, from above North's Camp" (UPRM and OMCA)
445. "Looking into Weber, from Heights" (Not Available)

No. 12. Utah Series

446. "Coalville, Weber Valley" (UPRM and OMCA)
447. "Coalville, Weber Valley" (UPRM and OMCA)
448. "Quaking Aspen Grove, White Pine [C]anyon" (UPRM and OMCA)
449. "Looking across Cottonwood Lake, July 16" (UPRM)
450. "Old Sawmill, Parley's Park" (UPRM)
451. "Party on Snow White Pine [C]anyon, Aug. 1" (UPRM and OMCA)
452. "Looking into White Pine [C]anyon" (Not Available)
453. "Looking into Weber Pine [C]anyon" (Not Available)
454. "Distant View, Ripple Lake, White Pine [C]anyon" (UPRM)
455. "Looking into Cottonwood [C]anyon, from Mount Emma" (Not Available)
456. "Fishing Party, Ripple Lake" (UPRM and OMCA)
457. "Tourists at Ripple Lake" (UPRM and OMCA)
458. "Among the Pines, White Pine [C]anyon" (UPRM and OMCA)
459. "O. C. Smith and Party, White Pine [C]anyon" (UPRM and OMCA)

460. “Cottonwood [C]anyon, from Mount Emma” (UPRM and OMCA)
461. “Tourists at Ripple Lake” (UPRM)
462. “Snow, August 26, White Pine [C]anyon” (UPRM)
463. “Looking into Parley, from Mount Emma” (UPRM and OMCA)
464. “Ripple Lake, White Pine [C]anyon” (UPRM and OMCA)
465. “On Wasatch Mountains” (UPRM, OMCA, and USU)
466. “Eph. Hank’s House, Parley’s Park” (UPRM and OMCA)
467. “Judge Snyder’s Residence, Parley’s Park” (Not Available)
468. “Be[a]ver Dam, White Pine [C]anyon” (UPRM)
469. “Be[a]ver Dam, White Pine [C]anyon” (Not Available)
470. “Be[a]ver Dam, White Pine [C]anyon” (Not Available)
471. “Be[a]ver Dam, White Pine [C]anyon” (UPRM and OMCA)
472. “Be[a]ver Dam, White Pine” [C]anyon (UPRM and OMCA)
473. “Miner’s Residence, Bingham [C]anyon” (UPRM and OMCA)
474. “Mormon Cottage, Parley’s Park” (UPRM)
475. “Snow and Timber Line, Uinta Mounts.” (UPRM and OMCA)
476. “Brigham Young’s Residence” (UPRM)
477. “Theatre, Salt Lake City” (UPRM, which has an alternate view, and OMCA, which has two alternate views)
478. “Great Tabernacle, Salt Lake City” (UPRM, which has an alternate view, and USU)
479. “Great Salt Lake City” (UPRM)
480. “Deseret Store, Salt Lake City” (UPRM and OMCA)
481. “Mormon Family, Salt Lake City” (UPRM, which has an alternate view, and OMCA)
482. “Brigham Young’s House, Salt Lake City” (UPRM)
483. “Breaking Ground for Utah R.R.” (Not Available)
484. “Sheep, Utah” (UPRM and OMCA)
485. “Miner’s Residence, Bingham [C]anyon” (UPRM and OMCA)
486. “First Grist Mill, Utah” (UPRM and OMCA)
487. “Green Monster Copper Mine” (UPRM and OMCA)
488. “Mormon with Three Wives” (Not Available)
489. “Saw Mill, Bingham [C]anyon” (UPRM and OMCA)
490. “Entrance to Copper Mine” (UPRM and OMCA)

No. 13. Salt Lake Valley Series

491. “Taylor’s Mill, Ogden” (UPRM and OMCA, which has an alternate view)
492. “Woolen Mill, Ogden” (OMCA)
493. “Taylor’s Mill Station, Ogden” (UPRM)
494. “Mouth of Weber from Uintah” (UPRM)
495. “Bridge, Ogden” (UPRM and OMCA)

496. “Corinne, from North West” (OMCA)
497. “Corinne, from South West” (UPRM and OMCA)
498. “Uintah Hotel, Corinne” (UPRM)
499. “Montana Street, Corinne” (UPRM and OMCA)
500. “Station Buildings, Corinne” (OMCA)
501. “View on Montana Street, Corinne” (UPRM)
502. “Steamer on Bear River” (UPRM and OMCA, which has an alternate view)
503. “Looking towards Brigham City” (UPRM and OMCA)
504. “Bear River Corinne” (UPRM)
505. “Bear River Bridge, Corinne” (UPRM and USU)
506. “Ferry across Bear River, Corinne” (UPRM and OMCA)
507. “R.R. Bridge from Ferry, Corinne” (UPRM and OMCA)
508. “Distant View of Corinne” (UPRM and OMCA)
509. “Salt Lake Valley, Corinne” (Not Available)
510. “Salt Lake Valley” (UPRM and OMCA)
511. “Passenger Train, Corinne“ (UPRM, which has an alternate view, and OMCA)
512. “Wasatch Mountains from Bear River” (Not Available)
513. “Paymaster’s Car, Blue Creek” (OMCA)
514. “Slaughter House at Camp, Blue Creek” (OMCA)
515. “Great Trestle Work, Prom[o]ntory” (UPRM and OMCA)
516. “Carmichael’s Cut, Prom[o]ntory” (OMCA)
517. “Sale Lake, from Trestle Work” (UPRM and OMCA)
518. “Carmichael’s Cut, Prom[o]ntory” (Not Available)
519. “Salt Flats, from Bent’s Work” (UPRM and OMCA)
520. “Hall’s Camp Prom[o]ntory” (OMCA)
521. “Salisbury’s Cut, Prom[o]ntory” (UPRM, which has an alternate view, and OMCA)
522. “Great Bend, Prom[o]ntory” (OMCA and USU)
523. “Mack’s Cut, Prom[o]ntory” (UPRM and OMCA)
524. “Cut No. 4, East of Prom[o]ntory” (OMCA)
525. “Trestle Prom[o]ntory” (Imperial View, OMCA)
526. “Caves of Prom[o]ntory” (UPRM and OMCA)
527. “Graders Breaking Camp, Prom[o]ntory” (OMCA)
528. “Distant View of Great Trestle” (UPRM and OMCA)
529. “Cut Near Blue Creek, Prom[o]ntory” (UPRM and OMCA)
530. “Boarding House Cavern, Prom[o]ntory” (OMCA)
531. “Engine on Great Trestle, Prom[o]ntory” (UPRM and USU)
532. “Over-Hanging Cliff, Prom[o]ntory” (UPRM and OMCA)
533. “Dead Fall, Prom[o]ntory” (UPRM and OMCA)
534. “Assembling to Lay Last Rail” (OMCA)
535. “Junction of Rails, Prom[o]ntory” (UPRM and OMCA)

536. “Prom[o]ntory from West” (UPRM and OMCA)
537. “Ceremony of Laying Last Rail” (OMCA)
538. “Morning before Laying Last Rail” (UPRM and OMCA)
539. “Chinese at Laying Last Rail” (OMCA)
540. “Laying Last Rail” (OMCA)
541. “Scene before Laying Last Rail” (UPRM, which has an alternate view, and OMCA)
542. “Getting Ready for Laying Last Rail” (Not Available)
543. “Group of Officials at Laying Last Rail” (OMCA)
544. “Eating House, Prom[o]ntory” (UPRM and OMCA)

No. 14. California Series

545. “Summit Sierra Nevada[s], Snow Sheds” (UPRM)
546. “Donner Lake, Distant View” (UPRM)
547. “Summit, Old Emigrant Road” (UPRM)
548. “Summit, C.P.R.R., Looking West” (Not Available)
549. “Donner Lake and Snow Sheds” (UPRM and USU)
550. “Snow Sheds, Looking West from Summit” (UPRM)
551. “Donner Lake, from Old Ced[a]r” (UPRM and USU)
552. “Mountain Ced[a]r, Summit C.P.R.R.” (UPRM)
553. “Hydraulic Gold Mining” (UPRM)
554. “Hydraulic Gold Mining, Gold Fields” (UPRM and USU)
555. “Hydraulic Gold Mining, below Bank” (UPRM, OMCA, and USU)
556. “Hydraulic Gold Mining, Miners at Work” (UPRM)
557. “Lake Anna, Sierra Nevada[s]” (UPRM)
558. “Mountain Scenery, Sierra Nevada[s]” (Not Available)
559. “Colfax Station, C.P.R.R.” (UPRM and OMCA)
560. “Colfax, Front Street” (OMCA)
561. “White Oak Carlin” (UPRM and OMCA)
562. “Like Oak Carlin” (UPRM and OMCA)
563. “Long Leaf or Nut Pine” (Not Available)
564. “General View of Colfax” (UPRM)
565. “Live Oaks, Sacramento Valley” (Not Available)
566. “Round House, Rocklin” (UPRM and OMCA)
567. “Looking up K Street, Sacramento” (UPRM and OMCA)
568. “Sacramento Machine Shops” (OMCA)
569. “Sacramento Machine Shops” (UPRM and OMCA)
570. “Chinese Washing Clothes, Sacramento” (UPRM)
571. “C.P.R.R. Shops, Sacramento” (OMCA)
572. “K Street, Sacramento” (UPRM)

573. "Sacramento River and Pier" (UPRM)
574. "G Street, Sacramento" (OMCA)
575. "Chinese Quarters, Sacramento" (UPRM and USU)

No. 15. Groups and Indians Series

576. "Snake Squaws Making Toilet" (USU)
577. "Ute Squaws in Nevada" (UPRM and OMCA)
578. "Visiting Indian Camp" (UPRM and OMCA)
579. "Snake Chiefs" (OMCA and USU)
580. "Shoshone Indians" (UPRM, OMCA, and USU)
581. "Sick Squaw and Medicine Man" (USU)
582. "Squaws Gambling for Beads" (OMCA and USU)
583. "S. B. Reed" (UPRM and OMCA)
584. "W. and W. Camp, Weber" (UPRM and OMCA)
585. "Ella Seymour" (OMCA)
586. "Pay Day, Echo City" (OMCA)
587. "Group of Horsemen, Echo City" (OMCA)
588. "Alexander and Family, Utah" (OMCA, which has an alternate view)
589. "Frost and Morton" (UPRM and OMCA)
590. "Family Group, Utah" (UPRM and OMCA)
591. "O. C. Smith and Wife" (OMCA)
592. "Dan Tilden and Friend" (OMCA)
593. "S. B. Reed and Family" (OMCA)
594. "S. B. Reed on Horseback" (OMCA)
595. "Mr. and Mrs. Hill" (OMCA)
596. "Cashier and Clerks, Echo City" (UPRM and OMCA)
597. "Cashier's Office Echo" (OMCA)
598. "Mormon Bishop and Family" (Not Available)
599. "Entrance to Weber" (Imperial View, OMCA)
600. "Engineer's Camp, Weber, Near Tunnel No. 3" (UPRM and OMCA)
601. "Warner, Whitman and Gray" (OMCA)
602. "O. C. Smith's Clerks, Echo City" (OMCA)
603. "Group of Tourists, Echo City" (Not Available)
604. "Excursion Party at Reeds" (OMCA)
605. "Group of Tourists, Echo City" (OMCA)
606. "Group at S. B. Reed's Office" (UPRM and OMCA)
607. "Indian Squaws and Papooses" (USU)
608. "Dan Casement, Echo City" (UPRM and OMCA)
609. "Warner and Whitman Group, Echo" (OMCA)

610. "Mrs. S. B. Reed, Echo" (OMCA)
611. "Group of Engineers Echo" (OMCA)
612. "Miss Anna Reed" (UPRM and OMCA)
613. "Mrs. S. B. Reed, Sitting" (OMCA)

MISCELLANEOUS STEREOGRAPHIC VIEWS

Nine more stereo-view negatives are at the Oakland Museum of California. One of the images is of an unidentified bridge, and another is identified as "Interior of Paymaster's Tent, Laramie City." The final seven images are of individual portraits. Only three individuals are identified: Mrs. Lamb and Mr. and Mrs. Blair.

Large-Format Views

1. "Pony Engine." View shows Union Pacific Engine 3. (OMCA)
2. "Machine Shops, Omaha, Neb." (OMCA)
3. (Not Available)[11]
4. "North Platte Bridge No. 4" (OMCA)
5. (Not Available)
6. "Lime Kiln Cut Near Granite Can[y]on" (OMCA)
7. No description provided. View shows embankment no. 1, east of Granite Canyon. (OMCA)
8. "Entering Black Hills Carmichael's Cut Granite Can[y]on" (OMCA). *Great West Illustrated*, Plate I.
9. No description provided. View shows Great Embankment, Granite Canyon, looking west. (OMCA)
10. "Granite Can[y]on Embankment" (OMCA). *Great West Illustrated*, Plate II. "Granite Can[y]on, from the Water Tank."
11. No description provided. View shows construction train on embankment, Granite Canyon. (OMCA)
12. "Embankment No. 1 West of Granite Can[y]on No. 12" (OMCA)
13. No description provided. View shows Hall's Fill near Granite Canyon. (OMCA)
14. "Hall's Cut Sherman Station" (OMCA). *Great West Illustrated*, Plate V.
15. "Camel Rock near Buford Station U.P.R.R." (OMCA). *Great West Illustrated*, Plate III. "Granite Rock, Near Bufor[d] Station."
16. No description provided. View shows Mallory's Cut near Sherman Station (OMCA). *Great West Illustrated*, Plate IV.
17. "Reed's Rock Sherman Summit of U.P.R.R." (OMCA)
18. (Not Available)
19. "Dale Creek Bridge Perspective View" (OMCA)

19 1/2. No description provided. View shows man sitting on cut logs, above curve in railroad tracks with Dale Creek Bridge in distance (OMCA). *Great West Illustrated*, Plate IX. "Eastern Approach to Dale Creek Bridge."

20. (Not Available)
21. "Dale Creek Bridge from Above" (OMCA)
22. No description provided. View shows valley and bridge of Dale Creek (OMCA). *Great West Illustrated*, Plate VII. "Dale Creek Bridge, General View."
23. "Dale Creek from above, No. 2" (OMCA)
24. "Dale Creek Bridge from above No. 2" (OMCA)
25. "Dale Creek Bridge from Below" (OMCA)
26. (Not Available)
27. "High Rocks Mining District Dale Creek Can[y]on" (OMCA)
28. (Not Available)
29. "Devil's Gate, Dale Creek Canyon, near Silver Mines" (OMCA). *Great West Illustrated*, Plate X. "Devil's Gate, Creek Can[y]on."
30. "Western Approach of Dale Creek Bridge, Granite Cut" (OMCA)
31. "Rock Cut No. 3 West of Dale Creek Bridge" (OMCA)
32. "Cut No. 4 West of Dale Creek Bridge" (OMCA)
33. "Miller and Patterson's Work Cut No. 5 near Red Buttes" (OMCA)
34. "Miller and Patterson's Cut No. 6 East of Tie Pile" (OMCA)
35. "Eagle's Nest, Red Buttes' Station, U.P.R.R. Soft Red Sandstone, about 80 Feet High" (OMCA)
36. "Red Buttes or Vase Rock, Sometimes Called Deal Rock, near Red Buttes' Station" (OMCA). *Great West Illustrated*, Plate XII. "Dial Rock, Red Buttes."
37. "Gen. Grant and Party at Fort Sanders Summer of '68" (OMCA)

37b. "General Grant and Party at Fort Sanders" (OMCA). *Great West Illustrated*, Plate XI. "Gen. Grant and Party at Fort Sanders."

38. "Commissioners at Fort Sanders" (OMCA)

38b. "Commission at Fort Sanders" (OMCA)

39. "Round House and Machine Shop East Front Laramie" (OMCA)
40. "Machine Shops of Laramie from Wind Mill" (OMCA)
41. "Rear View of Laramie Shops from South East No. 4" (OMCA)
42. "Front View of Laramie Shops" (OMCA)
43. "Laramie Shops Rear View from South West" (OMCA). *Great West Illustrated*, Plate XI. "Laramie Machine Shops, from the Southwest."
44. "Clerical Excursionists at Laramie City 1868" (OMCA)
45. No description provided (OMCA). *Great West Illustrated*, Plate XV. "Laramie Hotel, Laramie City."
46. No description provided. View shows the interior of the Laramie machine shops. (OMCA)

47. (Not Available)
48. No description provided. View shows railroad hotel dining room at Laramie. (OMCA)
48b. No description provided. View shows interior of dining room at Laramie. (OMCA)
49. "Employees of U.P.R.R. at Laramie City" (OMCA)
50. "Employees of U.P.R.R. at Laramie Offices" (OMCA)
51. "Rail Road Hospital Laramie City" (OMCA)
51 1/2. "Wind Mill, Laramie City" (OMCA). *Great West Illustrated*, Plate XVI. "The Wind Mill at Laramie."
52. "Ware House of U.P.R.R. at Laramie City Grain Stored for Transportation" (OMCA)
53. "Among the Timber of the Laramie Mountains" (OMCA)
53a. *Great West Illustrated*, Plate XIII. "Snow and Timber Line, Laramie Mountains."
53b. "Valley of the Great Laramie from the Mountains" (OMCA). *Great West Illustrated*, Plate XIV. "Valley of the Great Laramie, from the Mountains."
54. No description provided (OMCA). *Great West Illustrated*, Plate XVIII. "Valley of the Little Laramie River."
54a. No description provided (OMCA). *Great West Illustrated*, Plate XIX. "Among the Timber at Head of Little Laramie River."
54b. *Great West Illustrated*, Plate XX. "Source of the Laramie River."
55. "Wyoming Station Engine No. 23 on Main Track" (OMCA)
56. "Mr. Bushnell and Party at Rock Creek Station U.P.R.R." (OMCA)
57. "Rawlins Hotel" (OMCA)
58. "Round House and Machine Shops at Rawlins" (OMCA)
59. "Construction Train at End of Track, Gen. Casement's Outfit, Gen. in Foreground" (OMCA)[12]
60. "High Bluff Black Buttes" (OMCA). *Great West Illustrated*, Plate XXI. "High Bluff, Black Buttes."
61. No description provided. View shows Black Buttes, the Union Pacific Railroad in the background. (OMCA)
62. No description provided. View shows Bitter Creek Valley from coal mines near the point of rocks. Miners in view with train in distance. (OMCA)[13]
63. "Bitter Creek Valley from Coal Mine near Point Rocks" (OMCA)
64. "Carmichael's Cut Bitter Creek Valley" (OMCA)
64b. No description provided (OMCA). *Great West Illustrated*, Plate XXIII. "On the Mountains of Green River."
65. "Valley of Bitter Creek Panoramic View No. 2"[14] (OMCA)
66. "Carmichael's Camp Bitter Creek Valley No. 2" (OMCA)
67. "Carmichael's Cut Bunny Rock Seen in Dark Strata near Top of Cut" (OMCA). *Great West Illustrated*, Plate XXII. "Burning Rock Cut."
68. (Not Available)
69. (Not Available)

70. "Bitter Creek Valley No. 3 Panoramic" (OMCA)
71. No description provided. View shows Carmichael's Cut on Bitter Creek (OMCA).
72. "On the Mountains of Green River Smith's Rock in Foreground." (OMCA)
73. "Carmichael's Camp Bitter Creek Valley." (OMCA)[15]
74. (Not Available)
75. "Bitter Creek Valley Panoramic View." (OMCA)
76. (Not Available)
77a. No description provided. View shows Green River Valley. (OMCA)
77b. No description provided. View shows Green River Valley (OMCA). *Great West Illustrated*, Plate XXIV. "Castle Rock, Green River Valley."
77c. "Mountains of Green River Valley" (OMCA)
78. "Temporary and Permanent Bridge Green River Citadel Rock in Distance" (OMCA)
79. No description provided. View shows Citadel Rock near Green River (UPRM)[16]
80. "No Side Cut Green River Carmichael's Work" (OMCA)
80 1/2. No description provided. View shows Bryan Station with Union Pacific Engine 65 seen from rear. (OMCA)
81. "Church Buttes Winter" (OMCA)
81a. *Great West Illustrated*, Plate XXVI. "Church Buttes."
82. (Not Available)
83. "Fort Bridger Judge Carter Store in Middle Distance" (OMCA)
84. "Fort Bridger" (OMCA)
85. "Officers of Fort Bridger Col Morrow Commanding" (OMCA)
85a. "Officers at Fort Bridger No. 2" (OMCA)
86. "Construction Train End of Track Near Bear River Gen. Casement's Outfit" (OMCA). *Great West Illustrated*, Plate XXXXIV. "Gen. Casement's Construction Train."
87. "Supply Trains at End of Track Last Siding." Photograph made in vicinity of Piedmont, Wyoming (OMCA). *Great West Illustrated*, Plate XXVII. "Supply Trains."
88. "Coal Bed of Bear River Perpendicular Vein of 7 Feet" (OMCA). *Great West Illustrated*, Plate XXVIII. "Coal Beds of Green River."
89. "Bear River City" (OMCA). *Great West Illustrated*, Plate XXIX. "Bear River City, Near the Coal Fields."
90. "Snow and Timber Line Uinta Mountains" (OMCA)
91. "Surveying under Difficulties Head of Bear River" (OMCA)
92. (Not Available)[17]
93. (Not Available)
94. (Not Available)
95. (Not Available)
96. "The Old Trapper at the Head of Bear River" (OMCA)
97. (Not Available)
98. (Not Available)

99. (Not Available)
100. (Not Available)
101. (Not Available)
102. "Tunnel at Head of Echo Miller and Patterson's Work" (OMCA)
103. "Miller and Patterson's Camp at Tunnel No. 2 Head of Echo Can[y]on" (OMCA)
104. (Not Available)
105. "Tunnel No. 2 Head of Echo" (OMCA)
106. (Not Available)
107. "Castle Rock Echo Can[y]on" (OMCA)
108. (Not Available)
109. "Steam Shovel at Hanging Rock Echo Can[y]on" (OMCA)
110. "Looking down Echo Can[y]on from Death's Rock" (OMCA). *Great West Illustrated*, Plate XXX.
111. No description provided. View shows the Grand Lodge of Odd Fellows holding a meeting, Echo Can[y]on. (OMCA)
112. "Odd Fellows Meeting Echo Can[y]on Near Temple Rock No. 2" (OMCA)
113. "Rock Great Eastern No. 2 Echo Can[y]on" (OMCA)
114. "Rock Great Eastern No. 2 Echo Can[y]on" (OMCA). *Great West Illustrated*, Plate XXXVIII. "Rock Great Eastern."
115. "Monument Rock near Mouth of Echo Can[y]on" (OMCA)
116. No description provided (OMCA). *Great West Illustrated*, Plate XXXI. "Monument Rock, Mouth of Echo Can[y]on."
117. "Pulpit Rock Mouth of Echo Can[y]on 117" (OMCA)
118. *Great West Illustrated*, Plate XXXIII. "Sphynx of the Valley."
119. *Great West Illustrated*, Plate XXXII. "Hanging Rock, Foot of Echo Can[y]on."
120. (Not Available)
121. *Great West Illustrated*, Plate XXXIX. "East End of Tunnel, Weber Can[y]on."
122. "High Rocks Weber Valley Mouth of Echo Can[y]on" (OMCA)
123. "Distant View of Pulpit Rock at Mouth of Echo Can[y]on or Sentinel Rock Weber Valley" (OMCA). *Great West Illustrated*, Plate XXXIV. "Sentinel Rock, Weber Valley."
124. *Great West Illustrated*, Plate XXXV. "Echo City, Looking up Weber River."
125. "Warner and Whitman[s] at Echo" (OMCA)
126. "Bromley's Residence Echo City" (OMCA)
127. "Cashier's Office Echo City" (OMCA)
128. "Directors of North Western R.R. at Echo City" (OMCA)
129. (Not Available)
130. (Not Available)
131a. No description provided. View shows a Mormon family in Echo City. Three women in foreground. (OMCA)

131b. No description provided. View shows Mormon family near Echo, Utah (OMCA).[18] *Great West Illustrated*, Plate XXXXVIII. "Mormon Family, Great Salt Lake Valley."
132. "Engineers Office Echo City" (OMCA)
133. "R.R. Station House at Echo City" (OMCA)
134. "Conglomerate Peak of Echo" (OMCA)
135. (Not Available)
136. "Ware House Echo City" (OMCA)
137. "Dan Casement and Clerks at Echo City" (OMCA)
138. "Rocky Mountain Glee Club Echo City" (OMCA)
139. "Conglomerate Peaks of Echo General View" (OMCA)
140. (Not Available)
141. (Not Available)
142. "Echo City from the South" (OMCA)
143. "Echo City from the Bluff Looking North" (OMCA)
144. (Not Available)
145. (Not Available)
146. "The Old Saw Mill Parley's Park" (OMCA)
147. "Ripple Lake White Pine Can[y]on Parleys Park" (OMCA)
148. "Head of White Pine Can[y]on Parleys Park" (OMCA)
149. "Looking down into Ripple Lake from Mount Emma" (OMCA)
150. (Not Available)
151. "The Old Grist Mill Utah" (OMCA)
152. "Bishop Snyder's Residence Parleys Park Utah" (OMCA)
153. No description provided (OMCA). *Great West Illustrated*, Plate XXXXIX. "Brigham Young's Cotton and Woolen Factories."
154. "Zions Cooperative Mercantile Institution Salt Lake City Store in which Brigham Has an Interest" (OMCA)
155. (Not Available)
156. "Brigham's Bath House Hot Sulphur Springs Salt Lake City" (OMCA)
157. "City Creek Can[y]on the Water Used by Citizens of Salt Lake City" (OMCA). *Great West Illustrated*, Plate XXXXVI. "City Creek Can[y]on, Near City Creek Falls."
158. "City Creek Can[y]on No. 2" (OMCA)
159. "Brigham Young's Theater Salt Lake City" (OMCA)
160. "Townsend House Salt Lake City" (OMCA)
161. Group of Officials" (OMCA)[19]
162. No description provided. Part of a panoramic view of Salt Lake City. (OMCA)
163. No description provided. Part of a panoramic view of Salt Lake City. (OMCA)
164. Mormon Tabernacle No. 2" (OMCA). *Great West Illustrated*, Plate XXXXX. "Great Mormon Tabernacle."

165. “Residence of Brigham Young” (OMCA). *Great West Illustrated*, Plate XXXXVII. “Residence of Brigham Young.”
166. “Salt Lake City from Top of Tabernacle” (OMCA). *Great West Illustrated*, Plate XXXX. “Salt Lake City, from the Top of the Tabernacle.”
167. “Temple Street Salt Lake City” (OMCA)
168. “Looking down Temple Street Salt Lake” (OMCA)
169. “California U.P.R.R. Stable or Corral Salt Lake City” (OMCA)
170. Bird’s Eye View of Cotton Wood Can[y]on No. 2” (OMCA)
171. “Bird’s Eye View of Cotton Wood Can[y]on” (OMCA)
172. “Brigham Can[y]on The Old Steam Saw Mill” (OMCA)
173. “Looking up Weber Valley from the Narrows” (OMCA)
174. No description provided (OMCA). *Great West Illustrated*, Plate XXXVII. “Wilhelmina Pass, from the East.”
175. “The Narrows of the Weber Can[y]on No. 1” (OMCA)
176. “Narrows of the Weber No. 3” (OMCA)
177. “Looking up Weber Valley from the Narrows” (OMCA). *Great West Illustrated*, Plate XXXXIII. “Weber Valley, from Wilhelmina Pass.”
178. “Narrows of the Weber No. 4” (OMCA)
179. “Coalville, Weber Valley” (OMCA). *Great West Illustrated*, Plate XXXVI. “Coalville, Weber Valley.”
180. “Weber Valley from below Echo City” (OMCA)
181. “Wilhelmina Pass” (OMCA)
182. “Sentinel Rock Weber Valley” (OMCA)
183. “Excursion Party at 1,000 Mile Tree Wilhelmina Pass” (OMCA)
184. (Not Available)
185. (Not Available)
186. “Looking down Weber Can[y]on from Slate Point” (OMCA)
187. “Bridge No. 32 Weber” (OMCA)
188. “Looking down the Weber near Bridge No. 32” (OMCA)
189. “Finger Rock Weber Can[y]on” (OMCA)
190. “Bird’s Eye View of Weber Can[y]on” (OMCA)
191. (Not Available)
192. “Tunnel No. 3 Weber with Engine” (OMCA)
193. “Eastern Portal No. 4 Weber Can[y]on” (OMCA)
194. “Looking up the Weber from the Top of Tunnel No. 4” (OMCA)
195. “Strawberry Ford, Weber Valley” (OMCA)
196. “Strawberry Ford Weber” (OMCA)
197. (Not Available)
198. (Not Available)
199. *Great West Illustrated*, Plate XXXXI. “Weber Can[y]on, from below Devil’s Gate.”

200. "Devil's Gate Weber Can[y]on Perpendicular Rocks 2,000 Feet High" (OMCA). *Great West Illustrated*, Plate XXXX. "Devil's Gate, Weber Can[y]on."
201. (Not Available)
202. "Temporary Bridge Devil's Gate Weber from Below" (OMCA)
203. "From Devil's Gate Looking East No. 2" (OMCA)
204. "Constructing Temporary Bridge at Devil's Gate Weber" (OMCA)
205. "Construction Bridge Weber Can[y]on at Devil's Gate" (OMCA)
206. "Combination Bridge Weber Can[y]on at Devil's Gate" (OMCA)
207. "Testing Combination Bridge Devil's Gate Weber Can[y]on" (OMCA)
208. "From Devil's Gate Looking East" (OMCA)
209. "Senator Patterson and Par[t]y on Devil's Gate Bridge" (OMCA)
210. "Temporary Bridge Devil's Gate" (OMCA)
211. (Not Available)
212. "Excursion Party on Devil's Gate Bridge" (OMCA)
213. "Mormon Toll Bridge at Mouth of Weber Can[y]on" (OMCA). *Great West Illustrated*, Plate XXXXII. "Mormon Turnpike Bridge, Mouth of Weber Can[y]on."
214. (Not Available)
215. "Salt Lake City Panoramic No. 1 from Wasatch Mts." (OMCA)
216. "Salt Lake from the Wasatch Mountains No. 3" (OMCA)
217. "Corinne Panoramic View No. 2" (OMCA)
218. "Corinne Panoramic View No. 3" (OMCA)
219. "Panoramic No. 1 Salt Lake Valley from Corinne Brigham City in the Distance" (OMCA)
220. (Not Available)
221. "Promontory Trestle Engine on Trestle West No. 3" (OMCA)
222. (Not Available)
223. No description provided. View shows a group of men standing by engine Jupiter of the Central Pacific Railroad. (OMCA)
224. "Engineers of U.P.R.R. at the Laying of the Last Rail Promontory" (OMCA)
225. "Laying Last Rail Promontory" (OMCA)
225b. No description provided. View shows a group of 21st Infantry soldiers and Union Pacific officials. (OMCA)
226. "Officers of U.P. Rail Road at Ceremony of Laying Last Rail at Promontory" (OMCA)
227. "East and West Shaking Hands at Laying Last Rail" (OMCA)
228. No description provided. View on Donner Lake in the Sierra Nevada Mountains, with snowshed tunnels in foreground. (OMCA)
229. (Not Available)
230. (Not Available)
231. No description provided. Hydraulic gold mining, California. (OMCA)
232. (Not Available)

233. “Machine Shops of C.P.R.R. Sacramento, California” (OMCA)
234. “Group of Ute Indians on the War Path” (OMCA)[20]
237. “Group at O. C. Smith Echo City” (OMCA)

Miscellaneous Large-Format Views

Two more negatives are at the Oakland Museum of California. One of the images is taken at Black Buttes, Wyoming, and the other has the title “Cozzens Hotel and Catholic Church Omaha.”

NOTES

INTRODUCTION

1. Although sometimes referred to as Andrew Joseph Russell, the author has never found an original source with his middle name. It was quite common for men at that time to take their father's first name as a middle name and the first name of A. J. Russell's father was, in fact, Joseph.
2. It should be pointed out that I was looking at Russell's description of the stereograph from his first series, with an earlier numbering system, Union Pacific R.R. Views Across the Continent, West from Omaha, "No. 187 View of Tunnel No. 4, from an Elevation of 1,000 Feet." In the later Rocky Mountain Scenery series, he corrected his mistake and listed it as tunnel no. 3.
3. Hayden, *Sun Pictures of Rocky Mountain Scenery.*
4. "Is That Dress White and Gold or Blue and Black?," *New York Times*, February 28, 2015.
5. Utah State University, A. J. Russell Photograph Collection. The largest collection of Russell's glass-plate negatives is in the A. J. Russell Collection at the Oakland Museum of California. The largest collection of original prints is in the A. J. Russell Views at the Union Pacific Railroad Museum, a privately held collection maintained by the Union Pacific.
6. For example, two excellent general histories of the Union Pacific are Bain, *Empire Express;* and Klein, *Union Pacific.*

CHAPTER 1

1. A Russell large-format, or sometimes referred to as imperial plate, negative was 10" x 13"—much larger than a stereo-view negative.
2. Examples include John Carbutt, stereo-view no. 209, "Laying the Rails of the U.P.R.R.—2 Miles a Day"; Alfred Hart, stereo-view no. 317, "End of Track, near Humboldt Lake," and stereo-view no. 333, "Curving Iron. 10 Mile Canyon"; and Alexander Gardner, large-format view no. 39, "Westward the Course of Empire Takes Its Way," in *Across the Continent on the Kansas Pacific Railroad.*
3. Nearly everything we know about Russell's panoramas comes from contemporary New York newspapers. See *Nunda News*, 1860–1862. *Nunda News* also ran historical pieces starting in the 1950s; see pieces from January 28, 1954, and September 18, 1969.
4. The two best published sources of Russell's Civil War photography are Williams, "Reappraising the Brady Legend"; and Davis, "Photography in the Civil War." Two other informative articles are Cooney, "Union Army's Forgotten Photographer"; and Gladstone, "First Army Photographer."
5. I found no original buildings after traveling the entire length of the line, and this was confirmed by staff at the Union Pacific Railroad Museum.

6. Secretary Browning may have been influenced by the negative press surrounding the substandard work of the Union Pacific, and a personal dislike for the Union Pacific vice president Thomas Durant. As well, Browning sought the advice and consultation of Jesse Williams, the Union Pacific's government director, who was being secretly bribed by the Central Pacific to undermine the Union Pacific. See Bain, *Empire Express*.
7. Russell also photographed Union Pacific employees, including individual portraits, for resale to these same employees. See these entries (all from 1868) in Smith, Transcript of Diaries: May 31–June 6, June 13–18, June 20–26, July 18–24, August 1–7, August 15–21, and August 29–September 4. See also Willumson, *Iron Muse*, 50, 192. The transcript of Smith's diaries was created by Phyllis Morris in 1976. The current location of the original diaries is unknown, and the transcription is in private hands. I am indebted to Dr. Willumson and the descendants of Smith for sharing this source.
8. Russell joined Clarence King's 40th Parallel Survey for an expedition to the Uinta Mountains in the summer of 1869. O'Sullivan was the official photographer for King's survey and the two men photographed together during this trip. Most of Russell's negatives ended up with King's survey and were printed with the King survey mounts. See Jurovics et al., *Framing the West,* 181.

CHAPTER 2

1. *Nunda News*, January 11, 1952.
2. *Nunda News*, June 9, 1860, and December 13, 1956; Williams, "Truth be Told," 38; and Williams, "Reappraising the Brady Legend," 3.
3. *Nunda News*, October 29, 1953, and September 18, 1969; *Corning Journal*, April 22, 1903; and 1860 Census.
4. Williams, "Reappraising the Brady Legend," 3; and Walther, "Landscape Photographs," PhD diss., 60.
5. *Geneva Gazette*, November 26, 1858; and *Livingston Republican*, May 26, 1859.
6. Sandweiss, *Print the Legend,* 52–57; and Oettermann, *The Panorama,* 313–44.
7. *Geneva Gazette*, November 26, 1858.
8. *Nunda News*, January 28, 1954.
9. Ibid., January 15, 1870.
10. Ibid., June 9, 1860.
11. *Buffalo Express,* quoted in the *Nunda News*, December 15, 1860. The painting discussed is housed at the Steuben County Historical Society. Willumson, *Iron Muse*, 148.
12. Walther, "Landscape Photographs," 61–62; Naef and Wood, *Era of Exploration,* 201–2; Biographical Directory of the United States Congress, s.v. "Van Valkenburg, Robert Bruce," accessed January 3, 2017, bioguide.congress.gov; and *Nunda News*, December 15, 1860, and June 29, 1861.
13. For a discussion of Civil War panoramas, see Huhtama, *Illusions in Motion*, 19, 264–67, 275–76.
14. *Hornellsville Journal*, quoted in the *Nunda News*, December 14, 1861.
15. The loss was stated to be one hundred dollars. *Nunda News*, January 4, 1862.
16. *Schenectady Evening Star and Times*, May 14, 1862; and *Livingston Union*, February 5, 1862.
17. *Rochester Union and Advertiser*, February 25, 1862; *Clinton Courier*, May 15, 1862; *Waterville Times*, May 2, 1862; *Wyoming County Mirror*, May 14, 1862; and *Broome Weekly*, September 3, 1862.

18. *Nunda News*, February 8, 1862.
19. *Medina Tribune*, March 12, 1863; Williams, "Truth Be Told," 38; *Nunda News*, September 18, 1969; Willumson, "Alfred Hart," 61.
20. *Medina Tribune*, March 12, 1863; *New York Clipper*, January 3 and June 13, 1863; *Western Reserve Chronicle*, February 25, 1863; *Urbana Union*, January 28, 1863; *Fremont Journal*, December 19, 1862; and *Elk Advocate*, November 4, 1865.
21. *Rochester Daily Union and Advertiser*, March 6, 1865; and *Naples Record*, December 20, 1879.
22. Huhtama, *Illusions in Motion*, 264–67, 275–76, 371; and Holzer and Neely, *Civil War in Art*, 183–96.
23. *Nunda News*, February 8, 1862; and Sandweiss, *Print the Legend*, 52–56, 76–77.
24. *Nunda News*, September 6, 1862.
25. *Broome Weekly*, September 3, 1862; Williams, "Reappraising the Brady Legend," 3; and Cooney, "Union Army's Forgotten Photographer," 32.
26. Williams, "Reappraising the Brady Legend," 3; and Gladstone, "First Army Photographer," 7.
27. Haupt, *Reminiscences of General Herman Haupt*, 256.
28. *Nunda News*, January 31, 1957, and March 2, 1961. Certainly he never mentions sketching behind enemy lines in his accounts, nor does it appear in any contemporary accounts of his Civil War service.
29. Davis, "Photography in the Civil War," 133–49.
30. Ibid., 138–39, 156–57, 162–65.
31. He was also the ordnance officer for the construction corps. Williams, "Reappraising the Brady Legend," 3–5; and Gladstone, "First Army Photographer," 7.
32. It was not, however, until after the war that Russell was reimbursed for this amount. Cooney, "Union Army's Forgotten Photographer," 34; Gladstone, "First Army Photographer," 8; and Williams, "Reappraising the Brady Legend," 4.
33. Kibbey, *Railroad Photographs*, 81–83.
34. Ibid., 83–87.
35. Crawford, *Keepers of Light*, 42–45.
36. Cooney, "Union Army's Forgotten Photographer," 34–35; Williams, "Reappraising the Brady Legend," 4, 5, 10; and Walther, "Landscape Photographs," 64. In addition, Russell also continued painting, especially railroad cars and engines, according to the *Nunda News*, January 24, 1863.
37. *Baltimore American*, May 25, 1863.
38. Williams, "Truth Be Told," 39.
39. Fels, *Destruction and Destiny*, 10–12; Gladstone, "First Army Photographer," 7; Cooney, "Union Army's Forgotten Photographer," 35; Williams, "Truth Be Told," 38; and Davis, "Photography in the Civil War," 157–59. Russell "action shots" can be found in Haupt, *Photographs Illustrative of Operations*.
40. Buberger and Isenberg, *Russell's Civil War Photographs*, plates 6, 90, 91, 106, and 107.
41. Williams, "Truth be Told," 38.
42. *Baltimore American*, May 25, 1863.
43. Davis, "Photography in the Civil War," 159.
44. Colonel Devereux to Colonel McCallum, February 24, 1864, RG 92, box 815, "Photographs," National Archives.
45. Cooney, "Union Army's Forgotten Photographer," 35.

46. Buberger and Isenberg, *Russell's Civil War Photographs*, plates 7–10, 14–23, 26–31.
47. Quoted in Davis, "Photography in the Civil War," 164.
48. Buberger and Isenberg, *Russell's Civil War Photographs*, plates 32–35, 39, 42–43, 45–47, 48–49, 52–66, 72, 73–79, 84–88, 90–93, 99, and 106; Russell, "Photographic Reminiscences of the Late War," 212–13; Williams, "Truth Be Told," 39; Williams, "Reappraising the Brady Legend," 3–5; and Cooney, "Union Army's Forgotten Photographer," 34.
49. Russell, "Photographic Reminiscences of the Late War," 212–13.
50. *Baltimore American*, May 25, 1863.
51. Walther, "Landscape Photographs," 63; and Hirsch, *Seizing the Light,* 109.
52. *Nunda News*, June 13, 1863.
53. In addition, a few of his images were reproduced as illustrations in *Harper's Weekly*, December 12, 1863.
54. Williams, "Reappraising the Brady Legend," 3; Williams, "Truth Be Told," 40; Cooney, "Union Army's Forgotten Photographer," 35; and Gladstone, "First Army Photographer," 8.
55. *Nunda News*, June 17, 1865.
56. Gladstone, "First Army Photographer," 9.

CHAPTER 3

1. Bain, *Empire Express*, 52–53, 57–77, 117–18, 87–94.
2. Pacific Railway Act of 1862 (12 Stat. 489); Pacific Railway Act of 1863 (12 Stat. 807); and Pacific Railway Act of 1864 (13 Stat. 456).
3. Bain, *Empire Express*, 99, 102, 128–30, 136–46.
4. Bain, *Empire Express*, 122–24, 173–76, 179; and Pacific Railway Act of 1864 (13 Stat. 456).
5. Bain, *Empire Express*, 238–40.
6. Willumson, *Iron Muse*, 29.
7. Kibbey, *Railroad Photographs*, 77; and Willumson "Alfred Hart," 66–67.
8. Mautz, *Biographies of Western Photographers*, 107; Kibbey, *Railroad Photographs*, 52–63; and Willumson, "Alfred Hart," 61–66.
9. Willumson, "Alfred Hart," 66–67.
10. For a more detailed description of the conceptual framework of Hart's images, see Willumson, *Iron Muse*, 31–40, 67–88.
11. Willumson, *Iron Muse*, 5, 84–88.
12. Willumson, "Alfred Hart," 66–67.
13. "Photography as Applied to Business," *Photographic Times* 1, no. 4, April 1871, 49.
14. Willumson, *Iron Muse*, 34.
15. Bain, *Empire Express*, 227, 247.
16. Ibid., 254–55.
17. Ibid., 256.
18. Klein, *Union Pacific,* 191–92.
19. Van de Logt, *War Party in Blue,* 80–101.
20. Bain, *Empire Express*, 290–95; and Brey, *John Carbutt,* 39–53.
21. Willumson, "Alfred Hart," 21–26.

22. Bain, *Empire Express*, 394; and Russell, *Great West Illustrated,* plate 5.
23. Brey, *John Carbutt,* 55–66, 181. See John Carbutt, stereograph, "Views of the Rocky Mountains and Vicinity—288. Carmichael's Camp in the Black Hills U.P.R.R."
24. Bain, *Empire Express*, 112–15, 117, 162.
25. Ibid., 161–62, 193–94. Although the railroad did eventually reach Denver, it was not until 1870. Klein, *Union Pacific*, 344–45.
26. Hannavy, *Encyclopedia of Nineteenth-Century Photography*, 570–72; and Walther, "Landscape Photographs," 24–26, 30–36.
27. Walther, "Landscape Photographs," 44–56.
28. Several tintype portraits from the Wide Awake Gallery, under Russell's name, have appeared on the market. See examples at Gunsight Antiques, gunsightantiques.com; Internet Antique Shop, tias.com; and Sheaff: Ephemera, sheaff-ephemera.com.
29. *Nunda News*, April 18, 1868.
30. Williams, "Great West Illustrated," 4–18.
31. The two communicated because Russell photographed Durant on at least two of his trips out West; Durant also sent to or received from Russell at least two telegrams, one of which was quite long, in 1869. Western Union Telegraph Co. 1869 Accounts, box 33, Leonard Railroadiana, University of Iowa Libraries.
32. For every mile of track laid, the Union Pacific obtained rights to coal for ten alternate sections of land on both sides of the line. In the 1870s and 1880s this coal would prove extremely lucrative. Gardner and Flores, *Forgotten Frontier,* 12–13.
33. There is no Union Pacific record indicating that Russell received a salary, nor is this mentioned in Smith's diaries. In fact, these diaries indicate that Russell often was cash-strapped, and Smith gave him loans on occasion. As well, Russell, coming and going at his leisure, seemed to have more power over his own affairs than Smith.
34. Willumson characterizes it as an "exclusive agreement" in *Iron Muse*, 49. Correspondence in the Leonard Railroadiana at the University of Iowa Libraries indicates that publishers contacted Durant asking for permission to use Russell's images. Also, while Russell was in the West in 1869, Durant made prints from his negatives and sold them. *Iron Muse*, 49, 89.
35. Bain, *Empire Express*, 481–83.
36. Russell took photographs of Durant during this time: see large-format view nos. 37 and 37b; Russell, stereo-view no. 146, "Bushnell and Party, Rock Creek"; and Bain, *Empire Express*, 508.
37. See, for instance, Russell, large-format view no. 102; Russell, stereo-view nos. 267, 333, 372, 374, 375, 380, 385, 394, and 398; and Russell's later images after the work was complete in 1869: large-format view no. 105 and stereo-view nos. 384, 386, 391, 392, and 401. Bain, *Empire Express*, 493, 535–36, 550–51; and Joint Resolution for the Protection of the Interests of the United States in the Union Pacific Railway Company, the Central Pacific Railway Company, and for Other Purposes, April 10, 1869, sections 2 and 3.
38. Pacific Railway Act of 1862 (12 Stat. 489), sections 3 and 4; and Bain, *Empire Express*, 270.
39. See, for instance, 1868 images such as Russell, large-format view no. 102; Russell, stereo-view nos. 267, 333, 372, 374, 375, 380, 385, 394, and 398; and their corresponding 1869 images: Russell, large-format no. 105 and stereo-view nos. 384, 386, 391, 392, and 401.
40. Willumson makes a similar point, pointing out that Hart and Russell were corporate photogra-

phers creating a corporate photographic archive. As such they had much less artistic license than commentators have assumed. *Iron Muse*, 5–6.

CHAPTER 4

1. Willumson, *Iron Muse*, 50–51.
2. Williams, "Truth be Told," 40.
3. Russell's equipment was leftover from the Civil War, including his 10" x 13" camera and darkroom wagon. During the Civil War, he owned this equipment rather than the army. Williams, "Reappraising the Brady Legend," 5. On April 18, 1868, Russell's hometown newspaper the *Nunda News* stated that he was in "the Rocky Mountains."
4. Bain, *Empire Express*, 476. There are at least two Russell stereo-views (nos. 104 and 107) with a partially finished guardrail on the trestle.
5. Russell, *Great West Illustrated*, annotated table of contents.
6. Smith, Transcript of Diaries, April 12–18, 1868. The transcript reads, "I assist a J. P. Roberts in taking 4 Views of Dale Creek Bridge." This is the first and only mention of Roberts, so I am assuming this is a transcription error and J. P. Roberts is A. J. Russell.
7. "Death of Mr. O. C. Smith," *Rock Springs Minor*, January 21, 1904.
8. Biographical information in Smith, Transcript of Diaries, beginning of 1871; Wikipedia, s.v. "Dillon, Sidney," last modified May 17, 2017, wikipedia.org/wiki/Sidney_Dillon; and Smith, Transcript of Diaries, January 26–February 1, 1868, and February 16–22, 1868.
9. These mountains are now commonly known as the Laramie Mountains, although Russell sometimes used Laramie Mountains, even when referring to the Medicine Bow Mountains, which are further south and west.
10. Bain, *Empire Express*, 377.
11. Ibid., 439–40.
12. Smith, Transcript of Diaries, July 4–10, 1869, and July 18–24, 1869.
13. Russell, *Great West Illustrated*, annotated table of contents.
14. *Leslie's Illustrated*, May 8, 1869.
15. "Mr. Russell gets some pictures of me finished up also of others." Smith, Transcript of Diaries, May 31–June 6, 1868.
16. Smith, Transcript of Diaries, June 7–13, 1868.
17. Ibid., June 28–July 4, 1868.
18. Hayden, *Sun Pictures of Rocky Mountain Scenery*, 75.
19. Hayden, *Report of the United States Geological Survey*, 128.
20. Russell, *Great West Illustrated*, plate 19; also large-format view no. 54a.
21. Hayden, *Report of the United States Geological Survey*, 128.
22. Dodge, *How We Built the Union Pacific Railway*, 31; Bain, *Empire Express*, 518; and Walther, "Landscape Photographs," 72.
23. Smith, Transcript of Diaries, September 6–12, 1868.
24. Russell, large-format view no. 59.
25. Russell, large-format view nos. 62, 65, and 70.
26. Smith, Transcript of Diaries, September 20–26, 1868. See Russell, large-format view nos. 64b, 72, and 77c; and Russell, stereo-view no. 197.

27. *Nunda News*, September 3, 1870.
28. Bain, *Empire Express*, 550–64, 569, 605.
29. Ibid., 125.
30. Ibid., 495.
31. *Deseret News*, December 16, 1868.
32. Even Nounan paid the tithing. Arrington, *Great Basin Kingdom*, 262–63.
33. Bain, *Empire Express*, 511, 541.
34. *Deseret News*, July 15, 1868.
35. Hayden, *Sun Pictures of Rocky Mountain Scenery*, 88.
36. Bain, *Empire Express*, 529.
37. Pulpit Rock was demolished in 1928 after becoming a potential safety hazard because it became unstable during the construction of nearby Echo Dam. *Salt Lake Telegram*, September 15, 1928.
38. Russell, *Great West Illustrated*, annotated table of contents.
39. Hannavy, *Encyclopedia of Nineteenth-Century Photography*, 1245; and Richards, *Savage View*, 6–18.
40. Hannavy, *Encyclopedia of Nineteenth-Century Photography*, 1245–46; and Richards, *Savage View*, 21–31.
41. Hannavy, *Encyclopedia of Nineteenth-Century Photography*, 1245–46; and Richards, *Savage View*, 33–45.
42. Richards, *Savage View*, 51; and Russell, stereo-view no. 357.
43. Russell, stereo-view no. 375 and similar Savage stereo-view.
44. Richards, *Savage View*, 51, 58.
45. Savage Diaries, May 18, 1869, Brigham Young University.
46. Williams, "Great West Illustrated," 11, 12; and Richards, *Savage View*, 51.
47. Russell, *Great West Illustrated*, annotated table of contents.
48. Smith, Transcript of Diaries, November 28–December 5, 1868.
49. *Nunda News*, December 12, 1868.
50. Bain, *Empire Express,* 551–56, 585.

CHAPTER 5

1. Kibbey, *Railroad Photographs*, 35, 37, 63, 66; and Bain, *Empire Express*, 65.
2. Kibbey, *Railroad Photographs*, 35.
3. Bain, *Empire Express*, 428, 448–50, 469.
4. Ibid., 501–2.
5. Ibid., 632–33.
6. Spude, *Promontory Summit,* 48–49.
7. Johnson, "Rendezvous at Promontory," 18.
8. Savage Diaries, May 4, 7, and 8, 1869, Brigham Young University.
9. *Deseret News*, May 19, 1869.
10. Savage Diaries, May 7, 1869, Brigham Young University.
11. *Deseret News*, May 19, 1869. The newspaper correspondent mentions seeing "advance pages" of volume 1 of *The Great West Illustrated.*
12. Thomas Durant to Henry Crane, April 22, 1869, MSS 159, box 12, Leonard Railroadiana, Uni-

versity of Iowa Libraries. Durant paid him four separate payments of $45.13, $99, $100, and $631.28 (to E. & H. T. Anthony & Co. for supplies). The $45.13 was probably for supplies and the $100 and $99, in all likelihood, were for expenses to travel to Utah. I am indebted to Dr. Willumson for pointing out these sources.

13. *Nunda News*, May 1, 1869, and September 18, 1969.
14. Leonard Eicholtz wrote on May 5, 1869: "Rode all night, and get to Blue Creek at 5 AM. Walked over to camp with Maj. Russel[l] Co. Photographer who came up to take views of Road." Eicholtz Diaries, box 3, folder 6, University of Wyoming.
15. *Alta California*, May 7, 1869.
16. Spude, *Promontory Summit,* 90; and *Leslie's Illustrated*, June 5, 1869. All subsequent times are local sun time. The sequence for Russell's images taken during the ceremony was deduced from a mix of Johnson's "Rendezvous at Promontory," Spude's *Promontory Summit,* contemporary accounts, and the images themselves.
17. Russell took at least twelve stereo-views as well as six large-format views. He recognized the monetary value of the stereo-views and only eleven are in series no. 13.
18. Savage Diaries, May 10, 1869, Brigham Young University.
19. Kibbey, *Railroad Photographs*, 87; and Spude, *Promontory Summit*, 155.
20. Russell, stereo-view nos. 534, 538, and 541.
21. Spude, *Promontory Summit,* 19–20; and Stillman, "The Last Tie," 77.
22. Russell, stereo-view nos. 541 (alternate view) and 539.
23. *Daily Alta California,* May 12, 1869; and Spude, *Promontory Summit,* 202.
24. Russell, large-format view no. 225.
25. Russell, stereo-view nos. 540 and 541.
26. Spude, *Promontory Summit,* 25.
27. *Deseret News,* May 19, 1869. Russell was misidentified in the *Deseret News* as "Maj. A. D. Russell."
28. Russell, large-format view, no. 227.
29. Johnson, "Rendezvous at Promontory," 30–32; and McGowan, "First Train West," 27. About this time Russell moved both his cameras northwest, looking east, closer to the Jupiter. Russell, large-format no. 223; and Russell, stereo-view no. 543.
30. *Leslie's Illustrated*, June 5, 1869; and *Harper's Weekly*, June 5, 1869.
31. Richards, *Savage View,* 58.
32. Johnson, "Rendezvous at Promontory," 31–32, 48.
33. Stillman, "The Last Tie," 77; and Bain, *Empire Express*, 662. In Hart's stereo-view no. 357 (fig. 5.10) one can see that Russell's large-format camera is mounted on a large tripod.
34. Russell, large-format view nos. 224 and 226.
35. Kibbey, *Railroad Photographs*, 45.
36. See, for instance, Sandweiss, *Print the Legend*, 160: "The Chinese were banished from the official visual records of the scene." On May 10, 2014, a new photograph was taken at the annual reenactment of the ceremony at the Golden Spike National Historic Site with several of the descendants of these Chinese workers. See "A 'Photographic Act of Justice' for Chinese Laborers at Golden Spike," *Salt Lake Tribune*, May 12, 2014. Russell, however, did have one stereo-view, no. 539, titled "Chinese at Laying Last Rail."
37. Bain, *Empire Express*, 206–9, 219–22.

38. "Transcontinental Railroad Postscript," *San Francisco Newsletter and California Advertiser*, May 15, 1869.
39. Maxwell, "Incidents in an Engineer's Life in the Far West," 118, Maxwell Papers, University of Delaware.
40. Willumson, *Iron Muse*, 47n32.
41. A price of fifty dollars is noted in Willumson, *Iron Muse*, 104; Bain, *Empire Express*, 659; Williams, "Truth be Told," 41; and Williams, "Great West Illustrated," 12.
42. "New York Correspondence," *Philadelphia Photographer*, 1869, 89; and Walther, "Landscape Photographs," 74.
43. George Opdyke to Thomas Durant, n.d., in private collection, quoted in Willumson, *Iron Muse*, 169.
44. *Deseret News*, June 23, 1869, and March 24, 1869; and Walther, "Landscape Photographs," 76.
45. WIlliam Henry Jackson wrote in his diary on August 21, 1869, that he "had a talk with Russell's printer and looked over his negatives and pictures." Jackson Papers, MSS 1541, New York Public Library. Smith, Transcript of Diaries, June 20–26, 1869.
46. *Leslie's Illustrated*, June 5, 1869.
47. Walther, "Landscape Photographs," 75. Other images used by *Leslie's Illustrated* in 1869 include "Windmill at Laramie, Wyoming Territory," on May 8, 1869, and "The National Grand Lodge of Odd Fellows Holding a Meeting in Echo Canyon," on October 9, 1869.
48. *Nunda News*, May 29, 1869.
49. *Deseret News*, July 7, 1869.
50. Kibbey, *Railroad Photographs*, 43.
51. *Deseret News*, July 7, 1869.
52. Savage Diaries, May 18, 1869, Brigham Young University.
53. *Nunda News*, May 29, 1869.
54. Bain, *Iron Muse*, 162–65; and Kibbey, *Railroad Photographs*, 67.

CHAPTER 6

1. Pacific Railway Act of 1862 (12 Stat. 489), section 4; and *Deseret News*, June 2, 1869, and May 26, 1869.
2. Bain, *Empire Express*, 594–95, 602.
3. The Union Pacific paid A. S. Pittman $846.43 for printing costs between April and December of 1869 and received $300.30 in sales. Thomas C. Durant, Accounting Records Checkbooks, box 12, Leonard Railroadiana, University of Iowa Libraries. See also Willumson, *Iron Muse*, 49n49, 89n46.
4. See, for example, Russell's "On the Mountain with the Tripod and Camera" and "Whoa January" in *Anthony's Photographic Bulletin.*
5. *Nunda News*, May 29, 1869, July 3, 1869, August 21, 1869, September 25, 1869, and January 1, 1870.
6. *Great West Illustrated*, annotated table of contents.
7. *Deseret News*, May 26, 1869.
8. Russell, large-format no. 207.

9. *Great West Illustrated*, annotated table of contents.
10. *Deseret News*, May 26, 1869. This newspaper complained loudly about this problem. The absence of further complaints would suggest it was completed shortly thereafter.
11. Savage Diaries, May 18, 1869, Brigham Young University. See Russell, stereo-view no. 483.
12. Savage Diaries, May 30–31, 1869, and June 1, 1869, Brigham Young University; and Richards, *Savage View*, 59.
13. Richards, "Other Promontory Photographer," 154.
14. Smith, Transcript of Diaries, May 23–29, 1869.
15. Smith, Transcript of Diaries, entries in 1869: July 18–24, August 1–7, September 4–10, October 10–16, October 30, and November 6.
16. *Nunda News*, July 3, 1869.
17. Russell, "On the Mountains with the Tripod and Camera," 33. See also *Nunda News,* September 18, 1969.
18. Bowles, *Our New West*, 59–60.
19. *Nunda News*, May 29, 1869.
20. *Nunda News* May 29, 1869. Willumson points out Russell's preoccupation with water, which shows up in many images of *The Great West Illustrated*, in *Iron Muse*, 99.
21. *Nunda News*, May 29, 1869. Russell invested in mines and got Smith involved as well. Smith, Transcript of Diaries, June 7–13, 1868, June 14–20, 1868, August 23–29, 1868, July 4–10, 1869, and July 18–24, 1869.
22. *Nunda News*, August 21, 1869. Russell's negatives looking out from the mountaintop must have been lost or broken as they are not included among his known photographs.
23. Smith, Transcript of Diaries, May 23–29, 1869.
24. *Nunda News*, September 25, 1869.
25. Ibid.
26. Russell and O'Sullivan had crossed paths in the Civil War. Horan, *Timothy O'Sullivan,* 35.
27. Hannavy, *Encyclopedia of Nineteenth-Century Photography,* 1017–20; and Horan, *Timothy O'Sullivan,* 35.
28. Jurovics et al., *Framing the West,* 181.
29. *Nunda News*, September 25, 1869. Russell's elevations are about a thousand feet too high.
30. For an insightful discussion comparing the work of these two photographers, see Jurovics et al., *Framing the West,* 177–80.
31. Jurovics et al., *Framing the West*, 181. Both Russell and O'Sullivan negatives are in Timothy O'Sullivan Images, U.S. National Archives. As well, several of Russell's King survey negatives appear in Russell's Union Pacific series.
32. Jurovics et al., *Framing the West,* 181–84. The Salt Lake City images, though, were probably taken in the late fall of 1868.
33. *Nunda News*, September 25, 1869.
34. *Nunda News*, September 25, 1869; and Smith, Transcript of Diaries, August 15–21, 1869.
35. Russell, stereo-view no. 459.
36. Smith, Transcript of Diaries, August 22–28, 1869. Examples of Russell stereo-views from this trip include nos. 451, 454, 456, 457, 459, 460, 461, 462, 463, 464, 465, and 475; and Russell, large-format view nos. 149, 170 no. 2, and 171.

37. Miller, *Photographer of the Early West,* 25–41.
38. Hannavy, *Encyclopedia of Nineteenth-Century Photography,* 765–67.
39. Jackson Diary, June 29, 1869, New York Public Library.
40. Jackson Diary, August 23, 1869, New York Public Library.
41. Jackson Diary, August 7, 1869, New York Public Library.
42. Jackson Diary, September 19, 1869, New York Public Library.
43. *Leslie's Illustrated,* October 9, 1869.
44. Russell, stereo-view nos. 315 and 316; and Smith, Transcript of Diaries, October 2–8, 1869.
45. Bowles, *Our New West,* 61, 205; and *Deseret News,* October 6, 1869, October 13, 1869, November 3, 1869, and November 10, 1869.
46. Smith, Transcript of Diaries, October 30–November 6 and November 21–27, 1869; Russell, stereo-view nos. 535, 536, and 544; and Spude, *Promontory Summit,* 47.
47. *Nunda News,* January 1, 1870.
48. Ibid.
49. It is possible that he took some of these images in the last week of April or the first week of May in 1869, but he had very little time then (and a late April snowstorm is rare in Omaha) as he hurried out to Promontory.
50. For further discussion of this topic, see Willumson, *Iron Muse,* 64–65.
51. *Nunda News,* January 1, 1870.
52. "New York Correspondence," *Philadelphia Photographer,* 1870, 82.
53. Russell, "On the Mountain with the Tripod and Camera," 129.

CHAPTER 7

1. *Leslie's Illustrated,* January 15, 1870.
2. The series ran from January 1 to March 26. Russell's images can be found in the March 5, 12, 19, and 26 editions.
3. Brown, *Beyond the Lines,* 148–52.
4. *Daily Graphic,* April 23, 1880.
5. See untitled article in the *Photographic Times,* December 1875, 296, which refers to Russell as the "photographer in chief to Frank Leslie's Illustrated Newspaper."
6. *Anthony's Photographic Bulletin,* 1884, 152–53; Watrous, *A Century of American Printmaking,* 20–21; and Brown, *Beyond the Lines,* 298n69.
7. *Nunda News,* June 11, 1870, and September 18, 1969.
8. *Moore's Rural New-Yorker,* November 22, 1873.
9. *Photographic Times,* December 1875, 296.
10. See Willumson, *Iron Muse,* 165–66. Samuel Bowles, Thaddeus Clapp, and F. V. Hayden all approached the Union Pacific for permission to publish his images. In Leonard Railroadiana, University of Iowa Libraries: Hayden correspondence, September 1, 1868, box 18; Samuel Bowles to H. C. Crane, February 2, 1869, box 5; and Thaddeus Clapp to H. C. Crane, August 24, 1869, box 31.
11. Klein, *Union Pacific,* 239–40.
12. Russell was paid at least $155 by Hayden for the use of his images. Smith, Transcript of Diaries, June 1871.

13. *The Great West Illustrated*, though, had higher-quality images. Cassidy, *Ferdinand V. Hayden,* 228; and Foster, *Strange Genius,* 197.
14. *Sun Pictures of Rocky Mountain Scenery*, vii.
15. *Sun Pictures of Rocky Mountain Scenery*, 112; and Pattison, "The Pacific Railroad Rediscovered," 33.
16. *Sun Pictures of Rocky Mountain Scenery*, 54.
17. Ibid., 72.
18. Ibid., 30.
19. See, for instance, *Sun Pictures of Rocky Mountain Scenery*, 105.
20. Ibid., viii.
21. Willumson, *Iron Muse*, 192n50.
22. Ibid., 212n22.
23. Smith, Transcript of Diaries, October 24–30, 1869.
24. Ibid., June 1871.
25. Smith, Transcript of Diaries, June 1871. According to the transcriptionist, by the beginning of 1871 Smith had already obtained the negatives.
26. Smith, Transcript of Diaries, July and August 1871.
27. Smith, Transcript of Diaries, April 1872; and Willumson, *Iron Muse*, 168–69.
28. Smith, Transcript of Diaries, November and December 1872; and "Death of Mr. O.C. Smith," *Rock Springs Miner*, January 21, 1904.
29. Willumson, *Iron Muse*, 210n1.
30. For an overview on Silvis, see Swackhamer, "J. B. Silvis."
31. Hannavy, *Encyclopedia of Nineteenth-Century Photography*, 1477–79.
32. Williams, "Great West Illustrated," 17; Pattison, "Westward by Rail with Professor Sedgwick," 338; and Willumson, *Iron Muse*, 170.
33. Russell to Sedgwick, April 8, 1876, Sedgwick Papers, University of California, Los Angeles. Russell addressed this letter to "Friend Sedgwick."
34. Sedgwick, *Catalogue of Stereoscopic Views of Scenery*. In the *Long Island City Star*: "We hope the professor will visit us again." Sedgwick stopped lecturing in 1879, probably because interest waned in photographic images of the American West. Sandweiss, *Print the Legend*, 174; and Williams, "Great West Illustrated" 17.
35. Willumson, *Iron Muse*, 167; and Smith, Transcript of Diaries, March 1872.
36. Willumson, *Iron Muse*, 167n24; and Smith, Transcript of Diaries, August 1872.

CHAPTER 8

1. FamilySearch, s.vv. "Russell, Andrew Joseph," "Duryea, Catherine Adelia," accessed March 30, 2018, familysearch.com; and "Death List of the Week," *New York Times*, September 28, 1902.
2. Ulysses S. Grant Papers, October 1, 1880–December 31, 1882, vol. 30, 484, Mississippi State University Libraries.
3. Current and Current, *Photography and the Old West*, 135; and Naef and Wood, *Era of Exploration*, 252.
4. Minnesota State Census, 1895, "Cora P. Cramb in household of A. L. Cramb." FamilySearch, s.v. "Cramb, Cora P.," accessed March 30, 2018, familysearch.com.

5. Naef and Wood were the first to articulate in a scholarly work, *Era of Exploration*, 12, that this era was "a golden age of landscape photography."
6. Hayden, *Sun Pictures of Rocky Mountain Scenery*, 18. For a further discussion of this idea, see Willumson, *Iron Muse*, 159–61.
7. *Leslie's Illustrated*, March 12, 1870.
8. See Naef and Wood, *Era of Exploration*, 73–76, 86.
9. The first historian to tackle this issue was Sandweiss in *Print the Legend*, 184–85. In *Iron Muse*, 3–4, Willumson makes a similar point that transcontinental railroad stereo-views are misunderstood because they usually are removed from the original context of their creation.
10. *Scientific American*, June 2, 1860, 361.
11. This is the major theme of chapters 1–3 in Sandweiss, *Print the Legend*.
12. His photographer was John K. (Jack) Hillers. Sandweiss, *Print the Legend*, 295.
13. Taft, *Photography and the American Scene*, 308; Earle, *Points of View*, 83: and Walther, "Landscape Photographs," 26–27.
14. Willumson mentions that Smith and Russell did a "lively business" in *Iron Muse*, 166. If nothing else, the sheer number of photographers who operated along the lines is a testament to their popularity.
15. *Leslie's Illustrated*, March 12, 1870.
16. Sandweiss was the first scholar to discuss in detail the marriage of words and images in the 1860s that led the viewer to a predetermined meaning. In *Print the Legend*, see chapter 5 and Sandweiss's discussion of Russell's large-format images, 171–77.
17. For a fuller description, see Sandweiss, *Print the Legend*, 156–70.
18. See Sherow and Charlton, *Railroad Empire Across the Heartland*, 5–21.
19. *Cheyenne Daily Leader*, May 14, 1869.
20. For examples, see the *Deseret News*, May 19, 1869; article by Russell in *Nunda News*, May 29, 1869; and *Leslie's Illustrated*, June 5, 1869. For an in-depth discussion of the symbolism of the railroad to the nation, see Willumson, *Iron Muse*, 4, 25, 58–62.
21. This topic is explored at length in the first two chapters in Athearn, *Union Pacific Country*.
22. Edwin, *Account of an Expedition*, 236–37.
23. For additional examples, see Meinig, *Shaping of America*, 76–77.
24. Raynolds, *Report on the Exploration of the Yellowstone River*, 154.
25. *Leslie's Illustrated*, February 19, 1870.
26. Stegner, *Beyond the Hundredth Meridian*, 6.
27. Beadle, *Undeveloped West*, 50. The Northern Pacific Railroad had to fight against this perception even as late as the 1880s; see Schwantes and Ronda, *The West the Railroads Made* 123–26.
28. *Leslie's Illustrated*, January 22, 1870.
29. Fleming, "Ridgway Glover, Photographer."
30. For a typical example, see *Leslie's Illustrated*, March 26, 1870, which reported that warlike Indians had attacked a party of men on a Union Pacific handcar.
31. In *Iron Muse*, 12, Willumson mentions that the Union Pacific had to fight against this negative characterization, but he does not explicitly link these efforts to Russell's photographic archive.
32. Sandweiss discusses these ideas at length in *Print the Legend*, 13–14, 154–71.
33. Hayden, *Sun Pictures of Rocky Mountain Scenery*, 33.

34. *Our New West*, 47. Bowles used several Russell photographs, and Russell photographed him at least once in stereo-view nos. 315 and 316.
35. In *Western American Survey*, 24–29, Snyder, however, argues that O'Sullivan and Bell, unlike other western photographers, did not attempt to "portray the American West as hospitable and inviting."
36. Some commentators have taken this idea too far, writing that Russell photographed mile after mile of track sequentially, as if documenting the entire length of the Union Pacific one glass-plate negative at a time. See Sandweiss, *Print the Legend*, 77.
37. For a fuller discussion of this topic, see Bain, *Iron Muse*, 162; and Sandweiss, "Views and Reviews: Western Art and Western History," in *Under an Open Sky*, ed. Cronon, Miles, and Gitlin, 190–91.

EPILOGUE

1. Sabin, *Building the Pacific Railway.*
2. See Perkins, *Trails, Rails, and War;* and Beebe, *Hear the Train Blow.* For a fuller description of how Russell's images were used during this time, see Walther, "Landscape Photographs," 5–9; and Willumson, *Iron Muse*, 174–77.
3. Pattison, "Pacific Railroad Rediscovered," 25–29.
4. Combs, *Westward to Promontory*, 6; and Williams, "Great West Illustrated," 18. The most thorough discussion of the negatives is in Willumson, *Iron Muse*, 174–75.
5. Pattison, "Westward by Rail with Professor Sedgwick," 334–39.
6. Today the collection is at the Oakland Museum of California, which purchased the negatives in 1969.
7. Two examples include Combs, *Westward to Promontory:* and Best, *Iron Horses to Promontory.*
8. *Era of Exploration*, 201–8.
9. Susan Williams's two articles about Russell's Union Pacific images, "Great West Illustrated" and "Truth be Told," unfortunately do not have footnotes.
10. For a summary, see the introduction to Willumson, *Iron Muse,* 1–10.
11. See the New York Public Library, Digital Gallery; the digital Utah State University, Nineteenth-Century Western Stereo-Views Collection; the digital University of Iowa Libraries, Levi O. Leonard Railroadiana; the online Library of Congress, Prints and Photographs Division; the Union Pacific Railroad Museum, A. J. Russell Views; and the Oakland Museum of California, Andrew J. Russell Collection. Not all the images available online, however, are high-resolution copies.
12. Russell's stereo-views have frequently appeared on eBay since the 1990s.
13. White, *Railroaded.*
14. White felt that government-subsidized railroads were built before they were economically feasible and a better system would have been slowly to build westward as the population expanded.

CATALOG OF RUSSELL'S UNION PACIFIC PHOTOGRAPHS

1. Willumson, *Iron Muse*, 47–42.
2. Ibid.

3. *Baltimore American*, May 25, 1863.
4. The Library of Congress has the largest collection of Russell's Civil War images.
5. Image quality varies quite a bit from image to image, not just fading, but also detail.
6. Sometimes this series has thirty images and sometimes it has thirty-one. Perhaps realizing that he had double-numbered images, Russell might have issued later editions with only thirty images.
7. Thankfully, no. 31 is the only time the Across the Continent, West from Omaha series double-numbered an image.
8. Although the alternate views frequently came with a letter designation on the image itself, this is the only instance where titles listed on the verso of the Rocky Mountain Scenery series had a letter added to a number.
9. In the stereo-views, no. 232 is the only instance where the OMCA negative number does not match up with the UPRM print number. The OMCA image listed as no. 232 looks more like no. 233.
10. Russell listed both the Weber [C]anyon Series and the Devil's Gate Series as No. 10, so here I have listed the latter series as No. 11.
11. There are three large-format images in the A. J. Russell Photographs at Yale University that would be good candidates for no. 3 and no. 5. These images were definitely taken around the same time as the other Omaha large-format images based on the amount of snow in the images.
12. Note Russell's photographic wagon on the right side of the image.
13. A panoramic view of Bitter Creek Valley is formed by nos. 62, 65, and 70.
14. The number at the end of the description ("No. 2" in this case) refers to a series of views of the same subject or even where three negatives can be combined to form a panoramic image.
15. A panoramic view is formed by combining nos. 73 and 75.
16. Another Green River view by Russell can be found in *Great West Illustrated*, Plate XXV. "Green River Valley, Looking down the River."
17. The next nine out of ten negatives are missing, which probably went to King's geological survey. Two versions are in *Sun Pictures*: "Moore's Lake: Head of Bear River," and "Lake at Head of Bear River," which shows Ryder Lake. Photo albums in the A. J. Russell Photographs at Yale University, however, show several more images, in some cases from the same spot as his stereo-views of McPheters and Ryder Lake.
18. The people in this image are sometimes identified as Mary and Samuel Ashton, surrounded by Mary's female relatives.
19. A group of Union Pacific officials, including Durant.
20. My theory is that Russell may have used this title jokingly. The "Utes" were probably Shoshone, and they have no weapons. As well, the image looks posed and includes an Anglo man.

BIBLIOGRAPHY

BOOKS

Ambrose, Stephen E. *Nothing Like It in the World: The Men Who Built the Transcontinental Railroad 1863–1869.* New York: Simon and Schuster, 2000.

Arrington, Leonard J. *Great Basin Kingdom: An Economic History of the Latter-day Saints 1830–1900.* Cambridge, MA: Harvard University Press, 1958.

Aspinwall, Jane L. *Alexander Gardner: The Western Photographs, 1867–1868.* New Haven, CT: Yale University Press, 2014.

Athearn, Robert. *Union Pacific Country.* New York: Rand McNally, 1971.

Bain, David Howard. *Empire Express: Building the First Transcontinental Railroad.* New York: Viking, 1999.

Beadle, J. H. *The Undeveloped West; or, Five Years in the Territories.* Philadelphia: National Publishing, 1873.

Beebe, Lucius. *Hear the Train Blow: A Pictorial Epic of America in the Railroad Age.* New York: Dutton, 1952.

Bell, William A. *New Tracks in North America: A Journey of Travel and Adventure Whilst Engaged in the Survey for a Southern Railroad to the Pacific Ocean during 1867–8.* London: Chapman and Hall, 1869.

Best, Gerald M. *Iron Horses to Promontory.* San Marino, CA: Golden West Books, 1969.

Bowles, Samuel. *Our New West: Records of Travel between the Mississippi River and the Pacific Ocean.* Hartford, CT: Hartford Publishing, 1869.

———. *The Pacific Railroad–Open: How to Go; What to See.* Boston: Fields, Osgood, 1869.

Brey, William. *John Carbutt: On the Frontiers of Photography.* Cherry Hill, NJ: Willowdale, 1984.

Brown, Joshua. *Beyond the Lines: Pictorial Reporting, Everyday Life, and the Crisis of Gilded Age America.* Berkeley: University of California Press, 2002.

Buberger, Joe, and Matthew Isenberg. *Russell's Civil War Photographs: 116 Historic Prints by Andrew J. Russell.* New York: Dover, 1982.

Cassidy, James G. *Ferdinand V. Hayden: Entrepreneur of Science.* Lincoln: University of Nebraska Press, 2000.

Combs, Barry B. *Westward to Promontory: Building the Union Pacific across the Plains and Mountains.* New York: Garland Books, 1969.

Crawford, William. *The Keepers of Light: A History and Working Guide to Early Photographic Processes.* Dobbs Ferry, NY: Morgan and Morgan, 1979.

Cronon, William, George Miles, and Jay Gitlin, eds. *Under an Open Sky: Rethinking America's Western Past.* New York: Norton, 1992.

Current, Karen, and William R. Current. *Photography and the Old West.* New York: Abradale, 1986.

Danly, Susan, and Leo Marx, eds. *The Railroad in American Art: Representations of Technological Change.* Cambridge, MA: MIT Press, 1988.

Darrah, William Culp. *Stereoviews: A History of Stereographs in America and Their Collection.* Gettysburg, PA: Times and News Publishing, 1964.

———. *The World of Stereographs*. Gettysburg, PA: Darrah, 1977.

Dodge, Grenville Mellen. *How We Built the Union Pacific Railway, and other Railway Papers and Addresses*. Denver: Sage Books, 1965.

Earle, Edward. *Points of View: The Stereograph in America—A Cultural History*. Rochester, NY: Visual Studies Workshop Press, 1979.

Edwin, James. *Account of an Expedition from Pittsburgh to the Rocky Mountains, Performed in the Years 1819 and '20*. Vol. 3. London: Longman, Hurst, Rees, Orme, and Brown, 1823.

Fels, Thomas Weston. *Destruction and Destiny: The Photographs of A. J. Russell; Directing American Energy in War and Peace, 1862–1869*. Pittsfield, MA: Berkshire Museum, 1987.

Foster, Mike. *Strange Genius: The Life of Ferdinand Vandeveer Hayden*. Niwot, CO: Roberts Rinehart, 1994.

Fowler, Don D. *The Western Photographs of John K. Hillers: Myself in the Water*. Washington, DC: Smithsonian Institution Press, 1989.

Francaviglia, Richard V. *Over the Range: A History of the Promontory Summit Route of the Pacific Railroad*. Logan: Utah State University Press, 2008.

Gardner, Dudley, and Vera R. Flores. *Forgotten Frontier: A History of Wyoming Coal Mining*. Boulder, CO: Westview, 1989.

Hannavy, John, ed. *Encyclopedia of Nineteenth-Century Photography*. New York: Routledge, 2008.

Hart, A. A., and Charles Shober. *The Traveler's Own Book: A Panorama of Overland Travel, from Chicago to San Francisco. . . .* Chicago: Horton and Leonard, 1870.

Haupt, Herman. *Photographs Illustrative of Operations in Construction and Transportation, as Used to Facilitate the Movements of the Armies of the Rappahannock, of Virginia, and of the Potomac, Including Experiments Made to Determine the Most Practical and Expeditious Modes to Be Resorted to in the Construction, Destruction and Reconstruction of Roads and Bridges*. Boston: Wright and Potter, 1863.

———. *Reminiscences of General Herman Haupt*. Milwaukee: Wright and Joys, 1901.

Hayden, F. V. *Preliminary Report of the United States Geological Survey of Wyoming, and Portions of Contiguous Territories, Conducted under the Authority of the Secretary of the Interior, by F. V. Hayden United States Geologist*. Washington, DC: Government Printing Office, 1871.

———. *Sun Pictures of Rocky Mountain Scenery, with a Description of the Geographical and Geological Features, and Some Account of the Resources of the Great West: Containing Thirty Photographic Views along the Line of the Pacific Railroad, from Omaha to Sacramento*. New York: J. Bien, 1870.

Hirsch, Robert. *Seizing the Light: A History of Photography*. New York: McGraw Hill, 2000.

Holzer, Harold, and Mark E. Neely, *Mine Eyes Have Seen the Glory: The Civil War in Art*. New York: Orion Books, 1993.

Horan, James D. *Timothy O'Sullivan: America's Forgotten Photographer*. New York: Bonanza Books, 1966.

Huhtama, Erkki. *Illusions in Motion: Media Archaeology of the Moving Panorama and Related Spectacles*. Cambridge, MA: MIT Press, 2013.

Jackson, William Henry. *Time Exposure: The Autobiography of William Henry Jackson*. New York: G. P. Putnam's Sons, 1940.

———. *William Henry Jackson's "The Pioneer Photographer."* Edited by Bob Blair. Santa Fe: Museum of New Mexico Press, 2005.

Jurovics, Toby, Carol M. Johnson, Glenn Willumson, and William F. Tapp. *Framing the West: The Survey Photographs of Timothy O'Sullivan*. New Haven, CT: Yale University Press, 2010.

Katz, Mark D. *Witness to an Era: The Life and Photographs of Alexander Gardner: The Civil War, Lincoln, and the West*. New York: Viking, 1991.

Kelsey, Robin. *Archive Style: Photographs and Illustrations for U.S. Surveys, 1850–1890*. Berkeley: University of California Press, 2007.

Kibbey, Mead B. *The Railroad Photographs of Alfred A. Hart, Artist*. Sacramento: California State Library Foundation, 1996.

Klein, Maury. *The Union Pacific: Birth of a Railroad, 1862–1893*. Garden City, NY: Doubleday, 1987.

Klett, Mark, and Ellen Manchester. *Second View: The Rephotographic Survey Project*. Albuquerque: University of New Mexico Press, 1984.

Margolis, David. *To Delight the Eye: Original Photographic Book Illustrations of the American West*. Dallas: DeGolyer Library, Southern Methodist University, 1994.

Mautz, Carl. *Biographies of Western Photographers*. Nevada City, CA: Carl Mautz, 1997.

Meinig, D. W. *The Shaping of America: A Geographical Perspective on 500 Years of History*. Vol. 3, *Transcontinental America, 1850–1915*. New Haven, CT: Yale University Press, 1998.

Miller, Eugene Arundel. *Photographer of the Early West: The Story of Arundel Hull*. Mill Valley, CA: Antelope Press, 2004.

———. *Railroad 1869: Along the Historic Union Pacific*. Mill Valley, CA: Antelope Press, 2009.

———. *A Traveler's Guide to Railroad 1869: Along the Historic Union Pacific*. Mill Valley, CA: Antelope Press, 2009.

Miller, Nina Hull. *Shutters West*. Denver: Sage Books, 1962.

Moat, Louis Shepheard, ed. *Frank Leslie's Illustrated History of the Civil War*. New York: Mrs. Frank Leslie, 1895.

Naef, Weston J., and James N. Wood. *Era of Exploration: The Rise of Landscape Photography in the American West, 1860–1885*. Buffalo, NY: Albright-Knox Art Gallery, 1975.

Oettermann, Stephan. *The Panorama: History of a Mass Medium*. New York: Zone Books, 1997.

Ostroff, Eugene. *Western Views and Eastern Visions*. Washington, DC: Smithsonian Institution Traveling Exhibition Service, 1981.

Palmquist, Peter E., and Thomas R. Kailbourn. *Pioneer Photographers of the Far West: A Biographical Dictionary, 1840–1865*. Stanford, CA: Stanford University Press, 2000.

Perkins, J. R., *Trails, Rails, and War: The Life of General G. M. Dodge*. Indianapolis, IN: Bobbs-Merrill, 1929.

Raymond, Anan S., and Richard E. Fike. *Rails East to Promontory: The Utah Stations*. Salt Lake City: Utah State Office, Bureau of Land Management, 1981.

Richards, Bradley W. *The Savage View: Charles Savage, Pioneer Mormon Photographer*. Reno, NV: Carl Mautz, 1995.

Russell, A. J. *The Great West Illustrated in a Series of Photographic Views across the Continent; Taken along the Line of the Union Pacific Railroad, West from Omaha, Nebraska*. New York: Union Pacific Railroad Company, 1869.

Sabin, Edwin L. *Building the Pacific Railway*. Philadelphia: J. B. Lippincott, 1919

Sandweiss, Martha A. *Print the Legend: Photography and the American West*. New Haven, CT: Yale University Press, 2002.

Schwantes, Carlos A., and James P. Ronda. *The West the Railroads Made*. Seattle: University of Washington Press, 2008.

Sedgwick, Stephen J. *Catalogue of Stereoscopic Views of Scenery in All Parts of the Rocky Mountains between Omaha and Sacramento*. Newton, NY: S. J. Sedgwick, 1874.

Serow, James E., and John R. Charlton. *Railroad Empire across the Heartland: Rephotographing Alexander Gardner's Westward Journey*. Albuquerque: University of New Mexico Press, 2014.

Snyder, Joel. *One/Many: Western American Survey Photographs by Bell and O'Sullivan*. Chicago: David and Alfred Smart Museum of Art, University of Chicago Press, 2006.

Sontag, Susan. *On Photography*. New York: Farrar, Straus and Giroux, 1977.

Stegner, Wallace. *Beyond the Hundredth Meridian: John Wesley Powell and the Second Opening of the West*. Boston: Houghton Mifflin, 1962.

Taft, Robert. *Artists and Illustrators of the Old West*. New York: Charles Scribner's Sons, 1953.

———. *Photography and the American Scene: A Social History, 1839–1889*. New York: Dover, 1938.

Tissandier, Gaston. *A History and Handbook of Photography*. London: Sampson Low, Marston, Searle, and Rivington, 1878.

Trachtenberg, Alan. *Reading American Photographs: Images as History; Mathew Brady to Walker Evans*. Boston: Hiss and Wang, 1989.

Van de Logt, Mark. *War Party in Blue: Pawnee Scouts in the U.S. Army*. Norman: University of Oklahoma Press, 2010.

Van Monckhoven, D. *A Popular Treatise on Photography: Also a Description of, and Remarks on the Stereoscope and Photographic Optics*. Translated by W. H. Thornthwaite. London: Virtue, 1863.

Wadsworth, Nelson. *Set in Stone, Fixed in Glass: The Great Mormon Temple and Its Photographers*. Salt Lake City: Signature Books, 1992.

———. *Through Camera Eyes*. Provo, UT: Brigham Young University Press, 1975.

Waldsmith, John. *Stereo Views: An Illustrated History and Price Guide*. Radnor, PN: Wallace-Homestead, 1991.

Watrous, James. *A Century of American Printmaking, 1880–1980*. Madison: University of Wisconsin Press, 1984.

Weber, Eva. *Ansel Adams and the Photographers of the American West*. San Diego, CA: Thunder Bay, 2002.

White, Richard. *Railroaded: The Transcontinentals and the Making of Modern America*. New York: Norton, 2011.

Willumson, Glenn. *Iron Muse: Photographing the Transcontinental Railroad*. Berkeley: University of California Press, 2013.

ARTICLES

Bowman, J. N. "Driving the Last Spike at Promontory, 1869." *California Historical Society Quarterly* 36, no. 2 (June 1957): 96–106.

Cooney, Charles F. "Andrew Joseph Russell: The Union Army's Forgotten Photographer." *Civil War Times Illustrated* 21, no. 2 (April 1982): 32–36.

Danly, Susan. "Andrew Joseph Russell's The Great West Illustrated." In *The Railroad in American Art: Representations of Technological Change*, edited by Susan Danly and Leo Marx, 93–112. Cambridge, MA: MIT Press, 1988.

Davis, Keith F. "'A Terrible Distinctness': Photography in the Civil War Era." In *Photography in Nineteenth-Century America*, edited by Martha A. Sandweiss, 130–79. New York: H. N. Abrams, 1991.

Fleming, Paula. "Ridgway Glover, Photographer," *Annals of Wyoming: The Wyoming History Journal* 74, no. 2 (2002): 17–23.

Gladstone, William. "Captain Andrew J. Russell: First Army Photographer." *Photographica* 10, no. 2 (1978): 7–9.

Haycox, Ernest, Jr. "'A Very Exclusive Party': A Firsthand Account of Building the Union Pacific Railroad." *Montana: The Magazine of Western History* 51, no. 1 (2001): 20–35.

Johnson, Michael W. "Rendezvous at Promontory: A New Look at the Golden Spike Ceremony." *Utah Historical Quarterly* 72, no. 1, (2004): 47–68.

Leonard, L. O. "At Promontory Sixty Years Ago This Month," *Union Pacific Magazine* 8, no. 5 (May 1929): 18–19, 34.

Masteller, Richard N. "Western Views in Eastern Parlors: The Contribution of the Stereograph Photographer to the Conquest of the West." *Prospects* 4 (1981): 55–71.

McGowan, Joseph. "First Train West." Excerpt from diary of Lt. John Charles Currier. *Sacramento County Historical Society Golden Notes* 15 (1969): 1–35.

"New York Correspondence." *Philadelphia Photographer* 6 (1869): 88–89.

———. *Philadelphia Photographer* 7 (1870): 82–83.

Pattison, William D. "Collector's Choice: The Photographs of A. J. Russell." *American West* 6, no. 3 (1969): 20–23.

———. "The Pacific Railroad Rediscovered." *Geographical Review* 52, no. 1 (1962): 25–36.

———. "Westward by Rail with Professor Sedgwick: A Lantern Journey of 1873." *Historical Society of Southern California Quarterly* 42 (1960): 335–49.

"Photosculpture." *Philadelphia Photographer* 4 (1867): 105–6.

Richards, Bradley W. "Charles R. Savage, the Other Promontory Photographer," *Utah Historical Quarterly* 60, no. 2 (1992): 137–57.

Russell, Andrew J. "A New Out-Door Camera Box." *Anthony's Photographic Bulletin* 1 (1870): 117–18.

———. "On the Mountain with the Tripod and Camera." *Anthony's Photographic Bulletin* 1 (1870): 33–35, 128–30.

———. "Photographic Reminiscences of the Late War." *Anthony's Photographic Bulletin* 13 (1882): 212–13.

———. "Whoa January." *Anthony's Photographic Bulletin* 5 (1874): 3–4.

Sedgwick, Stephen J. "Great Salt Lake." *Anthony's Photographic Bulletin* 1 (1870): 56.

Stillman, J. D. B. "The Last Tie." *Overland Monthly and Out West Magazine* 3, no. 1 (1869): 76–78.

Swackhamer, Barry A. "J. B. Silvis, the Union Pacific's Nomadic Photographer." *Journal of the West* 33, no. 2, (1994): 52–62.

Weinstein, Robert, and Roger Olmsted. "Epic on Glass." *American West* 4, no. 1 (1967): 10–23.

Williams, Susan. "The Great West Illustrated: A Journey across the Continent with Andrew J. Russell." *Streamliner* 10, no. 3 (1996): 4–18.

———. "'Richmond Again Taken': Reappraising the Brady Legend through Photographs by Andrew J. Russell," *Virginia Magazine of History and Biography* 110, no. 4 (2002): 437–60.

———. "The Truth Be Told: The Union Pacific Photographs of Andrew J. Russell." *View Camera* 9 (January/February 1996): 36–43.

Willumson, Glenn. "Alfred Hart: Photographer of the Transcontinental Railroad." *History of Photography* 12 (January–March 1988): 61–75.

DISSERTATIONS

Walther, Susan Danly. "The Landscape Photographs of Alexander Gardner and Andrew Joseph Russell," PhD diss., Brown University, 1983.

NEWSPAPERS

Chronicling America: Historic American Newspapers, 1863–1869. Library of Congress. ChroniclingAmerica.loc.gov.

Deseret News (Salt Lake City, UT), 1866–1869.

Frank Leslie's Illustrated Newspaper (New York City, NY), 1868–1870.

Harper's Weekly (New York, NY), 1863.

Moore's Rural New-Yorker (Rochester, NY), 1873.

New York Times (NY), 1902.

Nunda News (NY), 1859–1969.

Old Fulton New York Postcards. Old New York State Historical Newspapers, 1860–1969. FultonHistory.com.

Photographic Times (New York, NY), 1871–1876.

MANUSCRIPT COLLECTIONS

Brigham Young University, Harold B. Lee Library, L. Tom Perry Special Collections. C. R. Savage Diaries, 1855–1909 (MSS 1424).

Council Bluffs Public Library. Grenville Dodge Papers, 1855–1916 (collection B D6643, vols. 1–5).

New York Public Library. Manuscripts and Archives Division. William Henry Jackson Papers. Diary, June 22–September 27, 1869 (MSS 1541).

Smith, Oliver C. Transcript of Diaries, 1868–1872. Transcript created by Phyllis Morris, 1976. Private Collection.

University of California, Los Angeles. Charles E. Young Research Library. Department of Special Collections. Stephen James Sedgwick Papers (collection 301).

University of Delaware Library. Special Collections. James Riddle Maxwell. "Incidents in an Engineer's Life in the Far West." James R. Maxwell Papers, 1867–1900 (MS 170).

University of Wyoming. American Heritage Center. Leonard Eicholtz Diaries (collection 00238).

Utah State University. Merrill-Cazier Library. Special Collections and Archives. Michael W. Johnson. "The Golden Spike Ceremony Revisited." Michael Johnson Papers (MSS 372).

PHOTOGRAPH COLLECTIONS

Artstor. Andrew J. Russell Slide Gallery.

Boston Public Library. Print Department. Western Photographs.

Brigham Young University. Harold B. Lee Library. L. Tom Perry Special Collections. C. R. Savage Collection (MSS P 24).

Central Pacific Railroad Photographic History Museum Archive. Russell Stereo-Views. Cprr.org.

Church of Jesus Christ of Latter-day Saints. Church History Library and Archives (photographs PH1714, 4050, 4758, 3736, 3160, 1610, 1724, 3046).
Denver Public Library. Digital Collections. Western History and Genealogy.
George Eastman House International Museum of Photography and Film. Still Photograph Archive. Clarence King Survey of the 40th Parallel.
Library of Congress. Prints and Photographs Division. A. J. Russell Photographs (lots 3057, 4162, 4177, 4189, 4336, 7096, 9209, 11486).
Metropolitan Museum of Art. Works of Art. Photographs.
New York Historical Society. Library. Early American West Photograph Collection (collection PR 266).
New York Public Library. Digital Gallery. Robert N. Dennis Collection of Stereoscopic Views.
Oakland Museum of California. A. J. Russell Collection.
San Francisco Museum of Modern Art. Photography Collection.
Sweetwater County Historical Museum. Photographic Reference Files.
Union Pacific Railroad Museum. Photography Archives. Union Pacific Collection. A. J. Russell Views.
University of Iowa Libraries. Special Collections and University Archives. Levi O. Leonard Railroadiana (MsC159).
University of Utah. J. Willard Marriott Library. Special Collections. Multimedia Archives. J. Carbutt Photograph Collection (collection P0328).
———. J. Willard Marriott Library. Special Collections. Multimedia Archives. Stereograph Collection (collection P0066).
University of Wyoming. American Heritage Center. Clarice Whittenburg Papers (collection 00364).
———. American Heritage Center. Howard F. Greene Papers (collection 02123).
———. American Heritage Center. Photographic Subject Files.
———. American Heritage Center. Stereocards Collection (collection 10733).
U.S. Geological Survey. Photographic Library. A. J. Russell Collection.
U.S. National Archives and Records Administration. Still Picture Records Section. Special Media Archives Services Division. Records of the Office of the Chief of Engineers. Timothy O'Sullivan Images (record group 77).
Utah State History. Research Center of Utah State Archives and Utah State History. Classified Photograph Collection.
———. Research Center of Utah State Archives and Utah State History. Stereographic Views Photograph Collection.
Utah State University. Merrill-Cazier Library. Special Collections and Archives. A-board Historical Photograph Collection.
———. Merrill-Cazier Library. Special Collections and Archives. A. J. Russell Photograph Collection (collection P0651).
———. Merrill-Cazier Library. Special Collections and Archives. C. R. Savage Photograph Collection (collection P0038).
———. Merrill-Cazier Library. Special Collections and Archives. Nineteenth-Century Western Stereo-Views Collection (collection P0349).
———. Merrill-Cazier Library. Special Collections and Archives. Sun Pictures of Rocky Mountain Scenery Collection (collection P0019).

Weber State University. Stewart Library. Special Collections. Richard Roberts Photograph Collection of Railroad and Ogden History (collection P 12).

———. Stewart Library. Special Collections. Transcontinental Railroad Photograph Collection (collection P 56).

———. Stewart Library. Special Collections. Union Pacific Railroad Photograph Collection (collection P 4).

———. Stewart Library. Special Collections. Western Stereo-Views Collection (collection P 146).

Yale University. Beinecke Rare Book and Manuscript Library. A. J. Russell Photographs of the Construction of the Union Pacific Railroad (collection ZZc10 864u).

———. Beinecke Rare Book and Manuscript Library. WA Photos (collection 399).

GOVERNMENT DOCUMENTS

Raynolds, W. F. *Report on the Exploration of the Yellowstone River by Bvt. Gen. W. F. Raynolds*. Communicated by the secretary of war in compliance with a resolution of Senate, February 13, 1866. Washington, DC: Government Printing Office, 1868.

Spude, Robert L. *Promontory Summit, May 10, 1869, A History of the Site Where the Central Pacific and Union Pacific Railroads Joined to Form the First Transcontinental Railroad*. Cultural Resources Management, Intermountain Region, National Park Service, 2005.

INDEX

Page numbers printed in *italics* refer to images.